JUST AS DEADLY

You've heard of Ted Bundy and John Wayne Gacy. But have you heard of Amy Archer-Gilligan? Or Belle Gunness? Or Nannie Doss?

Women have committed some of the most disturbing serial killings ever seen in the United States. Yet scientific inquiry, criminal profiling, and public interest have focused more on their better-known male counterparts. As a result, female serial killers have been misunderstood, overlooked, and underestimated. In this riveting account, Dr. Marissa A. Harrison draws on original scientific research, various psychological perspectives, and richly detailed case studies to illuminate the stark differences between female and male serial killers' backgrounds, motives, and crimes. She also emphasizes the countless victims of this grisly phenomenon to capture the complexity and tragedy of serial murder. Meticulously weaving data-based evidence and insight with intimate storytelling, *Just as Deadly* reveals how and why these women murder – and why they often get away with it.

Dr. Marissa A. Harrison is a research psychologist, author, and associate professor at Penn State Harrisburg. Her studies on serial murder and human sexuality have been covered in popular media such as *The Washington Post*, *The New Yorker*, and *Time*.

ADVANCE PRAISE

"Dr. Harrison has clearly demonstrated her expertise on female serial killers. Her seminal work will stand the test of time, scrutiny, and reliability. Her scholarship, insightful analysis, and penchant for detail make this book the best on the market. Excellent reading for those interested in why and how women become serial killers."

Dr. Eric W. Hickey, author of *Serial Murderers and their Victims, 7th Edition*

"Dr. Harrison's masterfully crafted book is a comprehensive, engaging, and thought-provoking insight into female serial homicide. Through the interesting case studies provided, the reader gets an in-depth understanding of the factors that can contribute to serial homicide in females."

Dr. Clare S. Allely, author of *The Psychology of Extreme Violence*

"Fascinating, ground-breaking, and long overdue. Harrison fills the inexcusable gap in the serial murder literature with her own original research on female killers, in what is sure to become a seminal work in criminology. A must-read."

Patricia Pearson, author of *When She Was Bad: How and Why Women Get Away with Murder* and *Wish You Were Here: A Murdered Girl, a Brother's Grief and the Hunt for a Serial Killer*

"There are countless books on male serial killers but very little on female serial killers. Using a range of perspectives, Dr. Harrison's book corrects this deficiency and documents the similarities and differences between male and female killers. Highly accessible, extensively researched, and valuable to professional and lay reader alike."

Professor Frederick Toates and Dr. Olga Coschug-Toates, authors of *Understanding Sexual Serial Killing*

"*Just as Deadly* firmly establishes Dr. Marissa Harrison as the preeminent authority on the female serial killer. This is a welcome and necessary addition to the small but growing body of literature that scrutinizes age-old preconceptions about serial murder."

Enzo Yaksic, author of *Killer Data: Modern Perspectives on Serial Murder*

JUST AS DEADLY

The Psychology of Female Serial Killers

Marissa A. Harrison

Pennsylvania State University

CAMBRIDGE
UNIVERSITY PRESS

CAMBRIDGE
UNIVERSITY PRESS

University Printing House, Cambridge CB2 8BS, United Kingdom

One Liberty Plaza, 20th Floor, New York, NY 10006, USA

477 Williamstown Road, Port Melbourne, VIC 3207, Australia

314–321, 3rd Floor, Plot 3, Splendor Forum, Jasola District Centre,
New Delhi – 110025, India

103 Penang Road, #05–06/07, Visioncrest Commercial, Singapore 238467

Cambridge University Press is part of the University of Cambridge.

It furthers the University's mission by disseminating knowledge in the pursuit of
education, learning, and research at the highest international levels of excellence.

www.cambridge.org
Information on this title: www.cambridge.org/9781009158206
DOI: 10.1017/9781009158183

© Marissa A. Harrison 2023

First published 2023

Printed in the United Kingdom by TJ Books Limited, Padstow Cornwall

A catalogue record for this publication is available from the British Library.

ISBN 978-1-009-15820-6 Hardback

This book is dedicated to Kenneth Cutting, Dora Beebe, June Roberts, Chelsea McClellan, Bert Montoya, Tami Lynne Tinning, Linda Slawson, Josephine Otero, Dolores Davis, and George Shaw, and all the victims and their loved ones.

Contents

Preface

Late one night in 2015, I received an email from Sarah Kaplan, a reporter writing for *The Washington Post*. She had written around 11:00 p.m. asking if we could connect before 4:00 a.m. the next morning. She had read an academic paper about female serial killers in the United States that I had recently published in *The Journal of Forensic Psychiatry and Psychology*, and she wanted to talk about my findings.

As a professor just doing her job, I was surprised, but grateful someone had actually read my research. And I was still awake, so I emailed her back around 2:00 a.m., ready to talk even at that late hour. My phone rang instantly. When I answered, I believe I said something to the effect of, "Wow, it really is you . . ." Reading the impactful journalism that resulted from our conversation was one of the first times I realized just how much interest there is in the topic of serial murder.[1] Then, a few months later, I did an interview with journalist Emily Anthes that appeared in her *New Yorker* piece, "Lady Killers."[2] That's when I really knew how eager people are to learn about the who, what, why, where, and how of serial murder.

I did not set out in my career to study murder or serial murder, per se. Academic psychologists and psychology students are interested in exploring the many facets of human behavior and mental processes, and I am an evolutionary psychologist with a degree in biopsychology (now frequently called "behavioral neuroscience"). My research has typically focused on male-female differences in sexual psychology that stem from the vast differences in reproductive biology. My research interests have included attraction, kissing, and declaring love. When I started in this field, I did not foresee a path of research geared at understanding women who perpetrate cruel and barbaric murders of innocent people – killers whom researchers have called "sadistic human beings devoid of empathy, morality or conscience."[3]

So, how did I end up pursuing this line of study? Years ago, my friend, colleague, and licensed psychologist Tom Bowers of Penn State Harrisburg was studying mass murder with his clinical research team. Since all behaviors and mental processes can be viewed through an evolutionary psychological lens, I partnered with him (i.e., invited myself into the project because it was so interesting) to collect data and analyze reported triggers for mass murder. We found that almost all mass murders in our sample were perpetrated by men triggered by a status threat.[4] Men went on a murderous rampage because of job loss, economic loss, and being bullied. Read from an evolutionary standpoint, this makes sense. A threat to – or loss of – status would have had profound reproductive consequences for males in our ancestral environment (i.e., over millions of years of human evolution). We are not, of course, saying that people evolved to kill large numbers of helpless victims. Rather, we attempted to explain the evolved psychological forces that may have played a part in creating such unbridled rage with such tragic results.

At the time, I had a student named Erin Murphy taking several psychology courses with me. She was, as I recall, both a criminal justice and a psychology major. Since she knew I was on a team studying murder, she approached me and asked if I would do an independent study with her on serial murder. I said "okay!" with no hesitation.

The topic was immediately interesting, and Erin, a top student who demonstrated diligence and commitment, was the first to tell me about the paucity of research on female serial killers. When I investigated the topic myself, I corroborated her conclusion. With Tom and Erin's help, I designed a project to collect data about female serial killers who committed their crimes in the United States. Because of the marked lack of empirical (original) research on the topic, we attempted to fill in knowledge gaps by collecting broad data on demographics, background experiences, crimes, motives, and victims. Moreover, we attempted to examine mental health issues, which had been largely ignored in previous female serial murder literature. Because I am not a clinical psychologist, I brought two additional people on board to help interpret and present the mental health issues we found reported in female serial killers: a fantastic M.A. clinical psychology student, Lavina Ho (now a Ph.D. student who will likely graduate by the time of press), and Claire Flaherty, a clinician and licensed psychologist from the Penn State Hershey College of Medicine.

A testament to people's interest in serial killers, it was striking how detailed Erin's fellow psychology students wanted her reports to be when updating our undergraduate research class about her findings. Because this was a general, nomothetic endeavor, we were aiming to document aggregate data and present averages and frequencies. Still, my bright, dedicated, and very curious students wanted to hear all the details, as horrific and disturbing as they were. I recall Erin vividly presenting murder cases with methods ranging from poisoning to fire, and about victims ranging from infants to the elderly. The listeners hung on every word and asked for more, at times even prompting Erin to ask, "Are you sure?" In one instance, when the students pressed for more information, Erin described burning bodies. The students recoiled and literally yelped in horror. One said, "I can't unhear that!" And yet they always asked for more.

Why is this topic so interesting? It occurred to me that, viewing interest in murder through an evolutionary lens, it is perhaps adaptive – conducive to survival and thus reproduction – to attend to, learn about, and understand damaging and deadly behavior so you yourself can avoid it. What is interesting to us outright (in evolutionary terms, our *proximate* motivation) might be serving an unconscious, evolved survival mechanism (our *ultimate* motivation). Psychologists have studied this phenomenon, called *morbid curiosity*,[5] noting humans' strong tendency to attune to negative and even disastrous events. Subsequent to my work with Erin, I worked with M.A. clinical psychology student Erika Frederick (who has since graduated), studying morbid curiosity in relation to interest in serial murder so that we could better understand this phenomenon.[6] As a result, in addition to talking about serial murderer psychology, this book talks about the psychology of interest in serial murder.

It remains puzzling why there is a decided lack of research, particularly empirical endeavors, regarding female serial killers – a point I stress throughout this book. Perhaps this trend reflects the fact that serial murder itself is rare. Although a challenging task, Garry Rodgers, a retired forensic coroner and homicide investigator, estimated the probability of being murdered by a serial killer in North America as .0004%.[7] Rodgers emphasized that you would have a better chance of winning the lottery than encountering someone like Ted Bundy. Moreover, among serial murderers, only about one in six are female, mirroring overall homicide trends.[8] Going from this, we can estimate you have about a .000067% chance of being the victim of a female serial killer.

Yet, as of this writing, fewer than one in six legitimate research papers and books on serial murder are about female serial killers. Almost all research investigates male serial killing. While there are far more male serial killers documented, the scientific examination of female serial killers is still disproportionately less frequent. I cannot with certainty explain why this is, although I discuss several reasons why it might be, including a societal perception that women ought to be nurturing and are therefore incapable of such heinous crimes. Indeed, I will bet that you have heard of Ted Bundy and Richard Ramirez, and that you can even recount at least some of the nature and circumstances of their crimes.

But have you heard of Amy Archer-Gilligan?

§

Amy Archer-Gilligan was a serial killer. She was lauded for opening and running what can be considered one of the first nursing homes in the United States. Most patients who chose to live in her facility in Connecticut were elderly men who, in exchange for lifetime care, paid a lump sum of money or a weekly fee. On May 8, 1916, Archer-Gilligan was arrested. The following day, the *Hartford Courant*, a renowned Connecticut newspaper, ran the front-page story: "Police Believe Archer Home for Aged a Murder Factory."[9]

It was the keen investigative work of *Hartford Courant* journalist Aubrey Maddock that brought Archer-Gilligan's crimes to light. Maddock was the first to uncover the statistical improbability of so many deaths occurring under Archer-Gilligan's care – 64 since the home had opened, and 48 occurring between 1907 amd 1916. These were exceedingly high numbers considering the home's limited capacity.[10] Knowing that arsenic had been found in the exhumed bodies of victims, Maddock traced Archer-Gilligan's purchases. Arsenic poisoning creates widespread organ failure and is a painful, gruesome way to die, and Maddock discovered that Archer-Gilligan had bought a large amount of arsenic from Mason's Drug Store in Windsor, Connecticut, just before each death.[11] She had also bought a lot of morphine, which I will talk about later. Maddock brought his findings to the police, resulting in her arrest.[12]

It was estimated Amy Archer-Gilligan killed at least 20 elderly and infirm people. Moreover, she had somehow gotten named as the beneficiary of their life insurance and other resources. Investigators also found that she had obtained loans from victims right before they died, and that she had suspiciously withdrawn money from their bank accounts. Her victims included some who had died shortly after paying a substantial boarding fee for long-term care in her home.

Due to legal entanglements involved with presenting all the evidence, the prosecution decided to try Archer-Gilligan for the murder of Franklin Andrews only. In court, she defended herself, saying, "Of course a large number of the inmates died. Most of them were old and feeble when they came under my care."[13] But her logic did not hold, considering the evidence: the statistical improbability of so many people dying in such a short time in her care; her purchase of a large amount of arsenic; the fact that arsenic was found in the victims' remains; and the fact that she benefited from their deaths. On July 14, 1917, she was convicted on one count of first-degree murder and sentenced to death.[14] Wearing a black dress and a mourning veil, she sunk into her chair and wept as she heard the sentence. As she was led out of the courthouse, she reportedly clung to her daughter, moaning "Oh, Mary, my darling child!" over and over between convulsive sobs.[15]

On appeal, Archer-Gilligan was awarded a new trial due to errors made in the first. This time, in July 1919, she pleaded guilty and the sentence was changed to life in prison.[16] In 1924, she was declared insane and was committed to the State Hospital at Middletown, Connecticut, where she remained for the rest of her life.[17] Archer-Gilligan died of old age at Connecticut Valley Hospital on April 23, 1962, at about age 91, but her murderous deeds were memorialized forever in the popular play *Arsenic and Old Lace*.[18]

In a story about Amy Archer-Gilligan, in 1919, *The Daily Arkansas Gazette* asked, "Do women commit cold-blooded murder? Do women kill, as countless men in every age and clime have killed . . . with calm premeditation?" *The Gazette* added, "It can be demonstrated by mere adduction of fact that women kill just as men kill, or as other animals, male and female, kill."[19] This statement from more than 100 years ago speaks precisely to the purpose of this book.

§

Throughout the following chapters, I infuse case studies of female serial killers to illustrate themes such as background factors, victim characteristics, and mental health. I also include a few case studies of male serial killers to illustrate discussion points. For the cases I highlight, I have assembled the facts myself from publicly available, original sources. For some, I report directly what clinicians or criminologists have stated, with appropriate attribution. From my interactions with students, colleagues, and general audiences, I understand they expect these details when reading or hearing about serial killings. Hearing a name, the details of the crime, who the victims were and how they died, and conjecturing on an individual's murderous motives all hammer home the terrifying reality.

Yet I would be remiss if I did not emphasize that, in psychological research, we who engage in nomothetic research (i.e., studying large samples of people to create generalized understanding) have an ethical imperative, and make great efforts, to protect the identity of participants.[20] In my research papers, for example, even though we have analyzed information available to the public, I do not provide the names of serial killers whose data we used to create our reports. However, we do our best in every project to describe our exact methodology so the results can be replicated if desired. Stated another way, if you replicate our methods you are going to find the same cases we did to include in your own research.

Furthermore, giving the name of a killer might reinforce the notoriety they may have sought through their crimes. As information-age scholar David Brin said in his appeal to the media, "Killers want notoriety. Let's not give it to them."[21] Nonetheless, I validate that, for plausible psychological reasons I describe later, many readers genuinely wish to hear real-world case studies of serial murderers and their victims, not just statistics. Accordingly, I offer the disclaimer that the cases presented in this book may or may not have been included in our collective data.

This book is a science-based endeavor reporting on female serial killer psychology and crimes. For case studies, I always consulted primary sources and have provided links to them in notes. I gathered the information presented herein from various valid, reputable sources accessible via the internet, such as the Associated Press, newspaper archives, national and local news websites, historical societies, court documents, censuses, and marriage and death records. Where I describe previous research derived from academic sources or data-based or reference-based books in the field, I provide abbreviated notes; there is a References section at the back of the book, complete with academic source information.

At no point in the research or writing of this book did I draw from other college's databases, internet blogs, student projects, or opinion or nonprofessional posts. Unfortunately, in my many years of serial murder research, I have encountered too many books and blogs that provide no sources for their information. Similarly, some pieces appearing in popular blogs have taken data from my own work and presented it as their own or misattributed my findings to others. The information in this book is derived from empirical data, and the findings have been published in reputable, peer-reviewed scientific journals. To use someone else's data without citing them is not good science or form. To present cases without citations is just storytelling and may perpetuate myths. This book is based on science. We psychological scientists are empirical and practical, and we take critical care to attribute findings accurately to others.

The information provided in this book, unless otherwise specified, is about female serial killers who committed their crimes in the United States. It is possible that these descriptions do not apply to women who committed serial murder outside the USA, but, in a contemporary sample, I believe that one would find similar demographics, means, motives, and victims outside this country. This is an empirical question. To understand the topic more fully and accurately, future endeavors should explore female-perpetrated serial murder in other Westernized and non-WEIRD (Western, educated, industrialized, rich, and democratic) cultures.[22]

As you will find in the pages to come, I do not interview, otherwise interact with, or diagnose those with psychological conditions or those who have committed crimes. Serial murder is rare, and gaining access to interview serial murderers is exceedingly difficult. So I am quite happy to have been a data wrangler for well over 20 years. Moreover, I am a science writer, and more than 20 years ago I had to scrap any ambitions of crafting artful articulations in my writing endeavors. I do not purport to write in an eloquent style like the gifted Stephen King or Nancy Gibbs (a shout-out to two of my favorite writers). You will not get details about a dark and stormy night where the merciless butcher (insert dramaturgy here). I report just the facts. The reader's imagination can take it from there.

In all my years of exploring this disturbing topic, however, I have never become desensitized to the sheer awfulness of planned murder. Rather, I have become more sensitized. Reading about and studying these crimes is jarring. The murder of anyone is horrible; these crimes usually involve the deaths of people who are very young, very old, or helpless. These victims suffered horribly and unnecessarily. Documenting these crimes can take a toll on any author. After I wrote the description of violent serial killer Dana Sue Gray's crimes and elderly victims for this book, I had to take the remainder of the day off. The same thing happened when I wrote about baby Chelsea McClellan, who was killed by serial killer Genene Jones and whose mother Petti McClellan-Wiese became a fierce advocate for murder victims. The murdering women whose stories appear in this book often brutally killed people who trusted them, with many victims incapable of fighting back.

The most common motive of female serial killers is monetary gain. What is the price of a life? According to Amy Archer-Gilligan in the early 1900s, the price of a life was a few thousand dollars in boarding fees or insurance money. Apparently, she deemed that it was worth poisoning older, often lonely people with arsenic.[23] Arsenic poisoning is cruel. It causes pernicious vomiting, severe diarrhea, kidney failure, encephalopathy (disease of the brain), multisystem failure, and death.[24] Her victims suffered before they died. That is not something one can get used to reading or writing about.

In the pages that follow, I stress that female serial killers are among us and can murder as many victims and just as cruelly as any male serial killer. I extend the caveat that the information herein is disturbing, but I endeavor to guess the reader is well aware of that fact. I present descriptive information on female serial killers, a comparison of the crimes of female and male serial killers, and my take, from an evolutionary point of view, on why people might find this phenomenon so fascinating. I also cover traumagenic and other psychological perspectives where I derived them from evidence-based literature. If we document incidents, patterns, antecedents, and consequences of serial murder and view the phenomenon through various psychological lenses, we increase the chance of prevention, or at least early detection.

We do not yet understand serial murder fully. But we do understand for a fact that women can be just as deadly as men.

You're the monster no one sees coming.

– US District Judge Thomas Kleeh to
Reta Mays, convicted serial killer and former
nursing assistant, at her sentencing for
murdering seven elderly veterans in her care.[1]

CHAPTER 1

Introduction: What Is a Serial Killer?

§

Kristen H. Gilbert is a serial killer. She was convicted of the first-degree murder of three disabled patients at the US Department of Veterans Affairs hospital in Massachusetts, where she worked as a nurse in the 1990s. She was also convicted of second-degree murder, having killed a fourth patient, and the attempted murder of two other patients. Gilbert is further suspected of killing, or trying to kill, other vulnerable people who were under her skilled care. In fact, so many patients died while Gilbert was on duty that her colleagues called her an "Angel of Death."[1]

Death was apparently not Gilbert's sole endgame. As *The Boston Globe* pointedly noted, "She liked to play the star." She "liked the thrill of medical emergencies" and "reveled in the excitement of emergency calls."[2] Gilbert also wanted to impress VA police officer Jim Perrault, with whom she had a relationship and said she was in love, by showing off her skilled medical heroics.[3]

Sources say Gilbert thrived on the excitement and medical challenge of treating a patient coding in a cardiopulmonary emergency. This explains her murder weapon of choice: epinephrine. Epinephrine is synthetic adrenaline that causes extreme tachycardia (accelerated heartbeat). To induce cardiac arrest, Gilbert, by all accounts a very skilled nurse, injected patients' intravenous lines with the drug epinephrine. According to Assistant US Attorney William Welch, "She caused patients to die because of the adulation she would get from coworkers . . . and her own personal thrill and gratification from saving individuals she put in distress."[4]

1

1.1 Kristen Gilbert in an undated photo. (Photo from Getty Images)

But, according to investigators, these were not her only motivations. One night in 1996, Gilbert reportedly asked her supervisor if she could leave early if her patient died. She was meeting up with boyfriend Jim. This patient was 41-year-old Kenneth Cutting, a blind, disabled veteran with multiple sclerosis who had no known heart issues. She proceeded to kill Cutting, a husband and a father, so she could leave early. This victim died of a heart attack – his tragic, early departure from this world occurring less than an hour after Gilbert requested an early departure from work for her romantic interlude.[5]

Gilbert's colleagues became increasingly suspicious and finally alerted authorities after a patient receiving a simple antibiotic treatment reported feeling nauseous and that he had a burning sensation after Gilbert flushed his IV line.[6] An investigation ensued, in which all 37 deaths that took place from 1995 to 1996 during Gilbert's shifts in Ward C were examined. When Gilbert was interviewed in March 1996, healthcare inspectors asked her, frankly, "Why are you the first one finding patients in distress?" She told them she had keen medical intuition.[7]

During the time of the investigation, Kristen Gilbert left work with a shoulder injury and began collecting workers' compensation. In her absence, the death rate on the evening shift markedly decreased. As the investigation progressed, she apparently grew desperate, making harassing phone calls to the VA hospital and fighting with her boyfriend, Jim Perrault. She even accused Perrault of being complicit in the investigation and kicked him in the testicles. Then, in October 1996, seemingly to derail the investigation, Gilbert called in bomb threats to the Veterans Affairs Medical Center. She was arrested for the threats and, two years later, sentenced to 15 months in prison for making them.[8] Yet her demeanor was not consistent. Even when she was identified as a murder suspect, Gilbert was not distressed by the seriousness of the allegations, according to her neighbor. Rather, she hoped that all pictures of her in the press were flattering and that Bridget Fonda would play her in a movie about her life.

Meanwhile, investigators exhumed the bodies of victims and found evidence of epinephrine. Furthermore, they found 85 doses of epinephrine unaccounted for in the VA Medical Center.[9] Overall, they determined that there was a one in 100 million probability of so many deaths occurring with Gilbert present.[10] In May 1999, she was arrested for murder.[11]

At trial, Gilbert pleaded not guilty, but the evidence was overwhelming. Fellow nurses testified that she was the first on the scene to the deaths and that they often found broken, empty bottles of epinephrine at the scene. The jury heard one survivor's account that Gilbert "put something in my arm" before his heart rate increased to 300 BPM and he passed out. Patient Angelo Vella died before trial, so his daughter testified that he had said he thought his heart was "going to explode."[12] As the US Attorney said, "The depth and cruelty of her evil had no natural boundary." Gilbert was, he added, "a cold-blooded serial killer."[13]

On March 14, 2001, Kristen Gilbert was convicted of murder and several other charges.[14] Since she committed crimes on federal property, prosecutors sought the death penalty as punishment, but in consideration of Gilbert's own children, jurors decided she should spend life in prison instead.[15] Gilbert received four life sentences for her crimes.

Ironically, however, had Gilbert received a death sentence, she would have been executed the same way she executed helpless, disabled veterans – by lethal injection.[16] Reflecting on the case just a few days after Gilbert's conviction, law professor David Rossman captured the horror of her crimes: "These good men . . . vulnerable men, there to be healed, all dead. What could be more frightening? More evil?"[17]

§

What is a serial killer? If you read five sources, you might get five different answers to this question. Although US Federal Bureau of Investigation (FBI) agent Robert Ressler's[18] use of the term "serial killer" decades ago made it more mainstream, there is, to my knowledge, no absolute definition available for "serial killer" or "serial murder." The FBI considers serial murder to be "the unlawful killing of two or more victims by the same offender(s), in separate events."[19] However, noted academics such as Eric Hickey, Stephen Holmes et al., and Amanda Farrell et al.[20] defined a serial killer as someone who has murdered three or more victims. In research conducted with my team in 2015, we adopted the definition of three deceased victims and added the distinction of them being intentional killings. Furthermore, to distinguish serial killing from mass murders or spree killing, we stressed that there must be a cooling-off period of at least one week between murders.

Indeed, the FBI website's information on serial murder is incomplete. It describes the modus operandi of the typical male serial killer. It ignores the fact that women can be just as deadly as men. All case examples presented are those of male perpetrators. In fact, almost all the experts who compiled the report were also men. In fairness, the group that assembled the FBI's information was a highly reputable and experienced team – likely some of the best experts in the world – working with the information they had at the time. However, newer research such as that published by my team in 2019 has elucidated drastic and statistically significant difference between the backgrounds, crimes, motives, and methods of male and female serial killers.[21]

At one time, authorities actually claimed that there were no female serial killers, and that serial murders were limited to sex-based crimes.[22] Even research[23] in the last 20 years has used the terms "serial sexual homicide" and "serial killer" interchangeably. And while the FBI report debunks the myth that all serial killers are motivated by sex, the examples provided in its report are largely sexual in nature. However, we know that the most common motive for female serial murderers is financial gain,[24] which is not mentioned in the report at all. The FBI report does underscore that "more research is needed to identify specific pathways of development that produce serial killers," but more research has since become available. It is time for the FBI and other law enforcement agencies to update their information, as other agencies look to this reference material when assessing murder cases in front of them.

The undeniable facts are these: women have been, and can be, serial murderers; their motives, crimes, and victims are almost always different to those of male serial murderers; and they have committed arguably some of the most disturbing clusters of murders the USA has ever seen.

§

Martha Patty Cannon was a serial killer. She committed among the most heinous crimes I have ever heard of in my many years of murder psychology research. People often ask me, "Which female serial killer's crimes do you consider the worst?" My usual answer is "all of them." But when pressed to name names, Cannon is typically at the top of the depraved list.

Also going by Lucretia P. Cannon, or simply "Patty," she was called "the wickedest woman in America" and "the most abandoned wretch that breathes."[25] Believed to have been born in about 1760, 16 years before the Declaration of Independence sparked the Revolutionary War, she was one of the first serial killers documented in the United States.

Cannon and her son-in-law, Joe Johnson, resided on the Delaware-Maryland state line, where they murdered and robbed people who patronized her tavern.[26] She was a prolific and equal-opportunity murderer throughout the early 1800s, reportedly killing men, women, and children of many ethnicities. She and her gang of thugs also kidnapped approximately 3,000 free Black people and sold them into slavery, separating them from their children, often shackling victims in her attic to await a buyer.[27] Scholars such as Richard Bell have referred to her crimes as a "reverse underground railroad."[28] Reports say that she strangled a three-day-old baby, burned other babies alive, and poisoned her own husband. Cannon also threw a child into a fireplace to stop the child from crying.[29] Patty Cannon was Black, and scholars contend that her ethnicity and gender prevented suspicion that she was engaging in these crimes.[30]

In 1829, a three-foot-long blue chest containing a man's bones was found buried on her property. The bones of others, including a child, were found in oak boxes. These discoveries led to her arrest for murder.[31] After she was in custody, one of Cannon's gang members, Cyrus James, told investigators that the buried remains were those of a well-known slave trader from Georgia whom she had shot and killed, keeping the $15,000 he had in his possession. James also said that he had seen Cannon kill a child by hitting them in the head with a wooden log.[32] Cannon confessed to killing more than two dozen people, including her own husband and child, but witnesses indicated she had murdered far more victims. At the age of approximately 70, Cannon died by suicide while in jail to avoid being put to death by hanging.[33]

Although one might question the accuracy of reports from 200 years ago, Mike Morgan, who wrote a biography about Patty Cannon,[34] stressed his confidence in the historical documentation he uncovered in his research. "Whatever you have had heard about her is probably true," he stated, "and even more so." He added, "Patty's heinous crimes equal, if not surpass the legend."[35]

Although we cannot explain what exactly drove Cannon to a life of horrible crimes, an obvious motive is the vast amount of money she earned from her kidnapping and slave-trading ring.[36] One can extrapolate that if someone is willing to kidnap, shackle, and sell another human being for profit, killing anyone who gets in the way does not seem far-fetched.

Digging into history, not much is available on Patty Cannon's past. *The Morning News* wrote a retrospective piece on Cannon in 1960. According to the report, she was victimized by her father, who was ultimately executed by hanging. Patty was said to have been tall, good-looking, and well-liked in her youth. She married Jesse Cannon, a captain in the Delaware militia, in 1791. At some point in their marriage, Jesse was found guilty of kidnapping free Black people. He was sentenced to the pillory, a wooden framework that the prisoner sticks their head and hands through for public display and shaming. Although the sentence was supposed to involve nailing his ears to the wood, it was reported that the governor of Delaware removed this part of the punishment because of Jesse's distinguished military service.[37] While it is unknown why Patty Cannon may have decided to kill her husband and child, it is clear that she was in charge of her gang by the early 1800.

A macabre liner note to Cannon's story is her bizarre postmortem journey. In 1902, her remains were unearthed from her grave outside the Sussex County Courthouse in Delaware in order to be relocated. Apparently, Attorney James Marsh had a "fascination" with her remains.[38] *The Morning News* ran a front-page story, "Found Patty Cannon's Skull," reporting that "the skull and bones are on exhibition at James A. Marshall's law office and scores of people are attracted there to see them."[39] After public display, Marshall took her skull home with him, and when he died, his son-in-law Charles Joseph reportedly hung the skull on a nail in his barn.

After Joseph's death, the new owners of the house, the Burtons, found the skull in a hat box in their attic. Mary Burton announced that she "didn't want any part of it."[40] They gave the skull to relatives of the Joseph family, who donated it to the Dover Public Library, where it was used as a display at Halloween. Cannon's skull now appears to be in the care of the US government at the Smithsonian Institution in Washington, DC. Or, a skull from another woman buried in Delaware at around the same time as Cannon, who was also about the age of 70 when she died, whose skull was once displayed, hung in a barn, and stored in a hat box, is at the Smithsonian.[41]

And this was the end of the first documented case of a serial killer in the United States that I have encountered. Imagine someone considered so depraved that Delaware State erected a commemorative road plaque warning, "Nearby stood Patty Cannon's House." Nonetheless, with crimes committed so long ago, we must concede that it may be impossible to determine what is fact and what is fiction.

§

Despite crimes of horror and magnitude, the names of female serial killers (FSKs) are virtually unknown to the public. When I give academic or public talks, I challenge audiences to name serial killers aloud. The names of male serial killers (MSKs) like John Wayne Gacy and Ed Kemper are invariably mentioned. But no one seems to have heard of Kristen Gilbert, Patty Cannon, or most other FSKs. Indeed, when asked to name a female serial killer, many people can only think of Aileen Wuornos, whose story earned notoriety when depicted in the 2003 movie *Monster* starring award-winning actor Charlize Theron.

Wuornos has been called "America's first female serial killer,"[42] but by all available definitions, she was not. Not only does this misnomer overlook the crimes of Patty Cannon more than 200 years earlier but also Wuornos does not quite fit the mold. Between 1989 and 1990, she shot men in the head and torso – killings she claimed were in self-defense as a hitchhiking sex worker. Active violence such as targeting and shooting strangers are not acts that fit the profile of a typical FSK. In fact, Wuornos' behaviors and crimes were largely of the kind considered typical of male serial murderers. That said, Wuornos robbed her victims after she shot them. Thus, at least one aspect of her crime was typical of FSKs – her motive for murder being money. I will return to her case later in this book.

While MSK crimes and profiles are the subject of countless academic volumes, murder by FSKs has been misunderstood, overlooked, and underestimated. One reason for this may be society's unwillingness to accept that women are capable of such heinous and gruesome crimes. Typical gender schemas categorize women as gentle, nurturing caretakers. Perhaps there is a type of morbid glass ceiling when it comes to women being recognized and remembered as callous murderers of multiple victims, and the only way it can be broken is when the murders are particularly violent or gory. To wit, Aileen Wuornos shot men in the head and dumped at least one body in a junkyard. Not only is she readily identified as a serial killer, but her story also became the subject of a major motion picture. Yet Amy Archer-Gilligan, whose covert, insidious methods turned one of the country's first nursing homes into a "murder factory,"[43] is largely unknown by name, despite the fact that her murders inspired the play and Hollywood movie *Arsenic and Old Lace.*

Journalist Patricia Pearson[44] posited that contemporary culture denies women's ability to be aggressive and violent. The sheer notion of a woman committing a planned string of murders is incomprehensible. This likely plays a factor when women get away with murder. In her work on FSKs, Deborah Schurman-Kauflin posited that "no one believes that a woman could kill multiple victims."[45] US District Judge Thomas Kleeh captured this ideology perfectly when sentencing serial killer nursing assistant Reta Mays for the murder of seven elderly veterans hospitalized in her care. He described Mays as the "monster no one sees coming." Similarly, when reporting on Amy Archer-Gilligan's arraignment in June 1917, one newspaper observed that "the spectators wondered how on Earth [the] State Attorney could ascribe such gruesome deeds to so pale and gentle a dove."[46]

Notably, while world-renowned forensic psychologist Eric Hickey[47] was one of the first authors on record to research and document the motives and crimes of female serial murderers, many of the solo or lead author researchers often cited for their work on FSKs are women: Deborah Schurman-Kauflin, a criminal profiler; Amanda Farrell,[48] whose work underscored how FSKs do not neatly fit into typical male serial murder classifications; Patricia Pearson, who authored an award-winning book on women who kill; and myself. This fact is open to interpretation, but perhaps it takes women to validate, underscore, and push society to accept the fact that women can be just as deadly as men.

Indeed, highly influential psychiatrist Hervey Cleckley's seminal writings about psychopathy[49] initially ignored women, as well. This is a substantial omission, as the perpetrators of many cases of serial murder have met the criteria for having, or are suspected to have had, psychopathy. As scholars have pointed out, Cleckley's 1941 book *The Mask of Sanity: An Attempt to Clarify Some of the Issues about the So-called Psychopathic Personality* did not discuss women psychopaths at all until the fifth edition of the book was released in 1976. Cleckley's omission may have been influenced by social stereotypes of women as warm and nurturing caregivers.[50]

Physical appearance can moderate perceptions of guilt just as powerfully as social stereotypes. Psychologists have understood for half a century that people experience the "halo effect" – meaning that they believe "what is beautiful is good."[51] Facially attractive people are judged to be more trustworthy, intelligent, socially competent, poised, and exciting.[52] In movies, for example, the good characters are likely to be physically attractive, and much more so than the bad characters.[53] And in the criminal justice system, it has long been common knowledge that a defendant who is good-looking has better chance of being found not guilty or of getting a less harsh sentence.[54] A halo effect around an attractive defendant can decrease the jury's and the public's perceptions of guilt. Tellingly, in 2015, my research team found that female serial murderers have typically been reported to be of at least average attractiveness.[55] When it comes to recognizing the guilt of FSKs, maybe people just do not think a good-looking woman is capable of committing gruesome murders with multiple victims.

§

Sharon Kinne is a serial killer. Guilty of heinous crimes, Kinne benefitted from her physical attractiveness several times in court before a guilty charge was finally brought. One newspaper story about Kinne exclaimed that she was "probably the prettiest defendant ever tried for murder" in Kansas City.[56] Louis Lombardo, the chief of operations for the prosecutor's office in Jackson County, Missouri, told a *Kansas City Star* journalist that at first he found her rather attractive – but added that his opinion changed as they worked the case.[57] "Ladies just weren't supposed to do what she did," said Jim Hays, a former local government official.[58]

The first time Kinne saw a jury, the year was 1961 and she was on trial for the murder of Patricia Jones, her ex-lover's wife. Despite physical and circumstantial evidence tying her to crime, Kinne was acquitted by an all-male jury in under two hours. After the not guilty verdict, the courtroom applauded.[59] In an eyebrow-raising epilogue, newspapers photographed Kinne giving autographs to, and taking photos with, the jury.[60]

The second time Kinne came to trial, it was for a murder that had actually taken place before the death of Patricia Jones. This time, Kinne was on trial for allegedly killing her husband, James Kinne, with a fatal gunshot to the head. At trial, Kinne blamed the gunshot on her daughter Danna, less than three years old, who she claimed was playing with the gun while Kinne got ready for a church event. She was found guilty of killing her husband, but the verdict was overturned by the Missouri Supreme Court because of jury selection issues.[61] She subsequently went through two more trials, resulting in a hung jury. As a prosecutor who worked on Kinne's case explained to a journalist, "Convictions are difficult to get . . . any time you are talking about non-motivated crimes committed by psychopaths."[62]

While I have not encountered any reports that Kinne had a formal psychiatric evaluation or any diagnosis, the prosecutor was not alone in his belief that Kinne was psychopathic. James Browning, one of the lead detectives on her case, said, "Guys really went for her, but I tell you what – I think she could kill you, then sit down to the table and enjoy a nice breakfast."[63] Indeed, Kinne had a long history of antisocial behavior, callous disregard for others (e.g., shooting her husband and blaming her toddler daughter), superficial charm, impulsivity, and lack of remorse. Moreover, while many of Kinne's relatives said they were afraid of her when she was angry, jurors found Kinne charming. People believed she was "the prettiest defendant ever," and people thought her "cool and expressionless" demeanor at trial meant that she was unruffled by false accusations.[64] Kinne showed signs and symptoms consistent with psychopathy – and she was not done killing.

While awaiting yet another trial, Kinne ran away with a new boyfriend to Mexico City, Mexico, where she killed once again. Kinne claimed that she met Francisco Paredes Ordonez at a bar. When he made sexual advances to her, she pulled a gun out of her purse and shot him – it was the same gun she had used to kill Patricia Jones.[65] The murder in Mexico earned her the nickname "La Pistolera" and a prison sentence. Reports were inconsistent as to the prison term she received, however, noting sentences of anywhere between 10 and 23 years.[66]

Law enforcement thought she had shot men before and gotten away with it. And, as it turned out, this time was no different. After serving only five years of her sentence, she escaped from prison on December 7, 1969. Some speculate that she used her good looks, once again, as an escape tool. She remains at large and would be in her 80s as of this writing.

1.2 Sharon Kinne with her attorney Martha Sperry Hickman and an unidentified man. (Photo from Bettmann Archive/Getty Images)

§

PSYCHOPATHY PRIMER

As a research psychologist, I am ethically compelled to stress that I am not a clinician licensed to make client diagnoses. I cannot go beyond my expertise. Yet even clinical psychologists must properly interview clients to make a legitimate assessment. Moreover, clinicians should not make assessments of public figures they have never properly interviewed, per the Goldwater Rule[67] and the *American Psychological Association (APA) Ethical Principles of Psychologists and Code of Conduct.*[68] Thus, I make no diagnoses in this book or elsewhere. Nevertheless, as Greg Hartley, an author and intelligence interrogator for the US military noted, you do not have to be a botanist to recognize poison ivy; a psychopath has readily identifiable traits and patterns.

Psychopaths pose great harm to society and can eventuate to being versatile and violent criminal offenders.[69] Many serial murderers like Sharon Kinne tend to exhibit behaviors and mental processes consistent with psychopathy, and their cases underscore the need for improved mental health issue recognition, understanding, and treatment. Thus, a brief primer of the concept is warranted.

While psychopathy is not an official mental health diagnosis, it includes both personality traits and antisocial behaviors.[70] Psychopathic traits include lying, manipulation, exploitation, callous disregard for the welfare of others, lack of remorse, and empathy deficits.[71] Hilda Morana and her colleagues[72] put it plainly: a psychopath is someone who knows facts but does not care. Furthermore, those with psychopathy tend to be fearless and impulsive risk-takers, with a documented lower perception of risk and a lack of fear for consequences.[73]

In *The Mask of Sanity*, Hervey Cleckley[74] describes how someone with psychopathy could appear to lead an ordinary life, pretending to have a normal, everyday existence. From their outer appearance, they seem highly functioning. They could appear very sincere, charming, and truthful, displaying typical emotionality. Yet this outward appearance masks a psychological milieu of callous disregard, impulsivity, irresponsibility, exploitation, and lack of remorse.[75] As Cleckley notes, they show "a gross lack of sincerity."[76] These deficits in remorse, empathy, and morality judgments may involve neural abnormalities.[77]

Psychopathy expert Robert Hare[78] suggested that, as a personality style, psychopathy evolved to promote social predation. As Hare suggested, "Psychopaths naturally slip into the role of criminal. Their readiness to take advantage of any situation that arises, combined with their lack of internal controls we know as conscience, creates a potent formula for crime."[79]

Some experts also believe that psychopathy may be an evolved, adaptive strategy.[80] A cheating adaptation requires the ability to conceal it in order to be successful.[81] The "mask of sanity" is an exercise of "affective mimicry" – it can help psychopaths appear to be normally functioning and to avoid detection while being socially exploitative.[82]

Many serial killers exhibit behaviors and cognitions consistent with psychopathy. Indeed, with the definition of serial murder encompassing three or more victims with a cooling-off period in between, it stands to reason that many serial murderers have mastered a "mask of sanity" to avoid getting caught after their first and second murders. Nonetheless, I do not think psychologists can say that all serial killers are psychopaths.

We do not have enough diagnoses or other information about older cases. But even from information we can derive from past reports, it is possible that serial killers like Patty Cannon and Ed Gein (discussed later) did not even try to portray a socially acceptable exterior – or could not have done so had they tried. Further, not everyone with psychopathy is a serial killer.

The most widely accepted and used measure of psychopathy is the Psychopathy Checklist-Revised (PCL-R), which measures interpersonal, lifestyle, affective, and antisocial behaviors and traits.[83] The PCL-R has been used to assess psychopathy in a few of the serial murderers mentioned in this book. Scores on the PCL-R produce two factors that work together to predict other psychopathology and maladaptive outcomes, including violent offences and recidivism.[84] Factor 1 of the PCL-R encompasses interpersonal and emotional characteristics considered to be pathognomonic (i.e., specifically characteristic) of psychopathy. These include superficial charm, feelings of grandiosity, deceitfulness, and a remorseless exploitation of other people, as well as a lack of emotional depth, empathy, or remorse for wrongdoing. Factor 2 encompasses antisocial behavior, including chronic irresponsibility, an impulsive lifestyle, and early-life behavioral issues.[85]

It is important to remember that having a psychopathic personality, or being diagnosed with mental illness, is different from being "insane" by the legal definition.[86] Hervey Cleckley[87] said that psychopaths have no reasoning deficits and have a typical awareness of the consequences of their actions. For example, when Cleckley was brought in as an expert witness at the trial of MSK Ted Bundy, he testified that Bundy – a psychopath who was skilled at presenting normalcy – was competent to stand trial.[88] Indeed, scholars have argued that most serial killers know the difference between right and wrong when they kill.[89]

When discussing psychopathy, it is important to note how the condition is depicted in relation to serial killers in pop culture. The portrayal of serial killers in films and television, for example, typically involves mixing psychopathy with psychosis, the latter of which includes delusions and hallucinations. But those who have worked on serial killer cases argue that these are not realistic portrayals, and clinicians and criminologists contend that such a mixture of high intelligence, psychopathy, and disabling psychosis (i.e., losing touch with reality) is very unlikely. Similarly, using words like "wacko" or "psycho" to describe serial killers is not accurate, as these words are often used as shorthand for "insane." Many serial killers such as Ken Bianchi, Jeffrey Dahmer, and John Wayne Gacy did not plead insanity or had their insanity plea denied.[90]

From a clinical perspective, psychopathic and psychotic have some opposite features. Someone who is psychopathic has a distorted emotional and moral compass, but they do understand how they ought to look to the social world. They work very carefully to present the mask of what society expects as normal.[91] In contrast, someone who is psychotic has lost their grip on reality and experiences a disrupted core experience of self.[92] They also have behavioral and cognitive deficits and can have a very difficult time managing their internal self in the outside world. It stands to reason that someone experiencing psychosis would not be able to perceive what is socially appropriate and effectively project a mask of sanity.

Some authors use the term sociopathy more than they do psychopathy, although the difference between psychopathy and sociopathy is not always clear and consistent across sources. Robert Hare, for example, explains that the term sociopathy may be preferred by some because psychopathy may be confused with psychotic, which suggests insanity.[93] Again, those with psychopathy are not insane by legal standards. Hare also suggests that some clinicians, sociologists, and criminologists may use the term sociopath because they believe the condition arises purely form environmental (social) circumstances. In contrast, those who feel that the condition is best viewed through a biopsychosocial framework may use the term psychopath. Moreover, some notable researchers contend that psychopathy and sociopathy fall on a spectrum. Eric Hickey[94] and colleagues argue that most MSKs are sociopaths who can express emotions but a small proportion of the group are psychopaths. (This has yet to be examined in FSKs.) It seems that experts do not necessarily agree on the definition of psychopathy. As a research psychologist, I take the biopsychosocial perspective, and thus use the terms psychopath and psychopathy, unless citing reports that explicitly use other terminology.

In sum, I have reviewed the definition of serial murder that I have seen academics typically incorporate in their research. Women's documented crimes most certainly fit this definition. Women are absolutely capable of committing serial murder, and they do. Yet societal and psychological forces continue to influence our perceptions and therefore our willingness to accept that women can plan and execute the cruel – often slow and painful – killings of men and women, young and old, vulnerable and infirm. In the pages that follow, I report aggregate data and additional case studies to illustrate key details about female serial murder, including a comparison between FSKs and MSKs and a psychological perspective regarding the motives, means, and makings of female serial murderers. But first, let us dive into the psychological forces that drive our interest in this most disturbing of topics.

CHAPTER 2

Why Are We Interested in Serial Killers?

§

Dana Sue Gray was a serial killer. In 1994, the unemployed nurse murdered elderly women by stabbing and choking them. One 87-year-old victim, Dora Beebe, was found in a pool of her own blood, strangled and bludgeoned to death with a clothing iron. Another victim, 86-year-old Norma Davis, was stabbed eleven times and strangled. The wounds to her neck were so deep she was nearly decapitated. After Gray murdered her victims, she stole their credit cards to feed her shopping habit.

Dana Sue Gray violently executed vulnerable women so she could buy expensive vodka and cowboy boots. She callously and brutally murdered people's mothers, sisters, wives, and grandmothers. And, if so inclined, today you can own Gray's underwear for $250. Autographed by Gray strategically in the crotch, the underwear is accompanied by her inmate number: W76776.[1]

§

Elizabeth Yuko recently reported for *Rolling Stone* magazine[2] that the sale of murderabilia, the "macabre artifacts" of criminals and crimes, has become quite a lucrative industry. She noted collectors' strong desire for serial-murderer artifacts such as a drawing of a deranged cartoon face and bloody knife by MSK Richard Ramirez ("The Night Stalker"). Self-portrait clown paintings by MSK "Killer Clown" John Wayne Gacy have been estimated in recent years to be worth thousands of dollars.[3] It seems that Western society sees serial murderers as "perverse icons."[4]

The curator of The Museum of Death[5] in Los Angeles, which collects and sells such artifacts, justifies people's interest in murderabilia as being legitimate and informative. Speaking to Yuko, the curator argued that, since museums collect and display artifacts related to presidential assassinations and the 9/11 terrorist attacks on the USA, collections of murderer artifacts should not be judged or viewed as aberrant. Nonetheless, another collector interviewed by Yuko conceded that procuring murderabilia "can be a dark hobby." Indeed, it should not be overlooked that the hobby (or profession) of collecting murder artifacts is extremely distressing to victims' families. As one victims' advocate stressed to Yuko, "It's one of the most nauseating and disgusting feelings in the world" to discover that people are profiting from memorabilia related to the criminals who murdered your loved one.[6]

Consumers spend hundreds of millions of dollars on media that is created to frighten them. According to *Forbes*, horror movies in particular make huge profits, taking in about $1 billion per year.[7] The carnivorous murder shark from the movie *Jaws* has terrorized audiences since 1975, and the franchise is reported to have taken in hundreds of millions of dollars. The 1973 movie *The Exorcist*, a story about demonic possession, has also raked in hundreds of millions of dollars, remaining popular throughout its half-century existence.[8] Similarly, serial murder is commodified.[9] Serial killer media is hugely popular, particularly on television and streaming services. The show *Mindhunter* on Netflix, which portrays fictional stories about FBI serial killer profiling, is critically acclaimed and an audience favorite.[10] Other programs such as *Dexter*, *Hannibal*, *Criminal Minds*, and *Killing Eve* continue to be fan favorites. They are consistently recommended for those who wish to travel down the dark and twisted paths of serial murderers and the law enforcement professionals who profile and track them.[11] Hundreds – if not thousands – of movies are also devoted to the topic, although some go directly to DVD or streaming. Eric Hickey reported that these movies and television shows appeal to consumers who want a greater in-depth understanding of serial murder and "the requisite gore."[12]

Whereas many of the aforementioned movies and programs are fictional – although perhaps infused with aspects of real cases for impact – there are countless programs, books, magazines, podcasts, and even comic books devoted to real-world serial killers and their stories. Collectively, these form the true crime genre.

Widespread interest in serial killers has even resulted in a robust industry of mass-produced collectibles that seem to memorialize and even make light of serial killing. *Psycho Killers*, a 1999 comic selling online for about $50, features Aileen Wuornos on the cover. One can find Ted Bundy, the Zodiac Killer, and Ed Gein action figures, each depicting killing and bloody action. Some are priced at well over $100. Interestingly, however, while there is an Aileen Wuornos action figure, it is difficult – if not impossible – to find figures representing the likes of Patty Cannon, Amy Archer-Gilligan, or Dana Sue Gray. Perhaps it is challenging to make an appealing resin model of an old grandma being choked with a telephone cord? Yet, through a quick internet search, you can easily find myriad macabre tributes to mutilating and murdering rapists. A T-shirt featuring a cartoon of Ted Bundy's abduction vehicle, for example, asks, "Do you want a ride?" I would bet large sums of money that the families of victims would not think this funny.

Admittedly, comedy is not a new approach to presenting serial murder phenomena. *Arsenic and Old Lace*, a 1939 Broadway play[13] and a 1944 movie[14] was a comedy said to be based on poisoner Amy Archer-Gilligan's serial murders. The prosecuting attorney from Archer-Gilligan's murder case, Hugh Alcorn, was invited to and attended the play's Broadway premier. Alcorn attended, but his son later told the *Hartford Courant* that his father did not like it: "He couldn't understand all the laughter over something he thought was a deadly serious matter."[15]

Scholars have argued that murderabilia desensitizes the public to the heinous nature of killers' crimes and to the suffering and cruel deaths of the victims. Research has indeed shown that, typically, the more one is exposed to an alarming stimulus, the less unsettling it becomes over time. This desensitization (decreased reactivity) or habituation has been demonstrated over the course of decades of cognitive, emotional, and physiological research.[16] Even victims of crime evince physiological and cognitive desensitization when watching a series of videos depicting real crimes.[17] Forensic criminologist Xanthe Mallett, for one, worries that society's increased immersion in stories of dangerous and violent true crime will also mean decreased sensitivity (i.e., desensitization) towards the suffering of the victims and their families.[18] One wonders if purchasers of an Ed Gein serial killer action figure with a shovel in his hands really think about the invisible, implied victim being exhumed in order for him to decapitate their bodies and harvest their body parts.

Around the world, there are various perspectives on the utility or damage of true crime and murderabilia. In 2021, I was honored to participate in an online debate with the University Philosophical Society (The Phil)[19] at Trinity College, Dublin. The position of "The House" was that true crime media is exploitative, and the desensitization of the public to the hideous nature of murder was brought up several times. I agreed. I took the position that true crime media – which can include videos, movies, books, and even merchandise – ignored victims' experiences in favor of profit, such as the sale of serial killer statues and T-shirts, and that this profit constituted exploitation. Skilled student debaters from Trinity College offered their own powerful opinions on this point. Passionately defending the rights and feelings of crime victims and their family and friends, honors student Erika Magan provided what I felt was the most intense statement of the night: "True crime keeps the pain alive." Student officer and editor Maggie Larson further argued that many programs take crime details too far, invading privacy without the victims' consent and noting that true crime stories reflect "the ultimate sense of entitlement to others' lives."

Nonetheless, there are valid arguments suggesting that some good can come from true crime media. In the debate social psychologist Amanda Vicary reminded us that true crime programs have resulted in new information being discovered about crimes and victims. In some cases, falsely convicted individuals were exonerated, particularly through the efforts of the *Innocence Project*.[20] In one example, the television show *America's Most Wanted* helped apprehend 17 people over time from "FBI's Top 10 Fugitives" lists, which included hardened murderers.[21] I myself am a fan of television programs like Oxygen's *Cold Justice* and Investigation Discovery's *Reasonable Doubt*, both of which use their experts and resources to pursue justice and truth without incorporating gore and exploitation.

While we know that people do get desensitized to violent crime – they do not always.[22] In fact, research conducted with my colleague Erika

Frederick has shown that serial murder and similarly horrid events are so shocking that humans have evolved to be continuously sensitive to these phenomena.[23] Paying attention to the most gruesome acts and actors may be an inherent, unlearned survival mechanism. As psychologist Dolf Zillmann argued in 1998, the fact that horror appeals to us serves as a form of protective vigilance. I recall when my research students wanted to hear every single, violent, disturbing detail of the FSK cases that Erin Murphy and I were compiling for our 2015 report.[24] Anecdotally, I can tell you that this information about serial murder continues to disturb me greatly, probably even more so over time.

§

Belle Sorenson Gunness was a serial killer. She was also a serial arsonist. Born Brynhild Paulson[25] and sometimes listed as "Bella,"[26] Gunness is also known as "Lady Bluebeard." Her crimes were gruesome and barbaric.

Gunness, originally from Norway, committed so many murders in the USA from the late 1800s through the early 1900s that authorities admitted that they would likely never know how many people she had killed. When dozens of bodies and body parts were discovered buried on her Indiana farm, the *Burlington Daily News* called her "the arch fiend living in her two-story house on the little hill," and it described the scene a "Death Harvest."[27] Thousands of people raced to the scene to watch the excavation of remains. Railroads ran special trips to the Gunness farm, where people hoped to witness the recovery of body parts. People even set up refreshment stands for onlookers, with "Gunness stew" for sale.[28]

Before arriving in Indiana, Gunness had lived in Chicago, Illinois, with her first husband, Mads Sorenson, their biological children, Axel, Caroline, Myrtle, and Lucy, and their foster daughter, Jennie.[29] In 1896, Caroline died of what was likely poisoning. In that same year, Gunness' unsuccessful confectionary business burned to the ground, and she collected insurance money. The family moved to Texas, where their home burned to the ground in 1898, and they again collected insurance money. In that same year, Axel also died of what was likely poisoning. Two years later, her husband died after exhibiting symptoms of strychnine poisoning, suspiciously on the one day that two insurance policies on him overlapped – conveniently adding to his wife Belle's insurance payout.[30]

Gunness, who had come from a family of farmers and was familiar with the lifestyle, took the hefty sum of insurance money and moved with her children to a farm in La Porte, Indiana. Soon after, the farm's boat-house pavilion and carriage house were completely destroyed by fire. She collected insurance money. Sometime after arriving in La Porte, Belle's foster daughter, Jennie Olson, disappeared. A young man with whom Jennie was friendly inquired about where she was, and Belle told him Jennie had gone to school in Los Angeles, California.[31]

In La Porte, Belle met Peter Gunness. They married on April 1, 1902.[32] Peter's infant daughter died within one week of their marriage, and Peter died within the year. The Indiana State Board of Health Certificate of Death lists the "chief cause" as fracture of the skull.[33] Gunness reported that he accidentally got hit in the head with a sausage grinder, but one of the children reportedly told a friend, "Momma brained Papa with a meat cleaver."[34]

Shortly after husband Peter's death, Gunness posted advertisements in newspapers looking for a male partner to be her companion and assist with running her farm. Authorities do not know how many men answered these "Lonely Hearts" ads with the hope of finding new love along with a new business venture, but it was quite a few. Apparently, a series of men visited Gunness, bringing most of their life savings with them, and all but one of them disappeared. The survivor, Ray Lamphere, had worked for Gunness and later told authorities about her wicked setup – murdering potential suitors and keeping their money. In 1908, *The New York Times* pronounced that "Mrs. Gunness was money mad."[35]

When Gunness visited an attorney to create a last will and testament,[36] she also mentioned to the lawyer that she feared Lamphere was obsessed with her and might try to harm her. "I'm afraid he's going to kill me and burn the house," she stated,[37] although she herself purchased several gallons of kerosene that day.[38] Indeed, the very next morning, her house mysteriously burned down to rubble. Her farmhand, Joe Maxton, woke up to the smell of smoke in the home, but reported that he was unable to wake up the Gunness family. He hurried to get help, but it was too late.

The bodies of Gunness' daughters, Myrtle Sorenson, Lucy Sorenson, and that of her young son Phillip Gunness,[39] born in either 1903 or 1904,[40] were found under a piano. The body of a headless woman was found in the house's charred remains. Witnesses described an overpowering stench of kerosene.[41] Witnesses claimed, and doctors confirmed during the forensic examination, that the dead body was too short to be Gunness – even taking into account the missing head. The deceased weighed only about 150 pounds and was about five feet three inches tall. Gunness was reported to be about 200 pounds and was about five feet seven inches tall.[42] Still, a dentist did testify that he made the gold tooth crowns and bridge found in the remains of the fire, but the teeth were not found with the head.[43] Since it seems more likely that the short, headless fire victim was not Gunness, it stands to reason she pulled her own bridgework out and left it in the house to prove her demise. Nevertheless, Belle Gunness was declared officially dead by the coroner.[44] She is listed in La Porte, Indiana records as having died on April 27, 1908, at age 48.[45]

John (Asle) Helgelien, the brother of one of the men who disappeared, was aware of his brother's correspondence with Gunness. John knew that his brother, Andrew, had left home to visit Gunness, and that shortly after arriving in La Porte, had withdrawn $3,000 from his bank account (that is about $97,000 today). When he did not hear from his brother, John traveled to the Gunness farm, arriving shortly after the fire. Along with Gunness' farmhand Joe Maxton, he searched in the debris from the fire, but they found nothing. But when they started to dig through garbage in the backyard where the farm hogs ate, they found Andrew's body and more. They immediately called authorities and reported their grim findings.[46]

The La Porte Sheriff's Office excavated the farm's hog pit and, over several days, found the dismembered remains of so many people, in so many severed parts, that the exact number of victims, and their identities, will probably never be known. Gunness used the skills of butchery that she had developed as a farmer to cut apart victims' bodies, and then buried their body parts.[47] The body of Jennie Olson, her foster daughter, was among those recovered from the yard. In Pine Lake Cemetery in La Porte, there is a headstone erected in memory of the unknown victims of Belle Gunness.

Ray Lamphere, who was arrested and convicted of arson but not murder, informed authorities that Gunness had indeed murdered dozens of men and took their money before disappearing. Speaking with a prison manager where he was incarcerated, Lamphere explained that after getting their money, Gunness poisoned most of the men, then bludgeoned them with a hammer. Some victims she dissolved in quick lime, speeding up decomposition, and some victims she disarticulated and buried in her yard.[48] Lamphere knew these details, it turned out, because he confessed to helping Gunness bury her victims. He said that victims' heads were generally buried in one location on the farm, and bodies were buried in another.[49] Lamphere also confessed that the woman found dead in the charred rubble of the farm was a housekeeper hired by Gunness only days before.

Her ruse successful, it seems that Gunness caught a train to Chicago. The Chicago Police oversaw the investigation, and the Assistant Chief stated his firm belief that the city was Belle Gunness' destination. "We are hunting for her in the theory that she lured her victims with matrimonial propositions, killed them, dismembered them and buried them," he said. "And we will arrest her for murder if we find her."[50]

Nellie Larsen, Belle Gunness' sister, conveyed her sentiments to *The South Bend Tribune*. According to the paper's report, Nellie believed Gunness was "a wholesale murderess" and that she "was so demonically possessed of lust for money that she would not have stopped at any degree of crime to enrich herself." Nellie also used the word "insane" to describe her sister, saying that she hoped it was indeed Gunness who died in the fire. It would, she expressed, "put an end to the misery which enveloped all the actions of her life."[51]

Although authorities did search for Gunness, she was never found. There were numerous sightings, however, through the 1930s,[52] and in 1931, there was strong speculation that a California woman named Esther Carlson was actually Gunness. Carlson had been arrested for poisoning a wealthy, elderly man named Carl August Lindstrom, for whom she had worked as a housekeeper.[53] When money disappeared from Lindstrom's bank account following his death, Lindstrom's son Peter asked for an autopsy. His father's body was reported to be "reeking of arsenic."[54] Esther Carlson not only had the same modus operandi as Gunness, she was also reported to look remarkably similar. Furthermore, she had in her possession a photograph of three children who resembled Gunness' own.[55]

2.1 Belle Gunness with her children. (Photo from Getty Images)

After Esther Carlson died of tuberculosis while awaiting trial in California,[56] an associate of Gunness' from La Porte, a man named Dennis Daly, identified the body. "That's Belle Gunness, unquestionably," he said, noting her high cheekbones. Still, authorities questioned the accuracy of an identification made decades after the time of Gunness' murder farm.[57] While the official story remains that Belle Gunness died in a house fire, the evidence shows that she disappeared into history.

Although clinicians do not have access to Gunness to interview and assess her, it is not a stretch to acknowledge that her reported personality and behaviors recapitulate the signs and symptoms of psychopathy. On the one hand, she was superficially charming and generous at church, with one source describing her as "intensely religious."[58] She adopted children in need and portrayed herself as a kind and lonely widow in personal ads. On the other hand, arson and insurance fraud seem to be the lesser of her crimes. She killed her husbands, children, and stepchildren, stole victims' life savings, murdered her suitors, fed their body parts to hogs, and manufactured a story to frame her farmhand for murder. The psychological evidence suggests that, with her disregard for danger, repeated and callous disregard for and exploitation of others, and commission of deadly violence, she may have been a psychopath along with possible other disorders. But "Hell's Belle" disappeared before anyone got a chance to diagnose her mental health formally.

Belle Gunness remains the focus of intrigue and forensic investigation even to the present day.[59] It seems that bludgeoning your husband with a sausage grinder, poisoning and burning your children, killing and dismembering at least dozens of people, feeding the remains of your victims to hogs, and ripping your own gold teeth out to cover a crime are jarring enough to capture onlookers' and readers' attention and curiosity for well over a century.

§

People have always been curious. The legendary psychologist and prolific writer William James[60] stated that curiosity is what drives us to seek novel, sensational experiences to learn about ourselves and the world. Curiosity can be viewed a positive force. It is a cognitive and physiological drive that causes us to explore, to learn, and to want to learn more.[61] On the other hand, some scholars argue that curiosity is an aversive cognitive state. That is, we are experiencing an information gap; we do not know what lies ahead of us, thereby causing discomfort.

Researchers suggest that curiosity triggers a dopamine-fueled drive to understand whatever mystery lies in front of us.[62] Dopamine is a craving and feel-good neurotransmitter in our brains that drives us to approach what is rewarding. Dopamine neurons are excited by new stimuli, and this motivates us to seek novel stimulation. That which activates dopamine in our brains also causes physical addiction.[63] With respect to the topic of serial murder, then, we can extrapolate that consuming true crime media may literally be addictive.

Humans have a negativity bias. If I told you, "I met a nice woman at work. She is a great teacher, she is funny, she suffers from intestinal worms, she has written three books, and she is a yoga instructor," I would bet that those unfortunate worms made the biggest impression. We pay attention to, emphasize, and repeat negative information more than we do positive information.[64] But negative information also stimulates our fight-or-flight physiology, including our emotional centers, stress hormones, and attention and decision-making brain circuitry.[65] In short, threatening stimuli definitively capture and focus our attention.[66] Our emotional physiology is old, evolutionarily speaking, and viewing or hearing of something dangerous and/or repugnant – including nonfiction or fictional entertainment – sounds the alarm, keeps us vigilant, and mobilizes us to action.[67]

It makes sense, therefore, that we pay attention to terrifying events and people. This is protective vigilance.[68] We can argue that we have an evolved drive to attend to that which can harm us so that we can avoid it should it come our way. Across millions of years of human evolution, people who have paid more attention to alarming events have left more descendants than people who have not.[69]

In fact, in several studies, people have chosen to view images of violence and death over other images. As social psychologist Suzanne Oosterwijk emphasizes, "people deliberately subject themselves to negative images."[70] In *Everyone Loves a Good Train Wreck: Why We Can't Look Away*, author Eric Wilson similarly asserts that when people witness or watch something terrible, such as motor vehicle accidents and graphic deaths, they cannot avert their eyes. "They can't miss the carnage. They are mesmerized by the savagery."[71]

Indeed, as stated above, many people showed up at her farm to watch the Sheriff's team dig up dismembered heads, torsos, arms, and legs from her hog pit of mutilated victims. Similarly, many dozens of people also watched on as victims' bodies were excavated from the properties of serial killers Dorothea Puente and John Wayne Gacy, both of whom I will discuss later. As evidence suggests, people get a visceral reaction to witnessing blood and gore.[72] In psychological terminology, even the visually and conceptually aversive might be appetitive in some form or another.

Apparently, we like it when we encounter negative stimuli. The great philosopher Aristotle is quoted as saying that we "enjoy contemplating the most precise images of things whose sight is painful to us."[73] I cannot tell you how many people approach me or otherwise contact me to share that they "love serial killers." I always hope and assume this means that they have a great interest in these criminals' psychology. Although, to be sure, some people do actually love serial killers. Sheila Isenberg interviewed women who have had long-term romantic relationships with serial murderers and authored a book[74] about them.

Taken all together, the evidence strongly suggests that we have morbid curiosity. That is, we simultaneously feel excitement, fear, and a compulsion to seek information and to know about horrid subjects that include, but are not limited to, death and terror.[75] In the media, the saying "If it bleeds, it leads"[76] conveys awareness among news entities that horrific and alarming content will secure viewer interest at the top of the news hour. Indeed, research shows that news stories about crime, accidents, and disasters are prevalent in competitive news outlets across many countries.[77]

Well-known psychologist Marvin Zuckerman and his colleagues were among the first research teams to publish studies about morbid curiosity. They argued that morbid curiosity is linked to the personality dimension of high sensation seeking. Sensation seeking is defined as the need for varied complex, stimulating, and novel experiences and the willingness to take risks, whether these are psychological, physical, or social, to gain such experiences.[78] Individuals who score high on measures of sensation seeking are those who are more likely to use alcohol and other substances, gamble, mountain climb, have risky sex, and seek unusual activities.[79] There is also strong evidence that links engagement in risky events to increased autonomic physiological arousal (i.e., fight-or-flight). Symptoms of fight-or-flight in this context include increased heart rate and respiration, heightened cortical activity, and the release of stress and arousal hormones such as adrenaline.[80]

Sensation seeking is common across people and cultures, suggesting that it is an evolved mechanism. Yet, like all psychological mechanisms that are a product of evolution, individual differences exist.[81] Suzanne Oosterwijk, for example, observed individual variation in response to negative images, and likewise, Zuckerman and colleagues reported individual variation in sensation seeking.[82] There is, however, a clear connection between morbid curiosity and sensation seeking. If an interest in horror (and murder in particular) serves a survival advantage, it makes sense that morbid curiosity serves as a mechanism of protective vigilance and a physiological call to action.

My colleague Erika Frederick and I set out to document the connection between morbid curiosity and interest in serial killers, as well as to document the connection between sensation seeking and interest in serial killers. We recruited men and women college-student participants and asked them to rate their interest in serial killers in addition to their interest in other morbid and non-morbid topics.[83] We asked the participants to complete the Curiosity About Morbid Events (CAME) Scale, developed by psychologists Marvin Zuckerman and Patrick Litle, which asks participants to rate their level of agreement with specific statements. The scale asks participants to rate their level of agreement with statements such as, "I think I would like to witness an execution," "It does not bother me to see extreme violence portrayed in movies or television," and "I would like to see an autopsy being performed." We also asked participants to respond to the Sensation-Seeking Scale, rating their level of agreement with statements such as, "I have tried some drugs that produce hallucinations or would like to," "Keeping the drinks full is the key to a good party," and "I like a lot of risky sports."[84] From the responses to these different scales, we averaged scores to calculate both an overall index of morbid curiosity and a sensation-seeking score.

What we found is that, for both men and women, those higher in morbid curiosity were more interested in the topic of serial killing, and those higher in sensation seeking were more interested in the topic of serial killing. Stated another way, those interested in serial killers have a heightened curiosity about morbid topics and demonstrate an overall interest in participating in and viewing risky and/or gruesome events and situations.

Cross-culturally, men traditionally have scored higher in measures of sensation seeking.[85] Men have more of the sex steroid hormone testosterone than do women, and increased testosterone is related to increased social vigilance, competition, dominance, and violence.[86] With this being the case, we would expect men to have heightened morbid curiosity compared to women. In keeping with previous research, our study found that men's morbid curiosity scores were, indeed, higher than women's scores. However, men's and women's sensation-seeking scores were the same. That said, we did find the expected association that both men and women with higher sensation-seeking scores also have higher morbid curiosity scores.

According to our study, those who were interested in serial killing also had a greater interest in learning about additional morbid and non-morbid topics. This finding suggests that morbid curiosity is an offshoot of curiosity in general. Yet these other interests were not statistically perfect predictors of serial killer interest, meaning that there are other factors beyond simple curiosity to explain why someone would want to learn about FSKs and MSKs.

Of course, morbid entertainment cannot itself hurt you, be it factual or fictional depictions, yet people are drawn to it. Evolutionary psychologists argue that our ancestral brain lacks the ability to distinguish between people and events who are actually in our lives and those we see portrayed in entertainment media such as on television.[87] This concept logically extends to morbid entertainment. Videos, books, and podcasts do not represent a threat in your immediate physical environment. But in evolutionary terms, our brains, having evolved over millions of years in conditions with no videos, books, and podcasts, still seem to respond to stimuli as if we were in the same environment as our ancient ancestors.

On the automatic and unconscious subcortical level, it is more conducive to survival for us to perceive a stimulus as an actual threat and activate physiological survival mechanisms just in case, as compared to taking even a split second longer to decide with cortical mechanisms that the threat is only occurring on our televisions. In other words, our brains reflect the idea that it is better to be safe than sorry, when being safe means remaining alive. In this context, then, it is interesting that evidence suggests people prefer horror entertainment that is more plausible.[88] It seems we actually *prefer it* when the threat feels more real.[89]

Research has yielded trait and personality factors associated with the consumption of horror media in general. For example, there is some evidence to suggest people who are higher in intelligence seek more horror entertainment.[90] There may also be experiential factors involved in the consumption or avoidance of horror media, such as having been victimized by violence in the past. Yet even as we continue to learn more through scientific research, we have yet to understand fully why the topics of serial murder and serial killers command the strong and continued attention of so many people.

What can be said with absolute certainty, however, is that they do. Whether it is through people showing up to watch as remains are exhumed by law enforcement, engaging with the thriving true crime genre, or exploring the disturbing world of murderabilia, serial murders and the killers who commit them tap into a strong current of morbid curiosity that exists in many.

CHAPTER 3

The Lives of Female Serial Killers

§

Dorothea Montalvo Puente was a serial killer. You would not likely derive this knowledge from the boarding house proprietor's appearance, as she was described as "ostensibly the essence of grandmotherly virtue." Curly and carefully molded grey hair, large-button sweaters and coats, and oversized glasses portrayed an image of innocence and care.[1] "Murderous Grandma" does not fall into our typical gender schemas, yet Puente ultimately came to be known as "Killer Granny" when it was discovered in the 1980s that she had murdered at least nine people, dismembered them, and buried them in her backyard.

Prior to the murders she committed at her boarding house, Puente was convicted for drugging three elderly people she met in bars and stealing their possessions.[2] She served about three years in prison, was released on parole, and took up where she left off with both of those activities and more.[3] Puente invited mentally ill, intellectually disabled, elderly, and indigent tenants in need of care and shelter to her lovely Victorian boarding house, known for its welcoming garden, on F Street in Sacramento, California. Social workers felt she was compassionate and were appreciative that she took in very difficult client cases.

After earning their trust, Puente murdered the vulnerable people who boarded with her, feeding them cake poisoned with the heavy sedative flurazepam (a drug that has greater effects on older adults).[4] As they lay incapacitated in their beds, she smothered her victims with pillows, then dismembered them and dumped their body parts into a mass grave in her verdant backyard.

3.1 "Death House Landlady" Dorothea Puente with SPD homicide detective John Cabrera, 1988. (Photo by Dick Schmidt/Sacramento Bee/Tribune News Service via Getty Images)

Puente hid her boarders' deaths so she could continue to collect their disability compensation checks, netting about $5000 a month. She forged letters to the US Social Security Administration to get her victims' government support checks sent to her address, and forged letters to loved ones that made them believe their family members were still alive.[5] When neighbors started complaining about a putrid odor emanating from her property, she told them that she had a sewer and dead rat problem that was causing the smell. Eventually, Judy Moise, a counselor for boardinghouse resident Bert Montoya, became concerned about his whereabouts, as he had intellectual disabilities and had gone missing.[6] Moise alerted the authorities, who made the grim discovery in her backyard.

Neighbors were in disbelief that the kindly older lady with the rose garden was a serial killer. Crowds and television trucks lined the streets as authorities exhumed the disarticulated remains of victims from that lovely yard.[7]

Some bodies were wrapped up in tablecloths "like a mummy," and one was in a plastic bag.[8] A body later identified to be 78-year-old Betty

Palmer was missing her legs, hands, and head.[9] Not all her victims wound up in her backyard, however. The body of yet another of her missing tenants was found near the Sacramento River in a box.[10]

At the age of 61, Puente was charged with murdering nine people.[11] She had fled as soon as the first body was found, but was soon captured.[12] Upon her arrest, she told authorities, "I used to be a very good person at one time." William Harder, who claimed to be Puente's grandson, corroborated her assertion. He said that Puente had not always been bad.[13]

Notably, William Harder is a murderabilia dealer who befriended both murderous cult leader Charles Manson and MSK Richard Ramirez. When pressed as to why he had no empathy for victims' families, Harder said, "That's not my job," and stated that there was no difference between collecting murderabilia and collecting US Civil War memorabilia. Among his inventory is a bobblehead of his grandmother, labeled "Dorothea Puente, The Death House Landlady." She is holding on to a stack of the checks she cashed after the deaths of her trusting disabled tenants.[14]

Indeed, Puente, who appeared grandmotherly and maintained an impeccable home while she used poison and suffocation to silence her victims, did it for the money. She preyed on the ill and infirm, and victimized people who knew her and trusted her. She got away with it for years. In court, her defense attorneys claimed that the tenants died of natural causes, claiming that Puente did not report them because she was afraid it would look suspicious and violate her parole.[15]

Mitigating factors in the case were drawn from her life story. She grew up as an orphan, for example, and her alcoholic, adoptive parents abused her and her many siblings. The *Los Angeles Times* reported that Puente's mother was a prostitute who died when Puente was 10, and that her father would hold a pistol to his head and threaten suicide in front of the children. After her mother's death, she spent time in an orphanage and many foster homes. At age 16, she was sexually abused. The jury also heard that, at times, she was kind and generous.[16]

Nevertheless, on August 26, 1993, at age 64, Dorothea Puente was convicted of the first-degree murders of Dorothy Miller and Benjamin Fink and the second-degree murder of Leona Carpenter. The jury was inexplicably deadlocked on six other counts of murder. She was sentenced to life in prison, narrowly escaping a death sentence, which would have meant execution by the gas chamber. The jury voted seven to five in favor of sparing her life. Once in prison without the chance of parole, reports say that she was called "Mom" by her fellow inmates. She apparently doted over them and cooked burritos for them.[17] Puente died at age 82 on March 27, 2011, in prison in Chowchilla, California.[18]

Despite efforts to introduce mitigating context in court, no one knows Puente's real story. Carla Norton,[19] who investigated Puente's background while writing a book about her in the mid-1990s, uncovered evidence that Puente at one point pretended to be a retired doctor. She told some people she was Egyptian and others she was Mexican. She had multiple aliases and spoke of having had many husbands. No one was certain of her true age. Puente was a murderer and a thief, but people were fooled by her "grandmother side." As Norton told the *Santa Cruz Sentinel*, "Sociopaths conceal that side very well. They are practiced and they have a vested interest in not advertising their criminal self."[20] While I am unaware of any psychological assessments of her, and I myself am not diagnosing her, her ability to present herself as a kind caregiver and grandma while murdering disabled individuals is consistent with behavior seen in psychopaths.

Indeed, Puente engaged in many behaviors typical of female serial killers.

§

In this chapter, and those that follow, I discuss research findings about FSK backgrounds, mental illness, crimes, and victims. The information I present here is based on my team's data collection. In 2014, we gathered information about a wide array of variables, and our sample size of FSKs is substantial considering the infrequency of these crimes. Although my team is not the first to study FSKs, studies using large samples of FSKs are rare, and some studies are at least a generation old. Seeking to collect information about as many FSKs as we could, our study is arguably one of the largest empirical (i.e., data collection) endeavors to be published on the topic. We also yielded some novel findings.

While there are many published studies of MSK crimes and psychology, there are very few scientific studies that gather original source material about FSKs in order to understand generalizations (i.e., nomo-thetic research) regarding FSK mental states, crimes, motives, and vic-tims.[21] There are a few case studies of individual FSKs (i.e., idiographic research), but while lone cases are rich sources of hypotheses and even treatment avenues, a sample size of one murderer cannot be generalized to describe the behaviors of all murderers. Moreover, we should keep in mind that experts feel there is an appreciable number of unsolved serial murder cases throughout the world.[22] There might be a certain type of serial killer whose motives and means are so different than others that they get away with their crimes.[23]

Unfortunately, very few researchers have access to actual case files or the ability to interview serial murderers. Forensic researchers, there-fore, often rely on newspapers, legitimate news websites and stories (e.g., Associated Press, ABC, CBS, NBC, FOX), historical societies, and court documents to derive data. This is called the mass media method of data collection, and it has been used to derive facts about people or events from the past or present when researchers cannot gain direct access.[24] Importantly, where there are previously existing studies that used clinical and interview data about serial murderers,[25] I have found that the infor-mation yielded by my mass media method studies, conducted with pub-licly available information, corroborates these findings almost exactly.

We know that sensationalism sells, and in the case of murder, news-papers might depict only what they deem "a good story" that will garner readership. We also live in an era where some people feel that "fake news" permeates our landscape – that the media present false or mis-leading information to manipulate the viewers and readers. Public fig-ures push this viewpoint, asserting the information is untrue when the media gives unfavorable reports.[26] Some scholars assert that there is a current "crisis of faith" in journalism.[27] Yet in my various research pro-jects, I have found information in the news to be factually consistent with courthouse records and transcripts, and I have found information to be fairly consistent across independently reported sources. Furthermore, unlike psychologists and criminologists who are investigating perpetra-tor psychology, reporters usually do not have a theoretical angle when writing their product.[28] I have not, for example, read any pieces on serial murderers where a newspaper reporter interjected words like "insane" or "psychopath" unless they were quoting legal proceedings or a clinical mental health expert. They report facts.

Our initial study generated a sample of 64 FSKs who committed their crimes in the United States from 1821 to 2008. That might not seem like a large sample for the social sciences, and indeed, at times the data were too scarce for meaningful statistical analyses. But serial murder is rare. It may be the case that only 2% of murders are committed by serial killers.[29] Using this estimate and taking one-sixth of that to be female-perpetrated, this leaves us 0.3% of all murderers to study. One would have to peruse about 20,000 murder cases to find a sample size of 64 FSKs.[30]

Fortunately, we were able to start with the news clearinghouse website Murderpedia.org,[31] where we could search alphabetically for FSKs. Acquiring the name of the offender, we consulted with an entry's noted primary sources for accuracy validation, and then performed internet and database searches for related newspaper articles, news network web stories, historical society collections, government documents, and court documents. We verified that each offender met our criteria: they had killed three or more people, had a cooling-off period of at least one week between murders, and committed their crimes in the USA.[32]

Of course, we did not simply "copy and paste" from Murderpedia. We used its list as a springboard for exploration of reputable, verifiable information sources. While we never found a mistake in Murderpedia .org's compilations, there has been a trend on the website in recent years toward incorporating information directly from Wikipedia or amateur blogs. Anyone can contribute to or edit this type of website, so this puts an even greater emphasis on the need to seek original sources. Moreover, as of this writing, the site had not been updated for a few years. Nevertheless, Murderpedia.org was a great asset as we began our research.

For this study, we only included verified FSKs, electing not to include suspected killers. We also did not include FSKs who committed their crimes with a partner, as we were interested in the psychology of the lone offender, and it would be difficult to parse each case and attribute motives and behaviors properly to each member of a pair. Notably, however, previous research has illuminated intriguing variations between lone killers and partnered killers. For example, partnered serial killers are less likely to be mentally ill but are more likely to engage in brutality such as kidnapping and using victims as sex slaves. Furthermore, women who were part of a serial killer pair were shown to have had more tumultuous upbringings than did FSKs who acted alone.[33]

The following is what we discovered about the lives of female serial murderers, including interpretation and case studies that build and expand on the original research and statistics my team published in the *Journal of Forensic Psychiatry and Psychology* in 2015.[34]

WHO ARE FSKS? DEMOGRAPHIC DATA ON FEMALE SERIAL KILLERS

Our dataset of 64 FSKs yielded important information about the demographics, professional careers, socioeconomic status, relationships, and even physical appearance of women who have committed serial murder in the United States. All but one FSK in our sample were born in the USA, for example. For those whose ethnicity was documented, almost all (about 90%) were White. Religious affiliation was seldom mentioned in cases, but in all instances when it was, the killer was noted as Christian.

FSKs have held a wide variety of jobs, including sex worker, drug dealer, psychic, food server, farmer, and Sunday school (religious) teacher. However, an alarming number of serial killers (39%) have worked in health-related positions (e.g., nurses and nurse's aides). In addition, more than one out of five has held another direct caregiver role (e.g., stay-at-home mother, stay-at-home wife, babysitter). That means that most (more than 60%) of FSKs were in charge of others' well-being, particularly of those who are vulnerable.

The majority of FSKs in our dataset were of middle-class socioeconomic status (55.3%), but some were lower-class (40.4%). Only a few (4.3%) were considered upper-class. Academic achievement was only available for 26 FSKs. Among these women, there was considerable variation in education: 34.6% had college/professional degrees, 19.2% had some college or professional training, 15.4% were high-school graduates with no further education, and 30.8% were high school dropouts. This means that the majority of FSKs had at least some postsecondary education. Notably, while intelligence is difficult to derive from news sources, descriptors were provided for 16 women, or 25% of our sample. Of these, eight were described by sources as being of average intelligence, two were described as having high intelligence, and six were described as having low intelligence or intellectual disability.[35]

Data on relationship status were available for most FSKs in our study. While they were actively killing, more than half (54.2%) were married, about a quarter were divorced, and the rest were in a romantic relationship or single. For those who had ever been married, they averaged two marriages, with about one in four FSKs having been married three or more times. The range of marriage frequency was one to seven marriages, meaning that among those who married, they married anywhere from one to seven times over the course of their lives. It seems that female serial killers are serial monogamists.

Over the course of our study, we were able find descriptions of physical appearance in about a quarter of our cases. Seven were reported to be attractive, with one killer being described as looking like actor Elizabeth Taylor, who was considered very beautiful. Ten were reported to have average looks. Five FSKs were noted to be overweight, and three were described as unattractive, through the use of such terms as "remarkably ugly" and "not particularly attractive." Taken from this, we can extrapolate that most FSKs have been deemed to be of at least average attractiveness. That said, the halo effect described in Chapter 1, in addition to societal disbelief that women are capable of such gruesome crimes, might aid women who have committed crimes over time in evading suspicion.

The age at which a FSK commits her first murder might be a key variable in the commission of these crimes. While our dataset included this information for most cases, we must remember that it is possible that some of a killer's crimes, including her first crime, may be unknown to police. Nevertheless, we determined that the mean age of a FSK's first act was 32, with a statistical standard deviation (SD) of 11.7 years.[36] The ages themselves demonstrated considerable variation, with FSKs ranging from 16 to 65 at the time of their first documented murder. However, about three-quarters of the FSKs in our sample were in their 20s or 30s when they first killed.

In addition to identifying key information about FSKs' ages at the time of their first murders, our study found that their average age when they were caught was about 39.25 (SD = 12.3). FSKs committed crimes, on average, over a 7.25-year span, but with noted variability (SD = 8 years). Some FSKs committed all their acts of murder in the same year, and at least one killed for over three decades before she was caught.[37]

§

"Jolly" Jane Toppan was a serial killer. She was a nurse "obsessed with death."[38] Her ambition, she is quoted as saying, was "to have killed more people – helpless people – than any other man or woman who ever lived." Toppan was born Honora (Norah) Kelley in 1857, the daughter of an Irish family who resided in the Boston area. When she was very young, her mother died of tuberculous, and her father Peter, known as "Kelly the Crack," died of alcoholism. She was adopted by Captain and Mrs. Toppan, whom she later poisoned.[39]

Toppan worked as a servant in her early life. She then began nurse's training at Cambridge Hospital in Massachusetts. She was called "Jolly Jane" because of her rosy cheeks and friendly demeanor, and she was "personally rather attractive." Nevertheless, colleagues developed disdain for her, as she lied, stole, spread gossip, and was "obsessed" with autopsies. Later, she secured work at Massachusetts General Hospital, but she was fired for dispensing opiate drugs too liberally.[40] In 1891, she got a job as a private duty nurse for wealthy clients, and she became admired for her compassionate nature and skills. Toppan made a lot of money for the time, although at least one report indicated that she augmented her personal finances by stealing from her victims.[41]

Former colleagues remember Toppan saying something to the effect that it is useless to keep old people alive. Her landlords were "feeble and fussy," for example, and so she killed them. But she did not kill the elderly only. Toppan also killed her foster sister, Elizabeth Toppan Brigham. Reports indicated that Elizabeth was always kind to Jane, but Jane resented her because she was attractive, married, and well-liked. One day, when the sisters went on a picnic, Toppan fed Elizabeth corned beef and taffy laced with the strong poison, strychnine. Death by strychnine is violent and painful. Elizabeth was likely terrified and aware of everything that was happening to her as she experienced painful muscle rigidity, including spastic arching of the back, an inability to breathe,

3.2 Serial killer nurse "Jolly" Jane Toppan may have murdered 100 people. (Photo from Getty Images)

and ultimate respiratory failure.[42] Toppan seemed to confirm this awful death when she revealed, "I held her in my arms and watched with delight as she gasped her life out."[43]

In a plot to marry her sister's widower, O. A. Brigham, Toppan moved in with him and killed his elderly housekeeper. "Jolly Jane" then poisoned Brigham and nursed him back to health to impress him. Apparently, however, he was not impressed enough to marry her.[44] Later, police became suspicious of Toppan when her current landlord's entire family mysteriously died. Toppan killed Mrs. Davis, moved into Mr. Davis' house and killed him, and then killed his two daughters with morphine and atropine poisoning. This triggered marked suspicion among surviving family members, who reported her to authorities. She was finally arrested on October 30, 1901, for the murder of Mary (Minnie) D. Gibbs, one of the Davis daughters.[45]

Authorities say that during her nursing training, Toppan experimented with the effects of morphine (an opiate narcotic depressant) and atropine (a stimulant at low doses and a depressant at high doses)[46] on her patients. This caused cycles of unconsciousness and alertness until they died. At the time, however, doctors dismissed the deaths of elderly patients as a product of heart disease, stroke, or even diabetes. Later, Toppan told authorities that she got a thrill from the killing. "No voice has as much melody in it as the one crying for life," she said, "no eyes as bright as those about to become fixed and glassy; no face so beautiful as the one pulseless and cold."[47]

She also killed friends and business acquaintances along the way. An investigator was quoted as saying, "If all of the suspicions involving the operations of Jane Toppan could be substantiated . . . the succession of murders will cover a wider range and be more astounding than any series of crimes perpetuated by one person in many years."[48] Toppan ultimately confessed to killing 31 people between 1885 and 1901, but the authorities estimated that she had killed many more. She later stated, "It would be safe to say that I killed at least 100 persons."[49] Toppan appears to have fulfilled her ambition to become one of the most prolific murderers on record.

In her confession, she said, "I have absolutely no remorse. Even when I poisoned my dearest friends . . . I did not feel any regret afterward. I cannot detect the slightest bit of sorrow over what I have done." Later, however, she changed her tone. She told physicians she was prone to violent outbursts and said, "I know I am not safe to be around. It would be better if I were locked up where I could do no one any harm."[50]

Psychiatrists at the time, called "alienists," examined Toppan twice. Dr. H. M. Quimby, Dr. George F. Jelly, and Dr. Henry R. Stedman were "insanity experts," and they unanimously declared her insane.[51] One report said that Toppan was deemed to have "mental degeneracy."[52] Another newspaper said that she was "declared a most remarkable specimen of degeneracy."[53] In addition to the murders she committed, she had written "a voluminous mass of letters" that was presented by authorities at her trial. The letters contained lies of wealth, planned trips around the world on a private yacht, and an engagement to a prominent man. *The Boston Post* stated that "the stories which she has told in these missives all border on the marvelous and seem to have been written with an absolute disregard for the truth."[54] *The Boston Globe* reported that after experts deemed Toppan "incurably insane" and Judge Bell gave the jury instructions for deliberation, she seemed pleased. It took the jury 20 minutes to decide she was not guilty by reason of insanity, and during that time Toppan "chatted, laughed and was exceedingly jolly."[55] In the end, Toppan was sentenced to life in Taunton Lunatic Asylum on June 24, 1902, with one headline declaring she was "Sent to the Madhouse."[56]

It is difficult to interpret Toppan's general insanity diagnosis through the lens of modern psychology, but it seems that mental health experts of the time believed Jane had lost touch with reality. One physician said that Jane also grew increasingly suspicious over time. An expert who examined Toppan told *The Boston Post* that hers was "one of the strangest cases of diseased mind he had ever seen."[57] While not diagnosing her, Toppan's symptoms may be indicative of schizophrenia, although the term and diagnosis were not introduced until after her assessment. She had reportedly lost touch with reality; expressed bizarre behavior (including kissing a dying patient experiencing a death rattle);[58] had an inappropriate affect (she liked autopsies and said that being in jail was the happiest she had ever been);[59] suffered from memory impairment (she told her lawyer that, at times, she had "great difficulty" remembering what she had done);[60] and experienced delusions of grandeur. Further, schizophrenia has a substantial genetic basis and is thus seen in siblings,[61] and Toppan's sister (unnamed) was also committed to an insane asylum.[62] Nevertheless, Toppan is no longer around to interview and assess.

Toppan's apparent delusions continued after institutionalization, along with her hallucinations. She was initially allowed to mingle with other patients, but as she developed more delusions and her violent outbursts became more frequent, she was confined to a padded cell. From her room she would scream about the dead victims coming back to exact revenge by poisoning her. When nurses brought her food, she would scream, "It is poisoned!" At one point, she wrote the hospital a letter that read, "I wish to inform you that I am alive in spite of the deleterious food which has been served to me." She also dug her nails into her own skin, causing bleeding, and said the injury was because one of her deceased victims injected morphine into her arm. At night, she screamed, "Fire! Fire!" – another way that she reportedly murdered her victims.[63]

Toppan was not idle during her time in the asylum, however. She wrote love stories.[64] In fact, Toppan told people that had she been married she would not have killed so many people.[65] Indeed, the New England Historical Society conjectured that her motive for murder was being jilted by her boyfriend when she was aged 16.[66] When Toppan died at the age of 81 on Wednesday, August 17, 1938, she had lived at the asylum for decades and become "a quiet old lady" in her later years.[67] One obituary for Toppan ran with the headline, "Famous Poisoner Dies Wednesday After Weird Life."[68]

§

Congruent with the data from our study, "Jolly" Jane Toppan was White, had a pleasant appearance, had at least some postsecondary education and training, and was a nurse and caretaker. We might further surmise, but cannot verify, that her Boston Irish heritage included Christianity, as most Irish immigrants to Boston in the 1800s were Roman Catholic.[69] Like the typical FSK from our dataset, she likely began killing in her 20s or 30s, but seems to have gotten away with it for about 15 years – longer than our reported mean, but still within about one standard deviation of it. Like many other FSKs, which I discuss in Chapter 4, Toppan had strong indications of severe mental illness.

It is unlikely that any one case will hit *all* the profile marks generated by our sample. Moreover, as stated at the outset of this book, Toppan's case may or may not be included in the sample from which we drew our statistics. Yet her case comes very close to our composite FSK profile extrapolated from our analysis.[70] I will talk about the complete profile later in Chapter 6.

THE DEVELOPMENTAL HISTORY OF FEMALE
SERIAL KILLERS

It is difficult to determine the precise developmental history of FSKs. In our data sample, for example, it is impossible to know whether cases that omit background information do so because there are no remarkable issues to present, or because the reporting agent or source just did not have this information available. When attempting to shed light on how women develop into serial killers, we must therefore interpret available information with caution.

In our sample of 64 FSKs, we found information about serious illness reported in the childhoods of only six women. Information on this topic was missing for most of the sample. In six cases illness was reported and the illnesses were blood poisoning and thyroid issues, head trauma, measles with long-term vision issues, scarlet fever, seizure disorder, and polio. With more sophisticated treatment and disease tracking available in the present day, and some conditions such as polio virtually eradicated, it is difficult to interpret these FSK data. We do know from research, however, that adverse childhood health problems increase the risk of health and behavioral issues in adulthood.[71] Pediatric specialists stress that adverse childhood experiences can have deleterious consequences on brain development, including neuroplasticity, which indicates the brain's ability to heal or adapt.[72] Stated another way, severe illness, abuse, or other adverse experiences when we are younger can change our brain's way of adapting to new information when we are older.

Relatedly, several FSKs are known to have had difficult family situations in their childhood. We found information for about a third of our sample regarding FSKs' familial environment growing up. With some overlap between conditions, there were instances of parental alcoholism, with an overrepresentation of alcoholic mothers as compared to women's prevalence of alcoholism in the general population. We also found instances of overly controlling parents and insulting and denigrating mothers. Five FSKs had mothers who were reported as absent or deceased, and one had a father who was reported as absent or deceased. Four FSKs were abandoned as children. Information within our sample about the physical and mental health of family members was sparse. As stated above, the absence of information may speak to non-access, or it can speak to the absence of the condition. While there is no way to determine this, it is clear that some FSKs experienced difficult family environments.

Of our sample of 64 FSKs, we found 20 cases (31.3%) in which the FSK was sexually and/or physically abused in her lifetime. This is about a third of our sample. In five of the cases, the FSK was both sexually *and* physically abused. In 30% of the women abused, the assault(s) occurred in childhood. As girls or women, they experienced being burned, beaten, and starved. Reported perpetrators were mothers, fathers, grandparents, and husbands or other romantic partners. I add the caveat that, after conducting research on this topic for several years, I feel that a prevalence of 31.3% abuse is likely an underestimate, but it is a clear indication of marked abuse in the developmental histories of many FSKs.

The long-term deleterious effects of childhood maltreatment have long been known, and it is a recurrent theme throughout this book. Poor outcomes stretch across health, psychological, relationship, and societal variables.[73] While a systematic review of childhood maltreatment outcomes is beyond the scope of this book, key findings are clearly relevant to the psychology of FSKs. Evidence suggests that childhood maltreatment changes the very architecture of the human brain, as the young brain must adapt to extreme, adverse experiences.[74] Some experts suggest that the physical and psychological abuse of a child inflicts "wounds that won't heal" because of the permanent effects on the brain.[75]

Notably, abuse impacts one's emotional processing, including the inability to recognize emotions in others.[76] And, indeed, a deficiency in emotional recognition has been documented in violent offenders.[77] Perhaps this offers a glimpse into why both FSKs and MSKs have a callous disregard for victims. Moreover, abuse decreases reward sensitivity,[78] meaning that increased stimulation would be needed to achieve a desired result. Perhaps this is why FSKs continue to murder for profit across various victims.

The tragic experiences of childhood maltreatment also negatively affect mental health throughout one's lifespan and can lead to the development of more than one psychiatric disorder.[79] Specifically, experts have suggested a traumagenic neurodevelopmental model that shows childhood adversity causes brain alterations. Affected regions include the frontal lobes (creating problems with decision-making), the hippocampus (causing memory and emotional reactivity issues), the hypothalamic-pituitary-adrenal (HPA) axis (which means an increased stress hormonal response), and the dopaminergic system (with increases in dopamine being associated with schizophrenia-like symptoms, emerging in later-life psychosis).[80] However, while there may be an indication of childhood abuse in the development of documented FSKs, it cannot be overemphasized that almost no one who experiences childhood trauma grows up to be a serial murderer.

§

Aileen Wuornos was a serial killer. She shot several men in the head and torso, stole their money, and disposed of their bodies carelessly.

Wuornos was born in 1956 in Michigan. Her father was a violent, convicted child molester who completed suicide by hanging while serving a prison sentence. Her mother, Diane, was 15 years old when she married Wuornos' father. She abandoned Wuornos and her older brother Keith to the care of their maternal grandparents after her husband's death. Wuornos' alcoholic grandmother and violent, volatile grandfather raised both children.[81] Wuornos told clinical examiners that her grandfather sexually abused her, as did one of his friends.[82] She also reported having an incestuous relationship with her brother.[83]

Years later, a relative stated that, despite being a good student and doing well in school, Wuornos started acting out around age ten or eleven. She shoplifted and set a fire that burned her face.[84] When school officials recommended counseling for Wuornos, her grandmother declined to grant permission. When Wuornos got pregnant at age 14, she was sent to live at a home for unwed mothers. Staff reported her as hostile and unable to get along with others. She gave birth to a baby boy, whom she gave up for adoption.

At some point, Wuornos' grandfather, who some speculate was the father of her baby, completed suicide. She was eventually thrown out of the house and began living in the woods. At the age of 16, she began earning money as a sex worker and was reported to abuse drugs and alcohol.[85] She was arrested several times in the 1970s for disorderly conduct and assault around the same time that her maternal grandmother died by suicide and her brother died of cancer.

When Wuornos was 20 years old, she moved to Florida and met a man named Lewis Gratz Fell, whom she married in May 1976. Fell, whose age was around 70 at the time, had the marriage annulled two months later,[86] claiming that Wuornos was violent with him and squandered his money. Wuornos herself stated that he beat her with his cane.[87]

Wuornos resumed life as a sex worker. The *Tallahassee Democrat* reported that Wuornos was "a strong-willed woman . . . with a brown purse and a heart full of betrayal." As a highway prostitute, she chose her company carefully and then decided if it would be a "normal day" or a "killing day."[88] Eventually, after a string of murders in Florida brought her under suspicion, Wuornos was arrested in 1991.[89]

After her arrest, Wuornos told authorities that she did, in fact, shoot seven men, but that she did it in self-defense. She claimed that she had been raped so many times that she decided to carry a gun. She had a story about roughness or abuse from each of her victims. "After I killed the first couple I thought about quitting," she said from her jail cell, "but I had to make money to pay the bills. And I figured at least I was doing some good killing these guys . . . they would have hurt someone else."[90]

Psychiatrist Wade Myers and colleagues assessed Wuornos while she was incarcerated and determined that she had psychopathy, antisocial personality disorder, and borderline personality disorder.[91] During her murder trial, her uncle Barry claimed she was never abused.[92] Yet clinicians were not convinced by him. They asserted that "childhood attachment disruptions, severe psychopathy, other personality disorder pathology, and a traumagenic abuse history likely contributed to her having serially murdered seven victims."[93]

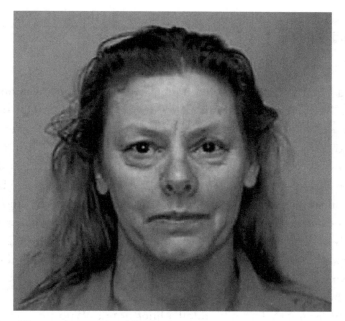

3.3 Aileen Wuornos in an undated Florida Department of Corrections photo. (Photo from Florida DOC/Getty Images)

When Wuornos was convicted for these multiple murders and sentenced to death, she canceled all appeals. In an interview with a local news station, she proclaimed, "I need to die for the killing of those people."[94] She continued, "I killed those men, robbed them cold as ice. And I'd do it again . . . I'm the one who hates human life and I'd kill again."[95] At the time, some people within the criminal justice system, the public, and the media argued that Wuornos might not have been competent for execution. *The Miami Herald's* Fred Grimm, for example, emphasized that her behavior was erratic and bizarre. Observers pointed to the fact that she fired her lawyer and instead appointed an evangelical horse trainer who claimed half the rights to movies about her life – actions that hardly demonstrate sound judgment. Many people felt she should have had additional psychiatric examinations.

Still, as Grimm said, "society shrugged off those mad, staring eyes,"[96] and Wuornos was executed on October 9, 2002. Her last words were, "Yes, I'd like to say I'm sailing with the rock. And I'll be back, like

Independence Day, with Jesus, June 6th, like in the movie. Big mother ship and all. I'll be back."[97]

§

Viewing Wuornos' life through a traumagenic lens, we might understand why her life followed an aberrant pathway. Undoubtedly, it can be difficult to have sympathy for a serial killer who has coldheartedly and violently terminated the lives of multiple innocent human beings. As one writer put it, Wuornos was "wounded but vicious,"[98] while investigators noted that she was "a killer who robs, not a robber who kills."[99] Nevertheless, she was a human being with a continued, toxic history of abandonment, neglect, paternal violence and suicide, incest, rapes, other physical trauma, and homelessness – and this list is not exhaustive. One cannot invalidate the suffering of her victims and their families, excuse her behavior, or offer absolution due to her having experienced profound childhood trauma. But we can pay attention to her circumstances for explanation and prediction.

Writer Kenneth Turan[100] added a liner note to Wuornos' story. The Hollywood movie about her life, *Monster*, won numerous, prestigious awards for acting and writing. Yet no one talked about Wuornos' story during any award acceptance speeches. "Admittedly," Turan wrote, "Wuornos is a tough person to thank." However, he added, not mentioning Aileen Wuornos perpetuated the way she had been marginalized and made invisible through her struggle – a facet of her developmental history that culminated in her terrible crimes. I agree with Turan. If someone had noticed and intervened on her behalf during her tumultuous upbringings, and if her grandmother had let her get the mental health counseling she needed, maybe her life would have taken a different turn. Perhaps there would have been no string of murders along the Florida highway system. Wuornos was, from childhood, abandoned, exposed to trauma, and raped to pregnancy. She had to learn to live in the woods and on the streets. She learned violence as a coping skill.

As we can see from Aileen Wuornos' case, traumagenic development may play a factor in becoming a serial killer, although we must remember that almost everyone who has ever experienced trauma has not become a serial killer. I continue in the next chapter about mental health and substance abuse issues in FSKs.

CHAPTER 4

Mental Health and Substance Use Among FSKs

§

Amy E. Duggan Archer-Gilligan, whom you met in the preface, was a serial killer. She was reported to have been a graduate of the School of Nursing at Bellevue Hospital in New York,[1] the first nursing school in the USA developed on English nursing pioneer Florence Nightingale's principles of training. The school was established the same year Archer-Gilligan claimed to have been born: 1873.[2] If she did, in fact, graduate from Bellevue, Archer-Gilligan must have been intelligent, and we can assume that, during her studies, she would have developed an advanced knowledge of how drugs affect the body.[3]

Archer-Gilligan ran one of the first nursing homes in the United States. Praised for her work, some called her "Sister Amy" for what they perceived as her compassionate and kind acts. Yet "Sister Amy" poisoned so many people in her care that the media and people around town eventually called her nursing home a "murder factory."[4] Although Archer-Gilligan was charged with five murders and only tried for one, authorities believed she killed far more. Because some relatives took their deceased loved ones far away for burial purposes, they never got an exact victim count.[5]

Evidence shows that Archer-Gilligan poisoned all but one of her victims with arsenic. She murdered Maud Lynch with strychnine. Amy probably even killed her two husbands, although she was only indicted in the murder of one: Michael Gilligan. Her first husband, James Archer, died suddenly, "taken with a spasm," in February 1910.[6] In November 1913, she married Michael Gilligan, who performed maintenance around her nursing home. He died in February 1914 just hours after having tea and crackers with Archer-Gilligan. Witnesses had seen him healthy and around town previously that week. Archer-Gilligan was the beneficiary of his estate, worth nearly $5,000 (about $100,000 today), although legal troubles consumed most of the money.[7]

The trial of Amy Archer-Gilligan attracted a lot of attention. Reports said it "was the most important poisoning case that has ever been tried in this country." The courtroom was always filled to capacity with spectators; authorities had to turn people away because there were no seats left in the courtroom. Many women attended, as did physicians and lawyers.[8] Although the medical and legal information was of interest, morbid curiosity was also likely in operation.

Archer-Gilligan's daughter Mary testified in court that her mother had been addicted to morphine since Mary was 13. Perhaps this explains why the *Hartford Courant* reported her purchase of a substantial amount of morphine at the local drug store.[9] Mary said that Amy "usually took six one-fourth grain tablets of morphine each morning and tablets four times a day."[10] Grain is a measurement from the old apothecary system, abandoned in the 1990s in favor of the metric system. One grain is 64.8mg,[11] which means that Archer-Gilligan began her morning with 97.2mg of morphine and topped off as the day went on. We know nothing about the purity of the morphine she took – reports simply named the drug – but experts report that even 30mg of immediate-release morphine increases risk of toxicity, and doses near 100mg can be fatal to those who are not tolerant of the drug.[12]

In other words, Archer-Gilligan had to have built up to the dosage that Mary reported, or she could have died. Indeed, up to 130mg of morphine was used as an anesthetic in the early 1900s.[13] Morphine, which is highly addictive, stimulates the body's opioid receptors to relieve pain.[14] We can conclude with reasonable certainty, therefore, that Archer-Gilligan typically felt little pain.[15]

In 1916, the *Harford Courant* reported that Archer-Gilligan was examined by psychiatrists after her arrest "to determine if she is mentally balanced," and that assessments of her mental condition were "conducted with unusual secrecy."[16] She was experiencing psychosis in prison. A former inmate who had already been released – and thus garnered no benefits from providing false information – testified that Amy walked around the prison corridors, talking to herself and repeating, "Oh dear, oh dear, why did I do it? What made me do it?"[17] State Attorney Hugh Alcorn was convinced that Archer-Gilligan had developed psychosis while behind bars because he believed her sane at the time of her arrest.[18] However, in addition to abusing drugs, testimony consistently showed that she had chronic and pervasive psychiatric issues.

In court, Katherine Duggan, Archer-Gilligan's sister, was asked if she thought Amy was "crazy or just saturated with morphine." The *Meriden Morning Record* reported that "Miss Duggan held to her statement that she believed Amy had never been right but at times was in her right mind and at times insane."[19] In fact, Archer-Gilligan frequently feuded with Katherine, although Archer-Gilligan trusted her sister enough to transfer her assets to her the day she was arrested.[20]

Another of Archer-Gilligan's sisters, Mary Malahan, described bizarre behavior to the court. Malahan related one incident in which Archer-Gilligan shipped 30 bottles of ketchup to her parents for no reason. She further reported that, at times, Archer-Gilligan seemed to have trouble walking and spoke so strangely it was difficult to carry on a conversation with her. Archer-Gilligan thought people were watching her, and she developed an obsession that the people of Windsor, Connecticut, were persecuting her.[21]

The evidence did not end there. Archer-Gilligan's daughter Mary said that her mother liked to have imaginary conversations on the telephone when it was disconnected. She also "talked at random." Witnesses described Archer-Gilligan as being very generous to service staff and her church, noting that she claimed God told her to be. She appears to have been obsessed with cabs (short for *cabriolet*, a horse-drawn taxicab, also called a *hack* at the time). The *Hartford Courant* reported that Archer-Gilligan had "hack mania" and would hire cabs for no reason. She apparently hired ten cabs for her wedding to James Henry Archer in 1896,[22] but the cabs sat unused outside the church.[23] Archer-Gilligan would also hire and send empty cabs to the funerals of people she did not know. Indeed, she was similarly obsessed with funerals. In one bizarre instance, Amy had to be carried out when she began screaming at a stranger's funeral. She also liked to play sad funeral music on the piano.[24]

Testimony regarding Archer-Gilligan's mental state reached far into her past. Before operating her nursing home, Amy Archer-Gilligan had been dismissed from a teaching job because administrators "were not satisfied with her disposition towards scholars." Annie Ryan, Archer-Gilligan's housemate from those days, told the court that she would "have nervous and crying spells for no reason." Ryan testified that Archer-Gilligan would buy goods from a bakery wagon as it passed the school, dismiss the schoolchildren, and have a picnic. During that time, she liked to hire horses for no reason.[25]

Reports indicate that Archer-Gilligan had a family history of mental illness, as well. Her sister and brother were both in in-patient psychiatric care (then called insane asylums). The *Hartford Courant* reported that Archer-Gilligan had three second cousins who were declared insane. Her grandfather and uncles were committed to insane asylums for life. In these cases, reportedly, her relatives were committed quite some time after the onset of their psychiatric symptoms, which worsened over time, evidencing progressive conditions. With so much mental illness in the family, Archer-Gilligan's sisters said they were ashamed and reluctant to have her committed.[26] Sadly, it stands to reason that you might not be reading about Archer-Gilligan in this context if mental illness had less of a stigma and she had received proper treatment for her symptoms.

At her first trial, Archer-Gilligan was found guilty of the murder of Franklin Andrews, although she was awarded a new trial when a higher court found errors in the proceedings. At the second trial, Archer-Gilligan's attorney Benedict Holden came ready with an insanity defense. He claimed that she had mental illness, which was exacerbated by drug use. She was therefore incapable of premeditated murder. Archer-Gilligan pleaded guilty to second-degree murder. The judge in the case, John Keeler, accepted the plea, agreeing that there were doubts to Archer-Gilligan's sanity, and therefore ability to premeditate, during the time leading up to Franklin Andrews' murder. Judge Keeler sentenced her to life in prison, but Archer-Gilligan was later transferred to the "state hospital for the insane."[27]

In contrast to the violent and painful death she caused by arsenic, Amy Archer-Gilligan spent the rest of her days in relative peace, wearing a black dress trimmed with lace, sitting on a chair, and praying. She lived a long life to about age 93 – or 88 if you asked her.[28]

I have not encountered a formal mental health diagnosis of Amy Archer-Gilligan, and she cannot be diagnosed now because she cannot be interviewed by a trained clinician. In 2015, author Ron Robillard tried to obtain a copy of her psychiatric records, but the Connecticut Supreme Court prohibited their release, fearing it would set a dangerous precedent and would discourage people from seeking psychological help and disclosing personal information.[29] Amy Archer-Gilligan made the front page of the *Hartford Courant* yet again some 100 years after the newspaper first brought her crimes to light, the paper noting that "Her secrets stay sealed."[30]

Nevertheless, we can examine her symptoms. Archer-Gilligan engaged in chronic and persistent drug abuse. Based on this fact alone, it is not surprising that witnesses reported she was irrational at times, "walking in a dazed sort of way" or "in a stupor."[31] But even before it was detected that she abused morphine, she had delusions and engaged in bizarre behavior. Archer-Gilligan's cognitions and behaviors are consistent with those seen in someone diagnosed with schizophrenia, including delusions, obsessions, probable hallucinations, confusing conversations making sense to no one else, and executive dysfunction (issues with impaired judgment and considering consequences).

Furthermore, there was a history of progressive mental illness in Archer-Gilligan's relatives. Schizophrenia, a progressive brain disease involving brain deterioration, has genetic components.[32] Moreover, substance abuse is common in people with schizophrenia and worsens as the disease progresses.[33] Archer-Gilligan had to have built tolerance from chronic and repeated use of morphine,[34] or she would not have been able to take such a high daily dosage without overdose or death. In the case of Amy Archer-Gilligan, her attorney was likely right in that the confluence of mental illness and drug abuse created a perfect storm for murder.

§

Most of the FSKs examined by my team[35] committed their crimes in the twentieth century. Some committed their murders in the 1800s, and a few were active in the early part of the 2000s, but the majority of documented cases are from the 1900s. This may speak to crime prevalence trends; it may relate to increasing sophistication in investigative tech-niques from the 1800s forward; it could be an artifact of record availabil-ity; or it may reflect what has been deemed newsworthy and published in the media. Whatever the case, when these women were committing their crimes matters, and it must be kept in mind as we discuss mental illness and substance abuse in relation to FSKs.

Expert attention to psychological issues as well as diagnostic systems and techniques have changed over the course of time. Negative, nonsen-sical, and often barbaric attitudes towards individuals with mental illness dominated early America. For example, some experts argued that Irish immigrants were more susceptible to insanity, a position taken because some Irish immigrants had a difficult time adjusting to American life.[36] People struggling with mental illness may have been chained to walls and displayed to the public, lobotomized, or subjected to exorcism. Around the mid-1800s, advocates such as Dorothea Dix began arguing for reform, voicing the struggles of mentally ill Americans to the US government,[37] and clinicians urged that mental disorders be considered medical disorders. Efforts were then made to implement fair and com-passionate diagnoses, treatment, and care.[38]

Although this is by no means a comprehensive history of mental health stigma, diagnosis, and treatment, a brief primer of this inhumane and ineffective part of American history is necessary in order to interpret our data about FSK mental health and substance abuse. People living in many of the years covered by our research would not have received the same diagnoses that we see now, nor would they have had access to com-passionate care. The American Psychiatric Association's classification system *Diagnostic and Statistical Manual of Mental Disorders (DSM)*[39] was not published until 1952. Historical newspapers and court documents would not have had the information or language to talk about, for example, posttraumatic stress disorder (PTSD). We can argue, then, that the data we did find on mental health and substance use represent a minimum frequency.

It should be stressed from the outset that classifications and diagnoses continue to evolve. We still have work to do to develop a comprehen-sive, fair, and accessible avenue to mental health treatment. In the USA, the National Institute of Mental Health (NIMH) reported that, in 2019, less than half (about 45%) of more than 50 million Americans with any mental illness (AMI) received services.[40] Furthermore, it must be noted that having a diagnosed mental health condition does not automatically qualify someone as being "insane" in the legal sense.[41] In the US legal system, a defendant must not have known the difference between right and wrong at the time of their crime(s). Indeed, one major problem in court proceedings is that mental health professionals and legal teams may not have the same understanding of an issue.[42] For example, a clinician may not be able to answer questions about mental processes and psychological illnesses with an absolute "yes" or "no." However, despite the complexity of this concern, there is an ethical obligation to understand enough to be able to provide a functioning and fair evaluation and legal approach.[43]

Although individual case studies of FSKs exist, my team's study is one of the only attempts to document the prevalence of mental health issues in a large sample of FSKs.[44] Of the 64 FSKs in our sample, we obtained mental illness information for 25, representing 39.1% of the total sample.[45] However, these data points represent minimum frequency. This does not mean the remaining 60.9% of FSKs we studied did not have mental illness. As I can find no accurate mental illness prevalence from the nineteenth or early twentieth centuries for comparison, we can instead rely on current estimates from the NIMH for comparison (duly noting a likely variability in prevalence over time). In 2019, the NIMH stated that 20.6% of Americans had any mental illness diagnosable that year or in the previous year.[5] This means that, even in the absence of missing data, FSKs experienced mental illness about twice as frequently as others in the general population.

In addition to any mental illness, the NIMH presents statistics for the prevalence of serious mental illness in the USA. Serious mental illness causes severe functional impairments and interferes with major life activities. This classification includes schizophrenia spectrum disorder, bipolar disorder, and major depressive disorder.[46] Currently, the estimated prevalence of serious mental illness in the US is 5.2%. While we have no way of gauging "functional impairment" in our FSK sample, we might argue that mental illness accompanying serial murder would always qualify. In this case, even accounting for just our minimum frequency percentage of FSKs with mental illness, our data would suggest that the prevalence of serious mental illness in FSKs is more than seven times that of the rest of the population.

When viewing their entire life span, FSKs experienced a wide variety of mental illnesses. As my team and I reported in the *Journal of Forensic Psychiatry and Psychology* in 2015, FSK conditions included anxiety, antisocial personality disorder (ASPD), bipolar disorder, borderline personality disorder, dissociative disorder, hypochondria, mental illness undefined, mixed-personality disorder, intellectual disability, and major depressive disorder. Some FSKs experienced more than one mental disorder (i.e., comorbidity). These comorbidities included ASPD and PTSD; depression and PTSD; depression and dissociative fugue; and schizophrenia and factitious disorder imposed on another (FDIA, formerly known as Munchausen syndrome by proxy, or MSBP). Notably, these illnesses were not always labeled in modern terminology, but my research team – which included clinical psychologists (i.e., diagnosticians) – assessed reports and considered symptoms as understood in modern terms. Although these data are based on news reports rather than clinical interviews, a startling overrepresentation of mental illness emerged in the evidence we gathered.

§

Martha Woods was a serial killer. Although her name appears on many lists and blogs about FSKs, it was difficult to locate original sources of information about her life. According to *The Baltimore Sun*, Woods lived in Maryland, the wife of an Army Mess Sergeant stationed at nearby Aberdeen Proving Ground military base.[47] Authorities asserted that Woods cared for nine children, and seven of them died. Deceased victims include Woods' three biological children, her adopted son, her niece and nephew, and the child of a friend.[48]

According to *The Baltimore Sun*, records showed that Woods brought her adopted son Paul to various hospitals – including the prestigious Walter Reed Medical, Kirk Army Hospital, and Johns Hopkins – five separate times for medical emergencies. Dr. Felix Kavanaugh, who examined Paul twice, told the court that while Woods explained Paul's symptoms in detail, he could determine no medical issues.[49] Paul died in 1969 when Woods smothered him. Unaware of her crime, doctors attributed the death to sudden infant death syndrome (SIDS), a term created right around the time of Paul's death to replace the label "crib death." SIDS is the unexpected death, with an unknown cause, of an infant under the age of one year.[50]

Woods next brought her adopted daughter, Judy, to Johns Hopkins Hospital in Baltimore for problematic breathing. An observant physician, Dr. Douglas Kerr, recalled the previous death of Paul. He admitted Judy to the hospital and reviewed the medical and death records of the other children who had died in her care and whose deaths she had tried to pass off as SIDS. Dr. Kerr and colleagues determined that all the children were healthy and had died suddenly without explanation. Contemporary experts laud Dr. Kerr for his medical detective work. The US attorney for the case, Charles Bernstein, described what Dr. Kerr did as heroic. "Remember," Bernstein said, "at that time, you didn't accuse a mother of murder."[51] Once Judy was removed from Woods' care, she never suffered another symptom of dangerously low oxygen (cyanosis).[52]

Woods was ultimately charged with the murder of seven-month-old Paul and the assault of Judy, with experts at the time believing that her motive was to gain attention. In 1972, when she was 42 years old, Woods was tried in federal court because she and her military husband lived on US property. At a trial that lasted over six weeks,[53] prosecutors produced evidence that, in addition to Paul, six other children in her care, in separate events, presented with breathing problems in local hospitals and died. Woods' defense team tried to blame insecticides used at Aberdeen military base for causing the infants' breathing problems and deaths.[54] The defense also argued there was "overwhelming evidence of mental illness."[55]

But the defense did not work. On June 8, 1972, Woods was convicted by a jury of eight women and four men and received a sentence of life in prison.[56] Moreover, she received sentences for other offenses, including assault, with consecutive and concurrent terms totaling 75 years.[57] Prosecutors later admitted they were worried about getting a jury to believe that a mother could murder her own children.[58]

The Baltimore Sun reported that, when sentencing Woods, Judge Frank Kaufman said he hoped "during the years ahead doctors and or others will find it possible to discover why these acts were committed and will be able to treat or through other methods take such steps to insure they will not occur again."[59]

In 1999, she was still in prison in Texas at age 70. Federal Bureau of Prisons records indicate that an inmate named Martha Woods, the same age as the person in this case presentation, died on her birthday at age 73 on April 20, 2002.[60] Furthermore, there is a Martha Leeann Woods who died on that day buried in West Virginia with her husband, a decorated Army veteran. The veteran's obituary, however only mentions "his late wife," with no name listed.

§

Despite the fact that the other children's deaths were originally attributed to SIDS, experts know Martha Woods killed the other children and contend that she killed all seven children to gain attention. Experts have a "three baby rule." If a first child dies with an undetermined cause, it is considered SIDS. If a second child in the same family dies without a known cause, it is considered undetermined. If the third baby in the same family, they suspect homicide.[61] The "three baby rule" is sometimes known as Meadow's Law, named after pediatrician Sir Roy Meadow, who was one of the first authorities on Munchausen syndrome by proxy. However, the "three baby rule" has been more commonly attributed to Domenic DiMaio and Vincent DiMaio. In their 1989 textbook, *Forensic Pathology*, they said of this phenomenon, "While a second SIDS death from a mother is improbable, it is possible and she should be given the benefit of the doubt. A third case, in our opinion is not possible and is a case of homicide."[62]

Martha Woods' case led early researchers to publish work on parents who disguise murder with SIDS, including DiMaio and Bernstein's landmark article, "A Case of Infanticide," published in the *Journal of Forensic Science*.[63] In retrospect, in fact, Martha Woods is believed to have had Munchausen syndrome by proxy (MSBP), although this did not become a formal diagnosis until 1977.[64] MSBP is now known as a factitious disorder imposed on another (FDIA) in some diagnostic systems, as this newer label emphasizes a behavioral pattern, although the term MSBP is used more frequently in the literature cited in this book. MSBP is a form of child maltreatment whereby caregivers fabricate or induce symptoms of health issues of children in their care, including bleeding, apnea, seizures, vomiting, and rashes. These symptoms may emerge only in the presence of the caretaker, which is almost always the child's mother. In one disturbing case, for example, a woman was caught on camera in a hospital closing her daughter's nose and mouth to induce seizures.[65] In fact, a woman was involved in 92% of MSBP/FDIA cases reviewed by experts.[66] Notably, the individual imposing illness on another may have extensive medical or symptom knowledge,[67] as seemed to be the case with Martha Woods.

The impact on victims cannot be overstated. Children often undergo unnecessary, invasive medical tests and procedures to determine the cause of perplexing symptoms,[68] and as many as 10% of child victims die. Considered medical child abuse (MCA) or "medical battering," it is one of the deadliest forms of child abuse.[69] Moreover, MSBP/FDIA can be difficult to detect, as the caregivers are pathological liars – if they detect suspicion, they change physicians. MSBP/FDIA is also very rare, as are estimates of its prevalence, which appears to be about 0.3–0.5%.[70] Indeed, experts stress that there are probably no reliable statistics available for MSBP/FDIA.[71]

Clinicians believe that MSBP/FDIA occurs because the caretaker enjoys the role. A mother whose child is sick garners sympathy and attention, and earns praise that she is an excellent and devoted caretaker. Some researchers feel that those with this condition derive satisfaction from deceiving doctors and others whom they perceive to be more important than they are.[72] When it comes to serial murderers, some women might enjoy the role of grieving mother.

§

Marybeth Tinning is a serial killer. All nine of her children died, and authorities suspect she killed at least eight of them. It is unknown whether she ever received a formal diagnosis of MSBP. Nevertheless, events reported in newspapers at the time of her arrest are consistent with behaviors seen by those who are diagnosed with this mental disorder. Remember, as military interrogator Greg Hartley pointed out, you do not have to be a botanist to recognize poison ivy.

The Tinning family lived in Schenectady, a friendly city situated on the Mohawk River in upstate New York. Each of the Tinning children, born from 1967 to 1985, died: Jennifer, Barbara, Joseph, Timothy, Nathan, Michael (adopted), Mary Frances, Jonathan, and Tami Lynne. None of the children lived beyond the age of five. Jennifer, who died first, was eight days old when she died. She had meningitis and never left the hospital. Jennifer's death may be the only one that Tinning did not directly cause.[73] Tinning did, however, receive an outpouring of sympathy over Jennifer's death.

The number and circumstances of the other Tinning children's deaths were so puzzling to doctors that local pediatrician Dr. Dominick Mele thought she had a "death gene" in her family.[74] Tinning would have one child at time, and although the infant would be healthy, Tinning would soon show up at a Schenectady hospital with a dying or dead baby. Not knowing causation, confused doctors attributed the babies' deaths to SIDS. World-renowned pathologist Michael Baden said that suffocation could mimic SIDS in a postmortem exam.[75] A headline in the *Poughkeepsie Journal* citing Tinning's case read, "SIDS: A Killer's Best Alibi."[76] Doctors also suspected Reye's syndrome (increased brain pressure and fat accumulation within organs), which is sometimes confused with SIDS.[77]

Schenectady is not a large city. The tragic circumstances of Marybeth Tinning and her husband Joe became known to its residents, and Tinning received a great deal of attention. Strangers would come to the babies' funerals to hug the grieving mother. Joe's mother praised Tinning as a courageous mother. As reported by Joyce Egginton in her 1989 book[78] about the Tinning case, Tinning held herself together well and seemed to appear detached or even to be enjoying herself during the children's funerals. Enjoying the attention or benefits from a child's sickness or death is a key manifestation of MSBP,[79] and Egginton suggests that Tinning garnered a lot of attention by staging elaborate funerals for the babies. Between enjoying neighbors' attention and planning fancy funerals, it seems Tinning reaped the sympathy benefits of a mother with dead babies. As Egginton pointed out, perhaps getting pregnant again after each child's death was logical for Tinning.[80]

Tami Lynne was Tinning's last living child. As reported by *The Washington Post*, Tami Lynne would not stop crying one night shortly before

Christmas, so Tinning suffocated her with a pillow. Tinning rushed the child to a local emergency room and said she found the child unresponsive. It was too late for Tami Lynne, who was wearing pajamas decorated with little clowns. It was at this point that an anonymous caller phoned social services and asked, "How many more have to die before you do something?"[81] Police finally questioned Tinning, and she admitted to suffocating Tami Lynne, Timothy, and Nathan to stop them from crying. She said, "I smothered them each with a pillow because I'm not a good mother."[82] Tami Lynne is buried in Schenectady Memorial Park[83] with her grandparents, who both outlived their grandchildren by nearly 20 years.

At the time, all the babies seemed to be well cared for, so doctors did not suspect abuse. Tinning's husband Joe claims he never suspected anything, and he was not suspected because his wife was alone with each child when they died. In fact, Joe defended his wife despite the fact that she allegedly tried to kill him with anti-seizure medication in 1974 – an attempted murder for which she was never charged.[84] He did, however, suggest that she needed psychiatric help. Notably, one official mentioned that Joe did not seem involved with the children, and he even had trouble remembering their names.[85]

Not only did Marybeth Tinning try to retract her confession, she pleaded insanity.[86] And it seems to have worked to an extent. A jury found her guilty of smothering Tami Lynne – acting recklessly with depraved indifference, but not guilty of acting with the intent to cause death. She was sentenced to 20 years to life in prison. District Attorney John Poersch said he hoped that "Mrs. Tinning can get some help."[87] Meanwhile, although she was indicted in 1989 by a grand jury for the murder of Timothy and Nathan, a judge dismissed the charges on the grounds that the grand jury was not provided with complete information. Later attempts to indict her for the deaths of her other children were abandoned.[88] Tinning was released from prison in 2018 after being denied parole six times.[89] She is reported to be living in Schenectady[90] once again.

How did this happen? How did nine babies from the same parents die, and no one investigated the Tinnings? According to *The Washington Post*, one official claimed that nothing was suspicious because the doctors had attributed the babies' deaths to SIDS. Officials also blamed a lack of

4.1 Sheriff Barney Waldron escorts Marybeth Tinning to the Schenectady County courtroom. (Photo from Getty Images)

centralized records for a failure to detect a pattern. "I guess we were all in the position to do something, but it wasn't done," said the medical examiner, Dr. Robert Sullivan, adding, "I should have talked with more people." A local pathologist stated, "You get no points for sticking your neck out." [91]

§

The condition is rare, but MSBP is a statistically overrepresented mental illness in my team's research sample of FSKs. Going by the upper estimate of the disease's prevalence (0.5%) and noting that at least 3 of our 64 FSKs had MSBP (4.7%), we can argue that, even with minimum frequency statistics, FSKs are more than nine times as likely as the rest of the population to experience the disease.

MSBP/FDIA may be more readily detectable these days, as it has made its way into the popular media in the past few years with the case of Claudine "Dee Dee" Blanchard. Although not formally diagnosed when she was alive, some experts contend that Dee Dee's behaviors were consistent with this condition. Dee Dee lied about diagnoses and induced symptoms of severe illnesses ranging from muscular dystrophy to leukemia in her daughter Gypsy Rose. Because she had some health-care training, Dee Dee was able to fake conditions with accuracy, and she forced Gypsy Rose to use a wheelchair and a feeding tube and did not let her attend school. The Blanchards gained public sympathy and support for Gypsy Rose's illness. Dee Dee's case made the news and was the topic of several documentaries after she was stabbed to death by Gypsy Rose's boyfriend, Nicholas Godejohn.[92]

Let me stress, however, that most people with mental illness do not perpetrate violence,[93] let alone murder. Nearly everyone who has ever lived with mental illness has not become a serial killer. In fact, evidence suggest that those with mental illness are more frequently the victims of violence, not the perpetrators.[94] Yet, the public has a general misconception that people with mental illness are inherently violent, which can be exacerbated by the media.[95] In films we see mental health patients depicted as suddenly becoming mass murderers or serial killers,[96] an unlikely transformation.

Nevertheless, people with serious mental illness have a "modestly increased risk" of perpetrating violence, including targeting family members.[97] While there are some case studies documenting and under-standing psychiatric conditions in MSKs,[98] the literature is sparse on the topic for FSKs. Still, the data are telling. Some evidence suggests, for example, higher rates of mental disorders in women who commit violent acts, including domestic violence (abuse of one's intimate partner), which is certainly in line with FSKs killing husbands, children, and other relatives.[99] Moreover, these disorders include depression, posttraumatic stress disorder (PTSD), borderline personality disorder, and antisocial personality disorder (ASPD)[100] – all of which are represented in our sample of FSKs.

According to our data, some mental illnesses do seem to be overrep-resented in FSKs. The prevalence of ASPD, for example, is estimated to be 0.5–1% in women.[101] Using the upper estimate of this prevalence and noting the minimum frequency of 4.7% of our sample experien-cing ASPD, this suggests a nearly fivefold risk. However, our study used newspaper reports to identify FSKs' background and crimes. To meet the DSM-5 criteria for ASPD, the individual would have to have been diagnosed with a conduct disorder (CD) before the age of 15,[102] and we were unable to document with the connection or progression from CD to ASPD for any cases within our sample. Nonetheless, in 9.4% of our sample, future FSKs exhibited behaviors in childhood that are consistent with conduct disorder. These include bullying, noncompliance with rules, violence towards others, lying, and stealing. By today's standards, about 7% of girls in the USA have symptoms of conduct disorder.[103] Interpreting this information with caution, it seems that there is an over-representation of conduct issues in the childhoods of FSKs.

Relatedly, many FSK cases feature lying, exploitation, manipulation, callous disregard for the welfare of others, and a lack of remorse.[104] These traits are consistent with psychopathy, which is not a diagnosis itself. Examples of callousness are illustrated by such FSK statements as, "[the children] bothered me, so I decided to kill them," and "I like to attend funerals. I'm happy when someone is dying."[105] Moreover, FSKs may actually view themselves as victims – a clear sign that they may be processing their actions through the lens of psychopathy.[106]

Of course, multiple, planned murders are prima facie evidence for lack of a conscience and disregard for others, but it is important to note that a single FSK might not exhibit all the characteristics of psychopathy, nor would she always exhibit them. That said, psychopathy may play a role in victim targeting, as psychopaths take advantage of opportunities. Think of Belle Gunness conning suitor after suitor, or Kristen Gilbert targeting vulnerable victims allegedly so she could be a hero nurse. Of course, there are probably sociocultural factors moderating FSK crimes as well.

Several of the women in our study were identified as having major depressive disorder. Depression is typically associated with a lack of energy and motivation, inability to concentrate, feelings of worthlessness and listlessness, lack of interest in daily activities, absence of experiencing pleasure, and even suicidal ideation.[107] It is seemingly counterintuitive to associate depression with serial homicide. There is evidence, however, to suggest that depression is related to violence. In a study comparing a large sample comparing more than 47,000 depressed patients with more than 898,000 healthy controls, depression was associated with an increased risk of committing violent crime. This phenomenon was rare in women, as only 0.5% committed violent offenses after their diagnosis, but it remained significant even after controlling for sociodemographic factors.[108]

Depression that can progress to a violent extreme may be a manifestation of postpartum psychosis (PP) in women who have given birth. Postpartum depression would be nonpsychotic, but PP is a dangerous affective (mood) or manic condition in which new mothers experience paranoia, confusion, delusions, and mood swings. Experts feel that both the infant's and mother's well-being are jeopardized by PP.[109] Reviewing my team's original (unpublished) data, they show that FSKs who kill their own children (75%) use asphyxiation statistically more frequently than FSKs who do not kill their own children (34%).[110] Suffocating a baby – smothering them with a pillow or closing their nose and mouth – is an extreme form of violence. While acknowledging that depression rarely leads to violence, and that serial murder is also exceedingly rare, it appears that depression may precipitate homicide in some cases.

Other behaviors associated with mental health appeared to greater or lesser degrees in my team's data. The first is demeanor. Clinicians typically assess a battery of information about a client to draw their conclusions about mental state, and demeanor is one of the aspects they address. Granted, news reports cannot take the place of clinical interviews, but in 31 cases my team was able to find descriptions of FSK demeanor. Comments described FSKs with terms such as angry, bizarre, flat affect, flippant, grandiose, hyperactive, unstable, and even serene. While unstandardized descriptors made pattern recognition difficult, we can estimate a dysfunctional mental state in FSKs from some of the comments noted above.

While data were available for only 8 of the 64 cases reviewed (12.5%), my team was also able to find some information commenting on sexual adjustment. Sexual information does not necessarily speak to crime motives for FSKs, but can speak to an atypical mental state. Uncommon sexual behaviors reported were prostitution, barking like a dog during sex, and autoerotic asphyxiation (choking oneself during sexual activity, rumored to heighten sexual gratification).

A final behavior related to mental health that my team and I examined was reported substance abuse in FSKs. It is difficult to determine exact prevalence or extent of substance use from publicly available media reports, yet the data showed indications that about one-fourth of the women in our study abused drugs and/or alcohol. Because information was not available for the remaining cases, this number is once again an estimate of minimum frequency, as missing data are not necessarily evidence of absence. Yet the data are telling. The Substance Abuse and Mental Health Services Administration (SAMHSA) reported in 2019 that 7.7% of people in the USA had a substance use disorder.[111] From this comparison, it appears that FSKs had a threefold risk of abusing substances.

§

Margie Velma Bullard Barfield was a serial killer. In North Carolina in 1977, she dated a man named Stuart Taylor, forging checks from his account to fund her addiction to Valium and several other prescription drugs. When she became worried that he was onto her scheme, she laced his tea and beer with *Singletary Rat Killer* and *Terro Ant and Roach Killer*, both arsenic-based rat poisons. He became extremely ill, and when he died in a hospital a few days later, an autopsy revealed arsenic in his system.[112]

Prior to Taylor's death, several of Barfield's family members also died, including those previously in good health. When Taylor died, people grew increasingly suspicious at the number of deaths associated with Barfield. An anonymous call reported her to the police, saying, "Somebody's got to stop her."[113] She was arrested in March 1978 at the age of 45. That day, like many others, she had taken a powerful cocktail of painkillers, sedatives, and antianxiety and antidepressant medications. Later in 1978, Barfield was convicted of the first-degree murder of Stuart Taylor and sentenced to death.[114]

Barfield confessed to killing three other people before Taylor. She had laced her mother's soft drinks with poison after taking out a loan in her name. She also killed two elderly people for whom she was a caregiver: Montgomery Edwards, 94 years old, and Dollie Edwards, 84 years old. She poured rat poison into their cereal and drinks.[115] In addition, two of her previous husbands had died under similar circumstances. The body of one husband was exhumed, and authorities found arsenic in his remains.[116]

Arsenic is a corrosive poison. Ingestion causes a grueling death, with mostly gastrointestinal symptoms. There are, however, differences between chronic and acute arsenic poisoning. The person experiencing acute arsenic poisoning has a burning esophagus, tremendous abdominal pain, nausea, projectile vomiting, and explosive diarrhea. The intense bleeding in the gastrointestinal tract interferes with circulatory and cardiac function. They may experience mental status symptoms, including psychosis. They would feel numb, cold, drowsy, confused, and likely, very scared. They may experience seizures or fall into a coma before they die of multiorgan failure (e.g., digestive system, heart, kidneys, and lungs).[117] Since Barfield's victims died shortly after ingesting arsenic in their meals, we can infer that they died this way from acute arsenic poisoning.

Reports at the time argued that Margie Velma Barfield did not have "the face of a drug-crazed serial killer." She looked shy and had a nice smile and a "round figure." According to one outlet, she looked like someone who would dish out food at church picnics, hold her grandchildren, and gift them with hand-knit toy bunnies.[118] Her children, however, emphasized her drug habit, stating that she hid her pills in her yard, her bra, the toilet paper, the washing machine, and even in her hair rollers. According to her daughter Kim, you could hear "pills rattling around on her head" as she walked around.[119]

Some family members and fellow prison inmates suggested that after Barfield overcame addiction in prison, she was reformed, and "returned to her good self." She became known as "Death Row Granny," and she often consoled other inmates who were upset or agitated. But Robeson County District Attorney Joe Freeman Britt emphatically denied the change, stating that Barfield was not "some sweet little old grandmother." According to Britt, she remained an acute threat: "That woman is a cold-blooded killer." He emphasized that Margie Barfield is a con artist and cruelly killed others "for greed, for money" as she borrowed money from her victims and never paid it back, or forged checks from her victims. Britt added that "if she gets out, she'd kill again. Hell, she probably poisoned half the county, if we only had the resources to exhume all the bodies for autopsies."[120]

Like many other serial killers, Barfield suffered childhood trauma. Barfield's father was "violently abusive" to her and raped her when she was 13. Barfield's sister corroborated the fact that their father was violent, and Barfield was bitter that her mother never protected them. Despite introducing these details about her early life, the Governor of North Carolina denied Barfield clemency. He noted that death by arsenic

4.2 "Death Row Granny" Margie Velma Barfield confessed to killing several people with arsenic. (Photo from Getty Images)

poison is "slow and agonizing" and that "victims are literally tortured to death." Barfield was not saved from execution.

According to *The Washington Post*, Barfield got to choose how she would die in the gas chamber – lying down, sitting up and inhaling, or by lethal injection.[121] She chose lethal injection by sodium pentothal and a muscle relaxant. Barfield was executed by the State of North Carolina on November 2, 1984, wearing blue slippers and pink pajamas. Among her last words were "I am sorry."[122]

§

Although drug addiction does fuel compulsive behavior, almost everyone who has been addicted to substances has not turned to serial murder to fund their habit. Arguably, however, Barfield's story is testament to the worst-case-scenario damaging effects of addiction. Also, we know that people who experienced childhood trauma may turn to substance abuse as a coping mechanism. In other words, they may use substances to avoid the mental anguish associated with memories of a violent past.[123]

Many of the disorders and behaviors discussed in this chapter are difficult to treat. For example, antisocial personality disorder (ASPD) does not appear to respond to interventions very well.[124] There are no specific medications approved for its treatment, and there are no substantiated effective psychological treatments. There is, in fact, a lack of research on treatments for ASPD.[125] It is costly to hospitalize someone with ASPD, and they may be disruptive to hospital functions and other patients. Only early intervention in childhood conduct disorder, the precursor to ASPD, seems to be effective.[126] Similarly, schizophrenia requires lifelong treatment, and those who suffer from the disease need daily living support.[127] Those who suffer from the disease may experience suspiciousness as a symptom, which may interfere with medication adherence. Meanwhile, medication that can help with symptoms typically has adverse effects, including motor issues, seizures, weight gain, sexual dysfunction, and even cardiac problems.[128]

Examining our sample of FSKs more closely, reports indicate that in only six of the cases in which mental illness was known did the FSK undergo treatment. We can speculate about what might have been different had FSKs been more extensively helped – or been helped at all. But, arguably, mental health treatment is insufficiently accessible even in contemporary times, and we do not have scientifically perfect predictors of what – or how – mental illnesses would lead to murder. Thus, more research is needed for identification and effective treatment. If we can address clinical knowledge gaps, we can ensure the most appropriate courses of treatment for violent offenders with mental health issues. Perhaps we could save lives.

CHAPTER 5

FSK Crimes and Outcomes

§

Tammy Corbett (Eveans) is a serial killer. The Illinois resident confessed to her ex-husband Richard Eveans that she suffocated all three of her children while living in Brighton, Macoupin County.[1] Brighton is typically a quiet, rural area, known for a mysterious dish called Burgoo soup[2] and for having the largest collection of Sears & Roebuck[3] mail-order houses in the USA.[4]

Three-year-old Richard W. Eveans Jr. died on his birthday in 1989. Richard ("Ricky") was the third child to die in the Eveans household, and after reporting to the scene of death, Police Chief Jay Woolridge believed that "something unnatural" was happening in the household.[5] Tammy Corbett was arrested and pleaded guilty but mentally ill to charges of smothering and killing Ricky.[6] She was sentenced to 20 years in prison.

The deaths of Tammy Corbett's other two children were then investigated. It was initially believed that seven-week-old Robert Wayne Eveans died in 1987 from a skull fracture and resulting meningitis when his brother pulled him down from a table. It had been believed that two-week-old Amy Eveans died in 1988 of sudden infant death syndrome (SIDS).[7] However, Corbett's former husband Richard Eveans Sr. told authorities that Corbett had confessed to him that she murdered the other two children, as well.[8] Corbett was charged with murdering Robert and Amy. She was already in prison for the death of Ricky when she waived her right to a jury trial for the other murders, opting for trial in front of a judge only. During the trial, her ex-husband recounted her confession to him, and further informed the judge that his ten-year-old daughter from a previous marriage had heard Tammy say, "I hope you die," right before Ricky was murdered.[9]

A clinical psychologist who evaluated her reported that Corbett attributed having murdered her children to dreams of doing it. This psychologist believed Corbett had mood and thought disorders, as well as impaired judgment, stemming from previous accidents and the trauma of having being raped three times when she was a teen.[10] However, three clinicians interviewed her, and not one of them thought she was insane.[11]

At no point does it seem that the diagnosis of Munchausen syndrome by proxy (MSBP, as labeled then) was indicated for Corbett. However, language used by the prosecutors suggested this was possible. State's Attorney Vince Moreth told the jury that Corbett killed her children, Robert and Amy, to gain sympathy and attention as a grieving mother. As reported by the *St. Louis Post-Dispatch*, Moreth said, "It was as if somebody was addicted to drugs and used drugs to make them feel good. Tammy Corbett was addicted to attention."[12]

On two counts of first-degree murder, Circuit Court Judge Joseph Koval found Corbett guilty but mentally ill. Corbett was already serving 20 years in prison for murdering Ricky when she received a life sentence, without the possibility of parole, for murdering Robert in 1987 and Amy in 1988.[13] State's Attorney Moreth did not seem pleased with this decision, however, clearly having hoped she would receive a death sentence. He reminded reporters that she did not even bake a cake for Ricky on his birthday before she murdered him. "Life [in prison] without parole is not a loss," Moreth said, "but we have to pay for her all those years." He added, "The only way she gets out of prison is in a box."[14]

Corbett was sentenced to the maximum security Dwight Correctional Center in Illinois, an institution her lawyer called "a house of horrors."[15] In fact, early reports suggested that prison was not going well for Corbett. While there, she made friends with a convicted murderer named Sondra "Tear Drop" Banks. In letters that Banks shared with authorities, she said that Corbett had mentioned she was having problems with other inmates. When talking about a particular inmate, Corbett told Banks that if problems persisted, "I'm going to just tag her ass," and said she had made a knife out of a prison spoon just in case. Banks said that

Corbett was generally a nice person but added, "I've seen many dark sides of Tammy."[16]

Dwight Correctional Center closed in 2013, and it is unclear where Corbett was subsequently placed when inmates were shuffled to other Illinois prisons.[17]

It cannot be overemphasized that almost all people who have experienced a traumagenic environment do not escalate to serial murder. That being said, physical accidents and sexual abuse seem to have created a storm of maldevelopment for Tammy Corbett. In the case of Corbett, this contributed to her murderous mindset, which ultimately led to a gruesome string of murders that shook an otherwise ordinary town in Illinois.

§

The sheer horror of crimes committed by FSKs captures our attention. Our desire to know more about who, when, how, why, and what triggers our natural response mechanisms to pay attention to murders and other gruesome events such as car accidents. Through our morbid curiosity, which itself appears to be a by-product of protective vigilance, we are preprogrammed to attend to events that can harm us so that we can avoid them, live to see another day, and have the chance to reproduce. Our fight-or-flight mechanisms are activated even when alarming events turn out not to be an immediate threat. Physiologically, it is better to be safe than sorry.

Although consciously (at the level of the cortex) we know exactly what is going on when we watch TV or read a book, those first danger signals go also to our emotional center limbic system, particularly our amygdala, which moderates our fear response. Greg Hartley, author and military interrogator, gave a great description of this mechanism. He stated, "The amygdala gets the first vote, and it decides whether you go into fight or flight." Hartley continued, "If it mistakes a bear for a rock, you don't reproduce. If it mistakes a rock for a bear, well then, so what?"[18] Again, it is better to be alarmed when unnecessary than to not be alarmed when necessary.

In our research, my team examined the crimes of FSKs, including victim characteristics.[19] I describe these findings below, and I will add the research findings of other scholars to paint as complete a picture as I can. The FBI's current publicly available information about serial murder gives examples only of sexual serial homicide. FSKs murder different targets in different ways. By understanding crime trends and victim profiles, we may be able to facilitate detection of FSK activity and, importantly, we may also be able to prevent murders.

CRIME PLACE

With respect to crime location, more than a quarter of FSKs (28.1%) murdered in urban areas only, 17.2% in rural areas only, and 9.4% in suburban areas only. An appreciable number of FSKs (45.3%) spread their crimes across region types including the suburbs, making suburbia the serial murder scene for more than half the cases.

FSKs committed their crimes across 31 of the 50 states, although we interpret this with caution, as some crimes may have been committed before a territory became part of the United States. Estimates are challenging because the population obviously has changed over time. Going by sheer numbers, Illinois and Texas have had the most FSKs committing crimes there. However, we can rank order states with the most FSK crimes, controlling for population. The state with the most FSKs committing crimes therein was Illinois (eight FSKs committed crimes there – think of Tammy Corbett), followed by Georgia (four), Pennsylvania (four), New York (six), and Texas (eight).[20]

CRIME TIME

Of 64 cases of FSKs, almost all were from the 1900s (about 48%), with a few from the 1800s and from the 2000s. Data did show a 2.5-fold increase in FSK cases over the past 50 years, but, and this is just my take, I would more readily attribute this to increased detection than to criminal increase. We also must consider that there may be a certain type of FSK out there who just has not gotten caught yet.

§

Genene Jones was a serial killer. In the 1970s and early 1980s, she was a licensed vocational nurse (LVN) who was skilled at inserting intravenous lines into sick children's veins. On Jones' shift at Bexar County Hospital in San Antonio, Texas, dozens of babies mysteriously died. Children suddenly had seizures and stopped breathing. Many times, Jones would sit bereft at their bedsides in the pediatric intensive care unit. People who worked in the hospital started referring to Jones' 3:00 p.m. to 11:00 p.m. shift as the "Death shift." Eventually, colleagues and hospital administrators caught on to that fact that Jones had been present at the death bed of ten children who died of "sudden and unexplained" circumstances, but they could not prove she was responsible. Still, children were ten times more likely to die on her shift than on those of other nurses who worked in the pediatric ward.[21] To fix the "problem," the hospital decided to replace all LVNs with registered nurses and offered Jones a job elsewhere in the hospital. When she declined and quit, the mysterious deaths stopped.[22]

Jones then went to work at a pediatrician's office in 1982. Within about a month, eight children had medical emergencies, and one died: 15-month-old Chelsea McClellan, who stopped breathing during a routine checkup for a cold. As this point, Jones was accused of injecting the children with succinylcholine chloride, a muscle relaxant.[23] She was tried and convicted of murder for killing baby Chelsea,[24] and was ultimately also convicted for attempting to murder another child. Jones was sentenced to prison,[25] with prosecutors believing she had killed as many as 60 young children.[26]

While serving her prison sentence, Jones said to her parole officer, "I really did kill those babies," adding, "I look back now on what I did and agree with you that it was heinous, that I was heinous."[27] In 2017, when Jones could have been released from prison on her initial charges, prosecutors filed five new murder charges against her for children who were hospital patients ranging in age from three months to two years.[28] However, Jones did not want to be known as a serial killer and offered to plead guilty to lesser charges, even though that meant she would remain in prison. In 2020, she pleaded guilty to killing 11-month-old Joshua Sawyer.[29] He was in the hospital for smoke inhalation, but he died when Jones injected him with a fatal dose of the powerful anti-seizure medicine Dilantin.[30] His mother, Connie Weeks, read a victim's statement and told Jones, "I hope for you to live a long and miserable life behind bars. Goodbye."[31] It is unclear what happened with the other four murder charges.

Genene Jones is still in prison, but she will be eligible for parole when she is 87 years old. Yet according to veteran prosecutor Catherine Babbitt, "With this plea, the odds are she will take her last breath in prison." Babbitt

5.1 Former licensed vocational nurse Genene Jones in handcuffs after a pretrial hearing in 1984 (Photo by Getty Images)

then added, "If the parole board wants to deny her every time she comes up and keep her until she takes her dying breath, that's their prerogative and our preference. Why on earth would she be allowed to walk among us?"[32]

The motive for Jones' murders was reported as unclear. Some suggested she wanted to play hero by reviving some of the children she injected with toxic doses of drugs, and some suggest she killed children to emphasize the need for increased pediatric care.[33] While the latter feels particularly hard to imagine, she did inspire one future medical professional: Chelsea McClellan's mother. Petti McClellan-Wiese became a nurse and advocate, leading the campaign that resulted in additional charges being brought against Jones. She testified before every grand jury and attended every court hearing. In 2019, Petti died suddenly at the age 64, but she had never stopped fighting and made sure Jones faced justice for at least some of her crimes.[34]

§

MEANS

An understanding of how FSKs murder can help detect crimes and perhaps prevent future ones. We found that 50% of FSKs in our sample used poison[35] as their primary murder weapon.[36] Psychologists Wayne Wilson and Tonya Hilton[37] made the strong argument that using a low-profile method of murder such as poisoning likely contributes to FSKs being able to get away with their crimes for a long period of time. Criminal profiler Deborah Schurman-Kauflin[38] agreed with this viewpoint, emphasizing that the FSKs she interviewed tended to use poison or asphyxiation as less detectable ways of eradicating their victims.

§

Nannie Doss (Nancy Hazel) was a serial killer. Born in Alabama in 1905, she murdered many of her family members from the 1920s through the 1950s. She was first married at the age 16. But when two of her daughters with first husband Charles Braggs mysteriously died of what was thought to be food poisoning, Charles became afraid and left home with their oldest daughter, Melvina.[39] As *The Alabama Heritage* pointed out, this decision made him "lucky Charles."[40] Others close to her would not be so lucky.

In 1954, Doss lethally poisoned her fifth and final husband, Sam Doss, in Tulsa, Oklahoma. Authorities were suspicious and, while investigating Sam's death, discovered arsenic in his exhumed body. Nannie Doss, whom newspapers called, "The Giggling Granny," confessed that she had put the poison in his coffee. Oklahoma investigators then received reports that at least one other husband in her past had died of what was believed at the time to be food poisoning.[41] After Nannie Doss was arrested for killing Sam Doss, she eventually confessed to poisoning three of her previous husbands, all of whom she had attracted through "Lonely Hearts" newspaper ads. Husband Frank Harrelson of Alabama died after drinking rat poison in his liquor; husband Arlie Lanning of North Carolina died after suffering several days of vomiting from poisoned food and drink; and husband Richard Morton of Kansas died after he ingested coffee laced with rat poison. She is also suspected to have poisoned Morton's dog.[42]

Relatives of Arlie Lanning had been suspicious. After Arlie died, Nannie Doss burned their house down for insurance money, and then

Arlie's mother suddenly died. Although Arlie's sister was the beneficiary of his will, Doss forged the insurance check paid out upon his death and kept the money.[43]

While Doss admitted to killing her husbands, she always maintained that she "never killed blood kin."[44] "You can dig up all the graves in the country," she said, "and you won't find any more on me."[45] Yet the evidence paints a different picture. After Arlie's murder, Doss went to live with her sister, Dovie, but Dovie died suddenly soon after her arrival.[46] Next, Doss poisoned her mother, Lou Hazel, after Lou surprised her with a visit. It was reported that Doss felt Lou was getting in her way. Upon exhumation, arsenic was discovered in Lou's body, same as the others.

She also likely killed her two young grandchildren. Doss' daughter Melvina believes she saw her mother stab her newborn baby daughter with a stickpin, but thought she was hallucinating in a postpartum haze. A few months later, Melvina left her baby son, Robert, in Doss' care. Robert mysteriously died of asphyxiation, and Doss collected $500 insurance money from his death.[42] In this context, the nickname "Giggling Granny" seems especially cruel.

Reports called her "jovial," and "affable," even when she was signing confession statements, and noted that Doss was laughing and enjoying herself when being filmed during questioning by authorities.[47] Interestingly, newspaper reports also called her "stocky," "plump," "pudgy," "round-faced," and "buxom," and described the gap between her two front teeth.[48] One understands reporting on her demeanor, but one wonders about the nature of this fixation with her appearance. Perhaps it is because grandmothers are expected to have a certain appearance, but are not expected to murder.

Reports were inconsistent as to why Doss had killed her victims. Authorities said she collected between $500 and $1200 insurance money upon the deaths of her husbands,[49] but they also conceded that the sums she collected were not even enough to cover each victim's funeral. County Attorney Howard Edmondson conjectured that "she killed them because they rubbed her the wrong way."[50] And, in fact, Doss did complain about several husbands: Charlie would leave home too frequently (although she did not kill him); Frank drank too much; Harvey drank too much and was a philanderer; and Sam was too straitlaced and would

5.2 "The Giggling Granny" Nannie Doss being interviewed by Captain Harry Stege. (Photo by Getty Images)

not buy her a television.[51] Another report claims Doss gave a reason for killing husband after husband – she said, "I have been seeking perfect love for a long time."[52]

Before trial, Doss was held for in-patient psychiatric observation at Eastern State Hospital for 90 days. Doss had told examiners her father was extremely strict and would not let her socialize. In addition, she apparently sustained a substantial head injury when a train she was riding in abruptly stopped, and she hit her head on the metal seat in front of her.[53] If these accounts are true, it may indicate a traumagenic history that could have contributed to the development of a murderer. At the time, administrative psychiatrist Dr. Felix Adams who assessed Doss said he felt that "she does not know right from wrong or realize the consequences of her acts." Other psychiatrists agreed she was "mentally defective." Nevertheless, a jury at her "sanity trial" took literally just two minutes to declare her sane. Dr. Adams was stunned at the verdict and told reporters he was in disbelief that the prosecution, on whose behalf he typically testified, ignored his report. He said Doss was "of low mentality," and that she was "infantile" and had intellectual disability.[54]

Diagnostic systems and mental illness markers were different in the 1950s. Moreover, according to criminal justice experts, the M'Naghten rule, focusing on knowing right from wrong to determine culpability, was growing antiquated even in the 1950s. Experts were arguing for evaluations of self-control or medical evidence of mental illness.[55] Still, although I am not a clinical psychologist, criminologist, or insanity defense expert, I feel one is justified in questioning a sanity ascription to a woman who killed four husbands, her mother, her mother-in-law, her sister, and her two grandchildren – someone whom a conglomerate of experienced, high-profile psychiatrists said was infantile and mentally ill. Furthermore, whereas trial by jury is a right in the USA, laypeople deciding on a defendant's mental health seems unjust.

Doss escaped the electric chair through the negotiations of her attorney, and because she was never read her rights when accused of murdering Sam. She said she had, though, wanted the electric chair as her fate.[56] Doss served life in prison, where she was assigned to work in the prison's bakery – a curious assignment for a notorious poisoner.[57] On June 2, 1965, Doss died in prison of leukemia.[58] Interestingly, arsenic is a carcinogen that, in laboratory studies, has been linked to leukemia.[59] To be scientifically fair I should note that purified derivatives of arsenic have been suggested as a therapy for cancer.[60] Still, the purified form is not the kind you find in rat poison.

Doss' tombstone reads, "Beloved Mother."[61]

§

Eradication of the victim appears to be the typical endgame and the reason for FSK murders – not necessarily enjoyment of the act. In our study, my team and I found no evidence of necrophilia or other unusual engagement with victim remains, besides careless disposal, such as in the case of "Death House Landlady" Dorothea Puente, or in the case of Aileen Wuornos, who left at least one body in a junkyard. Amanda Farrell and her colleagues noted, "It is unlikely you would find a woman sexually assaulting a corpse or engaging in cannibalistic or vampiric activities."[62]

Still, there can be exceptions. "Jolly" Jane Toppan's motives and crimes, for example, had many commonalities with other FSKs. Yet in one aspect she was a counterinstance to the typical FSK: she liked to hold victims as they died and reported that she enjoyed the feeling of someone's life slipping away. In 1902, *The Saint Paul Globe* further reported that, when in custody for murder, Toppan told a panel of physicians assessing her mental state that hearing the death rattle in her first victim's throat was as sweet as music, and she kissed him when he was cold from death.[63] This is not your typical FSK modus operandi where victims are concerned.

When describing the victims of FSKs, some caveats are warranted. There are instances in which we do not know all the victims of a serial killer, such as in the case of Belle Gunness, where it is thought her hog pit was the resting place of up to 100 people. Another example is that of Genene Jones, who is suspected of killing up to 60 infants and children. In many cases, it is impossible to determine the age and sex of victims, even when remains are discovered. Further, there are very likely victims who have died at the hands of serial murderers not yet apprehended, or who may never be apprehended. Sadly, we will never know, and we may never have enough information to complete the picture. Thus, these data are interpreted with caution as representing minimum frequency.

FSKs on average typically kill between five and 10 victims. We documented known victims, although it is likely in many cases these women killed more victims. Our sample of 64 FSKs killed an average of 6.1 persons, with a wide variation (SD = 4.84; range of three to 31 victims). This mean number is similar to that found in previous studies.[64] Some researchers reported whole numbers (appropriately, as victims are people) versus decimals. Therefore, calculating a grand or pooled mean would not yield valid data. It is worth noting that there is very likely overlap in the cases my team investigated and those explored by other teams. It is against ethical practice to list the names of subjects in this type of project, so we do not know.

VICTIM AGE

We could not determine mean ages exactly, as several reports indicated generalities (e.g., all victims were elderly). Our sample of 64 FSKs was a mixture of those who killed adults only (about 45%; average of 6 victims), children only (about a quarter; average of 5 victims), and both adults and children (about a third; average of 7 victims). The number of victims was highest in the "both" category, but there was no statistical difference between mean number of victims between these three groups. Standard deviations show wide variability in mean number of victims.

VICTIM VULNERABILITY

In our sample of FSKs, more than half (54.7%) murdered children, and a quarter murdered those who were infirm or elderly. With overlap in victim type, about three-quarters of FSKs in our study killed at least one person who was vulnerable and powerless in their direct care.[65]

These victims had arguably no chance of fighting back. Kristen Gilbert was a skilled nurse who murdered disabled veterans with injections of epinephrine. Dorothea Puente was a landlady who poisoned and suffocated tenants with intellectual disabilities and mental illness and buried their bodies in her yard. Martha Woods murdered most of the infant and toddler children for whom she was providing care, including her own, inducing fatal breathing issues. Genene Jones, a licensed vocational nurse, quite skilled by all accounts, injected baby Chelsea, baby Joshua, and countless other infants and children with lethal doses of sedatives.

VICTIM FAMILIARITY AND RELATEDNESS

Almost all (92.2%) of the FSKs in our sample are confirmed to have known at least one of the people they murdered. Moreover, most (62.5%) FSKs in our sample were related to all or some of their victims by blood or marriage. Of the entire sample, 43.8% killed their own children, and 29.7% killed at least one spouse or committed partner (fiancé or boyfriend). Four FSKs killed their mothers, one killed her father and her mother-in-law, and others killed aunts, cousins, and nephews.[66] Again, we must keep in mind that murders do go undetected, particularly under the assumption that those who give care are not supposed to kill, so this list is probably an underestimate.

OUTCOMES: WHAT HAPPENS TO FSKs?

§

Kimberly Clark Saenz is a serial killer. Convicted of the murder of five dialysis patients and injuring five others in Lufkin, Texas, the ex-nurse and mother of two children could have received the death penalty in 2012.[67] However, Saenz is spending the rest of her life in prison, ineligible for parole.[68] Of being in a penitentiary forever, Saenz's attorney said, "It's not a special place, just another corner of hell. And she will be there the rest of her life."[69]

Saenz murdered five patients and made others gravely ill by injecting bleach into their intravenous lines as they received treatment in the Lufkin DaVita Dialysis Clinic, where she worked as a Licensed Vocational Nurse (LVN). Investigators believe she killed or harmed even more patients. During her employment at DaVita Dialysis, there was an exponential increase in emergency patient transports to hospitals, including 30 in one month, compared to 15 total transports in the two years prior.[70]

Defense attorneys argued Saenz was "a good nurse, a compassionate, a caring individual who assisted her patients and was well liked." Saenz had told a grand jury she was being railroaded by her incompetent place of employment. Nonetheless, investigators who examined Saenz's computer found records of internet searches on whether it was possible to detect bleach in dialysis lines and on bleach poisoning in general. Moreover, two witnesses saw Saenz use a syringe to extract bleach from a cleaning bucket she was using and inject the substance directly into the IV lines of two patients.[71]

Reports are not clear as to Saenz's motive, and I could not locate any information on clinical assessment of her psychological state. Still, evidence does point to a troubled past. Prosecutors believed that Saenz had marriage problems, and they believed she took out frustrations on patients.[72] She also had indications of substance abuse. Saenz swore in an affidavit that she had no previous felonies, but the District Attorney had evidence that Saenz abused prescription drugs and stole Demerol (a synthetic opiate pain killer with heightened potential for addiction and misuse)[73] from her previous employer, Woodland Heights Medical Center.[74]

Saenz lied about having been arrested in order to obtain a healthcare job at DaVita Dialysis.[75]

The impact on victims and their families cannot be overstated. Wanda Hollingsworth's mother was killed by Saenz. Wanda is also a nurse. She addressed Saenz in court: "You have disgraced your family and the medical field. I honestly say I hope you rot in hell."[76] She added that Saenz was "nothing more than a psychopathic serial killer."

A jury found Saenz guilty of capital murder on March 30, 2012.[77]

§

What became of the FSKs in our study?[78] We found that, like Kimberly Saenz or Lydia Sherman (discussed later), most (about 80%) were sentenced to prison. Of the FSKs that went to prison, less than a quarter received the death penalty for their crimes. Another 12.4% of our sample of FSKs were committed to mental health facilities. A few went to local jail, remained under house arrest, or were never caught.

Recall the cases of Sharon Kinne and Belle Gunness. Neither was heard from again. Whereas Belle is long gone, Sharon ("La Pistolera") would be a little over 80 years old as of this writing, perhaps enjoying her golden years on some beach in Mexico.

Most FSKs whose cases were included in our study were caught and faced justice. Of course, we must concede that there may be many FSKs out there who were never caught, and therefore their stories have not been memorialized in news and court documents. However, investigators have access to increasingly sophisticated forensic techniques and thorough profiles to help with detecting and catching a murderer.

CHAPTER 6

FSK Motives and Profile

WHEN SOMEONE HEARS the *what* of serial murder, they probably want to know the *why*. Why did this happen? What were the motives? It is difficult to know the operation of someone's mind, particularly someone who makes murderous decisions. Most of us cannot put ourselves in a murderer's shoes. Most people would not understand the mindset, for example, of Dana Sue Gray, who choked elderly ladies with phone cords so she could steal their money and buy cowboy boots.

When examining the motives of FSKs, we can ask the perpetrator why they committed the crimes. Or, if we have no interview access, we can go by what clinical reports, news reports, court documents, and historical societies have recorded as their motives. We can also gauge what the FSK herself has said, and we can report what authorities have derived from the evidence. Nonetheless, we might not ever have a perfect understanding of why someone would commit a string of murders, particularly of children, the elderly, and infirm victims.

In 2015, my team and I documented what was reported as the primary motives for 63 out of 64 of the FSKs in our sample – one FSK's motive was reported as "unknown."[1] For all others, we classified motives according to Ronald Holmes and Stephen Holmes' serial killer typology.[2] Consistent with the opinions of other authors, we found that FSKs do not neatly fit into this classification system that was constructed based on MSK crimes. We found that the most common FSK motive to be "hedonistic" (about half), which are murders for profit, comfort, or thrill. Other motives were "power-seeking" (about one-fifth) and "unspecified mental illness" (about one in 10), with rare examples of "visionary" (following command hallucinations), and "missionary" (ridding the world of undesirable people).

Other cases, however, did not fit into these proscribed categories. My team found that about 8% of FKSs murdered for revenge. We also created a new category we labeled "maintenance killer." Although rare, FSKs do murder to protect their own interests, i.e., the killings were arguably collateral damage along a destructive pathway. And in some cases, FSKs had more than one motive.

It is interesting, and speaks to the theme of this book, that classification systems were developed by experts for understanding male-perpetrated serial murder, but these systems do not adequately capture female-perpetrated serial murder. FSKs can certainly be just as deadly, and their cases merit deeper understanding. Still, I found Holmes and Holmes' categorization system, compared to other systems, best able to capture the motives of FSKs.

§

Kristen Gilbert, you will recall from the beginning of this book, is a serial killer. Her motives cannot be neatly categorized. Gilbert liked to create cardiac events in her disabled patients at the Veterans Administration hospital in Massachusetts so that she could play hero nurse and revive them from the brink of death. The desire to play hero would make her "power-seeking." Yet these actions also gave her a thrill, which could be considered "hedonistic." A court document[3] noted that Gilbert's primary motive was the "desire for attention," and that she was "showing off" for her hospital police officer boyfriend Jim Perrault. *The Boston Globe* reported that Gilbert was literally playing footsie with Perrault as she attempted to help patients in cardiac distress.[4] Showing off is further underscored by Gilbert's unfounded claims to be a relative of well-known murderer Lizzie Borden.

We also know that Gilbert killed at least one person, Kenneth Cutting, so she could leave her shift early to go out on a romantic date in early February 1996. Demonstrating the complexity of classification, this action could qualify as "hedonistic" if the choice to murder was made for her pleasure or comfort. Might it also qualify as "missionary" if the motive was to get a sick person "out of the way"? Of course, we can all agree that Kenneth Cutting deserved so much more than to be collateral damage for Gilbert's date night with her boyfriend. Cutting was a VA patient for many years and was known as being cheery and kind, with a sense of humor. Although blind, Cutting would regularly greet people with a smile and a compliment, such as, "Boy, you look good today!"[5] So how do we classify Gilbert's reasons for murdering him? The distinction between "power-seeking" and "hedonistic" feels unclear. Furthermore, reports show that Gilbert was treated for psychiatric issues, which included making violent threats against others and a suicide attempt. She was in and out of psychiatric hospitals at least seven times in the mid-1990s.[6] She thus had signs consistent with "unspecified mental illness."

In other words, while Gilbert[7] should likely be classified as a primarily "power-seeking" serial killer, her case is a great example of how FSK murders do not fit neatly into any single preexisting serial killer category.[8]

§

Other scholars have cautioned against using existing serial killer classifications for understanding FSKs. Forensic expert Sandie Taylor and colleagues[9] argued against the validity of classifying FSKs into mutually exclusive categories of "visionary," "missionary," "hedonistic," and "power/control." On a related point, as of this writing, I am uncertain if FSK motives are statistically more likely to span across multiple categorizations compared to MSK motives; this is an empirical question.

Profilers Michael Kelleher and C. L. Kelleher[10] argued for another classification system for FSKs: "black widows," "angels of death," "sexual predators," "revenge killers," "profit or crime killers," "team killers," "killers of questionable sanity," and "unexplained murderers." These categories, however, are not mutually exclusive. As an example, "black widows" often kill husband after husband for profit (i.e., inheritance, insurance money), although "black widow" is a nickname typically ascribed to FSKs who murder their husbands, like Judy Buenoano, whose case I describe below.

As pointed out by Emily Dryer-Brees,[11] no classification systems are really accepted as serial killer doctrine. Even categorizations such as "organized" versus "disorganized" serial murder yield inconsistent results. Sandie Taylor and colleagues analyzed 40 serial killers in one study and 40 serial killers in another.[12] They found most serial murders to have organization, but they likely differ in aspects of disorganization.

Yet there are certainly different types of FSKs. Recall the case of Patty Cannon, who killed people who got in the way of her kidnapping and people-selling business. Recall the case of Martha Woods, who killed seven infants and toddlers, victims of her probable Munchausen syndrome by proxy/factitious disorder imposed on another (MSBP/FDIA). Recall the case of Aileen Wuornos, who shot men in the head and torso and robbed them. Recall the case of Nannie Doss, who is suspected of having killed multiple people who just got on her nerves. While all unified by horrific deeds and high victim count, these are different types of crimes.

KILLING FOR PROFIT: AN EVOLUTIONARY MOTIVE?

The most common motive for FSKs to murder is money/profit. This differs markedly from what a large body of scholarly work has told us about MSKs, whose primary motivator is sex. Yet this makes sense, from the perspective of evolutionary psychology.

But what is evolutionary psychology? As Charles Darwin[13] wrote, many millennia of existence gave rise to anatomical adaptations that were best suited to a species' survival and reproduction. And just as our human bodies evolved, evolutionary psychologists contend our minds evolved to solve the issues we faced regarding survival and reproduction. We have innate, adaptive drives mediated by genes inherited from our early human ancestors. These drives motivate behavior that, under the circumstances of our ancestral environment, would have increased the likelihood of survival and reproduction. For example, why do we feel happiness? People who felt happy left more descendants. Apply this explanation to caregiver bonding, physical attraction, falling in love, etc.

Sometimes, however, what would have worked to a specified degree in the ancestral environment can take lesser or exaggerated forms now. Take jealousy, for example. Jealousy was adaptive in the ancestral environment, or there would not be jealousy today. Some jealousy throughout human history led to mate guarding and anti-mate-poaching tactics, ensuring mate retention, and increasing reproductive chances.[14] When extreme, however, jealousy is a primary motivator for murdering one's partner, and even of one's partner's allies, particularly among men.[15]

Jealousy is an adaptation that, when taken too far, can prove fatal. Adaptations can go off-kilter.

"Evolved," however, does not mean "genetically predetermined" or "absolute." Noting that there is an evolutionary contribution to serial murder is different from saying that we are genetically programmed to commit serial murder. Do people who murder leave more descendants? No. The human population would have been eliminated very quickly if that were the case. Yet in evolved human female psychology, there is a drive for ensuring access to mates with resources, as resources would have facilitated survival and reproductive success in the ancestral environment. And it is this drive for money that has become a pathological variant motivating resource/profit-seeking FSK murders.

For example, the data from my team's study of 64 FSKs showed that FSKs who kill for profit (and who could thus be classified as "hedonistic") were older at the age of their first kill than all other types besides "missionary" killers. Maybe as they aged, they did not feel financially secure and took extreme measures to gather resources – in this case, financial resources. Going back to the original unpublished data, I discovered that 92% of "hedonistic" killers in our sample were of low or middle socio-economic status, perhaps indicating the potential for financial issues. While there were virtually no reports available about financial distress being a trigger for female-perpetrated serial homicide, perhaps we are seeing the ancestral survival drive to accumulate resources gone haywire.

Evolutionary psychology all comes down to eggs and sperm. Take it a step back . . . way back . . . to conception. Robert Trivers' Parental Investment Theory attributes sex differences in evolved psychology to sex differences in reproductive biology.[16] Men produce millions of sperm daily.[17] It would make sense, then, for males in the ancestral environment to have sex with as many females as possible to increase the likelihood of insemination. This is not to say that modern men should go on an intercourse spree and inseminate everyone they meet. But it does mean that an increased desire for sex would have best served male reproductive purposes over the course of human evolution. Indeed, contemporary men still want more sex, more sex partners, and more sexual variety, and they prefer more one-night stands and consent to sex sooner than do women.[18]

On the other hand, as Trivers pointed out, women's reproductive opportunities are narrow. Women are born with a few hundred thousand eggs and will ovulate only about 400 eggs in their lifetimes,[19] from puberty until menopause. Women who give birth also experience obligatory lengthy parental investment, with internal fertilization, pregnancy, labor, childbirth, breastfeeding, and postnatal care. It makes sense that females in the ancestral environment would have to be selective, choosing the best mates for their limited reproductive opportunities. Choosing a mate with status and securing resources would give a female and her children the best survival chances in the environment of evolutionary adaptedness (EEA) – the social and physical selection pressures humans faced over millions of years.[20]

Women today certainly do not need a male mate with money to survive, or any mate at all. However, women still have unconscious drives that operate in the way we did over millions of years of evolution when we were primitive hominids. To wit, around the world, women still prefer mates with high status and resources.[21] Furthermore, children of fathers who have invested resources in their well-being have lower infant mortality rates and greater access to material and social resources that give them a competitive advantage in life.[22]

Yet even with evolved psychological mechanisms, individual differences exist.[23] We have different degrees of jealousy, attachment, love, and sex drive, and we each have a myriad of developmental experiences that shape who we are. But the basic, evolved drives are in place to maximize the likelihood of genetic representation in subsequent generations.

So, for FSKs, we can understand, ultimately, why money is a prime motive for murdering,[24] but that does not make it right. It does not excuse murder or deem murder a correct behavioral response. Not at all. It is an evolved drive taken to a morbid extreme. Think of "black widows" who murder their husbands – and other people – to collect an inheritance or insurance money, who then move on to their next victim. The drive to secure resources is innate in women. FSKs take it to a terrible degree and use murder for financial gain.

Of course, there are other perspectives on serial murder besides the evolutionary one. These include social, clinical, and traumagenic factors; I would never say that such circumstances are uninvolved or unremarkable in the making of a murderer. We do not develop in a vacuum. These, however, are all proximate motivators. They are immediate causal considerations. Evolutionary psychologists contend that there are ultimate, evolved forces at work in all human behavior and mental processes. To view serial murder only through an evolutionary, or clinical, or personality, or gender role framework would provide an incomplete assessment. As proximate and ultimate motivators are studied by various experts in psychology, criminology, and sociology, we can gain the most complete, accurate understanding of a behavioral phenomenon.

§

Judias "Judy" Buenoano was a serial killer. She was born in 1943 or 1945 in Texas as Judias Welty, or Anna Lou Welty, depending on what source you read. This "black widow" held many roles in her life beyond "murdering wife/partner" and "mother": she was a nurse, a food server, and later, a manicurist. In 1962, Judias Welty married a man named James Goodyear, a United States Air Force sergeant. Her last name, "Buenoano," which she took some time after her marriage, was an imperfect Spanish variation of James' last name. James Goodyear adopted her son Michael, and they had two other children together. A few months after Goodyear returned from a tour as a pilot in Vietnam, however, he experienced a mysterious illness and died in a military hospital in Florida. As a result of James Goodyear's death, Judy Buenoano was the beneficiary of multiple insurance policies.

James Goodyear was just the first of several murders. In the late 1970s, Judy Buenoano moved to Colorado with her then boyfriend, Bobby Joe Morris. In 1978, Morris became ill with the same symptoms that had afflicted James Goodyear. Like Goodyear before him, Morris died, and Buenoano was once again the reported beneficiary of three separate life insurance policies totaling about $85,000.[25] Then, in the late 1970s, Judy's son Michael Goodyear joined the military. However, he became gravely ill with what was diagnosed as arsenic poisoning. The toxin affected his limb mobility. As a result, he had to wear heavy arm and leg braces. A few years later, in 1980, Buenoano took her son canoeing on the East Bay River near her Florida home. The canoe capsized and Michael drowned, weighed down in the river by his braces. Buenoano once again received an appreciable survivor's benefit payment. Reports are inconsistent, but figures range anywhere from $20,000 to $100,000.[26] She later gave authorities four different accounts of what happened that day, including the explanation that it was a snake falling into the canoe that caused it to capsize.[27]

Even aside from murder, reports suggest Buenoano was a suboptimal mother. A relative indicated that Buenoano was embarrassed of Michael, who probably had an intellectual disability. One of Michael's friends from the military testified that she called Michael "stupid," "dumb," and "idiot." She was also overheard calling Michael a "little bastard." Moreover, neighbors from when Michael was a child said he had no toys at home – Buenoano would frequently leave Michael and her other children alone in the house to go out, and they would fall asleep in front of the television.[28]

In the 1980s, Buenoano began dating a man named John Gentry, whom she met at a mud wrestling match. She reportedly took out a $500,000 life insurance policy on him.[29] Soon after, Gentry sought treatment at a local hospital for extreme nausea and vomiting. Buenoano claimed to have been giving him vitamins, but vitamin capsules containing paraformaldehyde (found in disinfectants) were later found in her home. Gentry did recover from the illness, but then his car exploded, injuring him very seriously. Authorities then became very suspicious of Buenoano, and they investigated other deaths tied to her.[30]

James Goodyear's body was exhumed, as was Bobby Joe Morris' body, and investigators determined that arsenic was in their systems. Buenoano was arrested. She was convicted in April 1984 and given a life sentence for killing Michael Goodyear and a 12-year sentence for planting a bomb in John Gentry's car.[31] Later, in 1985, she received a death sentence for killing James Goodyear in 1971 by arsenic poisoning. Investigators had evidence that Buenoano murdered Bobby Joe Morris, but they did not press charges once Judy was given a death sentence in Florida. Buenoano's two surviving children, Kim and James, asserted her innocence until the end.[32]

In the end, Buenoano had no final words as she faced her execution, although she spent the day before reading Mary Higgins Clark's novel, *Remember Me*, a story about a mother who blames herself for the death of her son.[33] At age 54, Judy was executed via the electric chair (known as "Old Sparky") by the State of Florida on March 31, 1998, the date on which Michael would have celebrated his 37th birthday. During the 38-second electrocution, reporters noted smoke coming out of her leg where an electrode was attached. [34] In her final moments, her limbs were destroyed, just as she had destroyed her son's limbs.

By the time she was caught, Judy Buenoano had murdered three people, and attempted to murder another, all for the insurance money. In all, she collected about $240,000 in benefits from the deaths she caused.[35] Over the years, she also started several house fires in order to collect insurance payments. Buenoano's foster daughter Debra Sims remembered her as a young mother yearning for a better life, often sewing sequins on dresses she never got to wear. Sims theorized that insurance fraud and murder were Judy's way of getting the money to have "finer things."[36] The prosecutor in Michael's murder described her motive as "twisted greed."[37] An unnamed relative said, "It's just my honest opinion, but I don't think she had any values on anything other than money."[38] "She cared nothing about anybody else's pain and suffering," asserted Attorney Belvin Perr, adding, "She rightly serves the title of Black Widow. Just like the spider, after she mated with her prey, she killed it."[39]

It is possible that that there is more to Buenoano's story, however. Judy Buenoano was reported to have had a traumatic upbringing. Her mother died when she was four years old, and she spent much of her youth living with various relatives and in foster care. She told authorities she was sexually and physically abused and often went hungry while in foster care. If true, although abhorrent, this would not be an unusual experience, as some reports suggest that as many as 40% of children in foster care are abused.[40] Eventually, her father remarried, and she lived with him and his new wife. According to Buenoano, her father and stepmother forced her to climb into the dumpsters of restaurants and grocery stores to find food. After running away at age 14, she was sent to reform school in Albuquerque, where records indicate she was a good student. She became pregnant with Michael at age 17.[41]

If these circumstances are true, Judy Buenoano, like many other FSKs, had a traumagenic upbringing. Yet we must concede that she has a history of lying. Indeed, Buenoano claimed she was the granddaughter of Geronimo,[42] the formidable and fearless Apache leader[43] – a claim for which there seems to be no record or basis. She also went by many names, including Anna Lou Welty, Ann Schultz, Ann Goodyear, and Judy Buenoano. Prosecutors argued that she changed names frequently so that insurance companies would not catch on to her being the recipient of a vast number of payouts. Moreover, on her marriage certificate to James Goodyear, she claimed to have been born in England rather than Texas. She also made herself older. She was a licensed practical nurse in Colorado, but she told people that she was a flight attendant, a doctor, and later, a psychologist. Nevertheless, her aunt confirmed, "She had a pretty rough childhood."[44]

§

KILLING CHILDREN

If FSKs primarily kill for money, which can be viewed as a pathological variant of ancestral tendencies for women to seek resources maximizing the chances that they and their offspring will survive, why would so many FSKs kill their children? If reproduction is the name of the game in evolution, isn't killing your children the exact opposite strategy? According to Richard Dawkins' concept of "genesmanship," an organism behaves in ways most suited to passing on its genetic legacy.[45] Seen from this perspective, then, killing your children is, indeed, the antithesis of genesmanship. Yet infanticide has been recorded throughout human history. A quick peek at the literature reveals scientific papers speaking to human infanticide everywhere from Ancient Rome, to Britain, to Italy, to Australia, to the Artic.

Nonetheless, murdering one's own children clearly indicates that an evolved caregiving mechanism is malfunctioning. It indicates that a motivator is not performing the way it evolved to perform – a malfunction similarly seen, for example, in the behavior of stalking, which researchers contend is an aberrant and dangerous courtship strategy.[46]

Murdering one's own children can be seen as an extreme outlier of the distribution of caregiving polygenic traits. As we know, individual variation exists in psychological mechanisms that are a product of evolution.[47]

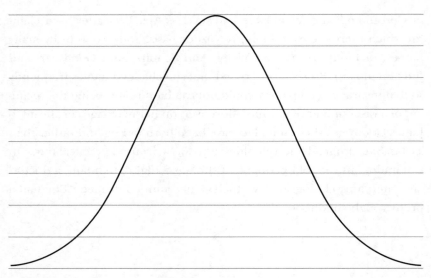

6.1 Bell curve representing a normal probability distribution

Think about a normal distribution – a bell curve – you may have encountered in a statistics course. Most behaviors and mental processes are captured by the optimal mean. The tails represent reduced or exaggerated manifestations of normal behavior. In the case of mothers, in the very middle of the normal distribution is the average (depicted by the highest point in the bell curve), where most are typically responsive and loving caregivers. To the right of that, heading towards one tail, you have mothers who are permissive, indulgent, overbearing, overinvolved, hanging on every detail of their child's life. At the extreme end, you might even see mothers with illness anxiety disorder over their child's well-being. On the other side of the curve, however, heading towards the other tail, you have mothers who harm their children. And way far down into that extreme, many statistical standard deviations away from the mean, you have mothers who kill their children – just like Judy Buenoano, Martha Woods, and Belle Gunness – or their grandchildren, like Nannie Doss.

Perhaps exploring infanticide in the non-human animal kingdom is warranted. Those who have witnessed infanticide among non-human animals describe it as horrifying.[48] Although it is disturbing to process, it may be an adaptive strategy, enhancing reproductive fitness by conferring resource benefits to the perpetrator.[49] For example, if a male tree squirrel kills juvenile tree squirrels that are unrelated to him, there would be more resources for his own offspring. This increases the chance that his offspring will survive and reproduce, thereby enhancing his fitness (meaning his genes will be passed down to subsequent generations).[50]

Decades ago, J. Boggess[51] argued that infanticide was a social pathology, and that in instances of overcrowding, non-human animals (e.g., langur monkeys) become psychologically disturbed and kill infants, with no reproductive advantage for the perpetrator. Although there has been pushback on this hypothesis from anthropologists, the pathological angle does seem to speak somewhat to FSKs killing their own children. FSKs already have a disturbed resource-acquisition drive. And some FSKs are killing their own offspring, thus directly eliminating their genetic fitness. There must be a psychological disturbance.

An older theory put forth by renowned anthropologist and primatologist Sarah Hrdy[52] argued that female-perpetrated infanticide of one's own offspring can eliminate competition for resources. She also argued that having "supernumerary" infants can trigger this response in the animal kingdom. Going back to my team's original FSK data, I found that 80% of FSKs who killed children killed their own children. And for those who killed their own children, the mean number of victims was 5.82. Where information was available for socioeconomic status of those who killed their own children, none were upper-class. Most were middle-class, and a few were lower-class.[53] As disturbing as it seems, it would not be a stretch to think that six children are "supernumerary" – there was likely some overcrowding in living quarters and limited resources were likely stretched.

Notably, infanticide seems to have different functions in different species, and its functions are not totally clear to scientists.[54] However, just because a behavior might be triggered by some evolutionary throwback mechanism does not make it correct or justified. In the human world, killing children is an aberrant manifestation on the extreme, suboptimal end of the distribution of parenting skills.

§

Rhonda Belle Martin was a serial killer. She was born on November 4, 1906. From 1934 to 1951, she killed six members of her family in

Alabama.[55] Victims included her three daughters, Emogene Garrett, age three; Carolyn Garrett, age six; and Ellyn Elizabeth Garrett, age 11. She also killed her husband George W. Garrett; husband Claude C. Martin; and her mother, Mary Gibbon.

George Garrett and their three daughters Emogene, Carolyn, and Ellyn were among the first of Martin's victims. Notably, the couple also had two other children who died very young, although information about them is sparse. Young Mary Adelaide Garrett (1930–1934) and Judith Charlene Garrett[56] (1938–1939) were buried in the same cemetery where newspapers say victim Ellyn Garrett (1932–1943) was also interred. According to *The Montgomery Advertiser*, Martin claimed that Mary Adelaide was born ill. Although there is no clear evidence that Martin was responsible for her first two daughters' deaths, it is not beyond reasonable doubt. Or one might wonder if Mary Adelaide's early death was natural but triggered something horrific in Martin, who subsequently killed all her girls in the same manner. *The Montgomery Advertiser* certainly speculated along these lines, asking, "Did something in her mind snap at the death of her invalid daughter?" Indeed, the obituary for 11-year-old Ellyn, known to have died at Martin's hand, indicated that she perished "after a long illness," which may mean this helpless little girl suffered with the effects of chronic arsenic poisoning.[57]

In total, Martin was married four or five times; one cannot be sure. But it seems that two of her husbands did not die by her hand: W. R. Alderman and Talmadge J. Gipson.[58] Information is sparse on Alderman. At age 40, Martin married Gipson in August 1947 – sometime after having killed George Garrett and their children.[59] However, their marriage lasted only five months. In March 1956, after Martin was accused of murder, Gipson told his story to *The Montgomery Advertiser* accompanied by a front-page photo of him, face in palm. He told reporter Joe Azbell, "The only thing I can figure that kept her from poisoning me is that I got shed of her too quick . . . or I didn't have no insurance." Gipson added, "I was working at the VA Hospital in Montgomery at the time and they could have detected the poisoning if I had got it." He also claimed he was so drunk when they got married that the judge asked him if he knew what he was doing.[60] Records indicate that Talmadge J. Gipson lived until 1989 when he died of natural causes at the age of 93.[61]

Less than two years after her marriage to Gipson, in 1949, Rhonda Belle married Claude Martin.[62] Apparently ignoring her marriage to Gipson, she was identified as a widow rather than a divorcee. Their marriage ended with Claude's murder, after which Martin, a food server, collected a total of $2,750 from three life insurance policies. Eight months after he died, she married his 28-year-old son Ronald, a Navy veteran. She poisoned him. Luckily, he survived, but he was left paralyzed from the waist down and had to remain in the care of a veterans' hospital.

When Ronald was admitted to the hospital and tests revealed traces of arsenic in his system, authorities began investigating all the suspicious deaths in Martin's family. They exhumed her six deceased victims.[63] Faced with the evidence, Rhonda Belle Martin confessed to putting arsenic-based poison (some sources say ant poison, some say rat poison . . . potat-o, potah-to) in the drinks of seven human beings – the six she murdered and the stepson/husband who lived. In a statement to the court, she admitted to putting poison in Emogene's milk in 1937. In 1939, she put arsenic in husband George Garrett's whiskey. In 1940, she poisoned Carolyn's milk, and did the same to Ellyn in 1943. In 1944, she served Mary, her mother, coffee laced with arsenic. Repeating her modus operandi, she also put arsenic in husband Claude Martin's coffee "three or four times," and later did the same to Ronald.[64]

In an odd coincidence, according to a story ran by the New York *Daily News*, Martin had lived across the street from Kilby Prison within view of a cell inhabited by "Mrs. Earl Dennison," a woman who was executed for killing her two-year-old niece with arsenic.[65]

While Martin told the court she had small insurance policies on each of her six victims, she claimed that this was not her motive.[66] "I don't know why I did it," she said, "I don't understand it. I didn't do it for the money. I loved my family. I guess I loved them to death."[67] Martin's attorney George Cameron attempted to use a mental illness defense, but the judge mocked his use of the word "schizophrenia," and then refused to recuse himself, despite having made clearly prejudicial comments in front of the jury.[68] Nonetheless, a psychiatrist from Birmingham, Alabama, testified at trial that he examined her and determined that she did, indeed, have schizophrenia. In his closing arguments, Martin's attorney pleaded, "Don't kill this crazy woman. Send her to prison

6.2 Rhonda Bell Martin confessed to putting poison in the drinks of her victims, including her children. (Photo by Getty Images)

as long as you can."[69] The all-male jury did not grant his request. Martin was convicted for having killed Claude Martin in 1951, and she was sentenced to death.

Contemporary legal scholars argue that the evolution of the M'Naghten insanity defense includes considerations of delusions (false beliefs). It also considers if the defendant "could have fairly been expected to exercise adequate reasoning abilities while in the throes of psychosis."[70] Delusions are a hallmark symptom of schizophrenia. Perhaps in today's era of increased understanding of mental illness, Martin would have met a different fate.

I am not diagnosing anyone. But I think you need not be a diagnostician to notice that Martin gave birth to five daughters in a short period of time (1930, 1932, 1933, 1934, and 1938), and it is therefore possible that she was suffering from postpartum psychosis (PP). When suffering from PP, the patient experiences bizarre, paranoid, or grandiose delusions, confusion, and mood swings. The patient exhibits "grossly disorganized behavior that represent[s] a dramatic change from her previous functioning," and "the safety and well-being of the affected mother and her offspring are jeopardized." It can be brought on by hormonal shifts, sleep deprivation, and stress.[71]

In the case of Rhonda Belle Martin, one might picture the rapidly changing hormonal milieu created by five pregnancies, as well as the sleep deprivation and stress one might have with five very young children – some with only a year between them. Moreover, if her first child was indeed very ill, this would have been a marked stressor. Homicidal behavior is rare in women with PP, yet the risk of PP increases in women with schizoaffective or bipolar disorder; Martin might have had either or both, as diagnostics were different in the 1950s. Additionally, risk increases for people with a previous PP episode,[72] and Martin had five children. There is, in fact, no evidence that Martin had any traumagenic background or bizarre behavior prior to the murders. And PP-related behaviors would be a dramatic change from behavior seen previously. It may be the case that Martin had an existing predisposition for schizophrenia spectrum, and the birth of each subsequent child, through no fault of theirs, exacerbated her symptoms. It is also possible that she had this predisposition, and the death of Mary Adelaide from illness triggered the expression of dangerous symptoms.

We shall never know if some of the Martin children might have been spared if there was a more extensive knowledge of mental illness in that era, particularly schizophrenia and postpartum issues. Yet trying to understand Martin's circumstances does not excuse her murders. In reviewing files for this case, I saw the marriage license of Rhonda Belle Garrett and Claude C. Martin, dated October 28, 1949.[73] To me, looking at his signature on the marriage license reinforced the victims' side of this story. One might presume that day was happy for him and that he had no idea what she would do to him only two years later. Rhonda Belle Martin showed victims no mercy, and those who experience arsenic poisoning, a type of heavy metal poisoning, suffer before they die. Symptoms include, but are not limited to, encephalopathy, demyelination of neurons, edema, vomiting and abdominal pain, bloody diarrhea, skin lesions, throat inflammation, and the breaking down of red blood cells.[74] Imagine the three young Garrett children enduring that. There are pictures of these beautiful children in newspapers of the time[75] – putting faces to the pain and crimes makes the circumstances of their deaths particularly difficult to process.

Holding on to a Christian Bible, Martin was executed by the Kilby Prison electric chair on October 11, 1957. I cannot verify it, but some sources say that Rhonda Belle Martin is buried in an unmarked grave near all her children. But she did leave a note inside her Bible asking for her body to be examined by physicians:

In death . . . I want my body to be given to some scientific institution to be used as they see fit, but especially to see if someone can find out why I have committed the crimes I committed. I can't understand it, for I had no reason whatsoever. There's definitely something wrong. Can't someone find it and save someone else the agony I have been through[?] Rhonda Belle Martin.[76]

§

Lydia Sherman was a serial killer. Known as "The Derby Murderess,"[77] she was a prolific poisoner. Sherman admitted to poisoning seven people – three husbands and several of her children – but, according to officials, this lethal nurse and caretaker may have murdered as many as 11 victims.[78]

Sherman was born in 1825 in New Brunswick, New Jersey. According to Connecticut and New England historical reports,[79] she was an orphan raised by her uncle. She married her first husband, Edward S. Struck, when she was about 17 years old.[80] Struck was a widower with two children, and some sources said he was about 20 years older than she.[81] The two had met at a "Methodist love feast."[82] Within seven years, the Strucks had six biological children, for a total of eight children in the family.

Edward had been a police officer in New York, but he lost his position. According to Lydia Sherman, he was accused of not doing his job during a saloon fight where a detective was killed. He then sank into depression and illness. He could not find another job, and it is not difficult to imagine they were pressed for money. In 1864, Sherman poisoned Edward with arsenic and killed him. A few weeks later, she poisoned and killed either two or three of their youngest children, depending on what source you read.

With husband Edward unemployed and now deceased, Sherman claimed she was struggling financially and did not have enough money to feed the children. Because of this strain on the family resources, she reported the children were "hurried into eternity."[83] Indeed, According to a report published in the *Harford Courant* on January 18, 1873, Sherman later confessed to her jailer that she had killed her children so they would not be burdens to her or "grow up to life's cares."[84] She was also quoted as saying that her six-year-old, four-year-old, and nine-month-old children "could do nothing for me or for themselves."[85] While these circumstances arguably fit models of infanticide in the non-human animal kingdom due to overcrowding and maternal supernumerary responses,[86] there is little doubt that a host of factors may have contributed to Lydia's decision to carry out the crimes, cover them up, and keep killing.

And kill she did. After the death of Edward and the children, Sherman got a job as a nurse. This was during the US Civil War, although no information was available as to whether she provided care for soldiers. Before long, Sherman's other three children had died. Reports indicate that only two, John and Cornelius, survived. Cornelius reported his stepmother to authorities as having caused his family members' deaths, but they did nothing.

After the US Civil War ended, Sherman took a job as a private nurse in Connecticut. Soon, she caught the attention of Dennis Hurlbut (called "Old Hurlburt"), an older widower with a considerable amount of money. Dennis Hurlburt married Lydia Struck on November 22, 1868.[87] It appears that his first wife had died on September 8, 1868, so he did not wait long.[88] Dennis Hurlburt's Last Will and Testament, written February 9, 1869, stated, "I give and bequeath all my real and personal estate . . . to my wife Lydia Hurlburt without reserve."[89] Shortly after, she poisoned his clam chowder.[90] Dennis died on January 20, 1870, with cause of death listed as cholera and acute diarrhea.[91] Cholera is a bacterial illness, the symptoms of which are similar to arsenic poisoning symptoms.[92] Later, the *New York Herald* later reported that, with a "cold heart," Sherman "hurled" Hurlburt into the grave and seized his property.[93]

Lydia Hurlburt did not wait long to get married again. On September 15, 1870,[94] at age 46, she married Horatio Sherman (sometimes reported as H. N. Sherman), aged 47. She did not wait long to poison again, either.

Shortly after their marriage, on May 12, 1871, the entire Sherman family of Derby, Connecticut, lay dead – hence Sherman's nickname "The Derby Poisoner." Lydia Sherman said she "only" meant to kill her new husband's children, Ada and Frankie, but Horatio died of poisoning, too.[95]

Right before he died, Horatio had not wanted to speak to his wife, and he mentioned something about arsenic to his brother George – which George later testified to at Sherman's trial. Mr. Sherman's friends were suspicious, and George was *very* suspicious. So, when Sherman was away visiting family, they contacted authorities to investigate. The Sherman family was exhumed.[96] Professor George F. Barker of Yale University (then Yale College) found "lethal quantities of arsenic" in their remains.[97] Authorities also investigated the murders of Lydia Sherman's two previous husbands, each of whom had died under similar circumstances.

Lydia Sherman was arrested for murder,[98] but claimed she was innocent.[99] And, in the end, she was only convicted for the second-degree murder of Horatio, with whom the prosecution could prove she was not on good terms. Horatio Jr. testified that his father and stepmother often argued. Sources say that Horatio Sherman would stay away from home in New Haven to avoid her. Noting that Horatio did not exactly immerse himself in refined culture and was "once found in a den with low people," the *Hartford Courant* suggested that "it probably would have been better for Mr. Sherman to have stayed in the den no matter how low its people."[100]

At trial, the *New York Herald* Reported, "Every seat in the courtroom that will accommodate probably four or five hundred persons was occupied by curious people who were anxious to get a glimpse of the accused."[101] Among their witnesses, investigators called a druggist named George Peck to the stand, who testified that Sherman had purchased arsenic rat poison from him.[102] Furthermore, a physician testified that, before he died, Mr. Sherman exhibited symptoms of arsenic poisoning, including vomiting and respiratory distress. Unfortunately, the prosecution could not show that she had administered the poison to her other victims, so the court would not allow information about the previous poisonings into evidence.[103] Yet one newspaper reported that Cornelius Struck, her suspicious surviving stepson from her first marriage, had the bodies of his father and siblings exhumed and tested while she was on trial in Connecticut. The examiners found arsenic.[104]

In the case of husband Horatio, Lydia Sherman was convicted of second-degree murder and sentenced by Judge Sanford to life in prison. On April 27, 1872, the *New York Herald* wrote, "If deliberate poisoning be not murder in the first degree we do not know what is," adding, "To kill by poisoning is the coolest and most deliberate act." Commenting on Sherman's sentence, the *Herald* went on to speculate that "the jury probably had a repugnance to hanging, and particularly to hanging a woman."[105]

After being in prison for about four years, Lydia escaped. The guard (called a "matron" at the time) left Lydia's cell door open because Lydia was in poor health and might have needed immediate assistance.[106] However, she was soon caught and returned to prison, where she died of cancer on May 16, 1878.[107] It is worth noting that arsenic exposure is associated with several types of cancer.[108]

There seem to be no psychological diagnoses reported for Lydia Sherman, although sources from 1871 said that she was supposed to enter an insanity plea. However, those who interviewed her said that she did not present as insane. A newspaper reported, "She does not affect to be moved by any insane impulse but talks like one who was entirely conscious of her innocence."[109] When closing arguments were being made in court, she wept openly, but this was momentary, and then she appeared to be indifferent again.[110] Sherman was callous; she killed her children when resources were scarce. She was perceived to be distrustful and jealous. Some say she killed husbands for their money.[111] Some argued that she just wanted her marriages to end.[112] While not attempting to diagnose anyone, it seems that having callous disregard for others, acting out emotions she thought appropriate to the situation, writing what some felt to be an embellished confession for attention, and executing multiple, planned murders, Lydia Sherman may have been a psychopath.

§

FEMALE SERIAL KILLER PROFILE

Knowing the "what" and "why" of previous serial murders can prove useful in identifying the "who" – the identity of subsequent perpetrators. Once investigators have several cases of murder and understand these killers' crimes and motives, they can create an offender profile. They examine the nature and characteristics of the killings they have committed, including victim traits and the mechanics of murders. They also consider the perpetrator's background information, such as psychological history, traumatic history, and criminal history. They then create a composite offender profile of statistically likely traits and behaviors that can be used to recognize other crimes and catch similar perpetrators.[113] Current classification systems for serial killers, and the FBI's currently available information, were developed through expert knowledge of male serial killers' crimes, including focusing on sexually motivated murders. Experts argue that these systems are inadequate to capture the essence of a female serial killer. Therefore, my team endeavored to create a FSK profile. Aggregating our data and observing trait frequencies, my team and I generated a data-based portrait of a female serial killer, published in the *Journal of Forensic Psychiatry and Psychology*.[114] We hope this may aid in investigations.

Our report suggested that a FSK is likely White and in her 20s or 30s. She has probably been married, perhaps multiple times, and she may be middle-class and Christian. Her appearance is likely to be normal; she is probably of average or above-average attractiveness. She probably holds a stereotypically feminine job and has a good possibility of being a nurse, other healthcare worker, or other direct caregiver in charge of those who are helpless (such as the elderly, the infirm, and children). She may have a traumagenic background, including parental issues, sexual abuse, or other physical abuse. There is a marked possibility that she suffers from some form of mental illness. People close to her are at risk, even her own children. She usually murders for profit but sometimes for power. She will most likely kill by poison or asphyxiation. There is a good chance she has murdered in the suburbs.[115]

Notably, our findings build on the seminal work of criminologist Eric Hickey, who was one of the first scholars to profile FSKs and to validate that women can even be serial killers.[116] As he put it, it is "myopic" to think otherwise. In 1986, Hickey developed an evidence-based portrayal of FSKs over time based on data from 22 cases and collecting interviews and other valid information sources. He found that FSKs most commonly kill in domestic and nursing contexts, and that financial gain is commonly a primary motive. Hickey also described the tumultuous upbringings of FSKs, as well as their psychopathology. While some of the statistics my team derived from our larger sample vary slightly from those presented by Hickey, and we did collect data on additional variables, our corroborating, converging evidence makes the composite of a FSK even more convincing and adds some unique findings and insights.

Experts emphasize, however, that a criminal profile is only "one investigative tool among many and is not a magical solution."[117] A summary of data, no matter how comprehensive, cannot predict who will become a FSK or detect a FSK with total precision. Still, profiles can be useful in that they allow investigators to focus their attention and identify potential suspects with parallel traits. Indeed, a team of researchers who conducted a meta-analysis of 40 years of research on offender profiling in 2018 determined that they had "moderate to strong accuracy" for connecting crimes to perpetrators.[118]

What can a profile accomplish? The *FBI Law Enforcement Bulletin*[119] summarized the characteristics of a successful criminal profile in a list that included moving a case forward, giving investigators new ideas, and helping catch an offender. However, profiling is not an exact science, and strict reliance on homology would not be a viable strategy.[120] For example, FSKs are not all uniform in their backgrounds, motives, and crimes. Nevertheless, as a research psychologist, my goal is to collect data and generate frequencies, averages, and probabilities in an attempt to describe and understand a given behavior or mental process. Hopefully, the data my team and I collected and summarized on FSKs will help investigators catch killers – and prevent more murders.

CHAPTER 7

Comparing FSKs and MSKs: Backgrounds and Mental Illness

§

Ed Gein is, most likely, a serial killer. Yet he committed crimes of a drastically different nature than any FSK I have read about in all my years of research. Gein confessed to killing two women, Mary Hogan and Bernice Worden, in the 1950s in and around Plainfield, Wisconsin. The third victim that would qualify him as a serial killer, per our criteria of three or more deceased victims, is his brother Henry, whom authorities are convinced he killed. Henry allegedly died while he and Gein were trying to extinguish a brushfire near their farm. Gein called the police after the fire was extinguished, stating that his brother was missing, and that he was alarmed. When police arrived on the scene, however, Ed lead them directly to Henry's body. Not only was he found in an area not burned by the brushfire, Henry had injuries to his head.[1]

Gein was suspected of killing others, as well, including two men who were hunting without permission on his neighbors' farm and were never heard from again. When searching Gein's home, investigators also found newspaper clippings about women who had disappeared in the area, and they found children's clothing – although there were no children living in the house. *The Twin City News-Record* reported that, when interrogated, Gein raised his hands like claws, snarled, and stated, "I've been killing for years."[2]

In 1957, as many as 150 investigators searched Gein's property. Among the disarray of all that Gein had hoarded through the years, they found the decapitated, disemboweled body of Bernice Worden hanging upside down by her ankles, said to be "dressed out like a deer."[3]

7.1 Ed Gein in handcuffs after his confession to murder. (Photo by Getty Images)

The Sheriff walked out of the house and vomited.[4] In all, authorities found the remains of at least 14 people, including Mary Hogan. They found 10 human heads in plastic and in a large, round box. One head belonged to an approximately 60-year-old woman, and one was that of a child. Facial skin was preserved as masks, displayed on Gein's walls at eye-level. Authorities found a belt made of women's nipples; a vest made of breasts; furniture upholstery made of skin; and a bowl made from the top of a human skull. They also found scattered pieces of skin, including vaginas. Further, they found a human heart in a pot, evidencing that Gein had engaged in cannibalism.[5]

Gein confessed to the murders of Worden and Hogan, whom authorities believe he mutilated after shooting. Gein claimed, however, that he did not kill the others; he obtained the other bodies and body parts through grave robbing from 1944 to 1952. He said he was in a "daze" when he committed his crimes. He also told crime lab authorities that he stole bodies, using their skin and acquiring female body parts to wear, because he wanted to be a woman.[6]

Ed Gein's crimes are said to have inspired horror films such as *Psycho, The Texas Chainsaw Massacre,* and *The Silence of the Lambs.*[7] Yet Sheriff Ed Kroll, who worked the case, said that it was "too gruesome to even talk about."[8] In 1958, Gein's farmhouse was destroyed by fire, with the general feeling, as one Plainfield authority put it, that the fire "was no accident."[9] The arson occurred shortly after rumors surfaced that Gein's house was going to become a tourist attraction. People were already visiting the house "out of curiosity," and a fence had been erected around it to prevent people from going inside.[10] Not explicitly approving of arson, but expressing relief, one Plainfield resident stated, "At least we know it won't be turned into a museum."[11]

How did this man develop into a killer who mutilated dead human beings?

Gein attended school to eighth grade but did not do well academically.[12] It has been reported that his father had alcoholism and was abusive, and that his mother Augusta was a religious zealot who repeatedly told Gein that all women were whores and that sex was evil and impure.[13] Mental health experts believe Gein had an unhealthy, dependent relationship with and an obsessive devotion to his mother. Gein's mother was extremely strict with her two sons, yet Gein adored her. When she died, he closed off rooms in the house she had occupied. He also may have killed his brother for arguing with his mother and disparaging her, although some suspected that Gein simply did not want to share the inherited farm with his brother.[14] Experts have speculated that Gein had incestuous feelings about his mother, suggesting that digging up bodies that reminded him of her was his way of bringing his mother back to life.[15]

As Ed Gein's lawyer stated, "I don't see how there can be any other conclusion but that the man is insane."[16] Gein had said, for example, that he "thought he was an instrument of God" when he shot Bernice Worden.[17] Ed Gein was diagnosed with schizophrenia by both prosecution and defense experts. In 1968, he was found guilty of first-degree murder due to insanity. He was ultimately placed in Mendota State Hospital.[18]

At Mendota State Hospital, Gein was said to be a model in-patient. Psychiatrist Dr. Gail Saltz speculated to *A&E Television* that incarcerators "may have been reminiscent of his mother," although she noted appropriately that she did not interview Gein so as to make a definitive conclusion.[19]

On July 26, 1984, Edward T. Gein, the "Butcher of Plainfield," died of cancer.[20]

Before and after his death, rumors circulated that Gein had a host of mental illnesses comorbid with schizophrenia. In 1957, *The Capital Times* of Madison, Wisconsin, ran the headline "Gein Gives Psychiatry a Field Day." The newspaper reported that, as the case became known, "psychiatric speculation continued unabated." Professionals and amateurs alike were ascribing necrophilia, transvestism (i.e., "cross-dressing"), and an Oedipus complex to Gein.[21]

However, a major red flag is that, in serial killer lore, Gein is "known" for having sex with dead bodies – necrophilia. Most people, including psychologists, take the term "necrophilia" to mean sexual attraction to, and sex with, dead bodies.[22] But while Ed Gein did keep women's genitals as souvenirs and wore them during his fantasies of being a woman, he never admitted to having sex with dead bodies. In fact, it is just as plausible that, because his mother was overly controlling, he murdered women and mutilated their corpses to take back some form of control. While it is possible that I am just missing it, I simply see no definitive proof of sexual interactions with dead bodies in valid reports. Indeed, every book I have seen suggesting that Gein engaged in necrophilia has done so with no citations for the information.

Gein was drawn to dead bodies, as even he described. Reports say Gein wanted to be a woman and transition into a woman's body,[23] something he stated explicitly.[24] He created and wore suits made from women's body parts, including genitalia and breasts, to wear and help him realize his wish. Tellingly of the times, one newspaper reporting on Gein pejoratively called him "sex-sick" simply for his desire to become a woman.[25] Psychologists know today that one's sense of gender – their sense of self as women, men, nonbinary, or genderqueer[26] – is separate from one's sexual attraction,[27] and this is a reason for society moving away from the term *transsexual* to the preferred term *transgender*. It strikes me that perhaps the concept of being transgender is so poorly understood, people would rather talk about necrophilia, no matter how tenuous the evidence.

Unfortunately, many books and other media pieces on serial killers, even "best sellers," give no citations or references for their work. This should be a warning to readers. The facts seem to have become distorted in the Gein case, so it stands to reason that this may occur across other serial killer cases. One high-priced book I encountered, for example, labeled the claim that Ed Gein engaged in necrophilia as a "fact," but gave no clarification or citations for this information. Moreover, this same book, awash in uncited Gein "facts," ran a list of Gein-related body-part jokes. It is easy to surmise that Mary Hogan's and Bernice Worden's families would not find humor in these jokes. It seems as though some authors and readers have become so desensitized to the victims' plight that it is acceptable to present murder, corpse abuse, and humor simultaneously – and with little insight into the actual facts of the case.

§

Although the primary aim of this book is to present information on FSKs, a comparison to MSKs illustrates the dramatic differences between their crimes. The case of Ed Gein illustrates just how different his crimes were compared to those of any documented FSK. In my career studying serial murder, I have found no information where a FSK has murdered to steal a penis, for example, or has created totems or costumes of male testicles or other body parts.

Along with my colleague Susan Hughes and then-graduate-student Adam Gott, I collected data on MSKs to compare to our existing FSK dataset. Being aware that data-driven comparisons between FSKs and MSKs are virtually non-existent, we gathered descriptive data from publicly available sources. Furthermore, as an evolutionary psychologist, I pursued the analysis of sex differences in serial murderers through an evolved psychology framework. That is, women and men have different behavioral tendencies due to evolved psychological processes, largely based on differences in reproduction, and we can make predictions about sex-specific tendencies.[28] I explain our general findings below, and later, I devote a separate chapter to the evidence that supports our evolutionary predictions.

Starting with the dataset we had for FSKs, we repeated the same information-gathering process for MSKs, using valid news reports, court reports, and historical society publications. My team and I found it important to peruse original, reputable sources to control for the evolution of legend – such as the idea that Ed Gein had sex with dead bodies, a "fact" everyone "knows." A critical thinker will always ask, "How do you know that to be true?" or "From where did you get that information?" I would hope that consumers of stories that are supposed to depict true crime indeed want the material to be *true*.

Since there is an established connection between age and crime, we selected each MSK's age at first murder to match those of each FSK in our sample. We also tried to match year of first murder between each FSK and MSK, as historical forces can influence behavior. There was high statistical reliability among the pairings we did yield; in other words, they matched well. We verified that each MSK met the definition of serial killer – three or more victims with a cooling-off period of at least one week between kills. In all, my team and I ended up with 55 pairs of FSKs and MSKs ($N = 110$) who committed their crimes in the United States between 1856 and 2009. Although this might not seem like a high sample size for the social sciences, considering the rarity of serial murder, we felt that this was an appreciable number.

My team's aim was to elucidate, with empirical data, as many FSK–MSK differences as we could, hoping that this information might aid in the detection of perpetrators and the prevention of murder. Below I report on the findings from our 2019 study, and you can find all exact statistical analyses in the original publication in *Evolutionary Behavioral Sciences*,[29] a scientific journal published by the American Psychological Association (APA). Unless otherwise noted, each of these comparisons yielded statistically significant associations or differences. In the information that follows, I add interpretations and supporting research in context.

RELATIONSHIPS, EDUCATION, AND SOCIOECONOMIC STATUS

There are major demographic distinctions between FSKs and MSKs. Identifying these statistically different factors can help investigators narrow down their search for a perpetrator. Moreover, psychologists can examine these characteristics further to understand the risk of becoming a murderer.

In terms of relationship status, murderous ends aside, FSKs have had a more successful romantic history. Most FSKs (about 57%) were in at least one committed relationship during the span of time in which their crimes were committed. By contrast, most MSKs were not in a relationship (only about 32% were). These MSKs were single, divorced, or widowed.

There was a difference in educational attainment between FSKs and MSKs. The majority of FSKs (54%) attended at least some college, but nearly three-quarters of MSKs (73%) earned a high school diploma as their highest achievement. Examining socioeconomic status, most MSKs – more than two-thirds – were lower-class. The majority of FSKs were middle-class. MSKs were more likely to be lower-class than were FSKs. Nonetheless, compared to estimates of the general population, there was an overrepresentation of lower-class individuals among both FSKs and MSKs.[30]

MENTAL ILLNESS

We found mental health information for two-thirds of the total sample, and a startling picture emerged. Whereas mental illness was very common in both FSKs and MSKs, our data showed that MSKs were more than twice as likely as FSKs to experience mental illness. For MSKs for whom information was available, 89.5% had reported mental health issues. That is nearly all. For FSKs for whom information was available, 42.6% had reported mental health issues. For mental illness, my team simply recorded "yes" or "no" for the purposes of this study, so an examination of what mental illnesses presented more in each sex was not possible here. This is an interesting avenue for further research.

I am uncertain why all serial murderers have not been viewed as having mental illness. By definition, a mental illness involves profound problems with emotions, thoughts, or actions causing interpersonal distress and/or problems socially.[31] Those with mental illness often exhibit unhealthy emotions (affect), and have difficulty controlling their emotions.[32] Serial homicide seems to me to be the epitome of dysfunctional responses.

A clarification is warranted. Data from my research show that mental illness, as defined in the *Diagnostic and Statistical Manual of Mental Disorders* (DSM), is present in both MSKs and FSKs at a prevalence beyond what we see in the general population. Still, I understand that some forensic experts see a distinction between the terms "mental illness" and "mental disorder." A forensic interpretation may be that "mentally disordered" refers to a normal mind malfunctioning, and "mental illness" refers to a disease of the brain, mind, and body. For example, it is argued that having delusions (false beliefs) is qualitatively different than having personality disorders (irrational thinking about certain circumstances) and may play a factor in legal culpability.[33] Seen from this perspective, serial killers may not be considered mentally ill but rather mentally disordered.

Nevertheless, even the US National Library of Medicine uses the terms "mental illness" and "mental disorder" interchangeably,[34] while in practice psychiatrists frequently contend with "fuzzy boundaries" between a "possible disease condition versus treating a variation of normal behavior."[35] Thus, while the distinction between these two terms is arguable, for serial killers the murderous end is the same. We may allow ourselves to consider whether someone with a "normal" mind is capable of killing another human being.

FSKs kill people they know, particularly those who are vulnerable and in their care, often for money. MSKs kill unfamiliar victims, often in cruel ways, and for sexual purposes.[36] Are these behaviors indicative of someone with a typically functioning mental state? Nonetheless, although women overall tend to have a higher prevalence of mental disorders compared to men,[37] in serial murder this is reversed when comparing an equal number of FSKs and MSKs.[38] Maybe there is a category of mental illness yet to be developed that will encompass murder and/or multiple murder. Clinical researchers should explore this sex difference more thoroughly.

Broadly speaking, researchers have identified sex differences in mental disorders. Compared to women, men experience more antisocial disorders and substance abuse issues and tend to externalize – they are disinhibited.[39] If we examined MSK data more thoroughly, would we find that MSKs disregard right and wrong, violate the rights of others, and act out their impulses more? Do MSKs exhibit behavioral problems beginning at a young age, as seen in those with ASPD? Compared to men, women experience more anxiety and mood disorders and tend to internalize – they have maladaptive self-regulation, manifesting in negative mood states, such as anxiety, fear, and depression.[40] Examining serial murderers more closely would we find that FSKs ruminate more (think repetitively about past negative experiences), increasing their perceptions of harm and conflict,[41] and act on their stressors?

It might simply be the case that the people in our study experienced diagnostic misses or errors. It might even be the case that missing data (i.e., information unavailable in our sources) explain the sex difference prevalence in serial murder. Maybe, as described in Chapter 1, at the time this information was reported in the news people were less likely to ascribe mental illness to women in general, as this notion violates our schema of mother, grandmother, or attractive woman. Or maybe in the past the crimes of MSKs were so typically overtly barbaric (e.g., rape, mutilated bodies), we felt MSKs must be mentally ill, whereas the crimes of FSKs were cold and calculated (e.g., poisoning), so FSKs must have uncompromised cognitive processes.

The National Institute of Mental Health (NIMH) estimates that 20.6% of Americans have or have had any mental illness (AMI) currently diagnosable, or diagnosable in the past year.[42] That means MSKs have more than a fourfold chance of having a mental illness compared to the population and are twice as likely as FSKs to have documented issues. FSKs have more than a twofold chance of having mental illness issues compared to the population. Of course, people with mental illness almost always do not harm other people, and mental illness itself would not be a sufficient cause for violence.[43] Among serial murderers – those who perpetrate such unfathomable harm – mental illness was arguably common. With data showing a marked overrepresentation in mental illness in serial murderers, and such a vast difference in mental illness prevalence in serial murderers, it would be prudent to continue this research.

My team and I could not find mental health information for the remaining third of the sample, however, so it is likely that these are minimum frequency data that underestimate the true prevalence of mental illness.

Many studies about serial murders and mental health are older, but keep in mind that serial murder is so uncommon, there are likely not new cases or information to analyze on a consistent basis. In addition, because FSKs have been largely ignored in the literature, many sources about this topic, including those speaking to psychological diagnoses, do not differentiate between FSKs and MSKs.

In 2014, forensic psychologist Clare Alley[44] and colleagues studied the prevalence of autism spectrum disorder (ASD) and head injury in serial and mass murderers. Although they found few previous studies with more than one subject and discovered that the use of standardized clinical assessments was rare, they were able to glean valuable information. They found a sample of 239 killers, 106 of whom had definite or probable ASD. Forty-eight of these were serial killers. Although they did not report the sex of the killers, they estimated that about 10% of all serial killers and mass murderers have ASD, and a similar percentage had a history of head injury. Although they cautioned that ASD or head injury alone would be an insufficient explanation for who becomes a serial killer or mass murderer, their work sheds valuable light on the different factors that might contribute to the making of a serial killer.

Helinä Häkkänen[45] is a forensic psychologist and researcher for the Finnish National Bureau of Investigation. She said that "major mental disorder is not usually considered to have a noteworthy role in serial homicide," but she did add that about a fifth of serial homicide offenders had a history of psychiatric treatment. Häkkänen conducted research with 45 repeat homicide or attempted offenders labeled "homicidal recidivists" (not necessarily serial murderers). Only one subject was a woman. Viewing her sample using our criteria for three or more victims, two subjects were probable serial killers (two previous convictions and being questioned for a third murder) and two were definite serial killers. She reported that 73% of this sample had received mental health services as an adult, and about a third had ongoing mental healthcare. Further, 89% were diagnosed with a personality disorder (most with ASPD), and 11% were diagnosed with schizophrenia. With results similar to what my team and I found in the United States, this Finnish study further shows that impactful mental health issues are more prevalent among serial killers than among the general population. Yet, with only one female subject in the sample, we cannot be sure exactly how FSKs differ from MSKs.

While many studies do not differentiate between MSKs and FSKs, there is still much to learn by placing our findings side-by-side with studies focusing on male offenders. For example, aberrant sexual thoughts and behaviors, either before or as part of a murder, appear to be very uncommon in FSKs. In MSKs, it is another story. In a study comparing 25 male serial sexual murderers and 17 male single-offense sexual murderers, more serial offenders (86%) compared to single offenders (23%) had violent, obtrusive sexual fantasies. Furthermore, those who committed sex-based serial murders had a higher prevalence of all paraphilias, with significantly more fetishism.[46] Although the definition of "paraphilia" has changed over time, it involves persistent, abnormal sexual interest or urges that cause marked personal distress to the self and can cause harm to the self or others.[47]

Researchers[48] believe that paraphilias lend a stimulus to these violent sexual fantasies and that eventually MSKs lose the inhibitions associated with acting out fantasy and probably engage in progressively more violent enactments. In fact, newer research suggests that a lack of inhibition is the most important factor in the development of sexually aberrant behavior, not the sexual arousal itself. Other behavioral indications of impulsivity, such as substance abuse, are common in those who commit sex crimes.[49] Researchers also suggested that the homicide itself may have become the paraphilia.[50] This is in line with paraphilias being associated with problems with impulse control/executive function.[51] It is important to stress that these behaviors are seldom, if ever, documented in FSKs.

Moreover, mental illness itself would not cause someone to commit a sexual crime.[52] Rather, fantasies fuel the inner compulsion, and the presence or diminution of mental health moderates control of the compulsion. Nonetheless, some violent offenders do have mental illness. As noted by forensic psychologist Eric Hickey, examiners may look for psychosis (losing touch with reality), anxiety, dissociative disorders (dissociative identity disorder, amnesia, and fugue), personality disorders, autism spectrum, and psychopathy.[53]

I did not expect to present an exhaustive literature review on MSK mental health for this book, but I am surprised at the lack of descriptive analyses to determine which, if any, psychological disorders are statistically overrepresented in MSKs.

§

John Wayne Gacy was a serial killer. He was also a psychopath. Known as the "Killer Clown," he wore a literal mask as he performed for children as his character Pogo the Clown, and he also wore a "mask of sanity" of the sort theorized by Hervey Cleckley[54] in his seminal work on psychopathy.

There are numerous sources of information available about Gacy, and some information is inconsistent, perhaps evincing that serial killer lore evolves. Nonetheless, I present information as I have found it in reputable sources.

Gacy was born in 1942. In a 2008 memoir describing his friendship with "Johnny," childhood friend Barry Boschelli described years of terrible parental physical abuse they both suffered. They were both a "punching bag" for their fathers.[55] John Stanley Gacy was extremely abusive to John Wayne Gacy (sometimes presented as Gacy Jr.) much more than to his other children, and it escalated as John Wayne Gacy got older. Gacy Sr. even threatened to kill his son.[56] Gacy's mother loved Johnny and tried to defend him, but it did not always work out well for her. At one point Mrs. Gacy told Boschelli to be careful of Mr. Gacy. It was clear she was afraid of her husband. John Wayne Gacy would block out the pain of his father's abuse, channeling his emotions to strength and stubbornness. Researchers have noted that psychopathy may stem, at least in part, from severely traumatized individuals "turning off" emotions as a coping mechanism.[57]

Gacy was hospitalized eight times between 1961 and 1967 for various issues including a heart condition, a fall, and car accidents. In one instance, he was in the hospital for 23 days with an unspecified head injury.[58] But while many of these injuries were likely related to the abuse at home, not all were. Barry Boschelli said that Gacy got hit in the forehead with a child's swing so hard that it knocked him unconscious one day on the playground. That is not the only time he experienced head trauma. In an interview, one of Gacy's sisters said that he had fallen down the stairs and hit his head, and then had episodes where he would pass out.[59]

Not all Gacy's childhood difficulties stemmed from abuse or injury. Throughout his life, Gacy struggled over his sexual orientation.[60] Gacy told a reporter that, when he was younger, he was not attracted to girls and thought of being a priest.[61] If Gacy lived in a time when homosexuality or bisexuality were more acceptable and had felt able to come out of the figurative closet, maybe 33 young men (at least) would not have died because of Gacy's rage against his own homosexual tendencies.

In addition, he said that his father thought he was feminine, even though his father named him after Western (cowboy) movie star John Wayne, whom one journalist called "a paragon of American masculinity." It is reasonable to assume his father was disappointed. He often disparaged Gacy and called him a "sissy," and Gacy's sister said, "Dad was just never pleased with how John was. He wanted John to be like him and he just wasn't."[62] In addition, Gacy used to dress in his mother's underwear.[63] When he was 10, Gacy showed Boschelli a bag of women's clothes he kept in his closet, but Boschelli told him to put them back in the closet where they belong.[64]

Notably, Gacy was not always known for telling the truth. Yet in a manuscript he wrote about his life, he described being sexually molested at age five. In an excerpt published in *The New Yorker* in 1994, Gacy wrote of visiting a neighbor with his mother and siblings. When other children were out of the room, the neighbor's 15-year-old daughter, who had intellectual disabilities, took off Gacy's clothes and, as Gacy stated, "fondled" him. The neighbor and his mother walked in on them and saw her "playing with" his penis. The neighbor rushed in, grabbed the girl, hit her repeatedly, and yelled at her for what she was doing. Gacy's mother hurriedly dressed him and rushed him home. Gacy said he was frightened and thought he was going to get beaten also. He said, "I was told not to be taking my clothes off with girls," adding, "I was told that what we were doing was dirty and wrong."[65] Gacy described how this made him self-conscious about removing his clothes in front of others. If true, we can think about Gacy's traumatic experience through the lens of learning theory. The first sexual encounter he had was forced on him, left him scared, and his mother told him it was dirty and wrong.

Gacy also claimed that a local male contractor molested him when he was nine years old. In an interview, Gacy's sister said that she remembered her father being incredibly angry and wanting his gun so he could shoot the contractor for something pertaining to her brother. Their mother told the sister that the guy "did something to him." Years later, Gacy's sister pondered if that event is "what happened to him" and what made him have "two sides."[66]

One might think about the profound impression these events had on Gacy's sociosexual development. Victims of childhood sexual abuse

(CSA) often experience subsequent maldevelopment. CSA victims have an increased risk of engaging in all types of criminal behavior, including violent and sexual crimes.[67] Furthermore, there is a gender effect whereby men who experience CSA perpetrate more sexual offenses. Yet, crucially, not everyone who is abused becomes a violent or murderous adult, and there is absolutely no evidence to suggest an adverse first experience with a woman would affect Gacy's sexual orientation.[68]

Gacy's crimes began early and can be traced back at least to when he was married to his first wife. In the 1960s, after graduating from Kentucky Fried Chicken's (KFC's) Chicken School, Gacy moved to Iowa to help run several restaurants owned by his father-in-law.[69] When Gacy's wife[70] went out of town in 1967, Gacy invited a 16-year-old boy to their home. They watched pornography and engaged in sodomy, for which Gacy was subsequently arrested. As reported in the *Des Moines Register*, psychiatrists who examined Gacy before sentencing diagnosed him with antisocial personality. While they found him competent to stand trial, they said he should be put under "firm consistent external controls." Noting that he was "unsocialized," they warned that he engaged in behavior that "brings [him] into conflict with society." "Persons with this personality structure do not learn from experience," they said, "and are unlikely to benefit from known medical treatment."[71]

Gacy pleaded guilty to a sodomy charge on November 7, 1968, and was sentenced to 10 years in prison.[72] His wife filed for divorce while he was in prison, but Gacy was deemed to be a model prisoner. He secured a donated golf course for inmate use and became a lead cook, supervising other kitchen workers.[73] After serving only about a year and a half of his sentence, he was paroled. If he had served his entire sentence, the fate of at least 33 young, murdered men and their families might have turned out very differently. Stated another way, if officials had listened to the psychiatrists and kept him under firm control, 33 young men might have been able to live their full lives.

Out on parole, Gacy moved to Chicago and lived with his mother. He married again in 1972. His second mother-in-law told the *Chicago Times*, "I was against the marriage from the beginning. He always seemed strange to me." She said she once saw Gacy fighting with a young man who yelled, "He tried to rape me!" She also lived with her daughter and son-in-law for a brief time and told reporters that the house always smelled strange, "like dead rats."

His second wife said Gacy had told her he was bisexual before they married, but she did not believe him.[74] She said he could not sexually function properly with women and that, before they separated, Gacy "started to bring home a lot of pictures of naked men." She found books in the house featuring gay men. She also found wallets around the house that belonged to teenage boys.[75] The second Mrs. Gacy filed for divorce on March 2, 1976.[76]

Indeed, from about 1975 onward, Chicago teenagers told the police that a man name John cruised the neighborhood and solicited young gay men from his black Oldsmobile.[77] Police saw many young men entering and exiting Gacy's Norwood Park Township home, but when questioned, they said nothing bad about Gacy, who had become a reputable contractor and business owner with many community ties.

Gacy's violent tendencies escalated. He kidnapped a 19-year-old man at gunpoint in January 1978. Gacy forced him to engage in brutal sex acts and held his head underwater in a bathtub repeatedly, causing him to lose consciousness. The victim reported the incident, but when Gacy was questioned by the police he claimed it was consensual. Gacy was released. Later, in March 1978, after soliciting 27-year-old Jeff Rignall with marijuana, Gacy rendered Rignall unconscious with chloroform, handcuffed him, and brutally sexually assaulted him.[78] When the attack was over, Gacy brought Rignall back to the park where they met, and left him there unconscious, bleeding from his rectum, and with facial burns from chloroform; the chemical also damaged his liver.[79]

Rignall later made it his mission to find his attacker, and he did eventually identify Gacy by his car. However, in May 1978, when Gacy was charged with misdemeanor battery, he simply paid Rignall $3,000 in a civil suit and did no jail time. Years later, Rignall's life partner Ron Wilder said in an interview that "Police didn't want to deal with gay rape."[80] It seems that Wilder was right. Reports state that at least three times parents of missing teenage boys from the area gave police Gacy's name as a suspect.[81] A neighbor even said that she occasionally heard screams coming from Gacy's home. She called the police, but when they responded, Gacy would tell them nothing was wrong.[82]

In fact, after Gacy was eventually caught, police came under intense scrutiny for not having paid attention sooner to reports and signs that linked Gacy to his crimes, including ignoring many families' pleas for police to help them find missing young male family members.[83] Gacy preyed on people he thought were powerless – those whom reporter Jay Levine described to *NBC/Peacock* as "voiceless, clout-less victims."[84] Officers typically told families it was most likely the young men had just run away from home. Gacy arguably relied on "luck" to avoid being caught – a documented characteristic of successful serial homicide offenders.[85]

But his luck ran out when he hurt a member of the Piest family. On December 11, 1978, 15-year-old Robert Piest's mother came to pick him up after his work shift at the local Nisson Pharmacy. They were going to celebrate her 46th birthday. Rob said to her, "Mom, wait a minute. I've got to talk to a contractor about a summer job that will pay me $5 an hour."[86] Rob, whose good looks were reminiscent of 1970s teen idol Shawn Cassidy, never came back. Elizabeth Piest grew increasingly concerned, drove back to her house, got her whole family and Rob's two dogs, and searched for him to no avail. She filed a missing persons report that evening.

Police Lieutenant Joe Kozenczak investigated. He learned quickly that Gacy's construction company had recently remodeled Nisson Pharmacy, and that Gacy was the person who offered Rob a job. Police searched Gacy's house. They found a film development receipt belonging to Rob's friend and coworker, Kim Byers. She had borrowed Rob's coat when she was working the cash register near the pharmacy doors during the chilly winter weather. Kim put the receipt in Rob's coat pocket and forgot about it. On December 15, investigators found that receipt, showing Rob had been at Gacy's house, and they eventually found Rob's blue puffy winter coat and other items in Gacy's house belonging to missing young men.[87] In the house, police smelled death.[88]

But Gacy was not yet arrested. Instead, a police detail followed him around town, where they caught him selling marijuana, and arrested him on December 21. While Gacy was in custody, police obtained a search warrant for his house. Police evidence expert Daniel Genty crouched into the crawlspace beneath Gacy's house. His flashlight illuminated movement in a puddle of sludge, which turned out to be living worms. He stuck his shovel into the mud and hit something. Genty said, "I pulled it up, and it's a bone, an arm bone." He yelled to fellow officers, "Charge him, I've got one!"[89]

Gacy, age 36, was arrested for murder on December 22, 1978.[90]

From December 1978 to April 23, 1979,[91] kneeling in a combination of soil and body decomposition "muck,"[92] police found the remains of 29 victims on Gacy's property, as well as the remains of four victims in nearby Chicago rivers. Examiners made great efforts to try to identify the victims. But because acid and lime had been poured on some of the victims, identification was not simple.[93] An anthropologist was brought in to help process remains, and a forensic odontologist was brought in to identify remains through teeth and dental records.[94]

Rob Piest was not identified until April 9, 1979. Nine young men remained unidentified at the time and were buried respectfully. Three were later identified. Decades later, in 2018, the National Center for Missing and Exploited Children released highly technical, forensic facial reconstructions of two of Gacy's still-unidentified victims, Body Number 10 and Body Number 13.[95] One hopes someone recognizes the young men in these hauntingly realistic sketches.

Victims had been handcuffed and raped repeatedly.[96] Many had been strangled with bunched-up paper, cloth,[97] or men's underwear shoved in their mouths and choked with rope around their necks. One report said Gacy used a stick with knotted ropes[98] (like a garrote) to strangulate. Medical examiner Dr. Robert Stein said that it was possible some of the victims had been buried alive after falling unconscious and just appearing dead after Gacy's strangulation attempts.[99] The opening to the crawlspace where they were found was itself sawed out and brought to the courtroom for Gacy's trial.[100]

On December 22, in a rambling statement that lasted hours, Gacy confessed to killing many young men after having sex with them, including Rob Piest.[101] Notably, incoherent and illogical speech can be a characteristic of psychopathy. It is as if psychopathic individuals do not, at times, know the difference between spoken speech and their own mental speech. Researcher Robert Hare has called this "mental Scrabble without an overall script."[102] Gacy also talked about himself in the third person,

7.2 Investigators remove a victim's remains from serial killer John Wayne Gacy's house, 1978. (Karen Engstrom/Chicago Tribune/Tribune News Service via Getty Images)

stating that "John" or "Jack" was the murderer.[103] Yet, in their search, police found a book in Gacy's home about the criminal justice system with bookmarked information on the insanity defense. They felt that Gacy was attempting to manipulate the court by pretending to have multiple personalities.[104]

On January 10, 1979, Gacy was indicted on seven counts of murder, aggravated kidnapping, deviate sexual assault, and taking indecent liberties with a child. Prosecutors sought the death penalty and execution via the electric chair. Gacy first tried to plead insanity and told the police an alternate identity had committed the murders. Defense attorneys tried to attribute crimes to his "hidden side" that was compelled to kill due to the chronic and severe abuse he suffered at the hands of his father.[105] But his insanity plea was rejected based on expert testimony. Still, he pleaded not guilty.

On April 23, Gacy was indicted for 26 additional murders, bringing the count to 33 victims.[106] The *Chicago Tribune* reported that at trial, both prosecution and defense witnesses claimed that Gacy experienced a host of abnormal psychological phenomena, with each expert's opinion not necessarily consistent with that of other experts. Defense experts testified he had borderline personality disorder; psychopathic personality; atypical psychosis; paranoid schizophrenia; and sociopathy. Prosecution experts testified that he had antisocial personality; mixed personality including narcissism; obsessive-compulsive quality; drug and alcohol use issues; histrionic character; and sexual sadism.[107] One psychiatrist also talked about necrophilia, as some suspected Gacy had sex with the men after he killed them.[108] Psychiatrists were at odds as to whether these disorders were present in Gacy all the time or just manifested in response to triggering events,[109] although we know what psychiatrists said in the 1960s about Gacy's mental state.[110]

Relatedly, one psychiatrist, Dr. Richard Rappaport, said that that Gacy "has a grandiose sense of self. He feels like he is the star. He has a pervasive sense of power and brilliance . . . that he is entitled to more than the average person." Rappaport drew from Cleckley's[111] work and said that Gacy wore a "mask of sanity. In reality it's only a mask . . . it covers up the insanity."[112] No experts could show, however, that Gacy lacked the mental capacity to know right from wrong at the time of the murders. On March 12, 1980, the jury took under two hours to find Gacy guilty. On March 13, he was sentenced to death. He was given 12 death sentences and 21 life sentences.[113] Judge Louis Garippo[114] set an execution date.

Gacy was on death row for nearly 15 years. During that time, he gave interviews with contradictory information and set up a phone number where people could pay to hear his confession. He called people collect, received numerous visitors, and answered about 27,000 letters.[115] He entertained fellow prisoners with "macabre jokes about his crimes."[116] During this time, Gacy pitied himself. He said, "I was made an asshole and a scapegoat . . . when I look back I see myself more as a victim than a perpetrator." He continued, "I was the victim," and he wondered "if there would be someone, somewhere who would understand how badly it had hurt to be John Wayne Gacy."[117] Before he was executed, Gacy told Corrections Department Spokesperson Nic Howell that his last words were going to be, "Kiss my ass." When Howell was asked if Gacy made apologies for anything, Howell answered, "Not a thing."[118] His last words were actually not about kissing his ass, but rather how the state was murdering him and that killing him would "not compensate for the loss of all the other lives."[119] On May 10, 1994, at 12:58 a.m., John Wayne Gacy, age 52, died by lethal injection.[120]

A postmortem exam revealed nothing remarkable about Gacy's brain. There was no evidence of the head injury he sustained as a child. This does not rule out him having neural functional and connectivity issues while alive. A psychiatrist who worked with Gacy in his last years has his brain in her basement, along with slices of his organs. It was Gacy's wish that his brain be studied, and Gacy's sisters allowed the psychiatrist to take it.[121] However, there are no accounts of his brain or organs being studied scientifically after the sisters granted this permission.

There is more to Gacy's story than is typically spoken about in the media. I would never defend Gacy's actions. Nevertheless, information about his childhood reveals a physically and psychologically traumatic development. I am a research psychologist. I cannot diagnose, but I can gather and present facts. One blaring fact is that he was sexually molested at least twice as a young boy. His sister corroborated that "something" did happen that caused her father to want to kill the contractor. Although Gacy was known to lie, since he never made any apologies for his crimes, even proclaiming his innocence for decades, I believe he did not fabricate these incidents. At no time did he ever try to explain away his behavior. I certainly can be wrong.

As Robert Hare noted, Gacy was clearly a psychopath. Superficial charm, callousness, lack of remorse, and avoiding blame are psychopathic characteristics.[122] When you are described as a psychopath by a leading contemporary expert on psychopathy, Hare, you must be a poster child for it. Although psychiatrists offered a host of diagnoses for Gacy, the common thread, even from reports in the late 1960s, was that he had ASPD with psychopathic features.

When Gacy was being investigated in 1978, the *Chicago Tribune* wrote "Murder suspect's '2 faces' revealed."[123] On one side, Gacy was boastful, but was outgoing, friendly, and plowed neighbors' snow-covered walkways without even being asked. He performed at children's parties as "Pogo the Clown," later earning him the nickname "Killer Clown." A public official who interacted with Gacy on the Norwood Park Township Commission said, "I believe he just had two personalities, one of which I never saw."[124] This is reminiscent of one of Hervey Cleckley's case studies, in which an individual was "nearly always in his mask of the grand and charming gentleman."[125] On the other side, when Gacy was unmasked he was a psychopath who bound, gagged, raped, and killed young men, leaving dead, victimized, human beings buried and decomposing under his house or discarded in a local river.

Journalist Alec Wilkinson interviewed Gacy for *The New Yorker* about a month before Gacy's execution, visiting him six different times, spending hours with him. Wilkinson said, "Gacy seemed unaware that he was in prison because he was a criminal. He seemed to think that I had come to see him because he was famous." Wilkinson's writing about his experience with Gacy illustrates *the mask of sanity* perfectly: "I often had the feeling that he was like an actor who had created a role and polished it so carefully that he had become the role and the role had become him." Wilkinson added that when interacting with him Gacy used "a catalogue of gestures and attitudes and portrayals of sanity" and noted that Gacy spoke "with deranged logic."[126]

Investigators said that Gacy was friendly when they spoke with him. However, investigators also said that Gacy never showed any remorse for his crimes, and Gacy blamed the victims who came to him for money, a job, or drugs. One detective added, "When it came time to dig up the basement, I think he was more concerned about us messing up his carpets."[127]

His father was consistently and progressively abusive to him, more so than with the other Gacy children, physically punishing, controlling, and humiliating him. Gacy Sr. also abused Mrs. Gacy, but she and Gacy Jr.'s siblings would put on a façade that nothing was wrong. One of his sisters told reporters that they were "normal as hell."

In addition, Gacy was hit in the head so hard that he was knocked unconscious, and as evidence suggests, he was hospitalized for it for more than three weeks. Although we do not know the exact location of impact, Gacy's friend remembers him being hit in the forehead. The forehead region houses the prefrontal cortex (PFC), the part of our brain with a critical role in social and moral behavior, emotional regulation, and impulse control. Although a postmortem examination revealed no injury or trauma, we cannot rule out that this blow to the head caused connectivity and functional issues. He was reported to have had more than one head injury. The physical abuse by his father could have exacerbated any physical insults, or physical insults could have exacerbated neural damage done by his violent father. Once someone sustains a concussion or other traumatic brain injury (TBI), structural and chemical changes in the brain can cause neurobehavioral issues[128] and make subsequent injuries even more dangerous.[129]

Gacy had a sexual orientation that, at the very least, was not completely heterosexual. He knew his father did not approve, and his trusted friend prompted him to put his women's clothes literally back in his closet. Gacy's two marriages and children also served as a mask to conceal his homosexuality. His first ex-wife said, "John came across very straight,"[130] but then he was arrested for performing sodomy on a young boy and she divorced him. Many years later, that victim died by suicide. Gacy's first ex-wife also told reporters in 1978 that he was charming but tended to "stretch the truth."[131]

Thus with Gacy we have an individual who experienced repeated blows to the head with potential impulse and emotional issues, struggling with sexual orientation, on whom physical abuse was used to control and humiliate, who had been conditioned that sex is dirty and wrong, with a family history of acting as if everything is normal and perfect. Under the cover of night in his home, Gacy humiliated, raped, tortured young people of the same gender as he, rendering them powerless, controlling them with restraints. During the day, he was the exemplary neighbor and business owner, and nothing seemed wrong. Of course, understanding an individual's traumagenic formative journey does not excuse later callous disregard, brutality, and murder. I also stress that nearly everyone who has experienced any or all these biopsychosocial traumas does not become a psychopath and a sexually sadistic serial murderer.

A quote by Annette Lachmann and Frank Lachmann[132] captures the essence of John Wayne Gacy's psychology. They stated: "Typically, the serial killer, brutalized and deceived in his childhood, inflicts this torture on his victims." They added, "In doing so, he attempts to redress his own painful early experience by reversing roles, temporarily revitalizing dead feelings, and momentarily restoring a traumatically depleted sense of self."

§

Within a book aimed at telling the stories of *female* serial killers, I certainly did not set out to write so much on John Wayne Gacy. Since his crimes were so gruesome, and since these events took place at a time at which media coverage had evolved to be arguably consistent, vigilant, and reliable, there is more reputable source information on him than I have typically seen for other cases. Gacy's story illustrates how vastly different the motives and crimes of MSKs and FSKs are. Still, we see that Gacy experienced profound childhood trauma, including sexual abuse, as many FSKs did. Furthermore, Gacy's case teaches us that there are profound dangers when not paying attention to previous crimes and other red flags. Psychiatrists gave stern warnings early on that he would cause problems in society and should be watched closely.

By comparing FSK and MSK motives, means, mental states, and victims, and by better understanding mental illness and treatment, we create a better approach to detection and prevention.

CHAPTER 8

Comparing FSKs and MSKs: Crimes and Victims

F EMALE SERIAL KILLERS MURDER DIFFERENT PEOPLE and in different ways than do men, but they are indeed deadly. At one point, experts argued that there were no FSKs, and that all serial homicides were sexual in nature. As of this writing, even the FBI's current website on serial murder gives examples only of sexual serial homicide. Yet, the victims of all serial killers met the same end. Still, people do seem to downplay serial murder committed by women. My team and I found that, statistically, the nicknames ("noms de guerre") given to FSKs more frequently emphasized their gender than nicknames given to MSKs.[1] I cannot confirm that these cases were a part of our aggregate data, but FSK examples are "Lady Bluebeard" and "Tiger Woman." We do not see nicknames for MSKs such as "Mr. BTK Strangler" or "Southside Strangler Man" pointing out the gender of the murderer. Eric Hickey, a leading expert on serial murder, argued that names for FSKs such as "Beautiful Blonde Killer" and "Old Shoe Box Annie" are "stereotypic, patronizing, and sexist."[2]

Our statistical analyses made our study unique in its direct comparisons of data for FSKs and MSKs. I know of no other studies presenting these empirical analyses. All differences reported here were statistically significant unless otherwise noted. It may help steer investigators in the right direction knowing that that one sex is much more likely than the other to have committed a suspected serial homicide they are investigating.

DIFFERENT PLACES

Comparing the locational data related to serial murder, MSKs are more likely to have murdered across multiple states, while FSKs are more likely to have committed the crimes close to where they were born. In my team's comparative sample of FSKs and MSKs, about one out of seven MSKs were born outside of the United States, but no FSKs were.[3] Most MSKs (more than two-thirds) committed crimes away from their birthplace, and 40% committed murders in multiple US states.

In contrast, only about a quarter of FSKs committed crimes away from their birthplace. Further, less than one out of five FSKs committed murders in multiple US states. Although there were no sex differences, many MSKs (about 46%) and FSKs (about 38%) targeted at least one of their victims in the US South, making that the most common area for serial killers to strike compared to in other US regions.[4] The US South has historically had among the highest crime rates in the country.[5] An explanation for this fact may be that the US South has typically had lower income compared to other US regions.[6] Researchers have documented that income inequality is related to crime.[7] Also, perhaps police staff and investigative techniques were not well enough funded to detect crime patterns, as legal scholars argue that underfunded police can lead to more crime.[8]

DIFFERENT VICTIMS

There are notable differences when it comes to the victim profiles of MSKs and FSKs, including their ages, the killer's familiarity with them, and how many the killer is likely to have murdered in a given time span. Congruent with previous research,[9] our data showed that almost all MSKs (85.5%) killed at least one stranger. In fact, before FBI investigator Robert Ressler's use of "serial killer" made the term more common, this type of homicide was called "stranger killings."[10] In comparison, only 14.5% of FSKs killed a stranger. Stated another way, MSKs are about six times more likely than FSKs to kill someone they do not know. We can see the error of broad-stroke conceptualization of all serial killers based on the crimes of only one sex. Furthermore, there was a stark difference in likelihood of stalking an unfamiliar victim prior to killing. MSKs were 18 times more likely than FSKs to stalk[11] victims. Nearly two-thirds of MSKs stalked at least some victims compared to only about 4% of FSKs.

Most FSKs (about 91%) in our sample killed at least one person they knew. Less than half (48%), but still an appreciable number, of MSKs killed at least one person they knew. Most FSKs (58%) killed at least one person they were related to by blood or marriage, but fewer than one in 10 MSKs (9%) killed a relative – of these, only one killed a blood relative and four killed their wives. FSKs were more than twice as likely to have killed their spouse or long-term, committed partner.

Data suggest that MSKs kill more victims than do FSKs. In our sample, MSKs killed between eight and nine victims, and FSKs killed about six. These are averages, however. We should not ignore the fact that some of the most prolific serial murderers in American history, such as Jane Toppan, Belle Gunness, and Patty Cannon, were women. Combined estimates from various reports suggest that, in total, these three women killed at least 100 people,[12] which is a higher victim count than that of infamous MSKs John Wayne Gacy, Ed Gein, and Ted Bundy[13] combined.

Although previous research, including my own,[14] showed that FSKs tend to commit crimes over a longer span of time before they get caught, in this sample, there was no statistical difference in kill span. MSKs' crimes lasted, on average, about 9 years ($SD = 11$), and FSKs' crimes lasted, on average, about 8 years ($SD = 8$), with marked variation for both.

Some reports did not identify exact age of victims, and some reports indicated that victims' age could not be identified with certainty. Think of John Wayne Gacy's or Belle Gunness' victims, recovered in a state of advanced decomposition, or recovered as body parts only. We categorized targeted victim age as "adults only," "both adults and children," and "children only." About half of FSKs targeted adults only more frequently than they did other groups. About half of MSKs targeted adults only, and almost half targeted both adults and children. MSKs were very unlikely (only about 4%) to kill children only. FSKs were seven times more likely than MSKs to kill children only.

Distribution of victim sex was different between FSKs and MSKs. FSKs most frequently killed both males and females. MSKs most frequently killed females.[15] Serial killers uncommonly targeted only the same sex as they are. Only about one out of eight FSKs killed women only, and only about one in six MSKs killed men only.[16]

DIFFERENT PRIMARY MEANS OF KILLING

As a part of our study, my team and I also examined and compared the most common ways that FSKs and MSKs kill their victims. Some killers used a mixture, but we documented their most frequently used method. Data showed that FSKs and MSKs murdered in somewhat similar ways but with differing frequencies. For FSKs, the most common method of killing was via poison (about 47%), but for MSKs, the most common method of killing was asphyxiation (about 47%). An appreciable number of FSKs also asphyxiated victims (nearly a third), but they also shot, stabbed, drowned, and beat (blunt force) victims to death, or allowed them to die through neglect. Only FSKs used drowning and neglect to kill. About a fifth of MSKs shot victims, and they also stabbed and beat victims. Few MSKs (7.5%) used poison to kill. Although uncommon for both, MSKs were four times more likely than were FSKs to kill victims by beating/blunt force trauma, and MSKs were more than twice as likely to shoot their victims than were FSKs.

§

Robert Lee Yates Jr. is a serial killer. He murdered at least 16 people, all vulnerable women whom he shot in the 1990s.

Born in 1952, Yates served in the Army and National Guard as a helicopter pilot. By all counts, he lived a fairly unremarkable life. He had two children with his first wife, but the marriage ended in divorce. Yates then married Linda Brewer, who thought he was a nice guy. They had four children together and lived in Spokane, Washington. Yates was described as a loving and doting dad who was deeply religious and never used profanity. He loved cars, the outdoors, and camping trips. He would go out hunting alone. But Yates, like so many serial killers, lived a double life.[17]

It turns out that Yates was hunting people. Instead of hunting in the woods, as his wife believed, he went cruising Spokane's red-light district in his vintage Corvette.[18] He would find vulnerable women, all sex workers, and invite them into his car and shoot them in the head or the heart. He covered their faces in plastic and then dumped their bodies along dirt roads and in vacant areas.[19] He may have put plastic over their heads to control the bleeding[20] and thus protect his beloved car.

Linda Yates claimed that she did not think her husband's solo hunting trips were unusual, although in hindsight, she did find it odd that he would dress nicely and wear cologne.[21] She also did not know Robert buried victim Melody Murfin only feet from their bedroom window – so he could see her "every day," as he later told authorities.[22] The Yates' daughter Sonja, however, told journalists that her mother was suspicious. "He would stay out until two in the morning. She wondered what he was doing."[23]

Women were turning up dead and being dumped along the Spokane River. Suspecting a serial killer, authorities in the Spokane area were searching for a murderer of female sex workers and drug users through the 1990s. Ultimately, the Corvette told on Yates. Late in 1997, Yates was pulled over in the Corvette by the police in a location where two people had been found dead, although he was not issued a ticket. In November 1998, Yates was pulled over by police again. A known sex worker was in his passenger's seat, but he told police she was a friend's daughter. Police closed in on Yates.[24]

Jennifer A. Joseph was found dead in 1997. She had died from several gunshot wounds, her body dumped in a farm field. Jennifer was last seen alive in a white Corvette with a White man driving. Yates had sold his Corvette in 1998, but police tracked it down. In 2000, investigators found blood on the seatbelt and seat, and carpet fibers from the Corvette matched fibers found on 16-year-old Jennifer's remains. They also found a mother-of-pearl button belonging to a blouse worn by her when her body was discovered. Obtaining DNA samples from John and Mi Hae Jones, Jennifer's parents, technicians found that it matched DNA extracted from the car.[25] On April 19, 2000, Yates was charged with first-degree murder.[26]

In 2018, *The Spokesman-Review* interviewed social worker Lynn Everson, who was the needle exchange coordinator for Spokane Regional Health District. Lynn knew most of the women Yates killed. She said, "If you look at the victims of serial killers, prostituted people are at the top of their list because they have no choice but to get into vehicles with strangers." To maximize the health and safety of prostitutes, Lynn kept a "bad tricks" list – those who choked, beat, stabbed, and raped women. She said, "Yates was on there."[27] Melanie Wilson, a friend of victim Melody Murfin, said, "You never know when you're going to meet a psycho."[28]

On October 19, 2000, Yates wiped away tears as he pleaded guilty to 13 murders.[29] He also pleaded guilty to one count of attempted murder of Christine Smith, whom he shot, but who managed to get away. Christine still had bullet fragments in her head. The evidence against him was damning. Overall, investigators had matched Yates' DNA to semen found on seven victims. Moreover, Yates' fingerprint was found on a plastic bag around a victim's head, and vegetation originating on Yates' property was found on the victims.[30] For these crimes, Yates was sentenced to 408 years in prison. He was subsequently convicted of two additional murders, at which point he was sentenced to death.[31]

When appealing Yates' death sentence, his attorneys claimed that he was mentally ill and suffered from a paraphilia – persistent, abnormal sexual interest or urges – and suggested that this explained his sex-based murders. But the prosecution was not buying it. As the Pierce County Prosecutor said, "I don't think Mr. Yates helps his cause by relying on the fact that he's a necrophiliac."[32] Nevertheless, Yates' death sentence was overturned in 2018 when the Washington Supreme Court struck down the state's death penalty.[33]

Despite Yates' conviction, there is much about his criminal history that remains unresolved. For example, he was also suspected in several unsolved homicides that took place in the areas where he was stationed in the Army and the National Guard during his 20-year military career.[34] He also had time "gaps" between his killings. He first murdered Patrick Oliver (the only man he is known to have killed) and Susan Savage, who were picnicking in 1975. He shot Stacy Hawn when he was on leave from the Army in 1988. He killed the other women in the 1990s.[35] However, homicide detective Vernon Geberth said that, most likely, "He didn't stop." That is, there were likely murders committed by Yates continuously since 1975, still undetected.

His is a gruesome track record. Among other aspects of the case, Detective Geberth felt that Yates probably experimented with various killing methods.[36] This is unsurprising. In a study I worked on with Enzo Yaksic[37] and several other noted scholars in the field, we found that successful serial killers are more likely to use multiple killing methods and various types of body disposal.[38] And although Yates dumped many women's bodies in fields, he also dumped some along a river and buried at least one in his own yard. With authorities believing there are more victims not yet found, it may be that he used other disposal methods as well.

It appears Yates lived a "normal" life when he was not committing murder. He was able to hold several jobs and had what was perceived as a typical family. As Jennifer Joseph's father said, "I just don't understand how somebody who has five kids . . . can do something like this."[39] While serial killer investigator Robert Keppel has cautioned that family dynamics are never fully known,[40] we can nonetheless see Hervey Cleckley's "mask of sanity" reflected in this case. Yates seemed ordinary when he was not killing.

With Yates' semen found on the bodies of his victims, there is an obvious sexual element to his crimes. While nothing can adequately explain such a killer's actions and behaviors, his developmental history may help contextualize his criminal profile. When Yates was a child, he was molested by an older boy. Criminologist Eric Hickey told *The Spokesman-Review*[41] this adverse event probably destroyed Yates' trust in people. A molested child is overpowered, and someone who was victimized may want to have power over others. According to Hickey, this could have been a factor in Yates' once having been a prison guard and then choosing a military career. Yates also worked at a smelting plant. A supervisor, Chazz Wellington, said of Yates, "If something didn't go his way, he would try to take charge." Wellington added that Yates would "overstep his boundaries."[42] Furthermore, Yates' grandmother killed her husband with an axe. Hickey said that it is possible the family has a genetic predisposition for violence.[43] It is also possible to learn from that experience that extreme violence is a solution to problems.

Although only one in five MSKs shoot their victims, Yates shot and killed his victims. Still, most FSKs do not use this means of murder.

§

DIFFERENT MOTIVES FOR MURDER

Just as FSKs and MSKs do not seem to kill in the same ways, they do not seem to kill for the same reasons. For example, 75% of MSKs in my team's study murdered primarily for sex, while only about 7% of FSKs did.[44] The most common primary motive that drove FSKs to kill was financial or material gain, found in 52% in our sample, whereas financial gain was the primary motive for only about 17% of MSKs in our sample. Stated another way, men are 10 times more likely than women to commit serial homicide with a sexual motive, and women are three times more likely than men to commit serial homicide with a financial/profit motive. Further, examining data from those in our sample who were in prime reproductive age (teens, 20s, and 30s) when they first killed, 80% of MSKs had a sexual motive, compared to only about 8% of FSKs. Examining data from serial murderers over age 40, nearly half (43%) of MSKs had a sexual motive – but no FSKs did.[45]

While there are clear differences in the crimes and motives committed by MSKs and FSKs, there are still some similarities worth noting. Let us return to the case of Robert Yates, for example. At first glance his activities seem to contrast starkly with serial murders committed by women. I have come across no instances of FSKs soliciting people who are sex workers, putting bags over their heads, and shooting them – with some kind of premortem or postmortem sexual contact transpiring. Yates' disposal of victims, though, was not unlike how FSK Dorothea Puente disposed of her victims. She recruited vulnerable tenants to live in her boarding house, killed them, and buried their bodies in her backyard though she disposed of at least one body near a local river. The difference here is a motive. We do not know Yates' full reasoning for committing serial homicide, but it was, at least in part, sexual. Puente killed for money – she stole her victims' government support checks (i.e., US social security disability). This difference speaks to evolutionary motives, which we turn to in Chapter 9.

OUTCOMES

Society deals with MSKs and FSKs differently, even though the crimes of FSKs can be just as heinous as those of MSKs. More than half of MSKs received the death penalty for their murders, but only a quarter

Table 1. US FSK and MSK Differences (from Harrison et al., 2019), $N = 110$

Female serial killers (n = 55)	Male serial killers (n = 55)
Probably in a romantic relationship at the time of killing	Probably not in a romantic relationship at the time of killing
Most have at least some college education	Most graduated from high school as their highest academic achievement
Most are middle-class	Most are lower-class
More than 40% have mental health issues	Nearly all have mental health issues
Seldom born outside the USA	Small percentage born outside the USA
Only about 15% killed at least one stranger	Almost all killed at least one stranger
Almost all killed at least one person they knew	Less than half killed at least one person they knew
The majority killed someone they were related to by blood or marriage	Only about 9% killed a blood or marriage relative
About six victims on average, with a wide range	Between eight and nine victims on average, with a wide range
Typically killed adults only; about a quarter killed adults and children. FSKs are seven times more likely than MSKs to kill children only	Typically killed adults only; about half killed adults and children; rarely kill children only
Most frequently killed males and females; uncommonly killed females only	Most frequently killed females; uncommonly killed males only
Most common method of killing was poison (nearly half), but about a third used asphyxiation	Most common method of killing was asphyxiation (nearly half), and about one in five shot victims
The majority murdered for financial gain	Most murdered primarily for sexual reasons
Most went to prison or jail	Majority received the death penalty
*About 13% kept souvenirs of crimes (n = 30)	Almost half kept souvenirs of crimes (n = 30)

Notes. Exact statistics are presented in Harrison et al. (2019) in *Evolutionary Behavioral Sciences.* *Data not appearing in Harrison et al. (2019) are discussed below.

of FSKs did. Nearly two-thirds of FSKs went to prison or jail. Of serial killers of both sexes in our sample, only four were placed in a mental health facility. One MSK in our sample escaped, and two FSKs remained at large.

FSKs VS. MSKs DIFFERENCES: THE BIG PICTURE

Table 1 gives a quick review of FSK and MSK differences based on our empirical study.[46] Please note we collected data only from serial murderers who committed their crimes in the USA.

OTHER FSK-MSK DIFFERENCES: OBSERVATIONS

In addition to the data-based comparison summarized above, I wanted to bring up some observations on sex differences in serial killer behavior I have made. Perhaps in the future, researchers can further explore these matters empirically.

WE CATCH MSKs. WE DETECT FSKs. MSKs leave a string of deceased victims with brutal injuries. With MSKs, we see an overt series of victim deaths. Gruesome murder is obvious. Victims' bodies are discovered or recovered, perhaps exhibiting marked brutality and sexual trauma. Perhaps a string of sexually violated and mutilated corpses is found. Media report numerous deceased victims with an unknown, monstrous perpetrator wreaking havoc on a city or town. Investigators then try to identify and catch the MSKs. Think of Robert Lee Yates.

FSKs, on the other hand, continue until someone suspects or detects something is amiss with a heretofore seemingly unconnected series of deaths. A series of deaths occur, which can appear accidental, but are caused by a covert perpetrator. Victims are vulnerable – typically elderly, infirm, or young children. Finally, a lightbulb goes on in a co-worker's, supervisor's, or family member's head. They have detected that a certain woman is the common denominator in the circumstances of a string of deaths. She was the nurse on shift at the time of all deaths; she is a mother whose third child has died suddenly; or she is a "black widow" who has lost multiple husbands.[47] What appeared to be accidental deaths are now examined closely, and cause of death is determined. The FSK is legally proven as having the motive, means, and the opportunity to have committed the crimes. Think of Kristen Gilbert or Amy Archer-Gilligan. In short, we typically catch male serial killers, but we detect female serial killers.

FSKs DO NOT TYPICALLY DEFILE DECEASED VICTIMS. As Amanda Farrell and her colleagues observed in 2011, "It is unlikely you would find a woman sexually assaulting a corpse or engaging in cannibalistic or vampiric activities."[48] There were some rumors that FSK Jane Toppan might have been sexually mounting her victims just after they died, but this is unsubstantiated. No such activity seems to have been reported with other FSKs.

This is not to say that body disposal, however, is always respectful – or even complete. It is not. Aileen Wuornos, for example, simply dumped her victims' bodies along highways or in the woods. Dorothea Puente buried her victims' bodies in her own backyard to hide their deaths. Some FSKs do not dispose of their victims' bodies at all. Diane O'Dell killed three infants and kept their bodies in her trunk for 19 years. Another infant's remains were found in her suitcase. The *New York Post* called her "Mommy Weirdest."[49]

Still, I have seen no cases of FSKs definitively characterized by necrophilia.

SOLO FSKs LIKELY DO NOT RAPE VICTIMS. I have never seen a case where solo-acting FSKs raped their victims. Partnered ("team") serial killers,[50] by contrast, have been known to commit violent sexual acts against their victims. For example, serial killers Debra Brown and Alton Coleman murdered eight people and committed seven rapes across three US states, with a victim count that included children. However, even in this instance, it was determined that Brown was "not a principal offender," and she was found guilty of only one of the murders.[51]

FSKs RARELY KEEP "TROPHIES". Many FSKs keep insurance money benefits and other resources gained from the deaths of victims. However, I have never seen a case in which a FSK kept trophies for the sake of memorializing her crime. My undergraduate research team and I collected data on serial murderers keeping trophies of their crimes perpetrated in the USA, with cases ranging back to the 1800s. The team cross-checked each other's findings, and I checked all findings later. This is part of a larger, ongoing project, but I would like to report interesting, tentative findings here. I thus used a random numbers table and selected 30 MSK and 30 FSK cases from our ongoing study to report on in these pages.

Data show that nearly half (46.7%) of MSKs kept souvenirs of their victims and crimes. These included heads, skulls, and other body parts; jewelry; lingerie and other clothing; and wallets and driver's licenses. However, we also included those who took and retained photos of the victims prior to murder or postmortem, the latter at times posed in sexual positions. MSKs might use these totems as stimuli to relive the "excitement" of the kill or the sexual elements of their murders.[52]

We found that only four out of 30 FSKs (13.3%) kept souvenirs of their victims. This low number was unsurprising to me, as the most common motive for female-perpetrated serial murder is financial gain, and kills are apparently the means to an end. In these cases, there would be no reason to take souvenirs to remember or fantasize about the crimes. I cannot be certain, but in three of the four cases where FSKs did keep victims' possessions, jewelry and make-up may have been taken for value or appearance, not because they belonged to a victim per se.

§

Jerome "Jerry" Henry Brudos was a serial killer. He kept women's body parts and undergarments, as well as photos of his murdered victims. Brudos committed acts of egregious violence against women, culminating in the slaying of four women in and around Salem, Oregon, between 1968 and 1969.

Brudos was born in 1939. He was fascinated by women's clothes – particularly shoes. He had found a pair of women's heels at a local trash dump when he was five years old. When his mother caught him wearing them, she confiscated and destroyed them. In 1956, when Brudos was 17, he beat a woman, took pictures of her naked, and stole her underpants. He was committed to a psychiatric ward. Later, in the 1960s, authorities found him lurking at Oregon State University wearing women's shoes and underpants.[53]

Brudos got married at age 22. He asked his wife to pose for nude photographs and engage in sexual acts she found bizarre. She did so at first, but later declined. He continued his obsession with women's clothing, breaking into homes and stealing women's undergarments.[54] Then, in 1968, Brudos used blunt-force trauma and strangulation to kill Linda Kay Slawson, a traveling salesperson who visited his home. He kept her body and dressed her in various undergarments. He cut off her foot and kept it so he could display shoes from his collection. Next, Brudos killed Jan Susan Whitney, had sex with her dead body, and took her remains to his workshop for posed photographs. He removed one of her breasts to keep as a souvenir. He then sexually assaulted and killed Oregon State University student Karen Elena Sprinkler and kept her breasts. He later kidnapped and killed Linda Dawn Salee. He dumped their mutilated bodies in local rivers.[55] Brudos also attempted to abduct 15-year-old Gloria Smith at gunpoint, but she fled and later identified him.[56]

Through this same time period, Brudos tried to date women at Oregon State University. In fact, it was because of this that he was eventually caught. After Oregon State student Karen Sprinkler was murdered, another woman student tipped the police that a man was soliciting dates from students. At the time Sprinkler disappeared, two students told the police they saw a large man dressed in drag (i.e., female clothes) in the University's parking garage.[57] He was investigated for suspicious activities at Oregon State, but authorities soon learned his crimes stretched far beyond trespass. Police found photos of the victims at Brudos' home, mostly of nude torsos, tying him to brutal murders. They also found photos of him wearing women's pantyhose and shoes. He confessed to raping and killing the young women in his photography darkroom, located in his home garage.[58] Linda Slawson's body was not found. Brudos said he threw her "over a rail somewhere."[59] Police believe he may have murdered as many as 12 women who went missing during his killing period.[60]

Although I am not a clinician and cannot ethically diagnose, and no one can diagnose mental health issues in the absence of proper interviewing and testing, we can examine the evidence and speculate what is happening in cases such as this one. Brudos told authorities that, as a child, he was abused by his whole family.[61] He also reported that his mother was domineering and had wanted a daughter instead of a son.[62] As early as age five, he attempted to dress like a girl; perhaps this was an attempt to gain his mother's love and acceptance, or perhaps he was exploring his gender identity. This early behavioral initiation seems to suggest gender issues and that shoes were not, at least at first, sexual to him. Later, he engaged in heinous acts of mutilation to possess women's body parts and photograph their torsos, perhaps as idyllic models of femininity for his emulation. He was seen in public several times dressing in women's clothing, underwear, and shoes. Some sources do say he had a shoe fetish, but I saw no information that it was shoes per se that brought him sexual gratification. Women's shoes, but also their clothing and bodies, were constants in his obsession.

Of course, nearly everyone who ever lived with gender identity issues has not committed murder. In terms of mental illness, he did admit to engaging in sexual sadism and necrophilia, although I encountered no reports of formal diagnoses. Sadism and necrophilia are both associated with loneliness.[63]

Forensic psychologist Faith Leibman[64] suggested that Brudos had a lifelong anger at his mother that he redirected at his victims. The family had an older son, and when Jerome was born, the mother was resentful she did not give birth to a daughter. Brudos reported that he was abused by both his mother and father, and his mother was controlling, rigid, and rejecting. This rejection of affection fueled his violent behavior. Leibman reported that one of Brudos' only friends in childhood, a little girl, became ill and died. This was an unfortunate form of abandonment by a female. He apparently had little trust in others, and he was consistently a loner with no friends and no one to confide in.

Despite his developmental history, seven mental health professionals testified that he was not insane and was competent to stand trial.[65] Rather than go to trial, however, Brudos pleaded guilty to three counts of murder. He received three life sentences.[66]

Later, in 1969, Brudos' wife Ralphene was charged with aiding her husband in the murder of Karen Sprinkler. An eyewitness claimed she saw Ralphene Brudos help her husband force a gagged woman into their home on the day that Sprinkler went missing. However, no one corroborated the eyewitness' story. In addition, a psychiatrist who examined Ralphene Brudos testified that she did not have a personality type suggesting she would participate in deviant sex acts like her husband did. She was found not guilty. She divorced Jerome Brudos, changed her name, and never let him see their two children.[67]

Jerome Brudos did not like prison. He was stabbed by a fellow inmate, leading to scars on his arm and back and poor blood circulation. Seemingly oblivious to the pain he caused his victims and their families when he raped and murdered women, defiled their bodies, and weighed their remains down with auto parts for disposal in the local Long Tom River, Brudos complained about being uncomfortable in prison. He said that being there was a burden, and that he was lonely, yet he also added that the prison was overcrowded, lamenting, "This place is just too damn full."[68]

Brudos died in prison of liver cancer in 2006.[69] When he died, Jan Whitney's sister said, "I am feeling relief." She emphasized, "He put my family through hell."[70]

§

A killer's practice of keeping trophies of murder victims may relate to their power or fantasy needs. This practice may also stem from a fear of being abandoned[71] – if you keep a part of someone's body or other personal possession, their essence remains with you. It is worth further exploring what psychological variables relate to trophy taking to elucidate the contents of a murderous mind.

FSK AND MSK SIMILARITY: SEXUAL TRAUMA IN COMMON

In this chapter, I have documented numerous differences between the means, motives, and victims of FSKs and MSKs. Still, a startling picture emerged with respect to something traumatic that many FSKs and MSKs have in common: they were victims of childhood sexual abuse (CSA). To address CSA experienced by serial murderers, it is important to understand what CSA is. I turn to the expert definition of CSA provided by RAINN (Rape, Abuse & Incest National Network at RAINN.org),[72] which is an anti-sexual-violence network. They defined CSA as any behavior that "intentionally harms a minor [child] physically, psychologically, sexually, or by acts of neglect." This can include sex of any kind, touching, fondling, exhibitionism, or "any other sexual conduct that is harmful to a child's mental, emotional, or physical welfare."[73]

As reported in *The Spokesman-Review*, when discussing the case of MSK Robert Lee Yates, criminologist Eric Hickey noted Yates' probable inability to deal with his anger about having been molested. Hickey said, "He doesn't know how to talk about it, so he buries it. The anger keeps fueling his fantasies, and that just pushes him over the edge." Hickey added that it is "very, very common" for serial killers to have been victims of CSA.[74] Of course, that would not be the only causal factor for someone to become a serial killer. In his book, however, Hickey also stressed it was a myth to think that all serial killers were sexually abused.[75]

But it was not until writing this book that it struck me just how many serial killers have experienced CSA – often repeatedly. Consider Robert Lee Yates, John Wayne Gacy, Margie Barfield, Aileen Wuornos, and Patty Cannon. If someone had helped them cope with their childhood trauma, we might have had fewer victims. These worst-case outcomes stress the need for early intervention and treatment.

Still, FSKs and MSKs typically commit quite different crimes with different motivations. By helping authorities recognize marked differences between them, we can aid in detection, apprehension, and perhaps prevention of future murders.

CHAPTER 9

The Behavioral Neuroscience of Serial Murder

WHY DOES SOMEONE COMMIT SERIAL HOMICIDE? The World Health Organization (WHO) and others have argued that interpersonal violence cannot be completely explained by any single factor. Rather, a multifaceted model is warranted to stress the impact of the interactions between individuals, the people around them, their community, and their society.[1] For this reason, in psychology, we promote a biopsychosocial model of understanding any behavior or mental process.

In this chapter and the ones that follow, I offer a glimpse into various perspectives regarding why someone would commit serial murder, and I offer a summary and syntheses of how we might view maldevelopment and lethal aggression through each lens. These perspectives are not mutually exclusive; for instance, you will see overlap in clinical and traumagenic factors. This chapter focuses on the biology of behavior, or behavioral neuroscience. Behavioral neuroscientists engage in reductionist techniques geared at understanding the neural, endocrinological, and genetic correlates and consequences of behavior and mental processes.

Whereas behavioral neuroscience is a rigorous, science-based field, this field started off mired in controversy. Early psychology was confused with pseudoscience such as phrenology, in which Franz Joseph Gall (1758–1828), a German physician, created a schema to determine how bumps in one's skull related to personality and behavior – even criminality.[2] Of course, this argument is just not true. However, we have come a long way since then, and contemporary behavioral neuroscientists have increasingly sophisticated, rigorous investigative techniques that facilitate deeper analyses. We can attempt to analyze what goes on physically – at the level of the brain – with those who commit crimes.

There are slim findings with respect to what transpires at the level of the brain in serial murderers. There are, however, excellent books and papers in the fields of psychology and criminology that describe biological mechanisms (e.g., frontal lobe issues) that contribute to violence, aggression, impulsivity, and compromised mood regulation. These factors can affect the decisions and behaviors of those who commit crimes.[3]

DIRECT BRAIN EVIDENCE: CASES SHOWING NEURAL ISSUES

There are very few studies[4] published that detail examinations, in vivo or postmortem, of the brains of serial murderers through direct means, such as by using brain imaging technique computed tomography (CT) scans and magnetic resonance imaging (MRI).

§

A CASE OF AN UNNAMED MSK. Researcher Richard Kraus[5] examined a MSK whom he did not name in 1995. Deductive disclosure may be possible here, but since Kraus did not name the perpetrator, I will not. The MSK was convicted of the murder of 11 women in the northeastern US. The MSK had "no hesitation" in admitting to all the homicides he committed. In this case, CT scans of his brain revealed ventricular enlargement. Ventricles are the brain's cerebrospinal-fluid-filled chambers, and enlargement of these means surrounding tissue atrophy, as commonly seen in psychological issues such as schizophrenia. CT scans of the MSK's brain also showed right temporal lobe damage and atrophy, and bilateral scars in the frontal lobes. Additionally, SPECT (single-photon emission computerized tomography) analysis showed reduced blood flow to the left parietal lobe. CEEG (continuous electroencephalography) showed bursts of "irritative patterns" in bilateral frontotemporal regions, more pronounced on the right side. All these issues were likely due to head trauma. MRI showed a healed, old skull fracture from a discus (i.e., athletic track and field) throwing accident. He also had a 47, XYY karyotype, and thus an extra Y chromosome, but tests showed that his testosterone (a masculinizing sex steroid hormone) was within normal levels.[6] Kraus summarized, "These clinical findings suggested that his aggressive and violent past could be associated with a matrix of genetic, biochemical, neurological, and psychiatric deficits."[7]

The MSK sustained a concussion from an accident. He reported that he had blackouts after the accident, accompanied by fainting, chest pains, nervousness, mood changes, and strong sex drive but decreased sexual performance. Later, he sustained another concussion when he was struck in the head with a sledgehammer.

A woman who claimed to have dated this MSK reported, "He wasn't weird, he wasn't rude . . . we just dated and went home."[8] Yet he had been in prison for arson, burglary, and for the manslaughter of a ten-year-old boy and the rape and murder of an eight-year-old girl. When he was released on parole, as quoted by Richard Kraus, a parole officer wrote that he was "possibly the most dangerous individual to have been released to this community in many years."[9]

Although the MSK's mother said that family had loved this person very much and never abused him, she thought she had spoiled him, and he did not behave as well as his siblings. When he was quite young, warning signs emerged. Describing this MSK to a newspaper, Kraus said that when the subject turned six, he was "completely unmanageable. His mother was beside herself. He was a bully, threatening others, running away from home, out of control." The other children nicknamed him "Oddie" and "Crazyboy," and he insulted teachers, tortured animals, and committed arson.[10] Animal cruelty, arson, and bedwetting make up the MacDonald Triad, a cluster of childhood behaviors thought to predict adult violence.[11]

The subject preferred to be alone, wandering away from school and home, and at age seven he was referred for mental health services after hitting other schoolchildren with an iron bar. Mental health professionals found that he indulged in a fantasy where he was another person who earned respect and had dignity.[12]

When he was age nine through ten, he engaged in theft and burglary. During that time, he was hospitalized for encephalomyelitis, which is inflammation of the brain and spinal cord. Later, although he did not perform well academically, he engaged in school sports. This is when he sustained a fractured skull during a track and field discus-throwing accident. However, his erratic and dangerous behavior preceded the injury, having emerged very early on.

In adulthood, one psychiatric report stated that he had an "emotionally unstable personality," and later, another stated that he exhibited "dissocial behavior."[13] He was married several times, and his wives described him as vacillating between being withdrawn and having fits of rage. He blamed some of his homicides on "uncontrollable rage." He also killed some of the victims because they resembled either his sister or his mother. Notably, while psychiatrists said that he had strong resentment towards his mother, Richard Kraus reported the MSK also had a genuine affection for her.

ANOTHER CASE OF AN UNNAMED MSK. In 1986, forensic psychiatrist Park Dietz[14] described one unnamed, White MSK in his 30s who had been charged with several murders committed somewhere in the United States.

This MSK had a very traumatic upbringing. His biological father, who was reported to have raped his mother, was executed for the murder of a police officer. On committing this crime, his father wrote that "the sensation was something that made me feel elated to the point of happiness." Moreover, even from a young age, the MSK physically resembled his homicidal father, and the MSK believed his father's essence lived inside him.[15]

His mother was married four times and had a series of short-term sexual partners. As a child, the MSK was exposed to sexually explicit pictures of his mother with an unknown man. The MSK experienced bedwetting (part of the MacDonald Triad) until he was 13. For wetting the bed, his mother beat him, ridiculed him, and called him "pissy pants" in front of others. He reported that he was forced to drink urine, burned with a cigar, and beaten repeatedly by one of his stepfathers, who also put his mother's head through a wall. He said he was knocked unconscious several times. The subject did not conceal his wrath towards his mother. He said he wanted to "blow the back of her head off" with a shotgun.[16]

He was in trouble with the law several times in his youth, committing vandalism, burglaries, and truancy. When he was 13, he was arrested for sexual contact with a seven-year-old girl and sent to reform school. As an adult, he was married and divorced four times, committing domestic violence against the first three wives. After numerous crimes, he was convicted of armed robbery and sentenced to time in prison.

Later, he molested his own seven-year-old daughter when she visited him in prison. When he was released, he married for the fifth time, although he also got a different woman pregnant. While in his 30s, he lived with his now 13-year-old daughter, whom he molested again and impregnated. After she had an abortion, he continued to molest her, and he also assaulted one of her friends. When she was 14, he sodomized this daughter to celebrate his own birthday.[17]

This MSK had sexual fantasies about killing his mother, and had fantasies about abusing, raping, and torturing young girls. His first victims were teen girls, and later, adult women, whom he beat, tortured, raped, and forced to play odd sex roles. He was sentenced to death for his murders. Dietz labeled this serial killer a "psychopathic sexual sadist."[18]

The subject of this report had sustained a severe head injury at age 20, falling into a coma. A CT scan showed sulcal widening and ventricular enlargements (i.e., evidence of cerebral atrophy).[19] In addition, neuropsychological tests, indirect evidence as described later, suggested frontal lobe damage. Repeated physical and psychological trauma in this MSK's history may have pushed him down a murderous path.

§

The two MSKs described above had documented head injuries with direct evidence of brain damage. Head injuries in serial killers appear to be overrepresented compared to population prevalence.[20] Using the mass media method, forensic psychologist Clare Allely and her team studied head injuries in serial killers and mass murderers. They found that about 10% of these perpetrators were reported to have sustained a head injury.[21]

Head trauma can cause brain bleeding and bruising, and brain hypoxia. A focal injury usually occurs in the frontal or temporal lobe, with widespread white matter (myelinated axon) shearing.[22] Axon shearing means that the part of the brain cells that transmits electric impulses tears, as a result of injury involving twisting and shifting of the head.[23] Frontal neural structures and their connectivity to other brain regions, including temporal structures, regulate executive functions, such as concentration, emotional control, planning, and moral and social reasoning, and judgment.[24] Brain injury compromises neurological structure, connectivity, and functioning and can therefore lead to behavioral deterioration and increases in impulsivity and violent criminal offending. Repeated head trauma is also associated with increased risk of depression, substance use, PTSD, social phobic, panic disorder, and agoraphobia.[25] Still, head injury is not an absolute determinant of violence or murder. Most people with head injuries do not commit murder, and many without head injuries do commit murder.

Indeed, not all serial killers have sustained head injuries. Furthermore, there are caveats to causal inference, as serial killers' head injuries may have been sustained in traumatic childhood circumstances, such as the MSK in Dietz's case study, and a cluster of adverse childhood experiences besides a head injury can cause maldevelopment. Furthermore, there are many events that happen in the formative years between childhood and adulthood, making it difficult to determine the exact pathway to serial murder.[26]

§

THE CASE OF JOSEPH VACHER. In 2011, scholar Jean-Pierre Luauté and colleagues[27] reported on serial killer Joseph Vacher, who, in 1898, confessed to at least 12 countryside murders in France. News reports from the time indicated that, beginning in 1894, Vacher may have killed at least 23 people. An American newspaper, *The Leavenworth Times*, reported, "Joseph Vacher had a passion for cutting the throats of shepherds and young girls – the bodies were always mutilated."[28] *The Baltimore Sun* said, "His rage was particularly directed against young girls. He first cut the throats of his victims with a knife and afterward mutilated them with a razor."[29] Some called Vacher "The French Ripper."

Alexandre Lacassagne, a renowned medical expert[30] and founder of modern autopsy and forensic procedures, worked on Vacher's case postmortem. Lacassagne oversaw legal medicine at the University of Lyon, France. Lacassagne and his colleagues founded many techniques used in modern forensic science, including systematic autopsies, blood spatter analysis, and securing the chain of custody for evidence.[31] This original team did not see any organic disturbance in Joseph Vacher's brain at the time of his postmortem examination.

Jean-Pierre Luauté and colleagues[32] reported, however, that a contemporary examination of retained biological material revealed that Vacher had lesions of the brain and the meninges (meninges are membranes

9.1 Front page of French newspaper *Le Petit Parisien*, October 24, 1897, depicts serial killer Joseph Vacher. (Photo by Leemage/Universal Images Group via Getty Images)

that protect the brain).[33] Examiners also found corpora amylacea (CA), small masses that can indicate neurodegeneration and/or evidence of infection or malignancy.[34] Vacher may have even had temporal lobe epilepsy. Thus, biological evidence suggests that severe brain disturbances contributed to Vacher's crimes. Luauté and his research team[35] reported that Vacher's sister had dementia, which can indicate inherited neurodegenerative conditions.

Moreover, news sources state that Vacher survived a suicide attempt. One newspaper reported that he "tried to blow out his brains with a revolver," and that the bullet was still lodged in his brain or skull.[36] It was also reported that he was bitten by a "mad" (rabid) dog in his youth. After a local doctor's herbal treatment, Vacher "became irritable and brutal."[37]

The motives for Vacher's killing were reported to be unknown, and some sources suggest that he just liked to kill. Vacher told authorities he killed one man because he wanted the man's shirt, and he killed others for their money. In one case, he killed a shepherd boy, hacked him into pieces, and simply continued on his way. Investigators found the bodies of victims exactly where Vacher said they were, but investigators believed he committed so many crimes he forgot just how many.[38] If he truly did forget, this may further evidence temporal lobe issues.

Joseph Vacher, "The Killer of Little Shepherds," was executed by guillotine for his crimes in Bourg-en-Bresse on December 31, 1898.[39] News reports at the time suggested that Vacher "simulated insanity" right before his execution,[40] but, per the reports of Luauté's team, his erratic behavior may not have been an act. It seems plausible that neurological issues including neurodegeneration contributed to Vacher's deadly impulsivity and explosivity.

THE CASE OF J. B. In 2008, neuropsychology researcher Feggy Ostrosky-Solís and colleagues[41] published perhaps the only neural examination of a FSK available: that of J. B., who killed at least 16 elderly women in Mexico.[42] J. B. was given the nickname "Mataviejitas," or "Killer of Old Ladies." Some sources suggested she committed as many as 36 homicides.[43]

J. B. came from an impoverished background. Her father abandoned the family, and her mother remarried. Her mother abused alcohol and was physically and verbally abusive to her. J. B. was not allowed to go to school, have toys or friends, and was forced to be a caretaker to her younger siblings. When she was 12, her mother "traded her" for three bottles of beer to an older man who tied her up and repeatedly raped her. J. B. later had a son, and her stepfather, who may have been the only positive force in her life, provided care for her son and her until the stepfather died at a young age. J. B. had four children with three different men, but her oldest son was killed in a street fight.[44]

Ostrosky-Solís and team report that, although J. B. provided for her family by selling candy and washing clothing, because of her height (she was nearly six feet tall), she became a professional wrestler. Her wrestling name was "La Dama del Silencio" ("The Silent Lady") because she claimed to be a quiet person. She worked as a wrestler and as a wrestling promoter for 13 years. J. B. may have gotten away with her crimes for years because of her height. Many people who witnessed a suspect leaving murder scenes assumed the killer was a man.

In the mid-2000s, although she had no criminal history, J. B. was accused of killing 12 elderly women, with the motive ascribed as burglary. In one case, what began as J. B. approaching an elderly lady and proposing to do her laundry for pay ended in a brutal murder. When J. B. asked for a higher wage than the woman was proposing, the woman said something about illiterate bitches wanting too much money. J. B. grabbed a stethoscope that was on the women's table and choked her with it. It was this murder that brought her into custody. She was apprehended by this woman's tenant and then arrested by police. When interrogated, J. B. confessed to strangling another woman with a stocking and another with a handkerchief. Both murders had taken place during arguments over money that J. B. had either asked to be paid in exchange for labor or had tried to borrow. J. B. told investigators that she "knew that killing people is by all means unacceptable,"[45] but that her actions were justified because these women insulted her.

During her years of wrestling, J. B. sustained no major head injuries. However, brain voltage (event-related potential; ERP) analysis did show differences between her and a control participant: J. B. had flattened response to various stimuli. In other words, she exhibited practically the same reaction to moral, neutral, pleasant, and unpleasant stimuli. Ostrosky-Solís and team took these findings and speculated that J. B. experienced amygdala changes that created psychopathic emotional processing.[46]

Psychological tests (indirect brain evidence) revealed that J. B. had deficits in executive functioning (e.g., impulsivity, flexible thinking, short-term memory), suggesting frontal lobe dysfunction. J. B. also scored high on some indications of affective dysfunction. When asked about her motive for killing one woman, she simply answered, "I got angry."[47] Her scores also revealed some anxiety and depression. Nonetheless, Ostrosky-Solís and colleagues reported that J. B.'s PCL-R of score of 25 (a measure of psychopathy) did not reach the cutoff for psychopathy. Notably, however, 25 is a cutoff score in some European countries,[48] and some experts contend that we should view psychopathy as falling on a spectrum.[49]

What made J. B. a murderer? Researchers suggested that her traumagenic history of physical, sexual, and verbal abuse, and lack of emotional and social support may have resulted in nervous system changes, particularly frontal abnormalities, in J. B. that created the propensity for violence.[50] J. B. indeed told investigators that she had a persistent resentment of her mother.[51] To the best of the authorities' knowledge, J. B. had no criminal history prior to middle age. Although no major head injuries were documented over the course of her wrestling career, one can speculate that repeated jarring and blows to the head,[52] accompanied by the physical abuse she sustained growing up, may have caused connectivity issues and therefore alterations in emotional regulation, perhaps beginning in middle age. Repeated head trauma does damage tissue and alter neurochemistry.[53]

It is worth noting that evidence suggests executive function decreases with age, and this may be attributable to connectivity diminution over time.[54] However, this almost always does not lead to serial murder.

In the end, J. B. was sentenced to 759 years in jail for the murder of 16 elderly women.[55]

§

Each of the above cases had documented evidence of neural damage or dysfunction. For at least a few serial killers, we see damage to parts of the brain that underly impulsivity, decision-making, and the understanding and control of emotions. In the case of Joseph Vacher, testing long after his death revealed marked brain abnormalities, and he had a family history of neurodegeneration. Further, he was subjected to an unknown, archaic treatment for a reported rabid dog bite; after this, Vacher was reported to have exhibited a personality change. It is unknown whether the treatment he was given indeed had toxic effects. In the case of J. B., evidence from testing brain signals showed impaired emotional response. Participation in wrestling matches, with head jarring, could have created neural damage undetected by the tests administered by neuropsychologists. We do not know, however, exactly how these individuals' neural issues translated to becoming a murderer. Neural dysregulation itself is an unlikely candidate as a lone cause of murder.

INDIRECT/IMPLIED EVIDENCE:
NEUROPSYCHOLOGICAL TESTING

Neuropsychological tests do not measure brain activity directly. They measure the presence, nature, and severity of compromise in decision-making, problem-solving, memory, mood, language, and other functions that may have resulted from brain injury or dysregulation.[56] These tests involve writing, drawing, and responding to questions. These assessments can help with diagnoses and establish a baseline for measurement of further decline or effectiveness of intervention.[57] Through neuropsychological examinations, clinicians make inferences about the brain's structure and function.[58]

§

THE CASE OF K. T. In 2013, psychologist Alessandro Angrilli and colleagues from University of Padova and 2CNR-IN Institute of Neuroscience in Italy[59] presented information on the cognitive and socioemotional state of a MSK. They administered tests of executive function to MSK K. T., who murdered at least five people over a seven-year timespan, bludgeoning and burning them. K. T. targeted sex workers, priests, people with substance abuse issues, and people who were homosexual. K. T. believed his victims were all sinners.[60]

Psychologists administered the Tower of London, a neuropsychological test involving planning object configurations, to assess K. T.'s executive function. Results revealed that he had "a mild deficit in planning." Other tests showed that he had intact moral reasoning, but he had impaired recognition of anger, embarrassment, and violations of social rules. Tests showed that K. T. did not meet the DSM-IV criteria for antisocial personality disorder.

K. T. was also administered the PCL-R (the measure of psychopathy). K. T. scored low for antisocial behavior on Factor 2 but scored 16 out 16 (100th percentile) for emotional detachment on Factor 1 (primary psychopathy). Angrilli et al. (2013) described K. T. as an emotionally detached psychopath and theorized that he had dissociation between emotions and morality.

§

In neuropsychological testing, clinicians administer a battery of paper-and-pencil or computer-based neuropsychological tests, and then infer brain injury or dysfunction. With increasingly sophisticated functional imaging techniques, the field of neuropsychology is growing to a point at which such testing may some day be automatically accompanied by real-time functional neuroimaging to identify problematic neural networks.[61]

CASES SHOWING NO NEURAL ISSUES

Just as the above cases evidence brain issues in serial killers, it seems there are just as many cases where an examination has shown no neural dysfunction.

§

THE CASE OF SURINDER KOLI. In 2012, forensic expert T. D. Dogra and his colleagues[62] presented one of the most comprehensive case studies of a serial killer I have ever seen. They used brain imaging and neuropsychological tests in their assessment of serial killer Surinder Koli. While an MRI of Koli's brain was unremarkable (nothing abnormal), the case paints an interesting picture.

In the mid-2000s, several children from Nithari, India, had gone missing. Forensic investigators found 19 skulls in the backyard of the house where Koli worked as a servant, as well as in the residence's sewer. He had murdered women, boys, and girls, engaged in sex acts with the corpses, and had cooked and eaten some of their breasts and arms. T. D. Dogra and colleagues reported that Koli showed no remorse. Although experts believe Koli committed the murders, and Koli admitted that the homeowner, Moninder Singh Pandher, knew nothing about the murders, both were sentenced to death for the crimes. News reports indicated that Koli received 12 death sentences and one acquittal for his crimes.[63] Curiously, Koli asked officials if death by hanging was painful. A man called a "butcher" of his victims, and who never expressed remorse, was worried about his own pain.[64]

Koli was of lower socioeconomic status. He attended school to seventh grade. His father died when he was young, but Koli reported that he got along well with his mother and siblings. He reported no psychiatric illness in his family. He was married with three children, although his first child died of illness, and he was unable to afford proper medical care for her. He said he had no close friends.

Koli worked as a domestic servant and caretaker, maintaining fairly regular employment. He had no criminal history, did not take drugs, and drank alcohol occasionally. Koli revealed to examiners that he was sexually abused around age 10–11 by a male in his 20s from the village. As early as age 14, he masturbated to fantasies about killing girls, having sex with their dead bodies, and mutilating them.[65]

When examined by clinicians, Koli was of average intelligence and had intact judgment. He maintained eye contact, exhibited rapport, and had normal response times to questions. He showed no signs of anxiety, had a normal pulse and blood pressure, and no abnormalities were detected in his nervous system functioning. He showed no thought, attention, or perceptual disturbances. There was no evidence of psychotic features. Still, he showed no emotions during four hours of testing, even when describing his family or his crimes. Dogra and his team reported that Koli was uncooperative on some of the psychological testing.

Dogra et al. said that "there was no question that masking or dissembling" was a key feature of Koli's personality. He engaged in deception as a mask, as he had "difficulties dealing with emotional situations and tended to use denial, avoidance, and escape into fantasy, mainly lethal ones." Koli's responses to psychological tests and questions indicated that he was vague, inconsistent, and avoidant. Dogra and colleagues concluded that Koli's profile was consistent with antisocial personality disorder (ASPD) and psychopathy. He had a callous disregard for others, he lied, violated social norms (particularly those of Indian culture), was aggressive, and killed. He was clearly a danger to others. He also had no remorse, no emotional reaction after murder, and used the same knives for household chores that he did for murder.[66]

Examinations of Koli, including an MRI, showed no "organic disturbance."[67] Stated another way, in this case, ASPD was diagnosed, and his behaviors and responses were consistent with psychopathy, but there was no evidence of underlying brain dysregulation. However, as this case also features cannibalism and necrophilia, this brain may not generalize to the brains of other FSKs or MSKs who do not eat their victims or have sex with corpses.

THE CASE OF JEFFREY DAHMER. As pointed out in 2017 by psychologist Sasha Reid, a lack of direct information about serial killer neurobiology may not be due to a lack of interest or effort.[68] The serial killer may decline participation in testing, be deceased, or their family may deny access. For example, MSK Jeffrey Dahmer murdered 17 men, had sex with their dead bodies, ate some of their body parts, and kept other body parts as souvenirs.[69] (I will provide more details about Dahmer's case later.) Dahmer's family did not wish for his brain to be an object of study. They petitioned the court to have his brain cremated with the rest of his body, and they won.[70] Nonetheless, as Reid pointed out, when Dahmer was alive, MRI and electroencephalography (EEG) tests revealed no neurological issues.[71]

THE CASE OF JOHN WAYNE GACY. Gacy sustained at least one head injury in his youth, requiring hospitalization.[72] He was also repeatedly physically abused by his father, which may have involved head trauma. However, reports indicate that a postmortem examination of John Wayne Gacy's brain showed nothing abnormal – no injury, swelling, atrophy, or tumor.[73] The psychiatrist who had possession of Gacy's brain reported that it was "normal."[74] It showed no ventricular enlargement or blockage.[75] Since this psychiatrist may still have Gacy's brain and slices of all his organs,[76] further analysis is possible with today's sophisticated imaging techniques. Still, the brain was driven home from the autopsy in the psychiatrist's Buick on the passenger seat in a jar.[77] A brain that has "ridden shotgun" in an unscientific transport and has been kept in a home basement may not have been handled or preserved well enough for examination to reveal conclusive evidence of dysfunction while the subject was alive.

§

With no evidence of brain injury, there must be more to these killers' stories. It could be the case that modern techniques are insufficient to detect minor brain differences that lead to major behavioral outcomes. It may be that serial murderers have no brain issues, and just chose to disregard the rights of others. In the case of postmortem examination, it is impossible to determine deviation or changes in function.

SO . . . WHAT DO WE KNOW ABOUT SERIAL KILLER BRAINS?

We know that there is an incomplete picture about neural functioning in serial murderers. From the cases above, only one of which was about a FSK, some direct evidence points to degeneration, disease, and brain response issues. Some indirect evidence points to executive function deficits. Some evidence suggests that head injury may be a factor. It seems, though, that just as much evidence suggests the absence of these issues. There is no overwhelming evidence to paint a comprehensive picture that the brains of serial killers have a unified pathophysiology that can explain or predict their crimes. Maybe there really is an overall lack of brain dysregulation in SKs, and that is why few reports exist on this topic. Scientific journals do not necessarily place great value on null results.[78] This is sometimes called the "file drawer problem,"[79] and it is estimated that 95% of studies with null results are filed away, never to be published. To maintain the rigor of science, we must yield when we have inconsistent, no, or very little, evidence. Evidence of absence is important.

This is not to say, however, that brain dysregulation does not contribute to the behaviors and mental processes of serial homicide offenders. I am confident, in fact, that there are functional neural factors involved. Someone who shoots multiple people in the head, asphyxiates several disabled people, smothers seven babies and enjoys their funerals, poisons disabled veterans, or buries bodies in their home crawl space does not have the executive functioning that the rest of us do. We would need more direct research with larger numbers of serial murderers to try to understand their pathophysiology. Of course, there is irony in that what would make the science more powerful would be the continuation of the horrible events so we could study and describe the neural workings of a greater number of perpetrators. And no one wants more serial murderers to exist. We also need to understand that, as noted by Sasha Reid,[80] the heterogeneity of serial killer presentation will make it unlikely that we will ever find a specific serial killer predisposition network in the brain.

There may be no way to derive neural evidence of serial murder. Surinder Koli killed nearly 20 people[81] yet showed no brain issues. Still, there may be a different neurological profile for a "successful psychopath" – those who have intact or even heightened cognitive abilities that allow them to use more covert approaches to goal attainment.[82] Following this viewpoint from experts on neurocriminology, there are likely serial killers out there who have high executive function and avoid detection *ad infinitum*. This theory is in line with our documentation of differences between aspiring, probable, and successful serial homicide offenders. Forensic researcher Enzo Yaksic and colleagues summarized that successful serial homicide offenders compartmentalize, take deliberate actions, have heightened aptitude and stamina, and make strategic, deliberate plans to selectively target victims. They also take active forensic countermeasures to avoid detection. Furthermore, successful serial homicide offenders can easily switch from being a murderer to being a normal part of society.[83]

BIOPSYCHOLOGY OF VIOLENCE, GENERALLY SPEAKING

We also must remember that serial murder is an atypical manifestation of lethal violence,[84] and suppositions about serial killers based on the neurobiology of other murderers or violent offenders may not inform the complete picture. Almost everyone who has ever lived with atypical brain structure, function, connectivity, neurotransmitter profile, and hormone profile has not committed murder, let alone serial murder.

Still, a general acknowledgement of the biology of violence is warranted. There are volumes of published science devoted to the biopsychology of violent behavior. For years, researchers have documented the

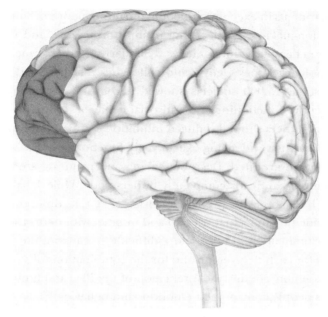

9.2 Digital illustration of the brain with the prefrontal cortex highlighted. Located in the anterior part of the cerebrum, the PFC supports executive function (e.g., attention, decision-making, emotional control, and social judgment). (Photo by Getty Images)

association between aggression and frontal lobes dysfunction.[85] In particular, many studies have shown relationships between prefrontal cortex (PFC) dysregulation and violent behavior. The PFC is the front of our frontal lobes, in the front of our cerebrum, behind our eyes and forehead.[86] It supports executive function, which is involved in inhibition (controlling responses to stimuli), attention, focus, and planning. These processes allow goal-setting and behavioral control, and they keep you on task.[87] Deficits in executive functioning (i.e., executive dysfunction) have been consistently linked with antisocial behavior and are considered key in the onset and maintenance of aggression and violence.[88] In fact, people with lesions to their PFC have increased violent attitudes.[89]

In 2013, psychologist and neuroscience researcher Stephane De Brito and colleagues studied executive function impairment in non-jailed individuals who had previously committed crimes. The researchers found that, compared to non-violent offenders, violent offenders with antisocial personality disorder (ASPD), with and without psychopathy, had impairments in executive function, including poor working memory and decision-making, not learning from punishments, and not adapting well to changing contingencies.[90] Similarly, a notable meta-analysis by criminologist James Ogilvie and colleagues that included 126 studies with some 15,000 subjects showed a robust association between poor executive functioning and antisocial behavior.[91] Moreover, violent criminal offenders showed reduced inhibition compared to non-violent offenders, further evidencing executive dysfunction.[92]

A caveat is warranted. Decision-making and planning are extraordinarily complex and not completely understood. While I have written generally here about the prefrontal cortex (PFC), its different divisions have specific functions that overlap and interact with neurotransmitters and other brain areas. It is therefore difficult to tease out the exact contributions for each PFC region and for the combinations of structures in the corticolimbic circuit (the interaction of the PFC and limbic regions that helps people control their emotions and behavior).[93]

In terms of violence, one area of research focus within the PFC is the orbitofrontal cortex (OFC). Simplified, the OFC is connected to limbic (emotional) brain areas and integrates responses to emotional stimuli. The OFC appears to play a role in rule use, reward valuation, and inhibiting cognitive, motor, and emotional responses. Stated another way, it helps integrate emotions, cognitions, and behaviors, facilitating competent decisions, preventing impulsivity, and allowing social flexibility.[94] Impulsivity and dysfunctional violence are related to reduced volume in the OFC and in the hippocampus, a limbic area.[95]

It is worth stressing here that frontal lobe issues can be linked to traumagenic experiences. Evidence suggests a traumagenic environment in childhood, something we have seen in many serial killers, interferes with OFC-amygdala (limbic) connectivity.[96] This means that childhood adversity can interfere with the ability to understand and regulate one's emotions and behavioral responses. Psychologist Jessie Lund and colleagues' systematic review of 36 studies yielded strong evidence of the connection between diminished executive function and adverse childhood experiences such as abuse, neglect, and exposure to intimate partner violence (IPV).[97] Again, trauma in childhood is continuously associated with suboptimal adult outcomes, including a proclivity for violence.

The understanding of the function of the PFC remains challenging to decipher. Tumors, strokes, closed head injuries, and other events affecting these frontal areas can cause substantial executive dysfunction and cognitive impairment.[98] But with no two injuries the same, analysis and mapping of distinct functions is challenging. In addition, although I have focused on neural regions here, most certainly, hormones and neurotransmitters (e.g., serotonin, dopamine) play a role in emotional regulation and impulse control.[99] Moreover, it is difficult to determine if those who perform well in laboratory tasks can execute optimal decision-making in real-life scenarios. Further research is needed.

Yet we know at least some information about the brains of violent offenders. We also understand that there are endocrinological, genetic, and epigenetic forces at play working in conjunction with the brain and with each other to moderate and mediate aggression. However, with virtually no research involving more than one serial killer's data, we are unable to generalize and say with certainty that "Serial killers have XYZ brain differences."

Even Aristotle would agree with the syllogistic logic that some serial killers have antisocial personality disorder (ASPD). ASPD involves frontal and limbic dysregulation, and therefore some serial killers probably have frontal and limbic dysregulation. But remember, not all people with ASPD are serial killers. Almost all are not. Furthermore, there is evidence of no dysfunction in the brains of those with psychopathy. Moreover, even though they are supposed to largely speak to the same concept, only one-third of people diagnosed with ASPD have psychopathy, and not everyone with psychopathy has ASPD.[100] As I tell my Physiological Psychology class often, "It's complex and not fully understood."

Even expert Robert Hare[101] questioned whether those with psychopathy had frontal lobe issues, and he was the creator of the Psychopathy Checklist (PCL), now known as the Psychopathy Checklist-revised (PCL-R). In testing these individuals with the Wisconsin Card Sorting Test (WCST),[102] Hare did not find deficits. It may be the case that damage to specific areas of the PFC, such as the orbitofrontal cortex (OFC), causes issues with negative and defense emotions, thereby motivating affective murders – those that are emotional and unplanned. Yet predatory murderers can have normal OFC and other frontal functioning.[103]

Many FSKs carefully plan their crimes – a trait of successful serial homicide offenders[104] – and would therefore be considered predatory.

In support of the idea that predatory murderers can have normal OFC and other frontal functioning, clinical expert and researcher Vanessa Pera-Guardiola and colleagues found that offenders with antisocial personality disorder (ASPD) who had higher PCL-R scores did not perform differently than controls on the Wisconsin Card Sorting Test (WCST), indicating no difference in executive function. Moreover, those with ASPD who had higher Factor 1 scores on the PCL-R (more psychopathy) performed better on the WCST. This research team suggested that psychopathy influences cognitive ability in those with ASPD.[105]

Indeed, in 2013, psychologist Andrea Glenn and colleagues argued that a diagnosis of ASPD is too broad and controversial, as it overlaps with other conditions.[106] In the DSM-5, a diagnosis of ASPD requires that the individual has a history of conduct disorder.[107] Subtypes of ASPD vary in marked ways, likely have different neural and genetic underpinnings, and can be influenced by substance use, anxiety, and other mental health conditions. ASPD is more behavior-based,[108] and psychopathy (not an official diagnosis in the DSM-5), has behavioral, affective, and interpersonal components.

Robert Hare also argued that the diagnosis of ASPD has "dubious validity." He stated that, among criminals, ASPD is quite common, but those with ASPD can have vastly different personalities, attitudes, and motives for engaging in criminal behavior.[109] It does not mesh well with other indicators of psychopathy. Hare stressed, "Most psychopaths . . . with the exception of those who somehow manage to plow their way through life without coming into formal or prolonged contact with the criminal justice system . . . meet the criteria for ASPD, but most individuals with ASPD are not psychopaths."[110] Hare also stressed that those with ASPD and those with psychopathy tend to perform differently on neuropsychological tests.

Even direct brain research measuring cognitive and emotional processing evinces differences between ASPD and psychopathy.[111] For example, using the measuring tools of fear-potentiated startle (FPS; measure of a startle reflex) and event-related potentials (ERPs; measures of the brain's electrical voltage), psychologist Marja Anton and colleagues showed that women offenders with psychopathy had an elevated reaction to threats but filtered out fear-based peripheral information in the pursuit of goals. Anton and the team noted that people with psychopathy have selective attention, becoming disinhibited when they have a great motivation to gain a reward. By contrast, women offenders with ASPD had less fear overall but displayed greater fear when cognitive load was increased. They suggested this response in those with ASPD might be an artifact of executive dysfunction.[112]

Still, little research to date measures the brain activity of serial killers directly. And of course, we know that not all psychopaths or people with ASPD are serial killers.[113] Moreover, of the limited number of case studies I have seen, only one report I have encountered describes a direct FSK brain examination. There have been several FSKs who committed crimes fairly recently, so I am not sure if contemporary, sophisticated neural analyses were not performed, or if the results are just not accessible, or if studies just show no results and remain unpublished, forever relegated to the file drawer.

Generally speaking, beyond serial killers, we can say confidently that some areas of the brain involved in executive function, such as the PFC, amygdala, hippocampus, and angular gyrus, probably show damage or dysregulation when someone has impairments in moral reasoning and demonstrates antisocial behavior.[114] Yet the science is still in progress.

Despite this caveat, researchers J. Arturo Silva and his team[115] have put forth a neuropsychiatric model of serial sexual homicide that they suggest speaks to almost all MSK cases. This model does not, however, speak to FSKs. A model is a prediction viewed through a cogent framework, and, admittedly, it need not include the data that test it. These researchers presented evidence that some individuals on the autistic spectrum have theory of mind (ToM) deficits, and that there may be a connection between serial murder, autistic psychopathology, and fantasy development. The authors believe that studying the functional neuroanatomy of autistic serial killers may be key to understanding their homicidal motivations. Still, this is not an empirical study in which they examined a sample of serial killers via MRI, fMRI, SPECT, or PET scans and found documented neural underpinnings of murder.

As Mark Palermo and Stefan Bogaerts[116] asserted, "There is no doubt that the brain is the organ of behavior," but we must be careful giving posthumous diagnoses of brain-related disorder (e.g., autism spectrum) to people who have committed crimes but have not been subjected to rigorous testing and modern diagnostics. Palermo and Bogaerts stressed that such ascriptions without science can create myths and perpetuate stigma. Moreover, there are ethical and legal issues in highlighting hypothetical connections between brain structure/function and crime, as there is potential for misuse, arguing neurological absolute determinants of crime.[117]

HEAD INJURIES AND GENERAL VIOLENCE

Head injuries that change the structure and function of the brain have long been linked with violent crime, and even with the persistence of violent criminal activity. Some researchers label these "acquired neuropsychological deficits."[118] Examining records for 16 male inmates on death row in California, for example, researchers found that 75% had a history of traumatic brain injury (TBI). In addition, all 16 men experienced family violence, with severe sexual and physical abuse in almost every case.[119] Along these lines, a meta-analysis of 24 studies showed a 51.1% average prevalence of TBI in an incarcerated sample of men and women. The 24 focus studies, emerging from six countries, reported TBI prevalence in incarcerated people ranging from 9.7% to 100%.[120]

In a recent comprehensive review of the literature, psychologist W. Huw Williams and team reported that TBIs are commonly associated with deficits in control, inhibition, and attention, as well as poor treatment outcomes. They suggested that emergency departments, family medicine, school, and mental health services could work together to identify and manage TBI with neurorehabilitation, which can increase the chance of improvement.[121]

GENES FOR VIOLENCE?

Is there a serial killer genotype? While the science to tell us what exact genes may predispose someone to commit serial homicide has not yet emerged, there is some research showing that violence against conspecifics is common across the animal kingdom, evidencing an evolved, genetic predisposition for killing.[122] There are also studies that show high heritability[123] in violence, but this may be different than murder.[124] And different still would be a predisposition to kill multiple people.

A genetic finding about violence and the MAO-A gene captured attention in the media in the mid-2000s. A variant of the MAO-A gene, sometimes known as "the warrior gene," was reported to be associated with violent aggression. Found on the X chromosome, this gene facilitates monoamine oxidase A production, a chemical that directs the breakdown (the oxidation) of the neurotransmitters dopamine, serotonin, norepinephrine, and epinephrine.[125] These neurotransmitters modulate many aspects of cognition, mood, and movement. Monoamine oxidase A metabolizes these neurotransmitters, and excessive monoamine loss can cause problems including depression.[126] These findings, however, were taken out of context by many media outlets, leading to a public (and dangerous) misinterpretation that having this gene was an absolute determinant of aggressive behavior. We must remember to contextualize findings – genes work in conjunction with other genes and with the environment to create an increased likelihood of a behavior.[127]

Other research shows the association between low MAO-A activity alleles (low repeats) and violent behavior. The MAO-A allele was associated with lower orbitofrontal volume (the OFC is part of the prefrontal cortex); reductions in limbic volume; reduced cingulate-related[128] inhibition,[129] and hyperactivity of the hippocampus and amygdala when recalling aversive stimuli. Stated another way, MAO-A low repeat alleles were associated with compromised emotional regulation and cognitive control. Similarly, low-activity variants of the MAO-A gene were linked to violent crime, weapon use, and gang membership.[130] While these findings have implications for executive dysfunction, it is worth stating again that the functioning of MAO-A is very complex.

Monoamine neurotransmitters may play a particular role in serial sexual homicide. This link has not been explicitly established, but evidence underscores a role for monoamines (i.e., dopamine, norepinephrine, serotonin) in both sexually impulsive behavior and violence. Monoamines are involved in an individual's perception of what is sexually attractive, their sexual motivation, and their sexual activity itself. Antidepressant drugs that affect monoamines can have the side effect of increasing or decreasing sexual cognitions and motivations.[131] Interestingly, studies have consistently shown monoamine dysregulation in individuals with paraphilia,[132] and those who commit serial murder have increased paraphilia.[133] Moreover, lower serotonin levels have consistently been linked to disinhibition, violence, and aggression, and drugs that increase serotonin, particularly selective serotonin reuptake inhibitors (SSRIs), are routinely used to treat sexual impulsivity and paraphilia.[134]

Nevertheless, in 2017, psychiatrist Andrzej Jakubczyk and colleagues showed that there was no link between MAO-A polymorphisms and history of sexual offenses. Further, precise ties between MAO-A polymorphisms and serial murder have not been established, and findings regarding "the warrior gene" are not necessarily associated with MSK and FSK typical traits. For example, MAO-A low activity expression (two repeats) was associated with antisociality; however, the two-repeat allele was not related to scores on a test of psychopathy.[135] Moreover, low activity expression of the MAO-A gene seems to be associated with aggression after being provoked,[136] which does not seem congruent with calculated homicides. This is, however, reminiscent of the case of J. B., a FSK who reacted with murder to women who insulted her.

While certain blogs and opinion pieces refer to MAO-A as a "serial killer gene," I have come across no studies directly assessing a particular serial killer's genomic makeup to crimes. We must await progress in this area of exploration for any such relation to be verified. Furthermore, we must keep in mind that it is necessary to consider the interaction with variants of the MAO-A gene with other genes and the environment to best study aggressive tendencies. Stated another way, it takes more than just an allele to make someone aggressive or a murderer.[137] Researchers and ethicists caution that any biological connection to behavior or mental process must be viewed in the context of environment, including cultural, societal, and economic conditions. The widespread attention to, and misinterpretation of, these findings prompted experts in the field to be very clear in their warnings about the limitations of their findings.[138]

Genes are composed of deoxyribonucleic acid (DNA), a unique molecular code for each person's structure and function.[139] DNA analysis may not directly tell us who has the potential to be a serial killer, but DNA left behind can help us catch a serial killer.

§

Joseph James DeAngelo Jr. is a serial killer. Known as "The Golden State Killer," he is a former police officer who murdered at least 13 people, killed pets, raped more than 50 women, and committed many burglaries

9.3 "Golden State Killer" Joseph DeAngelo in Sacramento Superior Court in 2019. DeAngelo was caught using Forensic Genetic Genealogy. (Hector Amezcua/Sacramento Bee/Tribune News Service via Getty Images)

throughout the 1970s and 1980s.[140] He was not caught at the time of the crimes, but was identified years later through genetic investigation.[141]

Authorities in the 1970s and 1980s felt that a string of murders, rapes, and burglaries in California was related. But they had only vague descriptions of a suspect – a stocky White man with larger than average legs, light skin, with brown or blonde hair, in his 20s or 30s. Authorities described the perpetrator's pattern as "explosive violence and then escape."[142]

DNA samples found at crime scenes did not match any in the US federal Combined DNA Index System (CODIS)[143] offender database.[144] But eventually DeAngelo was caught when investigators uploaded DNA obtained from a crime scene to GEDMatch,[145] an open-source genealogical database used for family history tracing. *The Los Angeles Times* reported that private data from two for-profit genealogy companies were also used in the operation.[146] Experts found DeAngelo's distant cousin and common ancestor and constructed his family tree. They eventually narrowed suspects down to Joseph DeAngelo and matched DNA he left on his car door while shopping at Hobby Lobby to the DNA he left at crime scenes.[147] DeAngelo, at age 72, was the first public arrest made as a result of using this investigative method,[148] known as Forensic Genetic Genealogy (FGG).[149] It has been reported that other criminals have been caught using this technique.[150]

Prosecutors claimed that DeAngelo had a history of faking mental illness and physical disability and that he was manipulative. In 1979, for example, when he was a police officer, he was caught shoplifting. He rolled around on the floor and pretended to have a heart attack. He told his colleagues he pretended to be "crazy" to avoid trouble. He was fired. Sacramento County Deputy District Attorney Thienvu Ho also reported that DeAngelo "feigned feeble incoherence" while being interviewed by authorities, even though they had observed him doing heavy yard work and riding his motorcycle shortly before.[151]

DeAngelo claimed he had another personality named Jerry who made him commit his crimes. "I didn't have the strength to push him out," DeAngelo said, "He made me. It was like in my head . . . he's a part of me. I didn't want to do those things. I pushed Jerry out and had a happy life."[152] However, there are no reports I can find where DeAngelo was formally diagnosed with dissociative identity disorder or any other disorder, and authorities suggest he was being manipulative.

Joseph DeAngelo appeared to have an aggressive, high sensation-seeking personality even before escalating to rape and murder. He dated Bonnie Colwell at Sierra College in the late 1960s. He coaxed her into engaging in risky activities, such as skydiving and riding fast cars and motorcycles. Colwell said DeAngelo was sexually "insatiable" and that he would break intercourse before he climaxed, and then return to the sex act and repeat. Colwell became frightened of DeAngelo's increasingly alarming behavior, ranging from cheating on college exams, to trespassing, to killing a dog, and she broke up with him. DeAngelo showed up with a gun at her house and demanded that she leave with him. Her father talked him down, but Colwell remained terrified of DeAngelo, causing her to take a leave of absence from the college they both attended.[153]

Some of DeAngelo's more sadistic behaviors seem to have manifested after this failed relationship. Experts say DeAngelo's hostile and resentful feelings towards Bonnie Colwell appear to be one of the driving forces of his crimes. DeAngelo raped and sodomized one woman in July

1978, and then he began crying. As conveyed in *The Los Angeles Times*, the report from Davis Police stated that the perpetrator was "sobbing" and said, "I hate you, Bonnie. I hate you, I hate you, I hate you." Later, he said to the victim, "I'll blow your fucking head off. I'll kill your fucking kids. I'll cut you."[154] Reflecting on DeAngelo's case, forensic psychologist Eric Hickey stated that "he obviously had a lot of anger towards women." He continued, "He hated women . . . he was very sadistic towards them."[155]

Former FBI Agent Brad Garret told *ABC News* that DeAngelo's modus operandi fits that of a sexual serial killer. He got progressively more violent, as his crimes went from robbery and rape to murder.[156] He would bind a woman victim, turn on her television, and cover it with a towel so he could see her in the glow of the TV while he raped her.[157] DeAngelo used a gun and blunt force to kill. Reflecting Hervey Cleckley's[158] observation that psychopaths are often dedicated to law and order and "traditional values" as a part of mimicking sanity, DeAngelo also had an attraction to uniforms: he was in the navy for 22 months during the Vietnam war[159] and then became a police officer.

Moreover, Garret said that DeAngelo was good at leading a "compartmentalized life," in that he worked for decades as a public affairs expert at a local supermarket and lived a typical life in Sacramento with his wife and three daughters.[160] His daughter wrote, "Growing up, I thought I had the best and most loving and attentive father in the world . . ." She continued, "The father I know and love is a good person."[161] Yet not only were DeAngelo's motives power, control, and sex,[162] his profile is clearly congruent with other successful serial homicide offenders who easily compartmentalize their lives and mix up their killing methods.[163] I am not diagnosing anyone, but evidence from media reports does suggest that DeAngelo's behaviors are consistent with the criteria for psychopathy.

Still, life in the suburbs may not have been exactly normal for DeAngelo. Neighbors nicknamed him "freak" and described him as argumentative, noting the regularity with which DeAngelo would yell and scream curses in their otherwise quiet neighborhood of Citrus Heights in Sacramento, California. When neighbors told reporters that DeAngelo was handy and even poured the concrete in his yard himself, a neighbor speculated that investigators were going to dig up the slabs in search of souvenirs he may have kept from his crimes.[164]

Indeed, DeAngelo had kept trophies of his crimes, including victims' identification, dishes, coins, and purses.[165] The items were later found in his bedroom, where authorities said he had a computer monitor with a towel over it. Investigator Paul Holes told Karen Kilgariff and Georgia Hardstark, hosts of the podcast *My Favorite Murder*, that he wondered whether DeAngelo was "pulling out any of those souvenirs and replicating the glowing environment from back in the 1970s" when he raped women with their televisions on.[166]

To avoid the death penalty, DeAngelo, also called the "East Area Rapist," pleaded guilty to 13 counts of first-degree murder. He also admitted to rapes he committed that were older than the statute of limitation and thus could not be prosecuted.[167] DeAngelo was sentenced to life in prison[168] An unnamed woman who, when she was age seven, watched him rape her mother, said that Joe DeAngelo was "proof monsters were real. I had met the boogeyman."[169] Debbi Domingo McMullan, whose mother was raped and murdered by DeAngelo, said, "Today the devil loses and justice wins."[170] The boogeyman left behind DNA, and justice was served.

§

There are only a few cases in available records where biological processes were investigated in actual serial killers, living or dead. Moreover, those cases studying the structure and function of the brain have not yielded very consistent evidence as to the precise neural makings of a serial murderer, and there have been no studies to date that have empirically demonstrated neural issues in a large-sample study of serial killers. No two serial killers are identical, of course, so identifying common neurological underpinnings may be difficult or impossible. Yet there is evidence as to what brain mechanism dysfunction underlies violence and impulsivity, even of a sexual nature. Unfortunately, however, to conduct studies that convincingly capture evidence, or evidence of absence, we must have access to an appreciable number of living serial murderers and subject them to the sophisticated neuroimaging techniques available today. While we are aiming for the body of knowledge to grow, we surely do not want the pool of serial murderers to grow.

CHAPTER 10

Psychosocial Factors that Make
a Serial Murderer

IN UNDERSTANDING ANY BEHAVIOR or mental process, it is best to take a multifaceted approach. What do we know about the mind of a serial murderer? What do we know about how other people, society, and institutions have influenced this person's psychology? In this chapter, I will examine clinical psychological, traumatic developmental, and sociocultural perspectives that may allow insight into the making of a serial murder. I include media dynamics and feminist perspective in this material. Because I have used these theories throughout this book, below is a summary snapshot of each perspective.

In psychology, we endeavor to ask why someone is who and what they are. That is an exceedingly difficult puzzle to solve, and no one has yet created a comprehensive model that would fully predict good behavior or bad behavior, including murder. Although we can speculate on contributions to a serial murderer's psyche, I cannot stress enough that it is statistically unlikely that someone who experiences any one of these factors, or even all of these factors, will become a serial killer.

CLINICAL PERSPECTIVE

I talked about mental health in the preceding chapters, but information bears repeating. Mental illness is not a motive for serial murder per se, and almost everyone who has ever lived with mental illness has not been a serial killer. It cannot be overemphasized that almost everyone with mental illness does not harm others. The odds of being murdered by someone with mental illness is about the same as winning the lottery, at about 1 in 60,000,000.[1] The serial homicide offending women and men whose data and stories are told in this book are extreme case studies. Still, mental illness can help answer the question of why serial murder is committed, and thus it is beneficial to examine serial murder through a clinical perspective.

Nearly 40% of the FSKs in our research had mental illness, and almost all MSKs in our research had mental illness. In addition, there were indications of serious mental illness, including disorders marked by anger, mood disturbances, distorted perceptions, and dissociation. And although psychopathy is not a separate diagnosis, it seems from the cases presented in this book that there is abundant evidence suggesting it is a common trait in serial murderers.

That is what we found in the records we examined; I would say the actual number of serial killers with mental illness is a lot higher. It is possible that mental illness was determined but not recorded properly in the initial newspaper reports, government records, court records, and historical society reports collected by my team and me. Yet, to be fair, even if mental illness was detected and diagnosed, the FSKs in our original sample largely did not receive mental health services (we did not obtain this information for MSKs). We know that we have still a lot of work to do in psychology to facilitate the recovery journeys of those with mental illness. It is possible that early treatment of mental illness can prevent homicide or other types of violence.

Although there are several published studies on MSK mental health, our study was one of the first to our knowledge to amass data on FSK mental health. Some other researchers' efforts are mentioned in this book,[2] but nomothetic (large sample) reports are rare. Idiographic (case study) reports of FSK mental illness in the scientific literature are also rare, but such reports can highlight mental illness in FSKs and incorporate traumagenic information in the etiology of each killer's violent development. I perused the literature for peer-reviewed, scientific, original report articles on this topic. I was not looking for others' syntheses. I wanted case reports written by clinicians who interacted with FSKs. I have had little success finding such. It is interesting that the two studies I found most readily identifiable in scientific journals provided case details for FSKs that do not exactly fit the typical FSK profile – Aileen Wuornos and J. B., who both had a modus operandi of explicit violence.

§

FSK Aileen Wuornos was mentally ill. Psychiatrist Wade Myers and colleagues[3] reported on their clinician assessment of Wuornos. She admitted to killing seven men, all over the age of 40, and to shooting them between one and nine times. Wuornos stole their money, electronics, and jewelry, and she disposed of most victims' bodies in wooded areas. At first, she claimed she killed the men in self-defense, but later reported in a documentary that she "was into the robbery biz" and that "there was no self-defense."[4]

This clinical team documented Aileen's traumagenic background, including her grandmother's refusal to give permission for Aileen to get counseling help in junior high school for her behavior problems.

The authors also examined her Department of Correction files, attempting to determine whether Wuornos were a psychopath, whether she had other personality disorders, and whether she were a sexual sadist. They used the Psychopathy Checklist-Revised (PCL-R) to gauge psychopathy. They reviewed Wuornos' court transcripts, reports, and testimony for criteria. Coded items included grandiose self-worth (she said she had sex with 250,000 men), lack of remorse (she said she did not care that the victims were dead and wished she could have reached her target number of victims), poor behavioral control (she attacked her friend with a shish kabob when they disagreed), and being manipulative (she used aliases, forged checks, and had multiple concurrent relationships).[5] They ascribed to Wuornos a PCL-R score of 32, which is above the cutoff of 30 for a psychopathy and put her in the 97th percentile of psychopathy.

Using the then-current edition of the *Diagnostic and Statistical Manual of Mental Disorders (DSM-IV-TR)*, Myers and colleagues diagnosed Wuornos with antisocial personality disorder and borderline personality disorder. They did not, however, support the theory that Wuornos was a sexual sadist or that her crimes were sexually motivated. They said there was no evidence that killing was sexually arousing for her.

Myers' clinical team affirmed that, as someone with psychopathy, Wuornos was emotionally callous, cruelly aggressive, and reactively and instrumentally violent. They also stated that, whereas borderline personality disorder probably did not directly contribute to Wuornos' murders, instability and sexual triggering could have lowered her inhibition. They concluded that disrupted childhood attachments and a series of developmental traumas, coupled with her extreme psychopathy and other mental illnesses, contributed to her committing crimes. Still, they underscored that Wuornos made "behavioral choices."[6]

§

FAKING IT? As seen with John Wayne Gacy and Joseph DeAngelo, and as noted by criminologist Jack Levin,[7] it is entirely possible that serial killers will try to fake mental illness. In psychology, faking mental illness by inventing symptoms is known as "malingering."[8] Levin talked about "Hillside Strangler" Ken Bianchi as an example. With his cousin Angelo Buono Jr., Bianchi raped, tortured, killed, and discarded the bodies of at least 12 women in the late 1970s in Los Angeles.[9] When Bianchi's apartment was searched, police found several books from which he could have learned how to feign mental illness, including multiple personality disorder (now called dissociative identity disorder, or DID). He had the book *Three Faces of Eve*, about a woman with DID. He watched the movie version of *Three Faces of Eve* and the movie *Sybil*, also about a woman with DID, many times.[10] Then, at one point after his arrest, Bianchi claimed multiple personality disorder as his defense. He said he had an alter ego, "Steve," who committed the murders. Bianchi pleaded guilty and was sentenced to life in prison. Buono was also sentenced to life in prison, where he died in 2002.[11]

Jack Levin conveyed that he felt that a manipulative, lying serial killer like Bianchi, with hope of getting a new trial or being released, would "never give up" manipulating victims, the public, law enforcement, prison systems, and criminologists. According to Levin, having power and control over victims, agencies, and even physically over Levin when they shook hands, made Bianchi feel superior.[12] Indeed, a news story in *The Bellingham Herald* in 2019 reported that Bianchi continues to be litigious. He has sued Washington State, the police, a county prosecutor, and the maker of a true crime novelty trading card with his face on it. He was convicted more than 40 years ago and is still filing appeals. One former police detective observed of Bianchi that "he has nothing else to do."[13] Perhaps he engages in these actions to try to have power. It seems that faking mental illness and trying to beat the system are extensions of the desire to take control over a situation.

TRAUMAGENIC PERSPECTIVE

Throughout the serial killer cases highlighted in this book, we see childhood exposure to sexual, physical, and emotional abuse. In cases like those of Wuornos, J. B., and John Wayne Gacy, for example, there was a substantiated, marked history of exposure to physical, emotional, and sexual trauma. Each of these individuals developed probable psychopathy and lethally violent behaviors. They also appeared to know the difference between right and wrong but committed heinous crimes regardless. They demonstrated indifference to negative events. Researchers and clinicians have specifically underscored that the confluence of traumatic experiences and mental health issues likely created violent proclivities in the FSKs they studied.[14] Although not everyone who has traumagenic and clinical issues is violent, and so few have escalated to serial murder, evidence is strong that these factors played a role in many of these cases.

Both Aileen Wuornos and J. B. were raped repeatedly by men. From a clinical-evolutionary perspective, it is plausible that exposure to such egregious violence perpetrated by men altered unconscious drives that ancestral females had to seek male partners with resources. Instead, these victimized women secured resources through victimizing others. Notably, while slender, short-statured, ancestral female hominids pursued male protection and resources for offspring and self-survival over millions of years in the ancestral environment, it is certainly not the viewpoint of evolutionary psychologists that modern women need a man's money, or a male partner, or any partner to survive. Moreover, interpretation from an evolutionary perspective does not condone a behavior. Just as importantly, there is no evidence that childhood events alter one's sexual orientation; Wuornos identified as non-heterosexual.[15]

Maltreatment in childhood, including sexual abuse, increases risk for later life psychopathology. Researchers believe that those who are abused experience epigenetic changes that increase risk for later-life psychological and behavioral issues.[16] ("Epigenetic" refers to a change in gene expression, but not in underlying gene sequence.)[17] Abused or neglected children can experience PTSD, psychosis, and personality disorders. These may manifest due to deficits in emotional understanding, altered sensitivity to threat, and decreased sensitivity to reward.[18] What this tells us is that we must do better in our society to protect children. When we do not, we risk the loss of one and many.

Nearly all the women portrayed in the FSK case studies in this book were victimized, with many instances of childhood sexual abuse (CSA). The same is true of the MSK cases presented. It is possible that these individuals are coping with their own perceived victimization through their crimes.[19] It is also possible that these individuals are lying about their experiences, but we have no compelling reason to doubt them with evidence to the contrary. Indeed, in many cases, interviewing clinicians believed them, or others corroborated their stories. Furthermore, for decades, clinicians have shared the opinion that it is rare for children to lie about being sexually abused.[20] Many children feel reluctant to disclose they have been abused, and up to 70% of victims do not disclose they have been abused until adulthood.[21]

SOCIOCULTURAL PERSPECTIVE

We do not live in a social vacuum. The world around us has a remarkable influence on who we are, how we feel, and what we do. Social, cultural, and historical context are all important to people's learning and development. We are an agent synthesizing a constant bombardment of information from various social forces. (We also, of course, contribute to societal forces.) We start off being dependent on our caregivers, looking to them for provisions and social instruction. We rely on others with more experience. As we grow, we synthesize the influences around us to learn how we ought to behave. Eventually, we take increased responsibility for our own behaviors and decisions.[22] For better or worse, external forces play a major role in our development throughout the life span.

The crimes of serial killers can thus be examined from a sociocultural viewpoint. In fact, researchers have demonstrated statistically that cultural and social factors can play a considerable role in the variations of MSK crimes.[23]

§

Ronald Dominique is a serial killer. Between 1997 and 2006, he killed at least 23 men in rural Louisiana. After eventually being arrested at a homeless shelter on December 1, 2006,[24] he confessed to killing the 23 victims found throughout six parishes in southern Louisiana.[25] Dominique said he could not remember if there were more.[26]

Dominique chose street hustlers and homeless men – people he could easily control – as his victims.[27] Lafayette Police Detective Randy Chesnut said that Dominique's victims "tended to be people who lived on the fringe."[28] Dominique's crimes were not impulsive. They were carefully planned and ritualistic – he killed for sex, power, and control. He tied up his victims, had sex with them, and strangled them to death with an extension cord. He kept his victims' urine as a trophy.[29] Other reports indicated that many victims were found without their shoes,[30] which he may have kept as trophies or to sell.

Sociologist Craig Forsyth, a crime mitigation expert, presented Ronald Dominique's case through a sociocultural lens. Although Dominique was loved by his family and friends, several factors stood out about his sociocultural development. Born in 1964, he once saw his mother having sex with her own brother while she was still married to Dominique's father. Forsyth asserted that this destroyed sexual boundaries for Dominique. Then, when Dominique sang in his high school's glee club, he reported – and former classmates corroborated – that he was ridiculed and bullied for being gay despite not being out of the closet. Because of this bullying, he found it difficult to go to school. He remained angry about this fact into his adulthood.[31]

When he got older, Dominique developed a heart condition and mobility issues. He was short in stature (about five feet five inches[32]), overweight, and used a cane to walk. He did not appear physically imposing. He also struggled with money, although he was helpful to his neighbors in the trailer park where he lived. They described him as generous.

At night, however, he seemed to take on a different persona. He performed drag at a local gay bar,[33] although reports indicated he was not liked very much on the gay scene. People even made fun of him for riding a motorized bike, calling him "Miss Moped." "To me, he seemed like an OK guy," said a man who knew him from a local gay bar. "But you could tell he was a little off. You could tell that there was definitely something different about him."[34]

Dominique was reported to have been involved in two rapes prior to becoming a serial killer. In 1993, he allegedly raped a homeless man who had a crack (drug) habit and history of mental illness. The police in the town where the crime was committed did not pursue charges. However, a second victim came to the same police in 1996, sharing a similar story and accusing Dominique of rape. Dominique was charged with aggravated rape in 1996 and went to prison on a reduced charge. While in prison, Dominique himself was raped "so brutally that his rectum was ripped."[35] He was released on November 7, 1996.

Dominique's first murder victim, 19-year-old David Mitchell, was found in a canal on July 14, 1997.[36] Craig Forsyth assessed that the trigger for Dominique becoming a serial killer was that the second rape victim had reported him to the police, and Dominique went to prison and was raped himself as a result. When he was released from prison, he subsequently asphyxiated the men he raped so they would not tell.[37]

Dominique killed people who had even less power than he did: men who lived a "high-risk lifestyle"[38] and who lived in or hung around low-budget motels known for drugs and prostitution. Police Captain Dawn Foret, who worked the case for two years, told reporters, "The majority of victims lived a transient lifestyle, a lot of them were homeless and involved in illegal drug activity."[39]

For sentencing purposes, the court hears arguments about mitigating circumstances which might include "a life which predisposed him or her to the crime."[40] When Craig Forsyth interviewed Dominique and investigated his background, a clear picture emerged of sociocultural turmoil. Despite being loved by family and friends, Dominique was exposed to incest, experienced poverty, was bullied about his sexual orientation, had poor health, consistently felt powerless in his dealings with people and institutions, and was raped.[41]

Dominique did not receive the death penalty. Instead, he pleaded guilty and is serving eight life sentences for murder.[42] Victim Chris Cunningham's brother Kurt said to Dominique, "I hope hell finds you fast."[43] Dominique is serving his sentences in the Louisiana State Penitentiary at Angola.

No one is looking to excuse serial murder. In Dominique's case, he sadistically murdered at least 23 vulnerable people who had trusted him enough to enter a sexual arrangement with him. What we can do as psychologists and criminologists is examine the many factors and levels of influence that may have pushed Dominique and other serial murderers down an aberrant path. Again, this does not excuse the behavior.

Sociocultural theorists contend that we must view behavior and mental processes as a product of how the self takes in information and responds to the world around us. Classic theory from Lev Vygotsky[44] stressed the importance of sociocultural and historical factors affecting human development. Likewise, Urie Bronfenbrenner[45] stressed the importance of complex interactions of ecological forces in human development. Dominique's sociocultural experiences were profound, disruptive forces in his life. Craig Forsyth asserted that, much like the dueling literary characters Jekyll and Hyde occupying the same person, Dominique was caught in between two different identities – the generous community member and the murderer.[46] Although I am not diagnosing anyone, Dominique's symptoms and dual identity are similar to what is observed in people diagnosed with psychopathy. And, of course, understanding Dominique's backstory does not diminish the agony the victims and their families suffered.

§

THE POWER OF THE MEDIA. While a component of sociocultural influence, it is worth elaborating specifically on the influence of the mass media. The media have the power to engage and terrify an audience,[47] but do they have the power to inspire crime? We might ask ourselves, what if culture – particularly the media – inspires serial murder? Evidence on this point is controversial,[48] but many studies over the years have suggested that exposure to media violence triggers aggression and crime. Such studies also suggest that the media provide information on the means of executing a crime and can therefore inspire similar styles of crime (i.e., "copycats"). In a 2020 analysis of more than 32,000 cases of homicide, political scientists Viridiana Rios and Christopher Ferguson[49] found support for the "copycat" theory in that media coverage influenced the probability of other criminals using similar techniques. However, they did not find support for the "trigger" theory – that is, they found no evidence that media coverage changes overall homicide rates.

Do these findings generalize to serial homicide? It is possible. Although I have not found empirical research speaking to this point (I have only seen analyses of copycat serial killers in fiction[50]), data do show that the media overemphasize atypical cases of violence and homicide.[51] Although he geared commentary towards coverage of mass murder in the media, researcher Grant Duwe's exploration of "body-count" journalism suggests that the media tend to "maximize the size of their audience and therefore their profits by catering to the public's fascination with rare and sensational acts of violence."[52] His theory can encompass media coverage of serial murder, as well. Serial murderers have a demonstrable cultural impact in the USA,[53] and the media seem to sensationalize and even come close to celebrating serial murder (e.g., murderabilia). It may be the case that some serial killers commit their crimes in the pursuit of this notoriety.

In 2016, sociologist Julie Wiest[54] conducted an analysis of how the USA and United Kingdom (UK) media portray serial murderers. She found that UK media sources portray serial killers as traditional monsters, or "savage, nameless animals that prowl neighborhoods and prey on innocent victims."[55] Furthermore, UK media sources highlight the victims of serial killers' crimes, placing lesser importance on the perpetrator. In the USA, however, serial murderers are portrayed as "fantastic monsters," having high intelligence, predation skills, and, arguably, celebrity status. Moreover, the media focus almost entirely on the perpetrator, largely ignoring the victims. Wiest connected her findings to the sentiments of author David Schmid who labeled being a serial killer in America as a form of modern celebrity.[56]

Take, for example, the murder trial of MSK Ted Bundy in 1979. One young woman told reporter Dan Sewell, "I don't know what it is he has, but he's fascinating. He's impressive. He just has a kind of magnetism."[57] Under the headline "All-American Boy on Trial," *The New York Times* reported on Ted Bundy's "hair and blue eyes, looking rather Kennedy-esque, dressed in a beige turtleneck and dark blue blazer, a smile turning the corners of his lean all-American face."[58] The article made him sound like a romantic hero or movie star rather than a serial killer who raped and killed dozens of women, including a 12-year-old junior high school student. In 2019, journalist Katie Dowd appropriately trashed Bundy's mythological image. As she put it, "Bundy was not special. He was not a genius. He was a pathetic misogynist so wounded by rejection he killed young women to feel powerful." She pondered, "Who benefits from humanizing any bit of this monster's life?"[59]

Certainly, many criminals become celebrities.[60] Yet, as criminologist Yvonne Jewkes and sociologist Travis Linneman underscored in their 2018 book, *Media and Crime in the US*, people in the USA "have a relentless fascination with serial killers."[61] Serial murder researchers Holmes and Holmes[62] reflected the notion that many serial murderers have become "societal icons," including David Berkowitz ("Son of Sam"), Ted Bundy, John Wayne Gacy ("Killer Clown"), Wayne Williams ("Atlanta Child Murders"), Gary Ridgway ("The Green River Killer") and Dennis Rader ("BTK"/"Bind, Torture, Kill"). Notably, there are no FSKs on this list. It seems only FSK Aileen Wuornos may have approximated this infamy among female serial murderers in the USA. Perhaps, as I suggested earlier, there is a brutality threshold for gaining public recognition as a serial murderer. It is also possible that the United States has a qualitatively different perception of serial murder compared to other countries, including being less willing to believe in women's hostility and culpability. In England, for example, it seems that everyone knows who Myra Hindley is. In the 1960s, she partnered with Ian Brady to commit the Moors Murders, which included the sexual abuse and murder of five children in the Manchester area.[63]

There have, in fact, been serial murder cases in which the perpetrator follows coverage of their own crimes in the media. Ed Gein saved newspaper clippings of missing people and later confessed to two murders of missing women whose bodies were found in his home.[64] "The Zodiac Killer," still at large, actually used area newspapers as part of his crimes. Thought to have killed more than 12 people in San Francisco, California, and beyond, he created and cut a cryptogram puzzle into three pieces and sent each piece to a different newspaper after he murdered a victim. The puzzles were Zodiac (i.e., astrologically) -themed, and detailed the killings. Zodiac challenged police, media, and the public to figure out his identity. According to police, "He liked publicity."[65] After more than

50 years, police and amateur sleuths are still trying to solve the case by breaking Zodiac's code.[66]

§

Dennis Rader is a serial killer. Known as the "BTK Strangler" ("Bind, Torture, Kill"), a nickname he gave himself, Rader used the media to assert his power and publicize his reign of terror over Wichita, Kansas, beginning in the 1970s. He killed at least 10 people, beginning in 1974 with the strangulation of Julie and Joseph Otero and two of their children, Josephine and Joseph Jr. When being arraigned on charges some 30 years later in 2005, Rader told the court that he entered the Otero home through the back door, cut the family's telephone lines (people typically had wired land lines then), and waited for them to return home. He strangled the Oteros with plastic bags and rope around their necks. He took 11-year-old Josephine to the basement. According to Rader, she asked, "What is going to happen to me?" He told her, "Well, honey, you're going to be in heaven with the rest of your family." Then he hanged the girl from a pipe and masturbated.[67] Police found Josephine's body partially clothed. Rader later told Kansas Bureau of Investigation (KBI) special agent Raymond Lundin that he targeted Josephine because he liked the dark eyes, hair, and skin of people who are "Hispanic."[68]

Standing before the court, Rader told Sedgwick County District Judge Greg Waller, "I had some sexual fantasies. That was after she [Josephine] was hung." When time allowed, Rader would pose victims' bodies in bondage positions, take photographs, and masturbate. Semen was found at scenes, although authorities did not report finding evidence of sexual assault of living victims. Rader sometimes stole victims' underpants and later wore them himself to reenact the thrill of killing.[69]

Rader communicated with Police Chief Richard LaMunyon, and the world, through the media. In the late 1970s, various media outlets would receive letters from an author who claimed to have committed unsolved murders.[70] Authorities say that Rader first put a letter about his crimes against the Otero family inside a book in the Wichita Public Library. Subsequently, he sent the media letters, poems, and even drawings, taunting them about his past murders and his plans for future ones.[71] In 1974,

Rader used the initials "BTK" in a poem about victim Shirley Vian, which he sent to *The Wichita Eagle and Beacon*.[72] He sent another letter to television station KAKE-TV in 1978, calling attention to a lack of current media coverage of his crimes. "A little paragraph in the newspaper would have been enough," the letter said. According to Chief LaMunyon, BTK appeared to be seeking recognition. Authorities confirmed that Rader checked news reports for coverage of his crimes.

In February 1978, newspapers reported receiving another letter from BTK. This time, he provided enough details about an unsolved murder for police to tie him to the slaying of 20-year-old Kathy Bright, who was murdered in April 1974. The story appeared on page 8 of *The Manhattan Mercury*, a local Kansas newspaper.[73] Another story about BTK, appearing in *The Wichita Beacon* in February 1978, ran on page 42.[74] One wonders how much it bothered Rader that he was no longer a front-page story.

On the 30-year anniversary of his first murders, a newspaper ran a story theorizing that BTK was dead. This apparently did not sit well with the attention-seeking Rader, who sent new letters to the media and left strange packages of details around Wichita. In March 2004, *The Wichita Eagle* received a package from BTK containing crime scene photos of the 1986 murder of Vicki Wegerle. In December 2004, a letter from BTK was found in Murdock Park containing victim Nancy Fox's driver's license.[75] Over time, claimed Chief LaMunyon, the tenor of BTK's letters to the media changed. His early messages contained anger and hurt. He wanted to make a name for himself. Rader suggested the *nom de guerre* "BTK," which stuck. His later messages, however, largely took the form of puzzles, seemingly geared at getting himself caught. These messages included an anagram of letters spelling "D RADER," as well as his house address number 6220.[76]

Years later, Rader was still using the media to his advantage – or so he thought. He asked the police to place a classified ad in a local newspaper, verifying that he could communicate with them by sending a computer floppy disk. "Be honest," he urged them. Per Rader's instructions, the police placed an ad that said, "Rex, it will be OK." Rader then sent a computer disk to a local television station containing information about clues to crimes. However, unbeknownst to him, the disk contained metadata that investigators traced to Christ Lutheran Church, where Rader

10.1 "BTK Strangler" Dennis Rader being escorted into the El Dorado Correctional Facility in 2005. Rader sent clues of his crimes to the media and police. (Photo by Jeff Tuttle-Pool/Getty Images)

was the congregation council president. The computer log revealed that "Dennis" was the last user.[77] Rader later said, "The floppy did me in."[78]

In addition, police had DNA samples that connected him to the murders. While the science did not exist in the 1970s and 1980s to solve the case, it did in 2005, and law enforcement had had the foresight to preserve their evidence.[79] Rader's daughter Kerri had recently had medical tests, and without her knowledge, authorities secured a court order to obtain a sample of her DNA from laboratory specimens for comparison. Kerri's DNA showed a 90% match to that found at BTK crime scenes.[80]

On February 25, 2005, police arrested Dennis Rader for crimes committed from 1974 to 1991. The pastor of Christ Lutheran Church was so stunned that Rader was under arrest, police had to repeat what they were telling him a few times.[81] One can only guess how the pastor processed the news that Rader, after strangling Marine Hedge, had put her body in the trunk of his car, driven her to the church, posed her body on the altar, and taken photographs.[82]

According to FBI agent Gregg McCrary and Chief LaMunyon, the BTK killer might never have been caught had Rader not opted to interact with the media again. Lieutenant Ken Landwehr, who headed the multiagency taskforce charged with catching BTK, affirmed, "Him sending that disk is what cracked the case. If he had just quit and kept his mouth shut, we might never have connected the dots."[83] Gregg McCrary, a retired FBI profiler, told *NBC News*, "Once he raised his head again and started gaming again, taunting the police . . . [it] breeds new life into this case."[84]

At his sentencing, Rader made a statement that, as noted by criminologist Jacqueline Helfgott,[85] seemed more like a press conference. He stated that he had many things in common with the victims, such as gardening, liking dogs, and writing poetry. He also alarmingly proclaimed that one of his young victims reminded him of his own children. This event, albeit bizarre, certainly fit in with Rader's attention-demanding modus operandi. At the end of his speech, he was sentenced to prison for ten counts of first-degree murder. He will be eligible for release in 2180, at age 235.[86]

Experts contend that Rader's characteristics are in line with those seen in psychopaths. Reflecting Hervey Cleckley's "mask of sanity," Rader was a contributing member of his community and church on one hand, while perpetrating vicious murders on the other. In fact, serial homicide researcher and expert Jack Levin said that Rader was "extraordinarily ordinary."[87] At the same time, as former FBI profiler Clint Van Zandt told *NBC News*, Rader is "someone who has no conscience, no guilt, someone who takes no responsibility for his actions."[88] A Wichita psychologist who worked with police on Rader's case, Howard Brodsky, said that during his hearings Rader had "a striking lack of remorse and emotionality. That's the keynote of a sociopath." He added, "This guy was an aberration."[89]

In an interview for *WebMD*, Jack Levin underscored how sexual serial killers have a pronounced need for control and power, and that victims' suffering makes them feel important.[90] Rader was sexually sadistically motivated by violent, misogynistic fantasies. He almost always targeted women, whom he would choke nearly to death, allow to regain consciousness, then choke again, gaining a thrill and a sense of power from his victims' suffering. When they were dead, he would sometimes masturbate into their underpants, with sadistic fantasies fueling his sexual gratification.[91] Of sexually sadistic killers like Rader, criminologist Jennifer Murray said they are "engrossed in a disturbing fantasy world of compulsive fixation on the absolute control over, objectification of, and the infliction of pain onto the victim."[92] Exerting his power through sexual dominance, assault, violence, and murder, Rader terrorized Wichita residents for decades before he was caught.

In 2005, psychologist Howard Brodsky said that Rader "wants to make himself interesting. He's very interested in his legacy, the books and movies that will follow."[93] Many years later, Brodsky remains correct in that Rader is still interested in his legacy. Rader still tries to garner media attention, and in 2017 told *The Wichita Eagle* that he was concerned about what will happen to his remains after he dies. He told the reporter, Roy Wenzl, that he wondered if his family would like to have his possessions when he passes. "I did write Kerri and ask her and the family if they would like my left-over art, poetry, papers, logbooks, journal, etc." Daughter Kerri Rader Rawson groaned as she told Wenzl that the family does not want his belongings, nor does she want them sold, which could cause more harm to his victims.[94] Rawson told a CrimeCon crowd in 2021 that she was disgusted by murderabilia, and she was particularly disturbed to learn that her father was autographing BTK crime scene photos and that these were desirable among collectors.[95]

§

In all my years of research, I have seen no cases in which FSKs taunt police and engage with the media as MSKs have. Further, I have seen no cases in which FSKs have retained copies of newspaper coverage of their crimes. Why might this be? One reason could be that there is no such coverage. Solo FSKs do not typically leave a string of grisly crime scenes behind, and thus do not fuel media and morbid imaginations in quite the same way.

FEMINIST PERSPECTIVE. In the course of my research, I have been intrigued by the question of whether my work could be considered "feminist." I endeavor to demonstrate that women are just as capable of serial murder as are men. Women might account for a small proportion of all serial murderers, but when they do kill, they poison, smother, beat, shoot, and drown babies, old people, and sick people. These crimes are just as deadly as those committed by men. It also may be the case that women commit many more serial murders and just do not get caught as frequently as men do. To begin with, we know that murder does not fit a gender stereotype for women. Additionally, a death might not appear as a murder when poison is used – FSKs' most commonly used means. They might just get away with it. Of course, this concept could never be tested, but it is a possibility.

Psychologist Amanda Farrell and her team[96] also offered some feminist perspective on FSKs. They pointed out that female serial murderers can be thought of as being in revolt against patriarchal society. FSKs target male spouses, children, and those in their care, perhaps as a rebellion against the traditional maternal role. Still, FSKs also target parents, siblings, aunts, and cousins, and those who simply get in their way. We can therefore see aggression beyond the confines of relational roles. In fact, FSKs most frequently target both male and female victims, and the endgame of death is typically more important than the players eliminated. Stated another way, FSKs typically kill people as a part of their plan to gain money or power, but whom they kill, as well as the dying process itself, seem less important. Think of Dorothea Puente, who killed tenants. She was a landlady who posed as a caregiver, but she poisoned and smothered disabled and underprivileged tenants for their government benefit checks. Her goal was profit; there is no evidence she had a personal issue with any of the victims.

On the other hand, there were indeed FSKs who murdered people because of who and what they were. Patty Cannon murdered a known slave trader and was reported to be proud of doing it. Jane Toppan killed landlords and her foster sister, people who held power over her in one form or another. Aileen Wuornos said she killed predatory men as a favor to society. As women's roles continue to change economically, politically, and socially, we can see if trends in FSK murders change.

PSYCHOSOCIAL FORCES: IN SUM

To summarize, researchers and authors have underscored that "structure and agency come together to create opportunity" for murder. To understand serial murder committed by women or men more fully, we certainly should examine the perpetrator's perceptions and cognitions, and consider how their experiences, particularly those that are trauma-genic, shaped their way of viewing and reacting to the world. We should also examine the roles of the family, economy, religion, and education in their lives.[97] Further, more broadly, we should examine the historical and cultural contexts of murder.[98] Serial killers do not develop and exist in a vacuum.

THE EFFECTS OF SERIAL KILLERS: VICTIMS AND BEYOND

Indeed, the crimes of serial murderers do not exist in a vacuum, either. In this chapter on suspected psychosocial influences *on* serial murderers, I wanted to validate the psychosocial influences *of* serial murderers. Victims' families, their friends, and their communities are affected profoundly and permanently by these murders. First, let me again underscore the sheer terror that the victims must have experienced in their final moments.

In this book, I have described the cruel murders of innocent people of all ages and genders. For example, prosecutors say FSK Kristen Gilbert injected hospitalized veterans with epinephrine, inducing cardiac arrest. The VA hospital where she worked could not account for nearly two-thirds of the epinephrine dispensed to Ward C during the time of her killings. An epinephrine injection would explain the fatal heart attack suffered by 72-year-old Francis Marier on December 20, 1995. Sources say Gilbert wanted to leave early on December 20, and when her request was denied, she took out her frustrations on Marier. Marier was more than a victim. He was a hero: a World War II veteran who, on D-Day in 1944, invaded Normandy with Allied forces.[99] We must also remember that, in addition to health issues, veterans already experience a high prevalence of posttraumatic stress disorder (PTSD), feelings of social isolation, and other major psychological issues.[100] Francis Marier, and all the victims, deserved so much better.

It is also difficult to imagine what victims' families and friends endure. Loved ones of murder victims are shaken, angry, confused, anxious, and feel as if their world has been turned upside down. They often wonder how they will go on living, and how what happened will forever change their life narrative.[101] Although not focusing on serial murder victims' families per se, psychologists Jennifer Connolly and Ronit Gordon reviewed years of research into the consequences of murder for victims' loved ones, experiences called being a "co-victim" or "survivor" of murder. In addition to their profound grief, families feel marked distress, including posttraumatic stress disorder (PTSD), anxiety, and depression. Families experience crisis at school, work, in their social lives, and among themselves. They cannot focus. They avoid gatherings, feel alienated, and friends may even avoid them, perhaps out of not knowing how to act with someone who experienced a traumatic loss.[102] In losing a loved one tragically, it seems one loses a part of oneself.

FSK Dana Sue Gray, an unemployed nurse, murdered elderly women in California in the mid-1990s. She stole their credit cards and went on shopping sprees. June Elizabeth Roberts, whom Gray knew socially, had just turned 66 years old in 1994. Loved ones were very worried, because they could not get in contact with her to wish her "happy birthday." So, they checked in on her in her home, only to find her dead in a pool of her own blood. Gray strangled Roberts with a telephone cord and bludgeoned her to death. Similarly, Dora Beebe was 87 years old when Gray struck her in the head multiple times with a clothing iron and strangled her with a telephone cord. These women were brutalized in their last moments. Gray stole elderly women's credit cards and bought perfume, shoes, sneakers, cowboy boots, and vodka. Family and friends listened in horror as details were discussed at Gray's trial.[103] Gray's victims suffered unimaginable trauma before they died, and it is difficult to imagine the trauma loved ones experienced when finding their loved one dead and the pain as they learned the gruesome details of these murders.

Gray was sentenced to life in prison for her crimes, but she makes money from selling her autographed underpants and her sketches, including a drawing of a butterfly and a skeleton.[104] Serial murder victims' families report that such commodification of murder compounds their hurt.[105]

FSK nursing assistant Reta Mays murdered infirm disabled veterans on her shifts from 2017 to 2018 at the Louis A. Johnson VA Medical Center in West Virginia. (I will discuss her case in more detail later.) The families of the victims of Reta Mays were grief-stricken and angry. They felt confused and betrayed, as Mays had spent time talking to and comforting these families as they visited their loved ones at the VA Medical Center. Robert Edge Jr. is the son of victim Robert Edge Sr., who was killed by Mays. Edge Jr. emphasized the pain Mays caused his family. By killing Edge Sr., Reta Mays had taken away a beloved father, grandfather, and great-grandfather. Robert Jr. said to Mays, "I do not forgive you. I would punish you with my own hands if it would do any good. I want you to experience what death feels like." Mays' victim Archie Edgell was married for more than 60 years. His wife, Frances, died about a year after he did. Her family believes she died from a broken heart.[106]

Families were present when Reta Mays was sentenced to seven life sentences, but certainly, as stated by Acting US Attorney Randolph J. Bernard, "No amount of prison time will erase the pain and loss that the families of these brave and honorable men have experienced."[107] Families stress that those who are murdered should not be solely remembered as victims. Of her father-in law who was killed by Mays, Amanda Edgell stressed that Archie Edgell "is not defined by how he died."[108]

Darla Sue Scott's family stressed that she was more than the victim of MSK Robert Yates. Scott's family members were seen wearing shirts with her picture on it, captioned, "Mommy," "Niece," and "Honey." Sunny Gale Oster was also more than a victim of Yates. Her family stressed that she was a beloved daughter and mother. The last thing Oster's stepmother said to her was, "Be careful, Sunny Gale. I love you." Sunny Gale said, "I love you, too."[109]

Psychologists argue it can be incomprehensible for family members to process that a loved one has been murdered. MSK Robert Yates murdered Melody Murfin and buried her in his own backyard. When addressing the court during Yates' trail, Murfin's two daughters asked, "How could you do that to us?" In court, victims' relatives called Yates a "sick monster."[110]

Victims' families show emotions ranging from anger to anguish. In the case of MSK Joe DeAngelo, Patti Cosper, whose mother was raped by DeAngelo, read to the court a victim impact statement on behalf of her mother, and then threw DeAngelo the middle finger.[111] Victim Katie Maggiore's brother also read an impact statement. DeAngelo shot and killed Katie and Brian Maggiore in 1978 while they were walking their dog. DeAngelo had shot Katie, who just turned 20 years old, in the head. Her brother stressed, "He had no idea how much Katie and Brian were loved."[112]

In some cases, families get no closure. John Wayne Gacy kidnapped, sexually assaulted, and brutally murdered 33 young men, defiled and discarded their bodies in his dirt crawl space, and left them decomposing. In the Gacy case, some families of missing young men only suspected their relative was a Gacy victim, but never received a positive identification. Other families have questioned the accuracy of identification of victim remains. For example, DNA evidence presented by victim Michael Marino's mother, Sherry, showed that the body identified as Michael's by the Gacy investigation team, and buried by Sherry and her family, could not be biologically related to her. According to her attorney, "This leaves Sherry with more questions than answers."[113] Research evidence consistently shows profound psychological pain for those like Sherry whose loved ones are missing, including enduring grief, PTSD, depression, and anxiety.[114]

The families of MSK Ronald Dominique's victims were also denied closure. It was extremely difficult to identify the bodies of victims left in bayous, garbage bins, and sugarcane fields in and around several Louisiana parishes, as some were eaten by rodents, and some decomposed after spending months exposed to the elements. Victim Wayne Smith's mother Angela said in court, "I really don't know if my child is dead or not because I did not get a chance to see my baby."[115]

Some families report feeling a little relief when the perpetrator is removed from society, never to hurt another person. Christine Duquette's brother, Henry Hudon, was murdered by Kristen Gilbert. Duquette wanted Gilbert to get the death penalty. However, Duquette appreciated that Gilbert's four life sentences would keep her away from the world forever. In her own grief, Duquette did not want others to meet the same terrible fate that her brother did.[116]

How about the people who helped catch serial killers? These murders also profoundly distress investigators. The sheriff investigating Ed Gein's grizzly house of victim remains ran to the sink to vomit, but he found Bernice Worden's decapitated head there. Her body was found hanging elsewhere by her heels. The sheriff had to run outside to compose himself.[117] One cannot fathom processing the imagery of Gein's house in person, with furniture upholstered with human skin, clothing made of human skin, skulls as dinnerware, and heads in plastic bags. Newspapers reported that no one wanted to stay very long in Gein's house.[118]

Officials had a similar reaction to John Wayne Gacy's murders. According to the *Chicago Tribune*, Cook County State Attorney Bernard Carey said that John Wayne Gacy's case was "one of the most horrendous I have ever had anything to do with."[119] Judge Louis Garippo quit right after sentencing Gacy to death.[120] Psychologists and criminologists argue that investigators of homicide feel pressure to solve cases and experience intrusive, unwanted thoughts about their cases. Investigators of murder are routinely distressed.[121]

What about people who assisted a serial killer investigation? Kim Byers put her film development receipt in her friend Rob Piest's winter coat pocket. The receipt was found in John Wayne Gacy's house and was an important key in linking Gacy to Rob's murder and the other crimes Gacy committed. Journalist Courtney Lund O'Neill is Kim Byers-Lund's daughter. In *Harper's Bazaar* in 2018, O'Neill told the story of her mother's involvement in the Gacy case. Kim, who became a physician and later a Lieutenant Colonel in the US Army Reserves, would be forever affected by these horrific murders, as was Courtney. Gacy was their "bogeyman." Byers-Lund said she was grateful for the feeling that prompted her to take that receipt out of the trash and save it. Through counseling, she came to feel that she and the spirit of her friend Rob Piest had somehow worked as a team "to stop the cycle of evil."[122]

Both Byers-Lund and O'Neill expressed the wish that society would tune in more to murder victims, such as Rob Piest, and pay less attention to the "monsters" who take their lives.[123] It is interesting that Byers-Lund, traumatized by the loss of her friend and her involvement in the notorious Gacy murder case, became a physician, a career involving healing.

How about the families of serial killers? John Wayne Gacy's family was in shock. His sister said, "I just can't believe it!" and continued, "We were an extremely close-knit family. We still are." On the last time she and Gacy saw each other, she said, "He was fine, the same as he always was."[124] Jerome Brudos' wife Ralphene was accused of helping him murder Karen

Sprinkler, but she was tried and found not guilty. Ralphene changed her name and never let Jerome Brudos see their children again.[125] Robert Yates' daughter Sasha was also in shock, exclaiming "What they went through – these families? How they feel about us? How much they probably hate us?"[126] In some instances, families of murderers may even face anger and blame for how their loved ones "turned out."[127] It is noteworthy that serial killers' families feel dismay, stigma, and uncertainty as to how and when to interact with others.

Dennis Rader's daughter Kerri Rawson authored a book about her experiences coming to terms with the fact that her father was BTK, one of the most notorious serial killers in American history: *A Serial Killer's Daughter: My Story of Faith, Love, and Overcoming.* In the book, she stated, "I struggled to comprehend the fact that the first twenty-six years of my life had been a lie. My father was not the man I'd known him to be." She added, "I wrestled with shame, guilt, anger, and hatred."[128] She told *The Wichita Eagle,* "I don't know of anyone who has a father like mine."[129]

Previously, Kerri had only known Dennis as a loving father, a Boy Scout troup leader, an Air Force veteran, and a man involved in his church. Kerri Rader Rawson did observe, however, that, at times "he could be very firm or have flashes of anger or outbursts that you weren't expecting."[130] Rawson said, "When your father is the BTK serial killer, forgiveness is not tidy."[131]

Still, when your family was brutally murdered by BTK, forgiveness is not forthcoming. Jeff Davis' mother was the kind and loving Dolores "Dee" Davis. She was Dennis Rader's final victim. Davis said he has no issue with Kerry Rawson writing about her father's (BTK's) crimes. However, he added, "Every time they [the media] shine the light on her, then part of that light, in his mind, shines on that little cockroach that masquerades as her father."

During Rader's trial, victims' families had to hear all the gruesome details of his crimes, and his photographs, drawings, and other souvenirs of his crimes.[132] At Rader's prison sentencing, Jeff called Rader "social sewage." He said, "My mother had been a beautiful person inside and out, and she's disregarded like a bag of garbage."[133] Davis stared at Rader while his sister, Dolores' daughter Laurel Keating, read a victim impact statement that included, "Remember that no one so evil should ever be able allowed to hold control over others."[134] Jeff Davis told the press, "He just nauseates me." Later, Davis said of his mother, "She was very, very special, with her modesty and grace and sincerity." He added, "She definitely was a person you didn't forget."[135]

BTK victim Nancy Fox's sister, Beverly Plapp, told reporters that she has emotional scars that will never heal from her sister's murder. She said, "As far as I'm concerned, Dennis Rader does not deserve to live. I want him to suffer as much as he made his victims suffer."[136] At sentencing, Plapp said, "This man needs to be thrown in a deep, dark hole and left to rot." She urged the court that Rader should "never, ever see the light of day . . . On the day he dies, Nancy and all of his victims will be waiting with God and watching him as he burns in hell."[137]

Charlie Otero was 15 at the time his parents and siblings were murdered by BTK. His brother Danny and sister Carmen arrived home from school a few minutes earlier and found his parents dead. Carmen was 13 years old when she cut the binding off the face of her mother, who was already dead. Because their phone was dead, the children ran to the neighbors to call the police. The Otero children told the police they were waiting for their other two siblings to arrive home from school. Police found those siblings murdered in the home. The surviving Otero children, now adults, watched in tears when crime photos were shown at Dennis Rader's trial.[138]

Charlie Otero said his whole life changed on that terrible day. Decades after his family was decimated by BTK, Charlie said that he could literally smell fear based on his horrible experience. He told reporters, "People exude a smell when they are really scared." He does, however, remember his family fondly. Charlie Otero said that with Rader behind bars, he was working on healing. "If there's a heaven, I want my mom and dad to look down and be proud," he says. "I want my family to know I'm going to make it."[139]

Communities are markedly affected by serial murder, too. Sources say that Wichita, Kansas, where BTK terrorized the community for decades, changed forever. After Dennis Rader was sentenced to prison, *The Wichita Eagle* said, pointedly, that it "is not really about where Rader goes from here. It's where we go from here."[140]

The victims of serial murderers must have experienced dread and pain in their final moments, and trauma from these crimes reaches beyond the victims to their families, friends, and even entire cities. Still, we hope that we can also ultimately see resilience[141] in those whose lives have been violated by the murders of their loved ones.

CHAPTER 11

Evolutionary and Converging
Perspectives of Serial Murder

EVOLUTIONARY PSYCHOLOGY is a subdivision of behavioral neuroscience. However, as an evolutionary psychologist, I wanted to devote special attention to the psychological viewpoint that influenced my decision to pursue research on the motives of FSKs and sex differences between the crimes of FSKs and MSKs. From the first Evolutionary Psychology course I took in college with Professor Gordon G. Gallup Jr. at the University at Albany, State University of New York, in the 1990s, I was hooked on this approach to studying behavior and mental processes. In fact, I was fortunate to stay at "UAlbany" for graduate study under Dr. Gallup's mentoring.

Of course, to me, all behavior and mental processes have evolutionary influences. Even with the first project on serial murder I undertook with colleagues,[1] I anticipated collecting an array of interesting data describing backgrounds, crimes, and motives of FSKs, but I also knew there would be opportunity to attempt to understand these FSK characteristics through their evolutionary underpinnings.

FEMALE SERIAL KILLERS MURDER FOR MONEY,
MALE SERIAL KILLERS MURDER FOR SEX

As I mentioned in Chapter 6, genesmanship[2] is an unconscious, evolved priority in all organisms. Our genes compel us to behave in ways that maximize our likelihood of leaving descendants and that can perpetuate our genes into subsequent generations. Ancestral persons who engaged in genetically mediated adaptive behavior left more descendants than those who did not, thereby altering the gene pool. Human sexual

psychology follows this premise. In his classic Parental Investment Theory, Robert Trivers[3] underscored the evolution of fundamental reproductive differences between women and men. He described how evolved
psychological mechanisms serve sex-specific interests in terms of maximizing reproductive fitness.

With males producing millions of sperm daily and being fertile from
puberty throughout the life span, seeking sex frequently with more
female partners increases the chance of insemination and reproduction.
I am not saying modern men have a free Darwinian ticket to be promis-
cuous. In the ancestral environment, males who sought sex more would
have left more descendants.[4] To this day, when compared to women,
men still want more frequent sex, increased partner variety, greater sex
act variation, more one-night stands, and will consent to sex sooner in a
given situation.[5] Men evolved to place a premium on sex.

In contrast, women are born with a few hundred thousand eggs and
will ovulate only a few hundred eggs in their lifetimes, beginning at
puberty and ceasing at menopause. Pregnant women experience a profound, obligatory parental investment, with pregnancy, childbirth, lac-
tation, and child-rearing. With such a limited reproductive opportunity
compared to males, females in the ancestral environment would have to
be choosy about the man they selected to impregnate them.[6] Moreover,
ancestral hominid females were smaller and more slender than hominid
males,[7] so females would have increased the chances of survival for themselves and their offspring by partnering with a male who had formidable status and resources to invest in the relationship and child-rearing.[8]
Even today, women around the world prefer mates with high status and
resources.[9] Women evolved to place a premium on resources. I am not
saying modern women need any partner. I am saying that over millions
of years of human evolution, ancestral females were probably better off
if they did have a partner.

When my team and I first began our research on FSKs, we observed
that financial profit was a primary motivator for FSK homicides.[10]
This corroborates the findings of other FSK researchers and teams,
although there is a limited body of existing work. It also fits the notion
of women's ancestral tendency to strive for resources. While murder is
obviously always horrific, the underlying drive to secure resources for

survival is nonetheless there. For example, Belle Gunness killed her husbands for insurance money and unsuspecting suitors for the contents of their bank accounts. Lydia Sherman killed children who used up "her" resources. I then took note of existing research documenting the predominantly sexual nature of MSK crimes and explored what it might tell us from an evolutionary perspective. While it is reproductively meaningless to kill a partner before or after sex, the sex drive is clearly there.

In 2019, my team and I gathered data and directly, empirically examined and compared the nature of FSK and MSK crimes to determine whether and how the data fit with Trivers' "parental investment theory." Our predictions were supported.[11] What we found aligned with evolutionary theory:

- MSKs have low access to resources, as evidenced by their low socioeconomic status. They are therefore less likely than other men to enjoy mate success in a normal way, as women worldwide prefer men with resources.
- MSKs' most common motive was sexual, and MSKs had a sexual motive far more frequently than FSKs.
- FSKs' most common motive for killing was profit, and FSKs had a profit motive far more frequently compared to men.[12]

In fact, the most common motive of FSKs has stayed persistent over time. Delving back into unpublished data from my team's original FSK study, it appears that the primary motive for FSKs was financial in the 1800s, 1900s, and 2000s, with no statistical difference between centuries.[13] This evidence suggests that FSKs' pathological drive for resources (i.e., greed) is timeless.[14]

FEMALE SERIAL KILLERS GATHER, MALE SERIAL KILLERS HUNT

When conducting this research, I also thought about victim selection. FSKs largely kill people they know – people around them. In some cases, they gain insurance money or other benefits from their victims' deaths. We thus can say that female serial killers "gather" victims. In contrast, MSKs stalk and murder strangers, sometimes keeping trophies of their kills. This is what hunters do. Is it possible that female serial killers are gatherers and male serial killers are hunters, following ancestral agrarian societal tendencies?

For about 95% of human history, we probably lived in hunter-gatherer societies.[15] Repeated social, ecological, and physical components of our ancestral environment gave rise to genetic-based mental and behavioral adaptations that would maximize our chances of survival and reproduction.[16] Perhaps it remains part of our unconscious psychology for men to hunt and women to gather, but in the case of serial murder, this is taken to a violent extreme.

Offering one of the only empirical comparisons of FSKs and MSKs (i.e., a comparison based on statistical analysis), my team found support for every hypothesis we tested regarding the hunter-gatherer model of serial murder. As reported in our article "Sex Differences in Serial Killers,"[17] we found that:

- FSKs are more likely to know their victims than MSKs.
- FSKs are more likely to enjoy financial gain from their crimes.
- MSKs engage in stalking more than FSKs do.
- MSKs kill strangers more frequently than FSKs do.
- MSKs are more likely to kill across a dispersed area away from their birthplace compared to FSKs.

It is worth noting that hunter-gather models of human ancestral living describe many dimensions of mobility, environmental harshness, and use of resources. It was not a one-size-fits-all environment for millions of years of human evolution. It is therefore difficult to describe blanket ancestral tendencies.[18] It is also worth emphasizing that humans have not evolved to be serial killers – not at all. Nor does evolutionary psychology explain the entire phenomenon of serial murder. Evolutionary psychologists think of evolved, unconscious drives as ultimate, distant motivators of human behavior and mental processes. There are countless other proximate influences on human psychology – including the neural issues, mental illness, trauma, and social forces presented in the previous chapters. Investigations from all these viewpoints contribute towards our understanding of what makes a serial murderer.

A behavior or mental process may recapitulate ancestral tendencies, but that does not mean it is good or correct. Further, individual differences certainly exist in the expression of ancestral tendencies.[19] I emphasize that I am not saying all human beings evolved to be serial killers.

PUTTING IT ALL TOGETHER: CONVERGING PERSPECTIVES

Even as an evolutionary psychologist, I strive to promote the notion that any human behavior is multifaceted and must be considered through a biopsychosocial lens for the best insight. Besides our evolved genetic makeup, our other physiological makeup plays a role in how we perceive, process, and act in the world, with variation in gene sequence and expression, brain regions, neurotransmitters, and hormones involved in, and influenced by, our functioning. Furthermore, all our personal experiences and beliefs about the world influence what we do. Our sociocultural world impacts us. Think of our family dynamics, friendships, schools, teachers, governments, and cultural phenomena and figures influencing our perceptions and decisions. Interacting with these forces alters our attributions and attitudes and contributes to our psychological health or dysfunction.

As noted by the World Health Organization and so many others, a single perspective regarding the pathway to murder will not provide a complete answer. We must consider the many forces that contribute to the growth and development of the human psyche. We might visualize, in general, a model of the proclivity for serial murder as portrayed in the figure below.

I use the term "proclivity for serial murder," because while all these factors may be at play for a given individual, the individual may not have the opportunity or means to commit multiple murders. Furthermore, it may be the case that some serial murderers were not influenced by some of these factors – I am not sure we will ever know. Also this model does not accurately capture overlap and multidirectionality. We do not have the evidence to support a hierarchy or magnitude of influence, each over the other. We also do not know which factors work more closely together, and which may be unrelated. Yet, even though this model will be a work in progress for the foreseeable future as psychologists, criminologists, and law enforcement professionals work to solve the mysteries of serial murder, it helps us visualize the forces at play in what may create a serial murderer.

11.1 Theoretical model of sources of influence in the pathway to becoming a serial murderer. Figure drawn by the author.

By viewing converging data, we can derive a better picture of why some-one might commit serial murder, but we are a long way from being able to predict what factors or combination thereof "act as an incubator"[20] to cre-ate a serial killer. Even with increasingly sophisticated neuroimaging tech-niques, neurocriminologist Adrian Raine[21] emphasized that we are not at the point in science where we could determine who is a serial killer, or who is even approaching that type of violence. Our biology interacts with our cognitions and our environment to create who we are.

CHAPTER 12

Our Understanding of Serial Killers Evolves

I N MY RESEARCH COMPARING FSKs AND MSKs, I found stark differences in their motives and crimes. They also had differences in
background. For example, FSKs are much more likely to have been in
a romantic relationship and typically have more formal education than
MSKs. Still, when one examines cases on a deeper level, we see that
FSKs and MSKs commonly have experienced a traumagenic upbringing.

As stated earlier, there is a major difference in how FSKs and MSKs
are suspected and eventually caught. Evidence suggests that we must
catch MSKs, but we must detect FSKs. For MSKs, victims, typically young,
single women, turn up missing or dead mutilated; it is obvious someone
committed a murder. That is almost always not the case for FSKs, where
a murder can pass as a natural death, or victim deaths may seem accidental until we put two and two together. In 1919, the *Daily Arkansas Gazette*
made the same observation when talking about FSK Amy Archer-Gilligan,
arguing how difficult it was to detect the crimes that had been committed:

> The bodies were not buried at Mrs. Gilligan's place. Men and women who
> died there were taken away by relatives and buried in graveyards near and
> far. Thus no accretion of corpses slept about the premises to rise at some
> fatal moment and mock the murderer.[1]

This observation resonates with the fact that 77% of FSKs in my team's
study primarily poisoned or asphyxiated victims. Deaths by these means
can be, and have been, mistaken as resulting from medical conditions.
Although we know that techniques of criminal investigation are evolving

with a great deal of sophistication, for confirmed or potential FSKs, it just may be the case that perpetrators' knowledge of detection techniques keeps down victim numbers, as the perpetrator feels they may get caught. Modern medical diagnoses and treatment, psychological diagnoses and care, and communication between agencies allow for detecting and tracking problems. For example, centralized medical records can reveal subsequent child deaths in the same family, or a string of unexpected deaths with related causes.

§

Reta Mays is a serial killer. She was a nursing assistant on overnight shifts at the Louis A. Johnson VA Medical Center in Clarksburg, West Virginia. A veteran herself, Mays murdered seven vulnerable men, ranging in age from 81 to 96. They had all served in the US Armed Forces in World War II, the Korean War, and the Vietnam War.[2]

Mays' weapon of choice was unprescribed insulin. Patients in Ward 3A experienced unexplained drops in blood sugar, which caused seven patients' deaths from 2017 to 2018. Four of her victims died within a three-week span. The VA Medical Center staff did not immediately investigate the causes of these hypoglycemic events, track insulin, or report any suspected patient harm. But finally, in June 2018, a hospital director reported a potential "Angel of Death" to the Veterans Affairs Office of the Inspector General. An investigation ensued that involved the Inspector General, the FBI, the West Virginia State Police, and the Greater Harrison Drug and Violent Crimes Task Force. Examining the case took more than 300 hours of interviews, reviews of thousands of pages of medical documentation, scouring of employee and visitation records, consultation with forensic and endocrinological experts, and victim exhumation.[3]

The Inspector General denounced the abject failure of the hospital staff to detect and stop the killings, stating that the Medical Center "did not consistently promote a culture that prioritized patient safety."[4] Similarly, VA sources told *CBS 13 News* that Mays had claimed to be a CNA on her job application, but a search could not locate her name in the state license database.[5] If it is indeed the case that she is unlicensed, logic dictates either the VA did not check on the validity of her nursing license, or they did check but let an unqualified person interact with vulnerable patients.

Investigators said that Mays used her computer at work to search for "female serial killers" to compare her victim tally to that of other nurses who have killed. She also watched the *Netflix* series, *Nurses Who Kill*.[6] Reports state that, as a nurse who kills, Mays would sit beside her patients' beds and watch them die slowly. In some cases, more than one insulin injection was needed to cause death. An examination revealed, for example, that she had injected veteran Archie Edgell with insulin four times. In each case, she would then watch doctors try to revive the patients.[7]

At first, Mays denied having anything to do with patient deaths. Later, however, she admitted to administering insulin to patients whom she deemed to be suffering so that they could die "gently." US Attorney Jared Douglas called the crimes "horrific."[8] "The patients did not go here to die," he pointed out. "They did not need mercy . . . It wasn't the defendant's call to make."[9]

Although between 11 and 20 veterans died under suspicious circumstances during the Mays' period of employment,[10] prosecutors felt they only had sufficient evidence to charge Mays with seven murders. In 2020, Mays pleaded guilty to each of them – seven counts of second-degree murder. She also pleaded guilty to one count of assault with intent to murder.[11]

As FBI Acting Special Agent in Charge Carlton Peeples noted, "It is beyond disturbing that someone would seek out the opportunity to work as a medical professional to aid the sick, and then twist their duty and willingly end the life of their patients."[12] Indeed, her victims had families who will never recover from the loss. Norma Shaw, for example, was married to George Shaw, a 59-year-old victim of Mays. He was a veteran who spent 31 years serving his country in the United States Air Force.[13] Norma Shaw said Mays "took my life away."[14] Norma and her grieving family had the added stress of having to keep their knowledge of George's murder a secret while the investigation was ongoing.

As Acting US Attorney Randolph Bernard said, "These men are heroes in our community, state, and country, and deserved so much more."[15] So did their families.

With the hope of securing a less severe sentence, Mays' attorney described mitigating circumstances to the court. Mays herself served in

12.1 Norma Shaw with a photo of her husband, military veteran George Nelson Shaw Sr. Nursing assistant Reta Mays pleaded guilty to murdering George and six other patients at the Louis A. Johnson VA Medical Center in West Virginia. (Jeff Swensen for *The Washington Post* via Getty Images)

the West Virginia Army National Guard in Iraq and Afghanistan in a noncombat position in the 1092nd Engineer Battalion, repairing chemical equipment.[16] She experienced military sexual trauma and PTSD from her service,[17] as well as depression, postpartum depression, and anxiety.[18] Mays' attorney argued that injuries she experienced on the job at the VA, sometimes from agitated patients, exacerbated her stress. Moreover, her children were allegedly substance abusers and her husband had been arrested and convicted for child pornography offenses and sent to prison.[19] Mays stated that she gained a sense of control from ending patients' lives prematurely.

Notably, however, US Attorney Jared Douglas said, "Any reason the defendant gives is woefully inadequate."[20]

US District Judge Thomas Kleeh agreed with Douglas that mental health issues did not explain or justify the murders.[21] Declaring that she knew what she was doing, he told Mays, "You're the monster no one sees coming."[22] In 2021, at age 46, Mays was given seven life sentences, one for each of the murders, plus an additional 20 years for the assault of an eighth patient. Judge Kleeh said that others overcame life obstacles far more substantial than Mays experienced but "none of these other folks are killers, let alone serial killers."[23]

§

Of course, increased medical knowledge may help us catch FSKs, but this reasoning does not hold true for most cases of MSKs. It may have been more difficult to detect poisoning and other passive methods earlier in history, but the ability to observe a string of mutilated corpses has remained constant.

So, over time, we have gotten better at detecting and apprehending perpetrators. But it is difficult to determine with certainty whether female- or male-perpetrated serial murder is increasing, decreasing, or remaining at the same level. In our original FSK data, of 64 perpetrators we found that most cases ($n = 17$) dated from the 1980s, with only nine happening between 1990 and 2008.[24] With respect to FSKs, there is limited information out there compared to MSKs. Of course, with access to serial killers for interview purposes virtually impossible, our data were limited to what we found in reputable, publicly available archival reports. There may be cases not reported on, and there also must be serial murderers that just have not been caught.

I went back into the original, unpublished FSK vs. MSK data and found something interesting. For FSKs, there was a statistically significant negative correlation between year of first kill and number of victims[25] – that is, the earlier in American history a FSK's crime started, the greater the number of murder victims she killed. This was not true for MSKs; there was no significant relation between year of first kill and number of victims.[26]

We may be able to attribute this phenomenon, at least in part, to the power of morbid curiosity. Perhaps the most sensational FSK cases withstood the test of time, and we were therefore only able to locate information about FSKs in the distant past because their crimes were so extensive, their notoriety is preserved through media reports. In addition, numbers may be lower in recent years because FSKs tend to operate in ways that the contemporary medical community had grown savvier about catching, so that poisoners and baby killers are wary, knowing they may be caught or apprehended before they kill repeatedly.

I thought it noteworthy that serial murder may decline at some point due to increasing inclusivity in society. Well-known biological psychologist Frederick Toates has, for many years, been researching and writing about the incentives of and motivations for sexual violence.[27] In a 2020 seminar on sexually motivated serial killers sponsored by The Open University Psychological Society (London), Toates suggested that with society's increasing acceptance of non-heterosexuality, we will see a decrease in male-perpetrated serial homicides.

As Toates pointed out, MSK Jeffrey Dahmer, born in 1960, murdered 17 men, with his sex-motivated crimes taking place from 1978 to 1991.[28] American attitudes towards homosexuality became increasingly negative from the early 1970s through 1990.[29] This overlapped with Dahmer's formative years when one's sense of sexual orientation typically emerges.

Medical examiner Jeffrey Jentzen and his colleagues served as psychiatric and forensic experts in Dahmer's case. They assessed him to be ambivalent about his homosexuality. On one hand, he was frustrated by his own homosexuality and channeled his anger into the sadistic murders of gay men who accepted his advances. He also dismembered victims: Jentzen et al. believed that this was both a mechanism of control and an attempt to see what made the gay men function. On the other hand, he kept victims' body parts and photographs of their naked bodies as trophies to use in reliving the thrill of these encounters.[30] Forensic expert James Davis added that Dahmer felt frustrated, empty, alone, and neglected, and he feared abandonment.[31] He killed people and kept parts of them because it was a better outcome than being abandoned by them. Furthermore, Dahmer enjoyed aberrant sexual acts, and murder was an erotic event to him.[32]

According to the Pew Research Center, as of 2019, 72% of Americans feel that society should "accept" homosexuality, increased markedly even from 2002 when reports still indicated that a majority was accepting.[33] If Dahmer had lived today, when attitudes towards homosexuality are more inclusive, he might have had a stronger sense of self-worth and felt less hostility. Those 17 men might have lived. As tolerance continues to grow, I agree with my colleague Frederick Toates,[34] and I feel we will see fewer serial murderers motivated by hatred of or shame at one's homosexuality.

Along these lines, and with a caveat that sexual orientation and gender identity are not the same concept, if Ed Gein had lived today, society's somewhat better attitudes towards transgender individuals might have left him more comfortable with undertaking the transition to being a woman. A majority of people in the USA would like increased protection for transgender individuals.[35] Had this already been in place, Gein might not have dissected victims and robbed graves to create the female body he wanted to inhabit.

What drives anyone to become a serial killer? Almost everyone who ever lived with mental illness or who experiences trauma has not been a serial killer. We know some patterns, we are aware of some likely causes, but we are not yet at a point where we can prevent all serial homicides. We can prevent some, as our detection methods have become very sophisticated. It is likely that many perpetrators have been stopped by investigators after their first or second murder, thereby preventing them from becoming a serial killer. Even if a murderer does cross the threshold of three victims, investigators have evolving approaches for determining their identity, such as when police caught the Golden State Killer because a distant relative was interested in their genealogy and sent a DNA sample to a commercial ancestry website for analysis.

The ability to detect or catch a murderer is considerable, commendable, and will continue to expand. I hope that our research on FSK patterns and the stark differences between the motives, means, and victims of FSKs and MSKs can aid in investigation if necessary. Much more than that, I hope it will never be necessary.

When delving into the backgrounds of both FSKs and MSKs for this book, it has not been lost on me as a research psychologist that these individuals almost always experienced some form of trauma, particularly sexual abuse, in their formative years. Investing in the promotion and maintenance of mental health and devoting intervention and treatment resources for at-risk and abused children can help the abused victim enormously. Such interventions may prevent a continued cycle of victimization violence, and even murder.

Although I am not a clinician, I wanted to suggest that it might be time to reconsider what we think constitutes insanity. Forensic psychologist Robert Hare[36] said that it has not been easy to distinguish between mentally ill murderers and psychopathic but sane murderers. Hare further said "sanity" has been debated for centuries. I feel the debate should continue. What is sanity? Cambridge Dictionary says that sanity conveys that the person is "showing good judgement and understanding."[37] Merriam-Webster Dictionary says that sanity means "soundness of health and mind."[38] Among other things, Belle Gunness bludgeoned her husband to death with a sausage grinder, killed her children, burned down her businesses and houses, killed dozens of men and fed their body parts to hogs, and then ripped out her own dental work and beheaded a stranger to fake her death. Does that sound like good judgment and a sound mind – sane – to the average person?

In the case of serial murderers, many have experienced childhood sexual abuse, other victimization, and trauma. Contemporary evidence is strong that such abuse changes the brain's structure and function. Recall that physical and psychological abuse inflicts "wounds that won't heal" because of the permanent impact on the brain. Such abuse impacts one's emotional understanding, impulse control, and decision-making.[39] It makes sense that an affected brain functions differently than an unaffected brain, and that someone who murders person after person is not showing sound mind or good judgment. I would never look for reasons to excuse serial killing – only to understand the phenomenon. The serial murder cases I presented in this book include among the most violent, vile acts perpetrated on fellow human beings that one could ever encounter. I am saying that someone who was sexually violated may have a quite different perception of right or wrong compared to people who were not violated. Moreover, there is evidence demonstrating irregularities in cortical and subcortical neural structures with deleterious behavioral, cognitive, and psychological outcomes for victims of childhood sexual abuse (CSA).[40] Maybe sanity is not possible in these cases. We can do better trying to detect, understand, prevent, and perhaps some day heal those who have been hurt.

What kinds of psychotherapy would work for serial murderers? Whereas that topic is far beyond my expertise, it stands to reason it would have to be a comprehensive, multifaceted approach to treatment developed specifically for each offender, as evidenced by the complexity of potential contributions to maldevelopment delineated in this book. Nevertheless, I would be remiss if I did not point out that, many decades ago, Hervey Cleckley[41] warned that a psychopath may not take part in any therapy with sincerity. Some scholars have therefore suggested we focus on trying to understand protective factors against the development of psychopathy, such as family support.[42] I know that clinicians work on each case the best they can with the tools they have.

I know it cannot erase pain, but I hope the families and friends of serial murder victims, and all murder victims, can find some solace knowing that psychologists, criminologists, and others in the justice system see you and hear you. We continue to strive to understand and prevent these horrible crimes.

THE MONSTERS NO ONE SEES COMING

In this book, I presented the psychology of FSKs through demographic, motivation, and crime data; through case studies; and by comparison with the behaviors and mental processes of MSKs.

The fact is that FSKs are often overlooked. As of this writing, they are researched infrequently. Nonetheless, from the research that does exist, we can see that FSKs poison, smother, and drown innocent victims who are typically too young, too sick, or too old to fight back. Using passive means of murder, they can go undetected. Judge Kleeh was right: a FSK is typically someone unexpected – "the monster no one sees coming."[43] They are nurses, mothers, and other caregivers. They likely kill for money but can do so for power and attention. Unlike MSKs, there is seldom a sexual motive.[44] We thus see concrete evidence that the crimes, motives, and victims of FSKs are different than those of MSKs, but that FSKs can be just as deadly.

Acknowledgments

I extend my appreciation to: the many students and colleagues who have helped with study design, data gathering, and information synthesis in my research; my alma mater, the State University of New York at Albany; Marywood University, for being part of my journey; the journals, editors, and peer reviewers who believed in and supported this science; Penn State University Libraries' resources and services; my colleagues at Penn State Harrisburg, who have supported my research; Eric Hickey, for opening the door for much-needed research on female serial killers; Frederick Toates, Olga Coschug-Toates, and other experts and journalists whose hard work is noted in this book; my friends at *The Phil*; my dedicated friends at the New York State Police and law enforcement everywhere, for their never-ending pursuit of justice; Elena Abbott, for her expert editing; the incomparable Janka Romero, Laura Simmons, and Charles Phillips at Cambridge University Press, and all at the University of Cambridge for this remarkable opportunity; my great-grandparents from South Shields, Tyne and Wear, England; and the readers of my research.

Notes

PREFACE

1 You can read Kaplan's 2015 article at: *The Washington Post* (March 6, 2015): www
.washingtonpost.com/news/morning-mix/wp/2015/03/06/inside-the-minds-
of-female-serial-killers/.

2 You can read Anthes' 2015 article at: *The New Yorker* (May 9, 2015): www.newyorker
.com/tech/annals-of-technology/female-serial-killers.

3 Warf & Waddell, 2002.

4 Harrison & Bowers, 2010.

5 Oosterwijk, 2017; Zuckerman & Litle, 1986.

6 Harrison & Frederick, 2020.

7 *HuffPost* (December 3, 2016): www.huffpost.com/entry/how-to-avoid-being-murde
r_b_8707446.

8 Hickey, 1991, 2010, 2016.

9 *Hartford Courant* (May 9, 1916, p. 1): www.newspapers.com/image/369106460/.

10 *Hartford Courant* (July 14, 1917, p. 3): https://www.newspapers.com/image/369409118/.

11 *Connecticut History* (May 8, 2016): https://connecticuthistory.org/windsors-murder-factory;
Hartford Courant (July 2, 1919, p. 7): www.newspapers.com/image/367383081/; *The Journal*
(May 9, 1916, p. 1): www.newspapers.com/image/675617421; *Windsor Historical Society* (July
16, 2018): https://windsorhistoricalsociety.org/amy-archer-gilligan-entrepreneurism-gone-
wrong-in-windsor.

12 *Hartford Courant* (May 9, 1916, p. 1): www.newspapers.com/image/369106460; *The New
York Times* (March 2, 1997): www.nytimes.com/1997/03/02/nyregion/whatever-went-
wrong-with-amy.html; *The Knoxville Journal* (April 30, 1950, p. 47): www.newspapers
.com/image/588247270.

13 *Hartford Courant* (May 11, 1916, p. 1): www.newspapers.com/image/369107207.

14 *Hartford Courant* (May 9, 1916, p. 3): www.newspapers.com/image/369106493.

15 *Evening Star* (July 14, 1917, p. 16): www.newspapers.com/image/332097684;
The Lancaster Examiner (July 18, 1917, p. 4): www.newspapers.com/image/567995277.

16 *Hartford Courant* (July 2, 1919, p. 7): www.newspapers.com/image/367383081/.

17 *Hartford Courant* (July 18, 1924, p. 4): www.newspapers.com/image/369384985.

18 *The Boston Globe* (April 24, 1962, p. 22): www.newspapers.com/image/433454011; *New England Historical Society* (2020) www.newenglandhistoricalsociety.com/arsenic-and-old-lace-not-funny-to-the-man-who-brought-a-serial-killer-to-justice/.

19 *Daily Arkansas Gazette* (July 27, 1919, p. 41): www.newspapers.com/image/141596789.

20 *American Psychological Association (APA)* (January, 2003): www.apa.org/monitor/jan03/principles.html.

21 *Salon* (August 13, 1999): www.salon.com/1999/08/13/nameless/.

22 See Rad et al., 2018.

23 *Hartford Courant* (April 17, 2014) www.courant.com/courant-250/moments-in-history/hc-250-amy-archer-gilligan-20140416-story.html.

24 Ratnaike, 2003.

EPIGRAPH

1 *NPR* (May 11, 2021): www.npr.org/2021/05/11/995885699/woman-who-murdered-7-veterans-in-va-hospital-gets-multiple-life-sentences.

1 INTRODUCTION: WHAT IS A SERIAL KILLER

1 *AP News* (November 27, 1998): https://apnews.com/article/9a6ebf9823b1c0fd8f-82631c9870afb6; *CBS News* (March 26, 2001): www.cbsnews.com/news/killer-nurse-gets-life/.

2 *ABC News* (January 7, 2006): https://abcnews.go.com/US/story?id=94953&page=1; *The Boston Globe* (October 9, 2000): http://cache.boston.com/globe/metro/packages/nurse/part2.htm; *The New York Times* (November 23, 2000): www.nytimes.com/2000/11/23/us/former-nurse-on-trial-in-patients-deaths.html.

3 *ABC News* (January 7, 2006): https://abcnews.go.com/US/story?id=94953&page=1; *The Boston Globe* (October 9, 2000, p. 12): www.newspapers.com/image/442016344.

4 *The Boston Globe* (March 9, 2000, p. 32): www.newspapers.com/image/428659016.

5 *The New York Times* (November 23, 2000): www.nytimes.com/2000/11/23/us/former-nurse-on-trial-in-patients-deaths.html.

6 *The Boston Globe* (May 15, 1999, p. 25): www.newspapers.com/image/441829567.

7 *The Boston Globe* (October 9, 2000, p. 13): www.newspapers.com/image/442016348.

8 *The Boston Globe* (October 9, 2000, p. 13): www.newspapers.com/image/442016348.

9 *The Berkshire Eagle* (November 25, 1998, p. 8): www.newspapers.com/image/533385899.

10 *The Boston Globe* (March 9, 2000, p. 32): www.newspapers.com/image/428659016.

11 *The Boston Globe* (March 15, 2001, p. 26): www.newspapers.com/image/443075617.

12 *The Boston Globe* (November 30, 2000, p. 35): www.newspapers.com/image/442155702.

13 *The Boston Globe* (March 27, 2001, p. 1): www.newspapers.com/image/442962840/.

14 *The Boston Globe* (March 15, 2001, p. 26): www.newspapers.com/image/443075617.

15 *The Boston Globe* (March 27, 2001, p. 1): www.newspapers.com/image/442962840/; *The Berkshire Eagle* (March 30, 2000, p. 7): www.newspapers.com/image/533423182.

16 *The Boston Globe* (March 15, 2001): www.newspapers.com/image/443075171/.

17 *The Berkshire Eagle* (March 19, 2001, p. 5): www.newspapers.com/image/533325752.

18 Ressler & Shachtman, 1992, p. 32.

19 *US Federal Bureau of Investigation (FBI)* (2005): www.fbi.gov/stats-services/publications/serial-murder.

20 Farrell et al., 2011; Hickey, 1991, 2016; Holmes et al., 1991.

21 Harrison et al., 2019.

22 Farrell et al., 2011; Holmes et al., 1991.

23 For example, Stone, 2001.

24 Hickey, 1991; Harrison et al., 2019.

25 *The Fall River Daily Herald* (February 23, 1882): www.newspapers.com/image/616914767.

26 *The Morning News* (April 6, 1981, p. 29): www.newspapers.com/image/157212941.

27 *Cape Gazette* (November 30, 2018) https://www.capegazette.com/article/sussex-county-serial-killer/159135; *The Cincinnati Enquirer* (February 6, 1882, p. 1): www.newspapers.com/image/31428905.

28 Bell, 2016.

29 *The Morning News* (September 2, 1960, p. 25): www.newspapers.com/image/155727298; *The Morning News* (December 1, 1982, p. 9): www.newspapers.com/image/160893825.

30 Bell, 2016.

31 *The Cincinnati Enquirer* (February 6, 1882, p. 1): www.newspapers.com/image/31428905; *The Morning News* (April 6, 1981, p. 29): www.newspapers.com/image/157212941.

32 *The Cincinnati Enquirer* (February 6, 1882, p. 1): www.newspapers.com/image/31428905.

33 *Cape Gazette* (November 30, 2018) www.capegazette.com/article/sussex-county-serial-killer/159135; *Delaware Online* (June 6, 2013): www.delawareonline.com/story/life/2019/06/13/legend-patty-cannon-wickedest-woman-america/1444450001.

34 Morgan, 2015.

35 *Cape Gazette* (June 7, 2015): www.capegazette.com/article/delmarva%E2%80%99s-patty-cannon-devil-nanticoke-book-tells-tale-serial-killer/84758.

36 *Cape Gazette* (November 30, 2018): www.capegazette.com/article/sussex-county-serial-killer/159135.

37 *The Morning News* (September 2, 1960, p. 25): www.newspapers.com/image/155727298.

38 *The Morning News* (September 18, 1985, p. 63): www.newspapers.com/image/157976004.

39 *The Morning News* (August 1, 1902, p. 1): www.newspapers.com/image/154703773.

40 *The Morning News* (September 18, 1985, p. 63): www.newspapers.com/image/157976004.

41 *Delaware Online* (June 13, 2019): www.delawareonline.com/story/life/2019/06/13/archives-patty-cannons-skull-now-spends-halloween-smithsonian/1444832001/.

42 *The Florida Times Union* (September 26, 2019): www.jacksonville.com/news/20190926/florida-serial-killings-from-aileen-wuornos-to-gary-ray-bowles-why-have-murderers-for-decades-chosen-daytona.

43 *Connecticut History* (May 8, 2016): connecticuthistory.org/windsors-murder-factory/.

44 Pearson, 1998/2021.

45 Schurman-Kauflin, 2000, p. 13.

46 *The Knoxville Journal* (April 30, 1950, p. 47): www.newspapers.com/image/588247270.

47 Hickey, 1986.
48 Farrell et al., 2011, 2013.
49 Cleckley, 1941.
50 Perri & Lichtenwald, 2010.
51 Dion et al. 1972; Dion & Dion, 1987.
52 For review, see Harrison & Hughes, 2020.
53 Smith et al., 1999.
54 Manthorpe, 2019.
55 Harrison et al., 2015.
56 *Great Bend Tribune* (June 18, 1961, p. 13): www.newspapers.com/image/69635240.
57 *The Kansas City Star* (February 10, 1974, p. 170): www.newspapers.com/image/676496232.
58 *The Kansas City Star* (February 3, 1997, p. 10): www.newspapers.com/image/684836058/.
59 *The Kansas City Star* (November 25, 1979): www.newspapers.com/image/677841808.
60 *The Salina Journal* (June 3, 1961, p. 2): www.newspapers.com/image/40711865.
61 *The Kansas City Star* (February 3, 1997, p. 10): www.newspapers.com/image/684836194.
62 *The Kansas City Star* (February 10, 1974, p. 170): www.newspapers.com/image/676496232.
63 *The Kansas City Star* (February 3, 1997, p. 37): www.newspapers.com/image/684836556.
64 *The Kansas City Star* (February 10, 1974, p. 170): www.newspapers.com/image/676496232.
65 *The Emporia Gazette* (October 19, 1965, p. 10): www.newspapers.com/image/10219448.
66 *The Kansas City Star* (February 3, 1997, p. 37): www.newspapers.com/image/684836556; *St. Joseph Gazette* (December 9, 1969, p. 1): www.newspapers.com/image/563289156.
67 *American Psychiatric Association* (August 25, 2016): www.psychiatry.org/newsroom/gold water-rule.
68 *American Psychological Association (APA)* (2017): www.apa.org/ethics/code.
69 Lynam & Gudonis, 2005.
70 Hare & Neumann, 2005.
71 Brook & Kosson, 2013; Hare, 1999; Lynam & Gudonis, 2005; Mullins-Nelson et al., 2012.
72 Morana et al., 2006.
73 Anderson et al., 2021; Bishopp & Hare, 2008; Hosker-Field et al., 2016; Snowden et al., 2017.
74 Cleckley, 1941/1988.
75 Hare, 1999.
76 Cleckley, 1988, p. 286.
77 Glenn & Raine, 2009.
78 Hare, 2001.
79 Hare, 1999, p. 87.
80 Glenn et al., 2020.
81 Harpending & Sobus, 1987.
82 Book et al., 2015.
83 Hare, 1991/2003, 2020.

84 Hunt et al., 2015; Tengström et al., 2000.
85 Abdalla-Filho & Völlm, 2020; Hunt et al., 2015; Patrick et al., 2005.
86 Hare, 1999.
87 Cleckley, 1941/1988.
88 Lilienfeld & colleagues (2018) remarked on Cleckley's profound influence in the field. Cleckley's perspectives on psychopathy have even made their way into the popular television show *Mindhunter*, which features investigations of serial murderers and their crimes. Further, Robert Hare drew from Cleckley's psychopath characterizations when he created the Psychopathy Checklist (Hare, 1991/2003; Lilienfeld et al., 2018).
89 Castle & Hensley, 2002.
90 Wahl, 2003.
91 Cleckley, 1988; Hare, 1999.
92 Sass et al., 2018.
93 Hare, 1999.
94 Hickey et al., 2018.

2 WHY ARE WE INTERESTED IN SERIAL KILLERS?

1 *The Los Angeles Times* (March 18, 1994): www.latimes.com/archives/la-xpm-1994-03-18-mn-35665-story.html; *New York Daily News* (May 31, 2014): www.nydailynews.com/news/crime/justice-story-dana-sue-gray-article-1.1810400 (url geo-restricted).
2 *Rolling Stone* (August 9, 2019): www.rollingstone.com/culture/culture-features/manson-murder-murderabelia-true-crime-collectibles-869058/.
3 *Observer* (October 29, 2018): https://observer.com/2018/10/serial-killer-art-lucrative-charles-manson-richard-ramirez/.
4 Wiest, 2016.
5 *Museum of Death* (2021): www.museumofdeath.net/.
6 *Rolling Stone* (August 9, 2019): www.rollingstone.com/culture/culture-features/manson-murder-murderabelia-true-crime-collectibles-869058/.
7 *Forbes* (October 27, 2019): www.forbes.com/sites/markbeech/2019/10/27/how-hammer-plans-to-revive-in-1-billion-horror-movie-market/?sh=7a33204648e9.
8 *Forbes* (October 3, 2019): www.forbes.com/sites/travisbean/2019/10/03/the-highest-grossing-horror-movies-of-all-time/?sh=2a64f710e4d3.
9 Jarvis, 2007.
10 *Rotten Tomatoes* (2021): www.rottentomatoes.com/tv/mindhunter.
11 *Men's Health* (March 29, 2021): www.menshealth.com/entertainment/g28701765/serial-killer-shows-like-mindhunter/.
12 Hickey, 2010, p. 189.
13 *Cottage Theatre* (2020): www.cottagetheatre.org/arsenic-and-old-lace.html.
14 *IMDb* (2021): www.imdb.com/title/tt0036613/.
15 *Hartford Courant* (April 17, 2014): www.courant.com/courant-250/moments-in-history/hc-250-amy-archer-gilligan-20140416-story.html.
16 Miles-Novelo & Anderson, 2020.

17 Di Tella et al., 2019.

18 *The Conversation* (August 16, 2019): https://theconversation.com/glamorising-violent-offenders-with-true-crime-shows-and-podcasts-needs-to-stop-121806.

19 *The Phil* (2017): http://new.trinitysocieties.ie/.

20 *Innocence Project* (2021): https://innocenceproject.org/.

21 *CBS News* (May 7, 2013): www.cbsnews.com/news/americas-most-wanted-host-john-walsh-on-cancellation-show-needs-to-be-on-tv/.

22 See Miles-Novelo & Anderson, 2020.

23 Harrison & Frederick, 2020.

24 Harrison et al., 2015.

25 *La Porte County Public Library* (2021): https://laportelibrary.org/at-the-library/explore-local/belle-gunness/.

26 *1900 United States Federal Census*: Ancestry.com.

27 *Burlington Daily News* (May 15, 1908, p. 5): www.newspapers.com/image/355482098.

28 *The Indianapolis Star* (November 11, 2017): www.indystar.com/story/news/history/retroindy/2017/11/10/female-indiana-serial-killer-comely-belle-gunness-loved-her-suitors-death/848023001/.

29 *The Pittsburgh Press* (May 10, 1908): www.newspapers.com/image/142179427.

30 *La Porte County Public Library* (2021): https://laportelibrary.org/at-the-library/explore-local/belle-gunness; *La Porte County Historical Society* (2021): https://laportecountyhistory.org/exhibits/belle-gunness.

31 *The Burlington Daily News* (May 15, 1908, p. 5): www.newspapers.com/image/355482098.

32 *Laporte County, Indiana; Index to Marriage Records Letters*: S – Z Volume V, W. P. A. Compiled by Indiana Works Progress Admin.; Book: R-O; p. 345: Ancestry.com.

33 *Indiana, U.S., Death Certificates*, 1899–2011: Ancestry.com.

34 *La Porte County Public Library* (2021): https://laportelibrary.org/at-the-library/explore-local/belle-gunness/.

35 *The New York Times* (May 5, 2007): www.nytimes.com/1908/05/07/archives/mrs-gunness-was-money-mad-sister-says-her-weakness-was-greed-may.html.

36 Her *Last Will and Testament* is filed under the name Bella Gunness, is dated April 27, 1908, and lists Myrtle Adophine Sorenson, Lucy Bergliat Sorenson, and Phillip Alexander Gunness as beneficiaries of all her property; *Indiana, US, Wills and Probate Records*, 1798–1999, Vol. E-G, 1895–1908, p. 809: Ancestry.com.

37 *Chicago Tribune* (March 1, 1987): www.chicagotribune.com/news/ct-xpm-1987-03-01-8701170475-story.html.

38 *The Seattle Times* (February 17, 2008): www.seattletimes.com/nation-world/unlocking-secrets-of-indiana-murder-farm/.

39 Myrtle A. Sorenson's death at age eleven is listed as occurring on April 28, 1908; Lucy B. Sorenson's death at age eight is listed as occurring on April 28, 2008; and Phillip Alexander Gunness' death at age four is listed as occurring on April 27, 1908; *Indiana, US, WPA Death Index*, 1882–1920, book H-14, p. 100: Ancestry.com.

40 *Indiana, US, WPA Death Index*, 1882–1920, H14, p. 100: Ancestry.com; *La Porte County Public Library* (2021): https://laportelibrary.org/at-the-library/explore-local/belle-gunness.

41 *Chicago Tribune* (May 14, 2008): www.chicagotribune.com/news/ct-xpm-2008-05-14-0805130697-story.html.

42 *Daily News* (November 1, 1987, p. 87): www.newspapers.com/image/491279835.

43 *The New York Times* (November 15, 1908):www.nytimes.com/1908/11/15/archives/gunness-teeth-identified-dentist-testifies-he-made-gold-crowns.html.

44 *Rushville Republican* (May 23, 1908, p. 3): www.newspapers.com/image/549005121.

45 *Indiana, US, WPA Death Index*, 1882–1920. Provo, UT, USA: Ancestry.com; Some reported Gunness died on April 28, 1908; *Chicago Tribune* (November 13, 1908, p. 2): www.newspapers.com/image/355258219.

46 *The Burlington Daily News* (May 15, 1908, p. 5): www.newspapers.com/image/355482098.

47 *The Republic* (May 8, 1908, p. 1): www.newspapers.com/image/128816390.

48 *Daily News* (November 1, 1987, p. 87): www.newspapers.com/image/491279835.

49 *The Indianapolis News* (July 19, 1930): www.newspapers.com/image/37486894.

50 *The South Bend Tribune* (May 7, 1908, p. 2): www.newspapers.com/image/513827223.

51 *The South Bend Tribune* (May 7, 1908, p. 2): www.newspapers.com/image/513827223.

52 *Chicago Tribune* (February 12, 2008): www.chicagotribune.com/news/ct-xpm-2008-02-12-0802120038-story.html.

53 *News-Pilot* (May 2, 1931, p. 2): www.newspapers.com/image/605748205.

54 *News-Pilot* (April 29, 1931, p. 1): www.newspapers.com/image/605685253.

55 *The Fresno Bee* (May 3, 1931, p. 35): www.newspapers.com/image/701098560.

56 *Chicago Tribune* (February 12, 2008): www.chicagotribune.com/news/ct-xpm-2008-02-12-0802120038-story.html; *Santa Maria Times* (April 30, 1931, p. 6): www.newspapers.com/image/629964716.

57 *News-Pilot* (May 7, 1931, p. 1): www.newspapers.com/image/605748246.

58 *The South Bend Tribune* (May 7, 1908, p. 2): www.newspapers.com/image/513827223.

59 *The Seattle Times* (February 17, 2008): www.seattletimes.com/nation-world/unlocking-secrets-of-indiana-murder-farm/.

60 James, 1890.

61 Kidd & Hayden, 2015; Litman, 2005.

62 Robinson & Berridge, 1993; Shin & Kim, 2019.

63 Berke & Hyman, 2000; Costa et al., 2014.

64 Baumeister et al., 2001; Bebbington et al., 2017.

65 Carretié et al., 2009.

66 van Steenbergen et al., 2011.

67 McCauley, 1998; Taylor, 1991.

68 Zillmann, 1998.

69 Harrison & Frederick, 2020.

70 Oosterwijk, 2017, p. 1.

71 Wilson, 2012, p. 40.

72 Carretié et al., 2009.

73 Zuckerman & Litle, 1986, p. 49.

74 *CNN* (September 28, 2018): www.cnn.com/2015/07/08/entertainment/serial-killer-lovers-the-seventies/index.html.

75 Zuckerman, 1994.

76 *The Hill* (July 12, 2020): https://thehill.com/opinion/technology/506947-news-industrys-bleeding-leads-good-for-business-bad-for-the-country.

77 Wang, 2012.

78 Arnett, 1994; Zuckerman et al., 1964.

79 Donohew et al., 2000; Zuckerman, 2007.

80 García-Sáinz, 2002; Roberti, 2004.

81 Kanazawa, 2010.

82 Oosterwijk, 2017; Zuckerman & Litle, 1986.

83 Harrison & Frederick, 2020.

84 Zuckerman, 1994; Zuckerman & Litle, 1986.

85 Cross et al., 2013; Zuckerman & Litle, 1986.

86 See Eisenegger et al., 2011, for review.

87 Kanazawa, 2002.

88 Clasen et al., 2020.

89 Evidence suggests that modern technology overwhelms our capacity to cope. For example, the prevalence of posttraumatic stress disorder (PTSD) triggered by *natural* disasters, such as hurricanes and earthquakes, is estimated to be 5–60 percent. PTSD triggered by *human-made* events, however, such as airplane crashes and modern warfare, is much higher at 25–75 percent s(Galea et al., 2005).

90 Clasen et al., 2020.

3 THE LIVES OF FEMALE SERIAL KILLERS

1 *Sactown Magazine* (August–September, 2009): www.sactownmag.com/the-life-and-deaths-of-dorothea-puente/.

2 *The Daily Breeze* (November 13, 1988, p. 2): www.newspapers.com/image/607714952.

3 *The Los Angeles Review of Books* (March 11, 2019): https://lareviewofbooks.org/article/hope-finds-well-dorothea-puente-archive/; *The Los Angeles Times* (March 28. 2011, p. 23): www.newspapers.com/image/193769983.

4 *RxList* (July 12, 2021): www.rxlist.com/dalmane-drug/patient-images-side-effects.htm.

5 *Daily Mail* (January 21, 2019): www.dailymail.co.uk/news/article-6616525/Grandson-Dorothea-Puente-laced-cakes-poison-says-shared-real-connection-her.html.

6 Norton, 1994.

7 Morbid curiosity piques interest in serial murder. A recent streaming program showed renovations to Dorothea Puente's "murder" home in Sacramento, *CBS 13 Sacramento* (October 24, 2019): https://sacramento.cbslocal.com/2019/10/24/dorothea-puente-home-featured-in-murder-house-flip-series/.

8 *The Daily Breeze* (November 13, 1988): www.newspapers.com/image/607714952.

9 *The Desert Sun* (August 28, 1993, p. 5): www.newspapers.com/image/244154983.

10 *The Napa Valley Register* (December 10, 1993, p. 13): www.newspapers.com/image/565102625.

11 *The Los Angeles Review of Books* (March 11, 2019): https://lareviewofbooks.org/article/hope-finds-well-dorothea-puente-archive/; *The Los Angeles Times* (April 1, 1989):

www.latimes.com/archives/la-xpm-1989-04-01-mn-830-story.html; *Times Advocate* (July 11, 1990): www.newspapers.com/clip/42889991/puente-arraignment/.

12 *The Napa Valley Register* (December 10, 1993, p. 13): www.newspapers.com/image/565102625.

13 *Daily Mail* (January 21, 2019): www.dailymail.co.uk/news/article-6616525/Grandson-Dorothea-Puente-laced-cakes-poison-says-shared-real-connection-her.html; *The New York Times* (March 28, 2011): www.nytimes.com/2011/03/28/us/28puente.html.

14 *Valley Public Radio* (February 5, 2019): www.kvpr.org/post/why-mans-bobblehead-collection-really-ticks-people#stream/0.

15 *The Los Angeles Times* (March 28. 2011, p. 23): www.newspapers.com/image/193769983.

16 *The Los Angeles Times* (October 14, 1993, p. 15): www.newspapers.com/image/712218442; *The Los Angeles Times* (March 28. 2011, p. 23): www.newspapers.com/image/193769983.

17 *The Desert Sun* (August 28, 1993, p. 5): www.newspapers.com/image/244154983.

18 *Santa Cruz Sentinel* (July 8, 1994, p. 49): www.newspapers.com/image/66378940; *The Los Angeles Times* (March 28, 2011, p. 23): www.newspapers.com/image/193769983.

19 Norton, 1994.

20 *Santa Cruz Sentinel* (July 8, 1994, p. 49): www.newspapers.com/image/66378940.

21 Other researchers have collected and presented data on FSKs. Eric Hickey's (1991/2010/2016) book *Serial Murderers and Their Victims* is the gold standard for understanding serial killing. Other endeavors include research by Keeney & Heide (1994), Kelleher & Kelleher (1998), Schurman-Kauflin (2000), and Farrell et al. (2011, 2013).

22 *Albuquerque Journal* (January 24, 2020): www.abqjournal.com/1406532/us-serial-killers-getting-away-with-murder.html.

23 Harrison et al., 2015.

24 For example, Farrell et al., 2013; Keeney & Heide, 1994 .

25 For example, Hickey, 1991, 2016; Holmes et al., 1991.

26 *Oxford Analytica* (2017): www.emerald.com/insight/content/doi/10.1108/OXAN-DB226032/full/html.

27 Zuckerman, E. (October, 2017): https://dspace.mit.edu/handle/1721.1/110987.

28 Lachmann & Lachmann, 1995.

29 *The Atlantic* (October, 2019): www.theatlantic.com/magazine/archive/2019/10/are-serial-killers-more-common-than-we-think/596647/.

30 Interestingly, our FSK sample size exactly matched that of Eric Hickey as he reported in his seminal 1991 book about serial murder.

31 *Murderpedia.org* (June 14, 2017): http://www.murderpedia.org/.

32 Harrison et al., 2015.

33 Gunn et al., 2014.

34 Harrison et al., 2015.

35 Harrison et al., 2015.

36 The standard deviation (SD) tells us the dispersion of scores with respect to the mean.

37 Harrison et al., 2015.

38 *New England Historical Society* (2020): www.newenglandhistoricalsociety.com/jolly-jane-toppan-killer-nurse-obsessed-death/.

39 *The Boston Globe* (June 23, 1902, p. 2): www.newspapers.com/image/430881982;*The Edwardsville Intelligencer* (August 18, 1938, p. 2): www.newspapers.com/image/26467039.

40 *Boston Magazine* (October 29, 2015): www.bostonmagazine.com/news/2015/10/29/jane-toppan/; *The Gothenburg Sun* (September 5, 1902, p. 5): www.newspapers.com/image/691976324.

41 *The Buffalo Sunday Morning News* (November 17, 1901, p. 17): www.newspapers.com/image/355521379.

42 *Centers for Disease Control and Prevention (CDC)* (April 4, 2018): https://emergency.cdc.gov/agent/strychnine/basics/facts.asp.

43 *Lowell Sun* (November 2, 2011): www.lowellsun.com/2011/11/02/for-10-years-jolly-jane-poured-her-poison/.

44 *The South Bend Tribune* (November 2, 1901, p. 7): www.newspapers.com/image/513481505.

45 *The North Adams Transcript* (October 30, 1901, p. 1): www.newspapers.com/image/545440176.

46 *RxList* (July 30, 2020): www.rxlist.com/atropine-drug.htm#clinpharm.

47 *Daily News* (May 21, 22017): www.nydailynews.com/news/crime/killer-boston-nurse-poisoned-family-1901-article-1.3182852 (url geo-restricted).

48 *The Sun* (2 November 2011): www.lowellsun.com/2011/11/02/for-10-years-jolly-jane-poured-her-poison/.

49 *The Edwardsville Intelligencer* (August 18, 1938): www.newspapers.com/image/26467039.

50 *The Saint Paul Globe* (July 6, 1902, p. 21): www.newspapers.com/image/84111710.

51 *Hartford Courant* (March 29, 1902, p. 1): www.newspapers.com/image/369473104.

52 *Kansas City Daily Gazette* (August 20, 1902, p. 3): www.newspapers.com/image/61552279.

53 *Kenosha News* (June 25, 1902, p. 8) www.newspapers.com/image/595184622.

54 *Boston Post* (March 28, 1902, p. 1): www.newspapers.com/image/68958384.

55 *The Boston Globe* (June 24, 1902, p. 1): www.newspapers.com/image/430882049/.

56 *The Southwestern Local* (June 27, 1902, p. 4): www.newspapers.com/image/678533457.

57 *Boston Post* (March 28, 1902, p. 1): www.newspapers.com/image/68958384.

58 *The Saint Paul Globe* (July 6, 1902, p. 21): www.newspapers.com/image/84111710.

59 *The Saint Paul Globe* (July 6, 1902, p. 21): www.newspapers.com/image/84111710.

60 *Chicago Tribune* (June 25, 1902, p. 7): www.newspapers.com/image/350217267; *The Salina Daily Union* (July 26, 1902, p. 6): www.newspapers.com/image/112411395.

61 Moran et al., 2013.

62 *The Boston Globe* (June 23, 1902, p. 2): www.newspapers.com/image/430881982.

63 *The Baltimore Sun* (October 23, 1904, p. 12): www.newspapers.com/image/372053435.

64 *The Inter Ocean* (October 17, 1904, p. 6): www.newspapers.com/image/34507298.

65 *Boston Magazine* (October 29, 2015): www.bostonmagazine.com/news/2015/10/29/jane-toppan/.

66 *New England Historical Society* (2020): www.newenglandhistoricalsociety.com/jolly-jane-toppan-killer-nurse-obsessed-death/.

67 *The Edwardsville Intelligencer* (August 18, 1938, p. 2): www.newspapers.com/image/26467039.

68 *The Morning Chronicle* (August 18, 1938, p. 1): www.newspapers.com/image/422516233.

69 *History.com* (August 21, 2018): www.history.com/topics/immigration/the-irish-in-boston.

70 The demographics we collected were in line with those reported by criminal psychologist Eric Hickey (1986, 1991, 2016), who has been one of the only researchers to report original material about FSKs. He conducted interviews where possible and examined case files for 64 FSKs who committed their murders in the USA. Schurman-Kauflin (2000) also interviewed seven FSKs. All were White. Four out of seven were direct caregivers. Both Hickey and Schurman-Kauflin determined the mean age of first kill to be in the early thirties, as did Farrell et al. (2011) who derived data on ten FSKs using the mass media method.

71 Dube et al., 2003.

72 Uchitel et al., 2019.

73 *American Academy of Pediatrics* (May 24, 2021): www.aap.org/en-us/advocacy-and-policy/aap-health-initiatives/healthy-foster-care-america/Pages/Trauma-Guide.aspx.

74 Hezberg & Gunnar, 2020.

75 *Dana Foundation* (October 1, 2000): www.dana.org/article/wounds-that-time-wont-heal/.

76 Catalan et al., 2020; Young & Widom, 2014.

77 Seidel et al., 2013.

78 Herzberg & Gunnar, 2020.

79 Hooven et al., 2012.

80 Read et al., 2014.

81 *Florida Today* (January 30, 1992, p. 4): www.newspapers.com/image/177202835.

82 *WFLA* (November 30, 2020): www.wfla.com/news/crime/this-day-in-history-serial-killer-aileen-wuornos-kills-first-victim-a-clearwater-man/.

83 *Biography.com* (July 27, 2020): www.biography.com/crime-figure/aileen-wuornos.

84 *Florida Today* (January 30, 1992, p. 4): www.newspapers.com/image/177202835.

85 *The Orlando Sentinel* (January 30, 1992): www.orlandosentinel.com/news/os-xpm-1992-01-30-9201300954-story.html.

86 *Florida Divorce Index, 1927–2001.* Florida Department of Health, FL, USA. Certificate Number 036782: Ancestry.com.

87 *Tampa Bay Times* (June 2, 1991, p. 13): www.newspapers.com/image/323263861.

88 *The Tallahassee Democrat* (August 18, 1991, p. 41): www.newspapers.com/image/247489362.

89 *The New York Times* (January 18, 1991): www.nytimes.com/1991/01/18/us/woman-is-arrested-in-a-series-of-killings-in-florida.html.

90 *The Tallahassee Democrat* (August 18, 1991, p. 41): www.newspapers.com/image/247489362.

91 Myers et al., 2005.

92 *Florida Today* (January 30, 1992, p. 4): www.newspapers.com/image/177202835.

93 Myers et al., 2005, p. 652.

94 *ABC News* (January 6, 2006): https://abcnews.go.com/GMA/story?id=124614&page=1.

95 *Calgary Herald* (October 9, 2002, p. 3): www.newspapers.com/image/486378707.

96 *The Miami Herald* (October 6, 2002, p. 1081): www.newspapers.com/image/647047368.

97 *Orlando Sentinel* (October 10, 2002): www.orlandosentinel.com/news/os-xpm-2002-10-10-0210100261-story.html.

98 *The Washington Post* (February 8, 2004): www.washingtonpost.com/archive/opinions/
2004/02/08/more-of-a-monster-than-hollywood-could-picture/179c7282-5e25-4eb5-
8980-c72aa90efdb0/.

99 *South Florida Sun Sentinel* (January 18, 1991): www.sun-sentinel.com/news/fl-xpm-
1991-01-18-9101030868-story.html (url geo-restricted).

100 *The Palm Beach Post* (March 21, 2004, p. 147): www.newspapers.com/image/134574512.

4 MENTAL HEALTH AND SUBSTANCE USE AMONG FSKs

1 *The Knoxville Journal* (April 30, 1950, p. 47): www.newspapers.com/image/588247270.

2 *Bellevue Schools of Nursing Records. NYU Medical Archives* (n. d.): https://archives.med
.nyu.edu/collections/bellevue-school-of-nursing.

3 I add a note here evidencing Archer-Gilligan's propensity to misreport the truth.
In the July 1870 US Census, the then young Amy Duggan is recorded as two years
old, making her born about 1868. In the June 1880 US Census, she stays on a typical
human aging track and is twelve years old. Unfortunately, the 1890 US Census was
damaged by fire and is unavailable. It seems Amy probably started misrepresenting
her age right around then. The June 1900 US Census recorded her birthday as October 1873 and her age 26. The April 1910 US Census recorded her age as 37, which
presents a picture of confusing temporal mathematics. This means she or someone
else lied about her age and had at least one bad math day, or the 1870 Census was
incorrect but prescient. Also, as of 1900 her parents were no longer born in Ireland;
they were born in Connecticut. *National Archives* (1996): www.archives.gov/publi-
cations/prologue/1996/spring/1890-census-1.html. US Census Year: 1870; Census
Place: Litchfield, Litchfield, Connecticut, Page: 73; Ancestry.com. Census Year: 1900;
Census Place: East Hartford, Hartford, Connecticut, Page: 236. Ancestry.com; US
Census Year: 1910; Census Place: Windsor Township, Hartford, Connecticut, Page:
176; Ancestry.com; Windsor Historical Society (July 16, 2018): https://windsorhistor-
icalsociety.org/amy-archer-gilligan-entrepreneurism-gone-wrong-in-windsor/.

4 *Hartford Courant* (September 13, 1916, p. 1): www.newspapers.com/image/369118434.

5 *Hartford Courant* (July 1, 1917, p. 20): www.newspapers.com/image/369404793; *Hartford Courant* (April 17, 2014): www.courant.com/courant-250/moments-in-history/
hc-250-amy-archer-gilligan-20140416-story.html (url geo-restricted).

6 *Hartford Courant* (July 14, 1917, p. 3): www.newspapers.com/image/369409118.

7 *Hartford Courant* (June 30, 2017, p. 7): www.newspapers.com/image/369404283.

8 *Hartford Courant* (July 1, 1917, p. 20): www.newspapers.com/image/369404793.

9 *Hartford Courant* (May 9, 1916, p. 1): www.newspapers.com/image/369106460/.

10 *Meriden Morning Record (Record-Journal)* (June 26, 1919, p. 3): www.newspapers.com/
image/675656397.

11 Lipman,1994.

12 *Centers for Disease Control and Prevention (CDC)* (February 17, 2021): www.cdc.gov/
drugoverdose/pdf/calculating_total_daily_dose-a.pdf; *European Respiratory Journal*
(2017): https://erj.ersjournals.com/content/50/3/1701091; *US Food and Drug*

Administration (FDA) (December, 2009): www.accessdata.fda.gov/drugsatfda_docs/label/2010/022195s002lbl.pdf.

13 Shearer, 1960.

14 *RxList* (August 13, 2021): www.rxlist.com/consumer_morphine_duramorph_arymo_er/drugs-condition.htm.

15 Maybe she was just bad at numerical calculations, including dosage and age.

16 *Hartford Courant* (September 13, 1916, p. 1): www.newspapers.com/image/369118434.

17 *Hartford Courant* (June 30, 2017, p. 7): www.newspapers.com/image/369404283.

18 *The Journal* (December 20, 1916, p. 10): www.newspapers.com/image/675691452.

19 *Hartford Courant* (June 25, 1919, p. 1): www.newspapers.com/image/367315459/.

20 *Hartford Courant* (May 11, 1916, p. 1): www.newspapers.com/image/369107207/.

21 *Hartford Courant* (June 25, 1919, p. 1): www.newspapers.com/image/367315459/.

22 *Rutland Daily Herald* (November 24, 1896, p. 3): www.newspapers.com/image/533410692.

23 *Hartford Courant* (June 25, 1919, p. 12): www.newspapers.com/image/367315459/.

24 *Meriden Morning Record (Record-Journal)* (June 26, 1919, p. 3): www.newspapers.com/image/675656397.

25 *Hartford Courant* (June 25, 1919, p. 12): www.newspapers.com/image/367315459/.

26 *Hartford Courant* (June 25, 1919, p. 12): www.newspapers.com/image/367315459/.

27 *Hartford Courant* (April 17, 2014): www.courant.com/courant-250/moments-in-history/hc-250-amy-archer-gilligan-20140416-story.html (url geo-restricted).

28 *Hartford Courant* (April 17, 2014): www.courant.com/courant-250/moments-in-history/hc-250-amy-archer-gilligan-20140416-story.html (url geo-restricted).

29 *Record-Journal* (January 25, 2015, p. D2): www.newspapers.com/image/675862929.

30 *Hartford Courant* (September 15, 2015, p. A1): www.newspapers.com/image/263701091/.

31 *Hartford Courant* (June 25, 1919, p. 12): www.newspapers.com/image/367315459/.

32 van Haren et al., 2008; *National Institute of Mental Health* (May, 2020): www.nimh.nih.gov/health/topics/schizophrenia/.

33 Khokhar et al., 2018.

34 Of note, archival sources say that the Bellevue Nursing School graduates' pin was designed by Tiffany & Co. and included a wreath of poppies to signify nurses' role in alleviating pain. Morphine is derived from poppies. Amy Archer-Gilligan alleviated her own pain with morphine, at least to a certain extent: https://archives.med.nyu.edu/collections/bellevue-school-of-nursing.

35 Harrison et al., 2015.

36 Horwitz & Grob, 2011.

37 *Penn Nursing, University of Pennsylvania* (n. d.): www.nursing.upenn.edu/nhhc/nurses-institutions-caring/history-of-psychiatric-hospitals/.

38 Suris et al., 2016.

39 Current edition: DSM-5 (American Psychiatric Association, 2013).

40 *National Institute of Mental Health (NIMH)* (2020): www.nimh.nih.gov/health/statistics/mental-illness.shtml.

41 Castle & Hensley, 2002.

42 Melton et al., 2018.

43 Melton et al., 2018.

44 Our results are in line with the limited, existing literature, mostly low sample size and case studies, that speak to mental illness background of FSKs (e.g., Myers et al., 2005; Ryan et al., 2017). Keeney & Heide (1994) studied fourteen FSKs and found that the majority had some form of mental illness, such as bipolar disorder, dissociative disorders, or personality disorders. Theirs is one of the only studies speaking to mental illness in an arguably large sample of female serial murderers.

45 The original source material we considered gave good general indications of FSK mental health. It may be possible that mental illness is simply assumed after the perpetrator is caught, as asserted by other FSK researchers (Farrell et al., 2011; Schurman-Kauflin, 2000), but I did not see psychiatric information editorialized by news sources.

46 *American Psychological Association (APA)* (December 1, 2019): www.apa.org/monitor/2019/12/new-hope; *Substance Abuse and Mental Health Services Administration (SAMHSA)* (April 30, 2020): www.samhsa.gov/find-help/disorders.

47 *The Baltimore Sun* (February 23, 1972, p. 9): www.newspapers.com/image/377108804.

48 *Justia US Law* (2021): https://law.justia.com/cases/federal/appellate-courts/F2/484/127/195191/.

49 *The Baltimore Sun* (March 10, 1972, p. 38): www.newspapers.com/image/377183440.

50 *Mayo Clinic* (2021): www.mayoclinic.org/diseases-conditions/sudden-infant-death-syndrome/symptoms-causes/syc-20352800.

51 *The Baltimore Sun* (August 8, 1999, p. 30): www.newspapers.com/image/173482212.

52 *Justia US Law* (2021): https://law.justia.com/cases/federal/appellate-courts/F2/484/127/195191/.

53 *The Baltimore Sun* (July 25, 1972, p. 28): www.newspapers.com/image/376994605.

54 *The Baltimore Sun* (February 15, 1972, p. 28): www.newspapers.com/image/377191062.

55 *The Baltimore Sun* (July 25, 1972, p. 28): www.newspapers.com/image/376994605.

56 *The Baltimore Sun* (June 9, 1972, p. 48): www.newspapers.com/image/377300558.

57 *The Baltimore Sun* (July 4, 1972, p. 33): www.newspapers.com/image/377326042; *The Baltimore Sun* (July 25, 1972, p. 28): www.newspapers.com/image/376994605; *Justia US Law* (2021): https://law.justia.com/cases/federal/appellate-courts/F2/484/127/195191/.

58 *The Baltimore Sun* (August 8, 1999, p. 30): www.newspapers.com/image/173482212.

59 *The Baltimore Sun* (July 25, 1972, p. 28): www.newspapers.com/image/376994605.

60 *The Baltimore Sun* (August 8, 1999, p. 30): www.newspapers.com/image/173482212; *Federal Bureau of Prisons (US)* (2021): www.bop.gov/mobile/find_inmate/byname.jsp.

61 *Poughkeepsie Journal* (December 17, 1990, p. 1A): www.newspapers.com/image/114236383.

62 DiMaio & DiMaio, 1989; for review see Milroy & Kepron, 2017.

63 Firstman & Talan, 1997; DiMaio & Bernstein, 1974.

64 Unal et al., 2017.

65 Carter et al., 2006; Meadow, 1977, 1995; Unal et al., 2017.

66 Abdurrachid & Marques, 2020.

67 Faedda et al., 2018.

68 Meadow, 1977, 1995.

69 Faedda et al., 2018; Hornor, 2021; Yorker, 1994.

70 McClure et al., 1996.

71 *Cleveland Clinic* (November 26, 2014): https://my.clevelandclinic.org/health/diseases/9834-factitious-disorder-imposed-on-another-fdia.

72 Alexander et al., 1990; Faedda et al., 2018; Meadow, 2002.

73 *The Washington Post* (March 1, 1987): www.washingtonpost.com/archive/politics/1987/03/01/over-years-couple-buried-9-children/f2c444b0-93bb-483a-8fd8-d4d5aa46a4ae/.

74 *The Observer* (September 24, 1989, p. 36): www.newspapers.com/image/259076890.

75 *Who Magazine* (August 14, 2018): www.who.com.au/notorious-murderous-mother-marybeth-tinning-to-walk-out-of-prison.

76 *Poughkeepsie Journal* (December 17, 1990, p. 1A): www.newspapers.com/image/114236383.

77 *National Institute of Neurological Disorders and Stroke* (March 27, 2019): www.ninds.nih.gov/Disorders/All-Disorders/Reyes-Syndrome-Information-Page.

78 Egginton, 1989.

79 Meadow, 1995.

80 Egginton, 1989; *The Observer* (September 24, 1989, p. 36): www.newspapers.com/image/259076890.

81 *The Washington Post* (March 1, 1987): www.washingtonpost.com/archive/politics/1987/03/01/over-years-couple-buried-9-children/f2c444b0-93bb-483a-8fd8-d4d5aa46a4ae/.

82 *Daily News* (March 20, 2011, p. 41): www.newspapers.com/image/576251327.

83 *Find a Grave*, memorial page for Tami Lynne Tinning (22 Aug 1985–20 Dec 1985), Find a Grave Memorial no. 12511, citing Schenectady Memorial Park, NY.

84 *Daily News* (March 20, 2011, p. 41): www.newspapers.com/image/576251327.

85 *The Washington Post* (March 1, 1987): www.washingtonpost.com/archive/politics/1987/03/01/over-years-couple-buried-9-children/f2c444b0-93bb-483a-8fd8-d4d5aa46a4ae/.

86 *The Observer* (Sep 24, 1989, p. 36): www.newspapers.com/image/259076890.

87 *Poughkeepsie Journal* (July 18, 1987, p. 6A): www.newspapers.com/image/114331436.

88 *Democrat and Chronicle* (Apr 19, 1990, p. 16): www.newspapers.com/image/137339554.

89 *The Journal News* (July 17, 2018, p. A5): www.newspapers.com/image/460188851.

90 I comment here on my fondness for Schenectady, New York. Schenectady County Community College (SCCC) was the first college at which I was instructor of record for a psychology course.

91 *The Washington Post* (March 1, 1987): www.washingtonpost.com/archive/politics/1987/03/01/over-years-couple-buried-9-children/f2c444b0-93bb-483a-8fd8-d4d5aa46a4ae/.

92 *Biography.com* (April 4, 2019): www.biography.com/news/gypsy-rose-blanchard-mother-dee-dee-murder; *Harper's Bazaar* (April 3, 2019): www.harpersbazaar.com/culture/film-tv/a26887708/the-act-dee-dee-gypsy-blanchard-murder-trial-timeline/.

93 *Harvard Medical School* (2021): www.health.harvard.edu/newsletter_article/mental-illness-and-violence.

94 Stuart, 2003.

95 Vitello & Hickey, 2006.

96 Kondo, 2008.

97 Labrum et al., 2021, p. 10.

98 Morana et al., 2006.

99 I went back to our original data and analyzed whether FSKs noted to have mental illness murdered more victims. My team and I did not examine this in our original study (Harrison et al., 2015). Women with mental illness killed a mean of 6.6 (SD = 5.6) victims; women without mental illness killed a mean of 5.8 (SD = 4.3) victims. The number of dead is slightly higher for women with mental illness, and this could be clinically meaningful, but the difference was not statistically significantly different (p = 0.507). Thus, whereas there is a good chance a FSK has mental illness, a FSK with mental illness does not necessarily kill more victims.

100 Stuart et al., 2006.

101 Black, 2015.

102 See Fisher & Hany, 2020.

103 Linder et al., 2016; Nock et al., 2006.

104 Hare, 1999; Lynam & Gudonis, 2005.

105 See Harrison et al., 2015.

106 Hare, 1999.

107 *American Psychological Association* (APA) (2021): www.apa.org/topics/depression.

108 Fazel et al., 2015.

109 Doucet et al., 2009; Sit et al., 2006.

110 $X^2(1, N = 63) = 8.11, p = .004$.

111 *Substance Abuse and Mental Health Services Administration (SAMHSA)(US)* (2020): www.samhsa.gov/data/sites/default/files/reports/rpt29392/Assistant-Secretary-nsduh2019_presentation/Assistant-Secretary-nsduh2019_presentation.pdf.

112 *New York Daily News* (May 2, 2009): www.nydailynews.com/news/crime/death-row-granny-article-1.378057 (url geo-restricted).

113 *New York Daily News* (May 2, 2009): www.nydailynews.com/news/crime/death-row-granny-article-1.378057 (url geo-restricted).

114 *The News and Observer* (March 17, 1978, p. 50): www.newspapers.com/image/653438218; *The News and Observer* (July 1, 1984, p. 1): www.newspapers.com/image/654307626/; *The Washington Post* (October 21, 1984): www.washingtonpost.com/archive/politics/1984/10/21/tears-might-have-eased-penalty/2dfae8cb-b1d1-477a-afba-c7d4ca62921b/.

115 *The News and Observer* (November 30, 1978, p. 52): www.newspapers.com/image/653479787; *Spokane Chronicle* (September 13, 1984, p. 2): www.newspapers.com/image/569891081.

116 *The Washington Post* (October 21, 1984): www.washingtonpost.com/archive/politics/1984/10/21/tears-might-have-eased-penalty/2dfae8cb-b1d1-477a-afba-c7d4ca62921b/.

117 Campbell & Alvarez, 1989; Tournel et al., 2011.

118 *New York Daily News* (May 2, 2009): www.nydailynews.com/news/crime/death-row-granny-article-1.378057 (url geo-restricted).

119 *The Washington Post* (October 21, 1984): www.washingtonpost.com/archive/politics/1984/10/21/tears-might-have-eased-penalty/2dfae8cb-b1d1-477a-afba-c7d4ca62921b/.

120 *The News and Observer* (July 1, 1984, p. 16): www.newspapers.com/image/654307775/; *The Washington Post* (October 21, 1984): www.washingtonpost.com/archive/politics/1984/10/21/tears-might-have-eased-penalty/2dfae8cb-b1d1-477a-afba-c7d4ca62921b/.

121 *The Washington Post* (October 21, 1984): www.washingtonpost.com/archive/politics/1984/10/21/tears-might-have-eased-penalty/2dfae8cb-b1d1-477a-afba-c7d4ca62921b/.

122 *The Boston Globe* (November 2, 1984, p. 5): www.newspapers.com/image/437442709.

123 Min et al., 2007.

124 Fisher & Hany, 2020.

125 Black, 2017.

126 Fisher & Hany, 2020.

127 *Mayo Clinic* (January 7, 2020): www.mayoclinic.org/diseases-conditions/schizophrenia/diagnosis-treatment/drc-20354449.

128 Patel et al., 2014.

5 FSK CRIMES AND OUTCOMES

1 *Associated Press News* (February 5, 1993): https://apnews.com/article/668305a6f3662a4193d7b605b429e97e.

2 *The Telegraph* (June 17, 2018): www.thetelegraph.com/news/article/What-is-it-Mystery-soup-burgoo-draws-delights-13001677.php; *Village of Brighton, Illinois* (October 13, 2018): www.brightonil.com/vnews/display.v/ART/5bae6cc5bef13.

3 From 1908 to 1940, one could order prefabricated houses through the Sears & Roebuck Catalog, including the "Pretty Priscilla," cutting costs and construction time; *Sears Archives* (March 21, 2012): www.searsarchives.com/homes/index.htm.

4 *Enjoy Illinois* (2021): www.enjoyillinois.com/explore/listing/carlinville-historic-district.

5 *St. Louis Post-Dispatch* (February 11, 1993, p. 16): www.newspapers.com/image/141609451.

6 *St. Louis Post Dispatch* (December 5, 1990, p. 12): www.newspapers.com/image/141280516.

7 *St. Louis Post Dispatch* (December 5, 1990, p. 14): www.newspapers.com/image/141279766.

8 *St. Louis Post-Dispatch* (September 25, 1990, p. 3): www.newspapers.com/image/141250787.

9 *St. Louis Post-Dispatch* (September 22, 1990, p. 8): www.newspapers.com/image/141245044.

10 *Court Listener* (n. d.): www.courtlistener.com/opinion/2003777/people-v-eveans/; *St. Louis Post-Dispatch* (February 2, 1993, p. 24): www.newspapers.com/image/141599742.

11 *St. Louis Post-Dispatch* (January 30, 1993, p. 19): www.newspapers.com/image/141590080.

12 *St. Louis Post-Dispatch* (February 2, 1993, p. 24): www.newspapers.com/image/141599742.

13 *St. Louis Post-Dispatch* (February 11, 1993, p. 1): www.newspapers.com/image/141609451.

14 *United Press International (UPI)* (February 10, 1993): www.upi.com/Archives/1993/02/10/Child-killing-mother-sentenced-to-natural-life/5129729320400/?spt=su.

15 *St. Louis Post-Dispatch* (February 11, 1993, p. 16): www.newspapers.com/image/141609451.

16 *St. Louis Post-Dispatch* (February 10, 1993, p. 27): www.newspapers.com/image/141609443.

17 *WILL Illinois Public Media* (December 15, 2014): will.illinois.edu/news/story/report-overcrowding-after-dwight-prison-closing.

18 *The Behavior Panel* (February 17, 2021): www.youtube.com/watch?v=LJfRU7FCm-W4&t=536s.

19 Harrison et al., 2015.

20 Harrison et al., 2015.

21 *KIRO7* (January 22, 2020): www.kiro7.com/news/trending/genene-jones-angel-death-picu-nurse-gets-life-1981-murder-11-month-old-boy/ERHKXIP4WVHFFEOUNX-6VWZ6AXM/.

22 *Texas Monthly* (August, 1983): www.texasmonthly.com/articles/the-death-shift-2/.

23 *Texas Monthly* (August, 1983): www.texasmonthly.com/articles/the-death-shift-2/.

24 *KSAT.com* (January 26, 2020): www.ksat.com/news/local/2020/01/16/watch-killer-nurse-genene-jones-makes-plea-deal-in-court-hearing/.

25 *Associated Press News* (January 16, 2020): https://apnews.com/article/4a94be60293bf-b54a7bf306f34f33285.

26 *USA Today* (January 17, 2020): www.usatoday.com/story/news/nation/2020/01/17/texas-killer-nurse-genene-jones-guilty-infant-death/4499258002/.

27 *ProPublica* (January 16, 2020): www.propublica.org/article/texas-baby-killer-pleads-guilty-to-a-new-murder.

28 *My San Antonio* (January 15, 2020): www.mysanantonio.com/news/local/article/Child-killer-Genene-Jones-is-expected-to-take-a-14977763.php.

29 *KSAT.com* (January 16, 2020): www.ksat.com/news/local/2020/01/16/watch-killer-nurse-genene-jones-makes-plea-deal-in-court-hearing/.

30 *WDBO* (January 22, 2020): www.wdbo.com/news/national/genene-jones-angel-death-picu-nurse-gets-life-for-1981-murder-month-old-boy/Pq2dkXPujoVzeT2fCKsBnK/.

31 *Associated Press News* (January 16, 2020): https://apnews.com/article/4a94be60293bf-b54a7bf306f34f33285.

32 *Associated Press News* (January 16, 2020): https://apnews.com/article/4a94be60293bf-b54a7bf306f34f33285; *CBS11* (January 16, 2020): https://dfw.cbslocal.com/2020/01/16/ex-texas-killer-nurse-genene-jones-pleads-guilty-in-1981-death-of-11-month-old/; *ProPublica* (January 16, 2020): www.propublica.org/article/texas-baby-killer-pleads-guilty-to-a-new-murder.

33 *Texas Monthly* (August, 1983): www.texasmonthly.com/articles/the-death-shift-2/.

34 *Dignity Memorial* (June 11, 2019): www.dignitymemorial.com/obituaries/gonzales-la/petti-wiese-8742023; *San Antonio Express-News* (June 20, 2019): www.expressnews.com/news/local/article/Petti-McClellan-Wiese-mother-of-Texas-child-14024941.php.

35 This includes lethal dosages and other misuses of drugs.

36 This is consistent with reports from Hickey (2016), Kelleher & Kelleher (1998), and from Schurman-Kauflin (2000). This is also consistent with analysis by Wilson & Hilton (1998), who examined FSKs from 17 different countries. They found 45.3% of FSKs in the USA and 64.6% of FSKs from other countries used poison for a murder weapon, including arsenic, morphine, strychnine, and forced drug overdoses. One caveat is that their US sample committed crimes from 1825 to 1997, and their "other countries" sample committed crimes from the 1580s to 1997. A difference between regions may be attributed to weapon availability.

37 Wilson & Hilton, 1998.

38 Schurman-Kauflin, 2000.

39 *News-Journal* (November 29, 1954, p. 1–2): www.newspapers.com/image/294216061.

40 *Alabama Heritage* (January 31, 2019): www.alabamaheritage.com/from-the-vault/the-giggling-granny.

41 *Star-Gazette* (November 28, 1954, p. 1): www.newspapers.com/image/277371977.

42 *Daily Press* (November 29, 1957, p. 11): www.newspapers.com/image/230981863; *The Knoxville Journal* (January 13, 1957, p. 82): www.newspapers.com/image/587619079; *The Spokesman-Review* (June 1, 1955, p. 1): www.newspapers.com/image/568441673; *Alabama Heritage* (January 31, 2019): www.alabamaheritage.com/from-the-vault/the-giggling-granny.

43 *Encyclopedia of Alabama* (July 29, 2014): www.encyclopediaofalabama.org/article/h-3619.

44 *The Anniston Star* (June 3, 1965, p. 4): www.newspapers.com/image/109557902.

45 *News-Journal* (November 29, 1954, p. 1–2): www.newspapers.com/image/294216061.

46 *Encyclopedia of Alabama* (September 5, 2015): www.encyclopediaofalabama.org/article/h-3619.

47 *Chillicothe Gazette* (November 29, 1954, p. 4): www.newspapers.com/image/292445216.

48 *Miami News-Record* (November 29, 1954, p. 1): www.newspapers.com/image/8253926; *News-Journal* (November 29, 1954, p. 1–2): www.newspapers.com/image/294216061; *Star-Gazette* (November 28, 1954, p. 1): www.newspapers.com/image/277371977.

49 *The Spokesman-Review* (June 1, 1955, p. 1): www.newspapers.com/image/568441673.

50 *News-Journal* (November 29, 1954, p. 1–2): www.newspapers.com/image/294216061.

51 *The Kansas City Times* (December 1, 1954, p. 7): www.newspapers.com/image/657725608; *News-Journal* (November 29, 1954, p. 1–2): www.newspapers.com/image/294216061.

52 *The Knoxville Journal* (January 13, 1957, p. 82): www.newspapers.com/image/587619079.

53 *The Anniston Star* (October 18, 2015, p. 29): www.newspapers.com/image/141775688.

54 *The Daily Oklahoman* (May 5, 1955, p. 42): www.newspapers.com/image/449640806; *The Spokesman-Review* (June 1, 1955, p. 1): www.newspapers.com/image/568441673.

55 *PBS Frontline* (2014): www.pbs.org/wgbh/pages/frontline/shows/crime/trial/history.html.

56 *The Daily Oklahoman* (March 4, 2012, p. 25): www.newspapers.com/image/452611949.

57 *The Anniston Star* (June 3, 1965, p. 4): www.newspapers.com/image/109557902.

58 *Tulsa World* (August 1, 2006) https://tulsaworld.com/archive/your-honor-the-plea-is-guilty/article_c75b75d2-6ca7-57fb-9594-9bdd0c26b424.html.

59 Pershagen, 1981.

60 Davison et al., 2002.

61 *Find a Grave* (May 12, 2007): www.findagrave.com/memorial/19354123/nancy-doss.

62 Farrell et al., 2011, p. 230.

63 *The Saint Paul Globe* (July 6, 1902): www.newspapers.com/newspage/84111710/.

64 Hickey (1991) stated that the 64 FSKs in his sample killed between 7 and 10 people. The 7 FSKs that Schurman-Kauflin (2000) interviewed killed a total of 36 known victims, for an average of 5.14 victims. Farrell et al. (2011) reported that the 10 FSKs in their study killed an average of 9 victims.

65 Our findings are in line with those from Kelleher & Kelleher (1998), Farrell et al. (2013) and Holmes et al. (1991). These researchers reported that FSKs tend to target children, the ill, and elderly victims.

66 Harrison et al., 2015.

67 *CBS News* (April 2, 2012): www.cbsnews.com/news/kimberly-saenz-former-nurse-convicted-of-killing-five-with-bleach-awaits-sentence; *The Monitor* (April 1, 2012, p. 22): www.newspapers.com/image/331723516.

68 *Lufkin Daily News* (April 2, 2012): https://lufkindailynews.com/news/local/article_df1a2c38-7d00-11e1-9b9c-0019bb2963f4.html.

69 *KRTE ABC9* (April 2, 2012): www.ktre.com/story/17311211/sentencing-for-saenz-begins-with-light-shed-on-domestic-issues/.

70 *The Daily Sentinel* (April 9, 2009): www.dailysentinel.com/news/local/article_d318975a-8994-5504-b1f1-361793b3aeda.html; *KIMA CBS* (March 4, 2012): www.kimatv.com/news/nation-world/gallery/nurses-bleach-injection-deaths-trial-begins-11-14-2015-230029540?photo=1; *KLTV ABC7* (June 2, 2008): www.kltv.com/story/8402949/woman-accused-of-injecting-bleach-into-dialysis-patients-arrested.

71 *CBS News* (April 2, 2012): www.cbsnews.com/news/kimberly-saenz-former-nurse-convicted-of-killing-five-with-bleach-awaits-sentence; *Daily Mail* (March 31, 2012): www.dailymail.co.uk/news/article-2123252/Nurse-Kimberly-Saenz-faces-death-penalty-murdering-patients-bleach.html.

72 *The Daily Sentinel* (April 8, 2012): www.dailysentinel.com/social_media/article_039148ba-81b8-11e1-8f98-001a4bcf887a.html.

73 *RxList* (May 3, 2021): www.rxlist.com/demerol-drug.htm.

74 *Lufkin Daily News* (April 30, 2008): https://lufkindailynews.com/news/article_0907829c-7589-50df-99ae-eaf8bae3c53b.html.

75 *KIMA CBS* (March 4, 2012): www.kimatv.com/news/nation-world/gallery/nurses-bleach-injection-deaths-trial-begins-11-14-2015-230029540?photo=1; *The Lufkin Dailey News* (August 26, 2015): https://lufkindailynews.com/news/local/article_ee34960c-811c-11e1-ba1d-0019bb2963f4.html.

76 *San Diego Tribune* (April 2, 2012): www.sandiegouniontribune.com/sdut-life-in-prison-for-ex-nurse-in-5-bleach-deaths-2012apr02-story.html.

77 *The Monitor* (April 1, 2012, p. 22): www.newspapers.com/image/331723516; *KRTE ABC9* (April 2, 2012): www.ktre.com/story/17311211/sentencing-for-saenz-begins-with-light-shed-on-domestic-issues/.

78 Legal experts refer to the outcome of a case as its disposition. See *Washington State Department of Social and Health Services* (n.d.): www.dshs.wa.gov/node/28996.

6 FSK MOTIVES AND PROFILE

1 Harrison et al., 2015.
2 Holmes & DeBurger, 1988; Holmes & Holmes, 2010.
3 *Justia US Law* (2021): https://law.justia.com/cases/federal/appellate-courts/F3/229/15/577356/ 0).
4 *The Boston Globe* (October 8, 2000): https://cache.boston.com/globe/metro/packages/nurse/part1.htm.
5 *The Boston Globe* (October 9, 2000, p. 12): www.newspapers.com/image/442016344.
6 *Associated Press News* (November 27, 1998): https://apnews.com/article/9a6ebf9823b-1c0fd8f82631c9870afb6.
7 When Gilbert was convicted, the death penalty was a possible sentence. Although Massachusetts does not have capital punishment, Gilbert murdered people on government property. As told by *The Boston Globe*, ironically, Gilbert would have been executed the same way she executed helpless, disabled veterans – by lethal injection. Instead, Gilbert received four life sentences for her crimes; *The Boston Globe* (March 15, 2001): www.newspapers.com/image/443075171/.
8 To gain another expert's perspective on Gilbert, I contacted my colleague Enzo Yaksic, co-founder of the Atypical Homicide Research Group. He corroborated, "FSKs do not neatly fit into the Holmes and Holmes' typology. The Gilbert case is a great example of that" (personal communication, 2021).
9 Taylor et al., 2012.
10 Kelleher & Kelleher, 1998.
11 Dryer-Brees, 2012.
12 Taylor et al., 2012.
13 Darwin, 1859.
14 Buss, 2000; Duntley, 2005.
15 Buss, 2000; Daly & Wilson, 1988; Duntley, 2005.
16 Trivers, 1972.
17 Johnson et al., 1980.
18 Schmitt et al., 2001.
19 Markovic & Markovic, 2008.
20 Bennett, 2018; Trivers, 1972.
21 Buss et al., 2001; Buss & Shackelford, 2008; Hughes & Aung, 2017; Trivers, 1972.
22 Geary, 2000.
23 Kanazawa, 2010.
24 Harrison et al., 2015; Hickey, 2016.
25 *Associated Press News* (February 9, 1998): https://apnews.com/article/b41d1b30de8b-72fa71c4022a4e074d0c; *New York Daily News* (December 31, 2016): www.nydailynews.com/news/crime/artist-fatal-insurance-frauds-exploded-face-article-1.2929932 (url

geo-restricted); *Pensacola News Journal* (May 13, 1984, p. 1): www.newspapers.com/image/267073570.

26 *CBS News* (March 30, 1998): www.cbsnews.com/news/florida-executes-black-widow; *New York Daily News* (December 31, 2016): www.nydailynews.com/news/crime/artist-fatal-insurance-frauds-exploded-face-article-1.2929932; *Pensacola News Journal* (May 13, 1984, p. 1): www.newspapers.com/image/267073570; *South Florida Sun Sentinel* (November 2, 1985): www.sun-sentinel.com/news/fl-xpm-1985-11-02-8502180566-story.html (url geo-restricted); *United States District Court, Middle District of Florida* (n.d.): www.flmd.uscourts.gov/black-widow.

27 *The Orlando Sentinel* (March 29, 1998, p. 14): www.newspapers.com/image/234505689.

28 All three quotations in this paragraph from *Pensacola News Journal* (May 13, 1984, p. 1): www.newspapers.com/image/267073570.

29 A logistical point: sources say it is possible to take out life insurance policies on nonrelatives if one can demonstrate one would experience financial hardship if they died, and if the insured person consents to it. *Forbes* (April 5, 2021): www.forbes.com/advisor/life-insurance/on-someone-else/.

30 *The Orlando Sentinel* (March 29, 1998, p. 14): www.newspapers.com/image/234505689; *The Seattle Times* (February 9, 1998): https://archive.seattletimes.com/archive/?date=19980209&slug=2733480.

31 *Independent* (March 29, 1998): www.independent.co.uk/news/no-tears-for-the-black-widow-of-death-row-1153231.html; *The Orlando Sentinel* (March 29, 1998, p. 14): www.newspapers.com/image/234505689.

32 *The Tampa Tribune* (March 30, 1998, p. 12): www.newspapers.com/image/340847169.

33 *The Tampa Tribune* (March 31, 1998, p. 9): www.newspapers.com/image/340850653.

34 *The Bradenton Herald* (March 31, 1998, p. 1): www.newspapers.com/image/720271696; *The Bradenton Herald* (March 31, 1998, p. 3): www.newspapers.com/image/720271696; *Florida Today* (March 31, 1998, p. 40): www.newspapers.com/image/174748542.

35 *CBS News* (March 30, 1998): www.cbsnews.com/news/florida-executes-black-widow/.

36 *South Florida Sun Sentinel* (March 29, 1998, p. 12): www.newspapers.com/image/239016719.

37 *CNN* (March 27, 1998): www.cnn.com/US/9803/27/black.widow/index.html.

38 *Pensacola News Journal* (May 13, 1984, p. 1): www.newspapers.com/image/267073570.

39 *The Orlando Sentinel* (March 29, 1998, p. 14): www.newspapers.com/image/234505689.

40 *YouthToday.org* (September 20, 2017): https://youthtoday.org/2017/09/abuse-in-foster-care-research-vs-the-child-welfare-systems-alternative-facts/.

41 *News-Press* (February 8, 1998, p. 35): www.newspapers.com/image/217500574; *Pensacola News Journal* (May 13, 1984, p. 1): www.newspapers.com/image/267073570.

42 *Pensacola News Journal* (May 13, 1984, p. 1): www.newspapers.com/image/267073570.

43 *History.com* (October 23, 2019): www.history.com/topics/native-american-history/geronimo.

44 *Pensacola News Journal* (May 13, 1984, p. 1): www.newspapers.com/image/267073570.

45 Dawkins, 1989.

46 Brüne, 2003; Duntley & Buss, 2012; Wakefield, 2005.

47 Kanazawa, 2010.

48 Rees, 2009.

49 Hrdy, 1979; Tuomi et al., 1997.

50 Weissenbacher, 1987.

51 Boggess, 1979.

52 Hrdy, 1979.

53 Middle-class, $n = 9$; Lower-class, $n = 3$.

54 Ebensperger, 2007; Hiraiwa-Hasegawa, 1988; Rees, 2009.

55 *The Montgomery Advertiser* (May 26, 1957, p. 1): www.newspapers.com/image/256253622/.

56 *The Montgomery Advertiser* (August 28, 1939, p. 3): www.newspapers.com/image/414020904.

57 *Alabama Journal* (August 3, 1943, p. 2): www.newspapers.com/image/415361806; *The Montgomery Advertiser* (March 18, 1956, p. 1): www.newspapers.com/image/262331364; *The Montgomery Advertiser* (May 26, 1957, p. 1): www.newspapers.com/image/256253622/.

58 *The Atmore Advance* (November 4, 2014): www.atmoreadvance.com/2014/11/04/black-widow-killer-had-ties-to-perdido/.

59 *U.S. County Marriage Records, Alabama*, 1805–1967, p. 360: Ancestry.com.

60 *The Montgomery Advertiser* (March 18, 1956, p. 1): www.newspapers.com/image/262331364.

61 *U.S. Social Security Death Index*, 1935–2014: Ancestry.com.

62 *U.S. County Marriage Records, Alabama*, 1805–1967, p. 314: Ancestry.com.

63 *The Huntsville Times* (October 11, 1957, p. 1): www.newspapers.com/image/554859337; *Messenger-Inquirer* (October 12, 1957, p. 1): www.newspapers.com/image/378458252; *The Robesonian* (June 5, 1956, p. 1): www.newspapers.com/image/42031709.

64 *Alabama Journal* (June 4, 1956, p. 2): www.newspapers.com/image/457444680; *The Montgomery Advertiser* (June 5, 1956, p. 1): www.newspapers.com/image/262324152.

65 *The Birmingham News* (October 11, 1957, p. 8): www.newspapers.com/image/574895590; *Daily News* (March 14, 1956. p. 3): www.newspapers.com/image/455060994.

66 *The Miami Herald* (October 12, 1957, p. 4): www.newspapers.com/image/619703890.

67 *The Montgomery Advertiser* (May 26, 1957, p. 1): www.newspapers.com/image/256253622/.

68 *Alabama Journal* (June 4, 1956, p. 1): www.newspapers.com/image/457444636.

69 *The Montgomery Advertiser* (June 5, 1956, p. 1): www.newspapers.com/image/262324152.

70 Johnston & Leahey, 2021, p. 1778.

71 Sit et al., 2006, p. 353.

72 See Sit et al., 2006, for review.

73 *US County Marriage Records, Alabama*, p. 314: Ancestry.com.

74 *National Organization for Rare Disorders* (2021): https://rarediseases.org/rare-diseases/heavy-metal-poisoning/.

75 *The Cincinnati Enquirer* (March 15, 1956, p. 1): www.newspapers.com/image/101067494/.

76 *The Huntsville Times* (October 11, 1957, p. 2): www.newspapers.com/image/554859354; *The Montgomery Advertiser* (October 11, 1957, p. 1): www.newspapers.com/image/256321493.

77 *The Meriden Daily Republican* (February 1, 1876, p. 4): www.newspapers.com/image/674789812.

78 *Hartford Courant* (April 30, 2014): www.courant.com/news/connecticut/hc-250-lydia-sherman-20140429-story.html (url geo-restricted); *New Haven Register* (January 10, 2015): www.nhregister.com/connecticut/article/The-Derby-Poisoner-The-story-of-Lydia-Sherman-a-11358691.php.

79 *Connecticut History* (March 10, 2020): https://connecticuthistory.org/lydia-sherman-the-derby-poisoner; *New England Historical Society* (2020): www.newenglandhistoricalsociety.com/lydia-sherman-the-derby-poisoner-commits-the-horror-of-the-century.

80 *Hartford Courant* (January 8, 1873, p. 3): www.newspapers.com/image/368951297.

81 *The Knoxville Journal* (August 4, 1946, p. 39): www.newspapers.com/image/587736602.

82 *The Meriden Daily Republican* (May 17, 1878, p. 2): www.newspapers.com/image/674760841.

83 *Hartford Courant* (April 30, 2014): www.courant.com/news/connecticut/hc-xpm-2014-04-30-hc-250-lydia-sherman-20140429-story.html (url geo-restricted); *The Knoxville Journal* (August 4, 1946, p. 39): www.newspapers.com/image/587736602.

84 *Hartford Courant* (January 8, 1873, p. 3): www.newspapers.com/image/368951297.

85 *New England Historical Society* (2020): www.newenglandhistoricalsociety.com/lydia-sherman-the-derby-poisoner-commits-the-horror-of-the-century/.

86 Boggess, 1979; Hrdy, 1979.

87 *US Connecticut Church Record Abstracts*, 1630–1920, Vol. 102, Shelton: Ancestry.com.

88 *US Find a Grave Index*, 1600s–Current: Ancesty.com.

89 *US Connecticut, Wills and Probate Records*, 1609–1999: Ancestry.com.

90 *New England Historical Society* (2020): www.newenglandhistoricalsociety.com/lydia-sherman-the-derby-poisoner-commits-the-horror-of-the-century/.

91 *US Federal Census Mortality Schedules*, 1850–1885, line 15: Ancestry.com.

92 *Centers for Disease Control and Prevention (CDC)* (October 2, 2020): www.cdc.gov/cholera/illness.html.

93 *New York Daily Herald* (January 13, 1873, p. 3): www.newspapers.com/image/329398728.

94 *US Massachusetts, Town and Vital Records*, 1620–1988: Ancestry.com.

95 *Hartford Courant* (July 3, 1871, p. 2): www.newspapers.com/image/369170878; *Hartford Courant* (January 8, 1873, p. 3): www.newspapers.com/image/368951297; *Hartford Courant* (April 30, 2014): www.courant.com/news/connecticut/hc-xpm-2014-04-30-hc-250-lydia-sherman-20140429-story.html (url geo-restricted); *US Connecticut, Deaths and Burials Index*, 1650–1934, FHL Film Number 3330: Ancestry.com.

96 *Hartford Courant* (July 10, 1871, p. 1): www.newspapers.com/image/369171492.

97 *Hartford Courant* (April 18, 1872, p. 3): www.newspapers.com/image/369420005; *The Knoxville Journal* (August 4, 1946, p. 39): www.newspapers.com/image/587736602.

98 Reports are mixed on how many murders Sherman was charged with initially. One outlet said she was charged only with the murder of Horatio Sherman. Another Outlet said she was arrested for 11 murders – three husbands and eight children. *Nashville Union and American* (July 14, 1871, p. 2): www.newspapers.com/image/80924065; *New York Herald* (April 26, 1872, p. 12): www.newspapers.com/image/9055562.

99 *Hartford Courant* (July 3, 1871, p. 2): www.newspapers.com/image/369170878.

100 *Hartford Courant* (January 20, 1929, p. 63): www.newspapers.com/image/369263710.

101 *New York Herald* (April 24, 1872, p. 12): www.newspapers.com/image/9055562.

102 *The Knoxville Journal* (August 4, 1946, p. 39): www.newspapers.com/image/587736602.

103 *Hartford Courant* (April 18, 1872, p. 3): www.newspapers.com/image/369420005.

104 *The Knoxville Journal* (August 4, 1946, p. 39): www.newspapers.com/image/587736602.

105 *New York Daily Herald* (April 27, 1872, p. 6): www.newspapers.com/image/329422152.

106 *The Meriden Daily Republican* (May 31, 1877, p. 3): www.newspapers.com/image/674757498.

107 *The Meriden Daily Republican* (May 17, 1878, p. 2): www.newspapers.com/image/674760841.

108 Tapio & Grosche, 2006 .

109 *The Pittsburg Daily Commercial* (November 16, 1871, p. 2): www.newspapers.com/image/85457336.

110 *New York Herald* (April 24, 1872, p. 12): www.newspapers.com/image/9055562.

111 *The Ottawa Citizen* (September 18, 1982, p. 79): www.newspapers.com/image/461750455.

112 *New York Herald* (April 24, 1872, p. 12): www.newspapers.com/image/9055562.

113 van Aken, 2015.

114 Harrison et al., 2015.

115 The composite appears in Harrison et al., 2015.

116 Hickey, 1986, 2016; Hickey was also the first researcher to describe data on a larger sample of FSKs ($N = 22$), collecting information from police reports, news articles, and texts.

117 Pinizzotto, 1984, p. 32.

118 Fox & Farrington, 2018, p. 1247.

119 *Federal Law Enforcement Bulletin* (August 5, 2014): https://leb.fbi.gov/articles/featured-articles/criminal-investigative-analysis-measuring-success-part-three-of-four.

120 Kocsis & Palermo, 2015.

7 COMPARING FSKs AND MSKs: BACKGROUNDS AND MENTAL ILLNESS

1 *The Minneapolis Star* (November 19, 1957, p. 13): www.newspapers.com/image/187862394; *News-Record* (November 18, 1957, p. 1): www.newspapers.com/image/444945183.

2 *News-Record* (November 18, 1957, p. 1): www.newspapers.com/image/444945183.

3 *Wisconsin State Journal* (January 3, 2020): https://madison.com/wsj/news/local/crime-and-courts/six-serial-killers-who-left-deep-scars-on-wisconsin/article_209a11f5-ae56-513f-b868-624362f241b5.html.

4 *New Zealand Herald* (October 24, 2000): www.nzherald.co.nz/world/who-was-the-mother-of-the-most-depraved-serial-killer-of-all-time/T75XZ2O7K7AGAP5LBGPKD-KHVV4/.

5 *Stevens Point Journal* (November 19, 1957, p. 1): www.newspapers.com/image/250495821/.

6 *The Daily Telegram* (November 21, 1957, p. 1): www.newspapers.com/clip/24219479/ed-gein-wanted-to-be-a-woman/.

7 *A & E Television* (February 11, 2021): www.aetv.com/real-crime/ed-gein-the-skin-suit-wearing-serial-killer-who-inspired-psychos-norman-bates.

8 *Sheboygan Press* (July 30, 2016): www.sheboyganpress.com/story/news/2016/07/30/sheboygan-pathologist-helped-ed-gein-case/87772724/.

9 *Sheboygan Press* (November 15, 1958, p. 13): www.newspapers.com/image/240094415.

10 *The Daily Press* (March 20, 1958, p. 1): www.newspapers.com/image/243791445.

11 *Stevens Point Journal* (March 20, 1958, p. 1): www.newspapers.com/image/250465303.

12 *Nashville Banner* (November 30, 1957, p. 3): www.newspapers.com/image/603316818.

13 *Biography.com* (2021): www.biography.com/crime-figure/ed-gein; *History.com* (2021): www.history.com/this-day-in-history/real-life-psycho-ed-gein-dies.

14 *The Minneapolis Star* (November 19, 1957, p. 13): www.newspapers.com/image/187862394.

15 *The Los Angeles Times* (May 4, 2001): www.latimes.com/archives/la-xpm-2001-may-04-ca-59065-story.html.

16 *The Daily Telegram* (November 21, 1957, p. 1): www.newspapers.com/image/299073824.

17 *Manitowoc Herald-Times* (November 15, 1968, p. 1): www.newspapers.com/clip/24095961/gein-judged-insane-after-murder/.

18 Hare, 1999; *The Oshkosh Northwestern* (November 14, 1968, p. 1): www.newspapers.com/image/247912156.

19 *A & E Television* (February 11, 2021): www.aetv.com/real-crime/serial-killer-ed-gein-was-a-model-patient-after-being-incarcerated-for-his-gruesome-crimes.

20 *Kenosha News* (July 27, 1984, p. 2): www.newspapers.com/image/597295799.

21 *The Capital Times* (November 22, 1957, p. 1): www.newspapers.com/image/518720302.

22 Aggrawal, 2009; *American Psychological Association* (2020): https://dictionary.apa.org/necrophilia.

23 Gein's gender identity (woman): was not congruent with the sex he was assigned at birth (male).

24 *The Daily Telegram* (November 21, 1957, p. 1): www.newspapers.com/image/299073824.

25 *Nashville Banner* (November 30, 1957, p. 3): www.newspapers.com/image/603316818.

26 Resources say there are many terms to describe one's "experience of gender that is not simply male or female"; *The National Center for Transgender Equality* (October 5, 2018): https://transequality.org/issues/resources/understanding-non-binary-people-how-to-be-respectful-and-supportive.

27 *American Psychological Association* (2011/2021): www.apa.org/topics/lgbtq/sexual-orientation.

28 Trivers, 1972.

29 Harrison et al., 2019.

30 *Pew Research* (December 17, 2014): www.pewresearch.org/fact-tank/2014/12/17/wealth-gap-upper-middle-income/.

31 *American Psychiatric Association* (2021): www.psychiatry.org/patients-families/what-is-mental-illness.

32 Gross et al., 2019.

33 See Kröber, 2016.
34 *National Institute of Mental Health* (2019): www.nimh.nih.gov/health/topics/men-and-mental-health.
35 Helmchen, 2016.
36 Harrison et al., 2019; Hickey, 2016.
37 *National Institute of Mental Health* (2019): www.nimh.nih.gov/health/topics/men-and-mental-health.
38 Harrison et al., 2019.
39 Eaton et al., 2012.
40 Eaton et al., 2012.
41 Shapero et al., 2013.
42 *National Institute of Mental Health* (2020): www.nimh.nih.gov/health/statistics/mental-illness.shtml.
43 See Stuart, 2003, for review.
44 Allely et al., 2014.
45 Häkkänen, 2008, p. 52.
46 Prentky et al., 1989.
47 *Psychiatric Times* (November 28, 2016): www.psychiatrictimes.com/view/dsm-5-and-paraphilias-what-psychiatrists-need-know.
48 Prentky et al., 1989.
49 Krasowska et al., 2013.
50 Prentky et al., 1989.
51 Abel & Osborn, 1992; Craig & Bartels, 2021.
52 Schlesinger, 2008.
53 Hickey, 2016.
54 Cleckley, 1941/1988.
55 Boschelli, 2008, p.146.
56 *The Capital Times* (February 26, 1980, p. 4): www.newspapers.com/image/519841345.
57 Porter, 1996.
58 *The Des Moines Register* (January 12, 1979, p. 6): www.newspapers.com/image/129206754; *John Wayne Gacy: Devil in Disguise* (March 25, 2021) Documentary on Peacock television: NBC News Studios.
59 *John Wayne Gacy: Devil in Disguise* (March 25, 2021) Documentary on Peacock television: NBC News Studios.
60 *Biography.com* (2021): www.biography.com/crime-figure/john-wayne-gacy.
61 *The New Yorker* (April 18, 1994): www.newyorker.com/magazine/1994/04/18/conversations-with-a-killer.
62 *The Capital Times* (February 26, 1980, p. 4): www.newspapers.com/image/519841345; *Northwest Herald* (May 9, 1994, p. 5): www.newspapers.com/image/195153763.
63 *A & E Television* (September 15, 2020): www.aetv.com/real-crime/john-wayne-gacys-childhood.
64 Boschelli, 2008.
65 *The New Yorker* (April 18, 1994): www.newyorker.com/magazine/1994/04/18/conversations-with-a-killer.

66 *John Wayne Gacy: Devil in Disguise* (March 25, 2021) Documentary on Peacock television: NBC News Studios.

67 Papalia et al., 2018.

68 As noted by Savic et al. (2010): "There is no proof that social environment after birth has an effect on gender identity or sexual orientation" (p. 41).

69 *The New Yorker* (April 18, 1994): www.newyorker.com/magazine/1994/04/18/conversations-with-a-killer.

70 It is important to point out that Gacy's family, including both his wives, repeatedly stated that they did not want to be named in reports about Gacy at the time of his arrest and trial. While their identities can readily be obtained elsewhere, I will not be naming them here, as they had nothing to do with the crimes committed.

71 *The Des Moines Register* (January 12, 1979, p. 1): www.newspapers.com/image/129206718/.

72 *Chicago Tribune* (December 23, 1978, p. 1): www.newspapers.com/image/386643314.

73 *John Wayne Gacy: Devil in Disguise* (March 25, 2021) Documentary on Peacock television: NBC News Studios.

74 *The New Yorker* (April 18, 1994): www.newyorker.com/magazine/1994/04/18/conversations-with-a-killer.

75 Herman et al., 1984.

76 *Chicago Tribune* (December 28, 1978, p. 5): www.newspapers.com/image/386643323.

77 *Chicago Tribune* (December 17, 2018): www.chicagotribune.com/history/ct-john-wayne-gacy-timeline-htmlstory.html; *Fort Lauderdale News* (January 10, 1979, p. 8): www.newspapers.com/image/233418448.

78 *The Boston Globe* (January 3, 1979, p. 8): www.newspapers.com/image/436846702.

79 *The New Yorker* (April 18, 1994): www.newyorker.com/magazine/1994/04/18/conversations-with-a-killer.

80 *John Wayne Gacy: Devil in Disguise* (March 25, 2021) Documentary on Peacock television: NBC News Studios.

81 *Albany Democrat-Herald* (December 28, 1978, p. 12): www.newspapers.com/image/441134949.

82 *The New Yorker* (April 18, 1994): www.newyorker.com/magazine/1994/04/18/conversations-with-a-killer.

83 Herman et al., 1984.

84 *John Wayne Gacy: Devil in Disguise* (March 25, 2021) Documentary on Peacock television: NBC News Studios.

85 Yaksic et al., 2021.

86 *Chicago Tribune* (December 23, 1978, p. 4): www.newspapers.com/image/386643321.

87 *Chicago Tribune* (December 17, 2018): www.chicagotribune.com/history/ct-john-wayne-gacy-timeline-htmlstory.html; *Harper's Bazaar* (October 31, 2018): www.harpersbazaar.com/culture/features/a24269889/john-wayne-gacy-kim-byers-lund-interview/; *John Wayne Gacy: Devil in Disguise* (March 25, 2021) Documentary on Peacock television: NBC News Studios.

88 *The New Yorker* (April 18, 1994): www.newyorker.com/magazine/1994/04/18/conversations-with-a-killer.

89 *Times Advocate* (May 9, 1994, p. 3): www.newspapers.com/image/571862318.

90 *Chicago Tribune* (February 17, 1979): www.newspapers.com/image/386658911/.

91 *Hartford Courant* (April 24, 1979): www.newspapers.com/image/368573571.

92 *Times Advocate* (May 9, 1994, p. 3): www.newspapers.com/image/571862318.

93 *The New Yorker* (April 18, 1994): www.newyorker.com/magazine/1994/04/18/conver-sations-with-a-killer.

94 *Chicago Tribune* (December 23, 1978, p. 5): www.newspapers.com/image/386643323.

95 *National Center for Missing and Exploited Children* (2018): www.missingkids.org/poster/ncmu/1184583; *National Center for Missing and Exploited Children* (2018): www.missingkids.org/poster/NCMU/1322532; *USA Today* (July 23, 2018): www.usatoday.com/story/news/2018/07/23/john-wayne-gacy-unidentified-victims-new-sketches/819914002/.

96 *Times Advocate* (May 9, 1994, p. 3): www.newspapers.com/image/571862318.

97 Herman et al., 1984.

98 *The New Yorker* (April 18, 1994): www.newyorker.com/magazine/1994/04/18/conver-sations-with-a-killer.

99 Herman et al., 1984.

100 *John Wayne Gacy: Devil in Disguise* (March 25, 2021) Documentary on Peacock televi-sion: NBC News Studios.

101 *Chicago Tribune* (February 17, 1979, p. 5): www.newspapers.com/image/386658911/; *The Dispatch* (June 6, 1984, p. 3): www.newspapers.com/image/340163666.

102 Hare, 1999, p. 142.

103 *Chicago Tribune* (December 17, 2018): www.chicagotribune.com/history/ct-john-wayne-gacy-timeline-htmlstory.html.

104 *John Wayne Gacy: Devil in Disguise* (March 25, 2021): Documentary on Peacock televi-sion: NBC News Studios.

105 *Journal Gazette* (March 13, 1980, p. 3): www.newspapers.com/image/82478609.

106 *Chicago Tribune* (December 17, 2018): www.chicagotribune.com/history/ct-john-wayne-gacy-timeline-htmlstory.html.

107 Herman et al., 1984.

108 *Chicago Tribune* (February 29, 1980, p. 3): www.newspapers.com/image/386790761.

109 Herman et al., 1984.

110 *The Des Moines Register* (January 12, 1979, p. 1): www.newspapers.com/image/129206718/.

111 Cleckley, 1941.

112 *Chicago Tribune* (February 29, 1980, p. 3): www.newspapers.com/image/386790761.

113 *Biography.com* (2021): www.biography.com/crime-figure/john-wayne-gacy.

114 Shortly after sentencing, on July 1, Judge Garippo resigned.

115 *The New Yorker* (April 18, 1994): www.newyorker.com/magazine/1994/04/18/conver-sations-with-a-killer.

116 *St. Louis Post-Dispatch* (March 10, 1981, p. 7): www.newspapers.com/image/139560353.

117 Hare, 1999.

118 *Lancaster New Era* (May 10, 1994): www.newspapers.com/image/565300364.

119 *The Los Angeles Times* (May 10, 1994): www.latimes.com/archives/la-xpm-1994-05-10-mn-55926-story.html.

120 *Chicago Tribune* (May 11, 1994): www.chicagotribune.com/news/ct-xpm-1994-05-11-9405110269-story.html; *Hartford Courant* (May 11, 1994, p. 2): www.newspapers.com/image/175520540.

121 *Chicago Tribune* (May 29, 2004): www.chicagotribune.com/news/ct-xpm-2004-05-29-0405290263-story.html.

122 Hare, 1999.

123 *Chicago Tribune* (December 23, 1978, p. 1): www.newspapers.com/image/386643314.

124 *The Atlanta Constitution* (December 28, 1978, p. 1): www.newspapers.com/image/398681310.

125 Cleckley, 1988, p. 202.

126 *The New Yorker* (April 18, 1994): www.newyorker.com/magazine/1994/04/18/conversations-with-a-killer.

127 *Fox News* (March 25, 2021): www.foxnews.com/entertainment/john-wayne-gacy-true-crime-doc-devil-in-disguise; *The Wrap* (March 26, 2021): www.thewrap.com/john-wayne-gacy-devil-in-disguise-detectives-interview/.

128 Tagge et al., 2018.

129 *Centers for Disease Control (CDC):* (February 12, 2019): www.cdc.gov/headsup/basics/concussion_whatis.html.

130 *Albany Democrat-Herald* (December 28, 1978, p. 12): www.newspapers.com/image/441134949.

131 *Chicago Tribune* (December 23, 1978, p. 1): www.newspapers.com/image/386643314.

132 Lachmann & Lachmann, 1995, p. 22.

8 COMPARING FSKS AND MSKS: CRIMES AND VICTIMS

1 Harrison et al., 2019.

2 Hickey, 2010, p. 274.

3 In our broader sample of 64 FSKS (Harrison et al., 2015), there was one case in which the FSK was born elsewhere but committed crimes in the USA. Within our matched sample of FSK-MSK pairs (Harrison et al., 2019), there were no FSKs born outside the USA.

4 Harrison et al., 2019.

5 *Security.org* (May 17, 2021): www.security.org/resources/homicide-statistics-by-state/; *US Federal Bureau of Investigation* (2012): https://ucr.fbi.gov/crime-in-the-u.s/2011/crime-in-the-u.s.-2011/offenses-known-to-law-enforcement/standard-links/region; *US Federal Bureau of Investigation* (2019): https://ucr.fbi.gov/crime-in-the-u.s/2019/crime-in-the-u.s.-2019.

6 *Center for the Study of Southern Culture* (May 26, 2020): https://southernstudies.olemiss.edu/study-the-south/more-pricks-than-kicks/.

7 Brush, 2007.

8 Rushin & Michalski, 2020.

9 This percentage is very similar to Eric Hickey's (2010) report that 91% of MSKs committing their crimes since 1975 have killed at least one stranger.

10 Ressler & Shachtman, 1992.

11 In this instance, stalking refers to instances of watching and following the victim repeatedly, waiting outside their home or workplace, and tracking their pattern of behavior and schedules.

12 *Biography.com* (2021): www.biography.com/crime-figure/belle-gunness; *Cape Gazette* (November 30, 2018): www.capegazette.com/article/sussex-county-serial-killer/159135; *New England Historical Society* (2020): www.newenglandhistoricalsociety.com/jolly-jane-toppan-killer-nurse-obsessed-death/.

13 *Biography.com* (2021): www.biography.com/crime-figure/ted-bundy.

14 Harrison et al., 2015.

15 Hickey (2016) also reported that MSKs typically target young women who are alone.

16 Harrison et al., 2019.

17 *7News.com.au* (December 23, 2019): https://7news.com.au/news/crime/wifes-shock-my-hubby-buried-a-body-in-the-backyard-and-was-living-a-double-life-c-619061; *The Seattle Times* (May 7, 2000): https://archive.seattletimes.com/archive/?date=20000507&slug=4019811.

18 *ABC News* (January 7, 2006): https://abcnews.go.com/US/story?id=95301&page=1.

19 *7News.com.au* (December 23, 2019): https://7news.com.au/news/crime/wifes-shock-my-hubby-buried-a-body-in-the-backyard-and-was-living-a-double-life-c-619061; *The Washington Post* (May 21, 2000): www.washingtonpost.com/archive/politics/2000/05/21/police-looking-for-worldwide-trail-of-death/bd4007d9-6f8c-48d9-b8f9-1a5080fe85ab/.

20 *The Washington Post* (May 21, 2000): www.washingtonpost.com/archive/politics/2000/05/21/police-looking-for-worldwide-trail-of-death/bd4007d9-6f8c-48d9-b8f9-1a5080fe85ab/.

21 *Herald Net* (November 10, 2000): www.heraldnet.com/news/yates-wife-visits-him-and-asks-why/.

22 *7News.com.au* (December 23, 2019): https://7news.com.au/news/crime/wifes-shock-my-hubby-buried-a-body-in-the-backyard-and-was-living-a-double-life-c-619061.

23 *ABC News* (January 7, 2006): https://abcnews.go.com/US/story?id=95301&page=1.

24 *The Seattle Times* (May 7, 2000): https://archive.seattletimes.com/archive/?date=20000507&slug=4019811.

25 *The Seattle Times* (May 7, 2000): https://archive.seattletimes.com/archive/?date=20000507&slug=4019811; *The Spokesman Review* (April 20, 2000, p. 7): www.newspapers.com/image/575485727; *The Washington Post* (May 5, 2000): www.washingtonpost.com/archive/politics/2000/05/21/police-looking-for-worldwide-trail-of-death/bd4007d9-6f8c-48d9-b8f9-1a5080fe85ab/.

26 *The Spokesman Review* (April 20, 2000, p. 7): www.newspapers.com/image/575485727.

27 *The Spokesman Review* (October 12, 2018): www.spokesman.com/stories/2018/oct/12/social-worker-who-served-yates-victims-supports-en/.

28 *The Spokesman Review* (April 20, 2000, p. 1): www.newspapers.com/image/575485727.

29 *The Spokesman Review* (October 20, 2000, p. 1): www.newspapers.com/image/575493081.

30 *The Washington Post* (May 21, 2000): www.washingtonpost.com/archive/politics/2000/05/21/police-looking-for-worldwide-trail-of-death/bd4007d9-6f8c-48d9-b8f9-1a5080fe85ab/.

31 *The Spokesman Review* (October 20, 2000, p. 1): www.newspapers.com/image/575545169.

32 *The Seattle Times* (May 16, 2013): www.courts.wa.gov/content/PublicUpload/eclips/5.17.13%20STimes1.pdf.

33 *The Spokesman Review* (October 12, 2018): www.spokesman.com/stories/2018/oct/12/social-worker-who-served-yates-victims-supports-en/.

34 *The Washington Post* (May 21, 2000): www.washingtonpost.com/archive/politics/2000/05/21/police-looking-for-worldwide-trail-of-death/bd4007d9-6f8c-48d9-b8f9-1a5080fe85ab/.

35 *The Seattle Times* (October 27, 2000): https://archive.seattletimes.com/archive/?date=20001027&slug=4049951.

36 *The Spokesman Review* (October 26, 2000, p. 2): www.newspapers.com/image/575545178.

37 Prolific author and researcher Enzo Yaksic is the cofounder of the Atypical Homicide Research Group.

38 Yaksic et al., 2021.

39 *The Spokesman Review* (April 20, 2000, p. 6): www.newspapers.com/image/575485727.

40 *The Seattle Times* (November 5, 2000): https://archive.seattletimes.com/archive/?date=20001105&slug=TTDO27G1Q.

41 *The Spokesman Review* (October 26, 2000, p. 2): www.newspapers.com/image/575545178.

42 *The Seattle Times* (May 7, 2000): https://archive.seattletimes.com/archive/?date=20000507&slug=4019811.

43 *The Spokesman Review* (October 26, 2000, p. 2): www.newspapers.com/image/575545178.

44 Harrison et al., 2019.

45 As reported by Papalia et al. (2018), people who experienced childhood sexual abuse (CSA) are more prone to criminal behavior than people who do not experience CSA, including sexual and violent crimes. Interestingly, there is a sex effect in terms of a stronger association for women CSA victims and violent crime and for men CSA victims and sexual crimes. While my team did not document CSA for the serial murderers in our sample, it is notable that, in serial murder generally, we do see extreme violence manifest in the form of murder for FSKs, and in sexual barbarism and murder for MSKs.

46 Harrison et al., 2019.

47 Maybe the "three baby" rule should apply to three husbands; one dead husband is sad; two dead husbands are suspicious; three dead husbands are probably murder.

48 Farrell et al., 2011, p. 230.

49 *New York Post* (May 21, 2003): https://nypost.com/2003/05/21/baby-slay-horror-n-y-mom-stored-bodies-for-19-yrs-cops/.

50 I chose not to study pairs of serial homicide offenders in my research. I could not correctly parse cognitions, motivations, and attributions for each of the pair from media sources. I validate, though, the importance of researching and understanding this type of offender.

51 *IndyStar* (n.d.): www.indystar.com/story/news/crime/2019/01/03/debra-denise-brown-no-longer-executed/2470845002/; *Dayton Daily News* (May 1, 1985, p. 7): www.newspapers.com/image/406835151.

52 The research of Friedel & Fox (2018) yielded a different picture. They studied a large sample of male repeat homicide offenders who committed their crimes in the USA from the 1970s onward. They reported that most offenders who met the definition of "serial killer" did not retain victim totems. However, as the number of a MSK's victims increased, the probability of their keeping totems increased. This phenomenon should be explored further.

53 *Statesman Journal* (March 29, 2006, p. 2): www.newspapers.com/image/202827029.

54 Leibman, 1989.

55 *Statesman Journal* (March 29, 2006, p. 2): www.newspapers.com/image/202827029.

56 *The Capital Journal* (June 2, 1969, p. 11): www.newspapers.com/image/316222322; *Statesman Journal* (June 28, 1969, p. 1): www.newspapers.com/image/198489686.

57 *Corvallis Gazette-Times* (March 27, 2009, p. 31): www.newspapers.com/image/383787262.

58 *Statesman Journal* (March 29, 2006, p. 2): www.newspapers.com/image/202827029; *Statesman Journal* (June 28, 1969, p. 1): www.newspapers.com/image/198489686.

59 *Statesman Journal* (June 28, 1969, p. 1): www.newspapers.com/image/198489686.

60 *Corvallis Gazette-Times* (March 27, 2009, p. 31): www.newspapers.com/image/383787262.

61 *Statesman Journal* (March 29, 2006, p. 2): www.newspapers.com/image/202827029.

62 *Corvallis Gazette-Times* (March 27, 2009, p. 31): www.newspapers.com/image/383787262.

63 Aggrawal, 2009; Palmero, 2008.

64 Leibman, 1989.

65 *Corvallis Gazette-Times* (March 27, 2009, p. 31): www.newspapers.com/image/383787262.

66 *Albany-Democrat Herald* (October 30, 1969): www.newspapers.com/image/441822121.

67 *The Capital Journal* (September 30, 1969, p. 1): www.newspapers.com/image/316233391/; *Corvallis Gazette-Times* (March 27, 2009, p. 31): www.newspapers.com/image/383787262; *Daily News* (June 28, 1970): www.newspapers.com/image/464656155.

68 *The Capital Journal* (June 7, 1979, p. 19): www.newspapers.com/image/316863275.

69 *Biography.com* (2021): www.biography.com/crime-figure/jerome-brudos; *The Oregonian* (January 10, 2019): www.oregonlive.com/politics/2014/07/salem_shoe-fetish_killer_jerry.html.

70 *Statesman Journal* (March 29, 2006, p. 2): www.newspapers.com/image/202827029.

71 Davis, 1998.

72 RAINN's support network includes a mobile app, online chat, and phone number to reach someone to talk through issues with, and for referral to long-term support. Please visit https://rainn.org/ for more information.

73 RAINN (n.d.): www.rainn.org/articles/child-sexual-abuse.

74 *The Spokesman-Review* (October 26, 2000, p. 2): www.newspapers.com/image/575545178.

75 Hickey, 2016.

9 THE BEHAVIORAL NEUROSCIENCE OF SERIAL MURDER

1 *World Health Organization* (2002): www.who.int/violence_injury_prevention/violence/world_report/en/summary_en.pdf.

2 Parker Jones et al., 2018; see Harrison & Hughes, 2020, for review.

3 For example, Miller, 2014; Raine, 2013. Neurocriminologist Adrian Raine's (2013) book, *The anatomy of violence: The biological roots of crime*, speaks to the biological causes of violent and deadly criminality.

4 Psychologist Sasha Reid (2017) did an excellent job collating information about the few direct examinations that yielded evidence of brain damage in serial killers, including cases detailed by Kraus (1995) and by Dietz (1986). I give credit to Reid's comprehensive work here, because despite my many years of conducting research on this topic, I previously had not come across these two highly informative case studies. I went back to the original reports by Kraus (1995) and Dietz (1986), and I consulted original source media for additional information.

5 Kraus, 1995.

6 Kraus, 1995.

7 Kraus, 1995, p. 17.

8 *Democrat and Chronicle* (January 6, 1990, p. 8): www.newspapers.com/image/136428705.

9 Kraus,1995, p. 12.

10 *The Buffalo News* (April 13, 1993): https://buffalonews.com/news/a-serial-killers-lessons-learning-from-the-atrocities-of-arthur-shawcross/article_d17ecf2d-6b5c-5d5d-ab38-518e525fdefb.html.

11 Parfitt & Alleyne, 2020; a recent review by Parfitt & Alleyne (2020) showed that each of these behaviors predicts later violent offending, and the presence of all three behaviors together is uncommon. The fact that the three behaviors together are not necessary for prediction of violence ostensibly negates the validity of the triad concept. More research is needed.

12 Kraus, 1995.

13 Kraus, 1995, p. 14.

14 Dietz, 1986.

15 Dietz, 1986, p. 484.

16 Dietz, 1986, p. 484.

17 Dietz, 1986.

18 Dietz, 1986, p. 487.

19 Kawasaki et al., 2010.

20 Reid, 2017; Stone, 2009.

21 Allely et al., 2014.

22 Williams et al., 2018.

23 *Johns Hopkins Medicine* (2021): www.hopkinsmedicine.org/health/conditions-and-diseases/traumatic-brain-injury.

24 Meijers et al., 2017.

25 Williams et al., 2018.

26 Reid, 2017.

27 Luauté et al., (2011b).

28 *The Leavenworth Times* (January 1, 1899, p. 6): www.newspapers.com/image/76598134.

29 *The Baltimore Sun* (January 2, 1899): www.newspapers.com/image/365266305.

30 Role, 1998.

31 Starr, 2010.

32 Luauté et al., 2011b.

33 *Mayo Clinic* (2021): www.mayoclinic.org/diseases-conditions/meningioma/symptoms-causes/syc-20355643.

34 Christian et al., 2005; Singhrao et al., 1993.

35 Luauté et al., 2011a.

36 *The Grand Island Daily Press* (February 18, 1899, p. 2): www.newspapers.com/image/693029687.

37 *The Leavenworth Times* (January 1, 1899, p. 6): www.newspapers.com/image/76598134.

38 *The Grand Island Daily Press* (February 18, 1899, p. 2): www.newspapers.com/image/693029687.

39 *The New York Times* (January 1, 1899): www.nytimes.com/1899/01/01/archives/french-ripper-guillotined-joseph-vacher-who-murdered-more-than-a.html.

40 *The Leavenworth Times* (January 1, 1899, p. 6): www.newspapers.com/image/76598134.

41 Ostrosky-Solís et al., 2008.

42 *The Guardian* (April 1, 2008): www.theguardian.com/world/2008/apr/02/mexico.

43 Suárez-Meaney et al., 2017.

44 Ostrosky-Solís et al., 2008, p. 1224.

45 Ostrosky-Solís et al., 2008, p. 1225.

46 Ostrosky-Solís et al., 2008.

47 *The Guardian* (May 18, 2006): www.theguardian.com/world/2006/may/19/gender.mexico.

48 Flórez et al., 2020.

49 Stone, 2018.

50 Ostrosky-Solís et al., 2008.

51 *BBC News* (April 1, 2008): http://news.bbc.co.uk/2/hi/americas/7323821.stm.

52 Even in wrestling meant as an "illusion of legitimate competition," *ABC News Australia* reported that "the physicality is real. Like stunt performers, wrestlers execute feats of athleticism." Thus, I add it is possible, even in fictional, simulated wrestling matches, that head snapping, bouncing, and twisting motions can cause neurological harm. Still, wrestlers do not typically become serial killers. *ABC News Australia* (2017): www.abc.net.au/news/2017-10-04/its-all-fake-right-a-professional-wrestler-explains-everything/9010474.

53 *Centers for Disease Control and Prevention (CDC)* (February 12, 2019): www.cdc.gov/headsup/basics/concussion_whatis.html.

54 Fjell et al., 2017.

55 *The Guardian* (April 1, 2008): www.theguardian.com/world/2008/apr/02/mexico.

56 *Stanford Health Care* (2021): https://stanfordhealthcare.org/medical-clinics/neuropsychology-clinic/what-to-expect/purpose-of-assessment.html.

57 *Cleveland Clinic* (October 15, 2020): https://my.clevelandclinic.org/health/diagnostics/4893-neuropsychological-testing–assessment.

58 Benton, 1994.

59 Angrilli et al., 2013, p. 489.

60 Per Angrilli et al. (2013), K. T. would be classified as a missionary killer per Holmes and Holmes' serial killer classification (Holmes & DeBurger, 1988; Holmes & Holmes, 2010).

61 Roalf & Gur, 2017.

62 Dogra et al., 2012.

63 *Hindustan Times* (March 26, 2001): www.hindustantimes.com/cities/noida-news/surinder-koli-spared-in-13th-nithari-case-101616780549841.html.

64 *One India* (September 11, 2014): www.oneindia.com/india/is-hanging-painful-asks-jittery-nithari-butcher-surinder-koli-1519514.html?ref_medium=Desktop&ref_source=OI-EN&ref_campaign=Topic-Article.

65 Dogra et al., 2012.

66 Dogra et al., 2012, p. 306.

67 Dogra et al., 2012, p. 311.

68 Reid, 2017.

69 *CNN* (April 30, 2015): www.cnn.com/2015/04/30/us/feat-jeffrey-dahmer-killer-explanation/index.html.

70 Reid, 2017, p. 55.

71 Palermo, 2008; Reid, 2017.

72 *John Wayne Gacy: Devil in Disguise* (March 25, 2021) Documentary on Peacock television: NBC News Studios.

73 Fox & Levin, 2011.

74 *Telegraph-Forum* (May 9, 2004, p. 12): www.newspapers.com/image/601396065.

75 Ventricles are interconnected cavities in the brain in which cerebrospinal fluid (CSF) is produced. CSF cushions the brain and removes the brain's waste products. Enlargement can indicate that the surrounding brain tissue has atrophied. A blockage can put dangerous pressure on the brain, creating a condition called *hydrocephalus. National Center for Biotechnology Information, U.S. National Library of Medicine Bookshelf* (2001): www.ncbi.nlm.nih.gov/books/NBK11083/.

76 *Chicago Tribune* (May 29, 2004): www.chicagotribune.com/news/ct-xpm-2004-05-29-0405290263-story.html.

77 *Telegraph-Forum* (May 9, 2004, p. 12): www.newspapers.com/image/601396065.

78 Null results are findings from a research study that did not turn out the way the researcher predicted.

79 Rosenthal, 1979.

80 Reid, 2017.

81 *Hindustan Times* (March 2, 2019): www.hindustantimes.com/delhi-news/surinder-koli-convicted-in-10th-nithari-rape-murder-case-sentencing-today/story-nqz71ND5efVNrqAzDiHuSO.html; Dogra et al., 2012).

82 Gao & Raine, 2010.

83 Yaksic et al., 2021; I (Harrison) was part of this team.

84 Reid, 2017.

85 Brower & Price, 2001.

86 *National Center for Biotechnology Information, U.S. National Library of Medicine Bookshelf* (September 20, 2020): www.ncbi.nlm.nih.gov/books/NBK545214/.

87 Blair, 2017; De Brito et al., 2013; Meijers et al., 2017.

88 Pera-Guardiola et al., 2016.

89 Cristofori et al., 2016.

90 De Brito et al., 2013.

91 Ogilvie et al., 2011.

92 Meijers et al., 2017.

93 Kovner et al., 2019.

94 Keuper et al., 2018; Nelson & Guyer, 2011; Torregrossa et al., 2008.

95 Kumari et al., 2009.

96 Goetschius et al., 2020.

97 Lund et al., 2020.

98 Wang et al., 2020.

99 Celada et al., 2013; Dalley & Roiser, 2012.

100 Abdalla-Fihlo & Völlm, 2020.

101 Angrilli et al., 1999, 2013; Hare 1991/2003.

102 Wisconsin Card Sorting Test (WCST) is a neuropsychological exam testing executive function, particularly cognitive flexibility and reasoning; *American Psychological Association (APA)* (2020): https://dictionary.apa.org/wisconsin-card-sorting-test.

103 Angrilli et al., 2013; Raine et al., 1998.

104 Yaksic et al., 2021.

105 Pera-Guardiola et al., 2016.

106 Glenn et al., 2013.

107 See Black, 2015, for review.

108 Glenn et al., 2013.

109 Hare, 1996.

110 Hare, 1996, p. 1.

111 Glenn et al., 2013.

112 Anton et al., 2012.

113 LaBrode, 2007.

114 Raine & Yang, 2006.

115 Silva et al., 2004.

116 Palermo & Bogaerts, 2015, p. 1564.

117 Giordano et al., 2014.

118 Schwartz, 2021.

119 Freedman & Hemenway, 2000.

120 Farrer & Hedges, 2011.

121 Williams et al., 2018.

122 Gómez et al., 2016.

123 Heritability is variability in phenotype attributable to genetic differences. Stated another way, it measures how genes can explain observable trait differences. *Medline Plus* (September 16, 2021): https://medlineplus.gov/genetics/understanding/inheritance/heritability/.

124 Viding & Frith, 2006.

125 *US National Library of Medicine* (August 18, 2020): https://medlineplus.gov/genetics/gene/maoa/.

126 Meyer et al., 2006.

127 Lea & Chambers, 2007; Wensley & King, 2008.

128 The cingulate is part of the limbic system and connects to the frontal lobes. It is "a connecting hub" for emotions, motivation, attention, cognitive control, and motor control. *Medline Plus* (July 23, 2021): www.ncbi.nlm.nih.gov/books/NBK537077/.

129 Cerasa et al., 2010; Meyer-Lindenberg et al., 2006.

130 Beaver et al., 2010; Stetler et al., 2014.

131 Kafka, 2003.

132 Kamenskov & Gurina, 2019.

133 Prentky et al., 1989.

134 See Kafka, 2003, for review.

135 Beaver et al., 2013.

136 McDermott et al., 2009.

137 Lea & Chambers, 2007.

138 Wensley & King, 2008.

139 People's genes vary from each other, and from those of other species, only by a very minor amount. But that small difference goes a long way in terms of making us each unique. *National Human Genome Research Institute* (2021): www.genome.gov/Pages/Education/Modules/BluePrintToYou/Blueprint3to4.pdf; *Medline Plus* (2021): https://medlineplus.gov/genetics/understanding/basics/gene/.

140 *CNN* (August 21, 2020): www.cnn.com/2020/08/21/us/golden-state-killer-sentencing/index.html.

141 *ABC News* (August 21, 2020): https://abcnews.go.com/US/living-witness-teen-dads-murder-confronts-golden-state/story?id=72473195.

142 *The Los Angeles Times* (December 8, 2020): www.latimes.com/projects/man-in-the-window-joe-DeAngelo-golden-state-killer-serial/; *The Sacramento Bee* (August 14, 2018, p. A7): www.newspapers.com/image/644054005.

143 *USFederal Bureau of Investigation* (FBI) (n. d.): www.fbi.gov/services/laboratory/biometric-analysis/codis/codis-and-ndis-fact-sheet.

144 Brown, 2019.

145 *GED Match* (2021): www.gedmatch.com/.

146 *The Los Angeles Times* (December 8, 2020): www.latimes.com/california/story/2020-12-08/man-in-the-window.

147 *The Los Angeles Times* (June 15, 2018, p. B4): www.newspapers.com/image/442272611.

148 *ABC News* (August 21, 2020) https://abcnews.go.com/US/living-witness-teen-dads-murder-confronts-golden-state/story?id=72473195.

149 Brown, 2019.

150 *ABC News* (August 21, 2020): https://abcnews.go.com/US/living-witness-teen-dads-murder-confronts-golden-state/story?id=72473195; Brown, 2019.

151 *SFGATE* (June 29, 2020): www.sfgate.com/crime/article/Golden-State-Killer-Joseph-DeAngelo-mental-health-15374517.php.

152 *Sioux City Journal* (June 30, 2020, p. A4): www.newspapers.com/image/670329892.

153 *Esquire* (July 5, 2020): www.esquire.com/entertainment/tv/a33169675/ill-be-gone-in-the-dark-joseph-deangelo/; *The Los Angeles Times* (December 8, 2020): www.latimes.com/projects/man-in-the-window-joe-DeAngelo-golden-state-killer-serial/.

154 *The Los Angeles Times* (December 8, 2020): www.latimes.com/projects/man-in-the-window-joe-DeAngelo-golden-state-killer-serial/.

155 *ABC7* (April 26, 2018): https://abc7news.com/forensic-psychologist-examines-mind-of-accused-golden-state-killer/3399573/.

156 *ABC News* (April 27, 2018): https://abcnews.go.com/US/fbi-agent-thinks-golden-state-killer-suspect-fits/story?id=54776471.

157 *New Zealand Herald* (May 28, 2018): www.nzherald.co.nz/world/terrifying-look-inside-golden-state-killers-bedroom-stocked-with-victims-trophies/FVLDQ2YZO6VT65T-GAW3GNC3KW4/.

158 Cleckley, 1941/1988.

159 *The Los Angeles Times* (April 26, 2018): www.latimes.com/local/lanow/la-me-golden-state-killer-what-we-know-deangelo-20180426-story.html.

160 *ABC News* (April 27, 2018): https://abcnews.go.com/US/fbi-agent-thinks-golden-state-killer-suspect-fits/story?id=54776471.

161 *ABC10* (August 25, 2020): www.abc10.com/article/news/crime/he-is-the-best-father-i-could-have-had-daughter-of-golden-state-killer-pens-letter-about-her-dad/103-9ed45271-875c-46f5-be12-41bda262c19c (url geo-restricted).

162 *ABC News* (April 27, 2018) https://abcnews.go.com/US/fbi-agent-thinks-golden-state-killer-suspect-fits/story?id=54776471.

163 Yaksic et al., 2021.

164 *The Los Angeles Times* (April 27, 2018, p. A8): www.newspapers.com/image/425887590.

165 *The Desert Sun* (June 2, 2018, p. A11): www.newspapers.com/image/436970497.

166 *New York Daily News* (May 25, 2018): www.nydailynews.com/news/crime/creepy-detail-revealed-search-golden-state-killer-home-article-1.4010343 (url geo-restricted).

167 *CNN* (August 21, 2020): www.cnn.com/2020/08/21/us/golden-state-killer-sentencing/index.html; *Sioux City Journal* (June 30, 2020, p. A4): https://www.newspapers.com/image/670329892; *The Sacramento Bee* (May 15, 2018, p. A1): www.newspapers.com/image/644534470.

168 *CNN.com* (August 21, 2020): www.cnn.com/2020/08/21/us/golden-state-killer-sentencing/index.html.

169 *ABC57* (August 19, 2020): www.abc57.com/news/the-nightmare-has-ended-victims-address-the-golden-state-killer-in-court.

170 *CBS13 Sacramento* (August 20, 2020): https://sacramento.cbslocal.com/2020/08/20/family-members-of-murder-victims-assail-golden-state-killer-joseph-deangelo/.

10 PSYCHOSOCIAL FACTORS THAT MAKE A SERIAL MURDERER

1 Taylor & Gunn, 1999.

2 Hickey, 1986, 2016; Keeney & Heide, 1994.

3 Myers et al., 2005.

4 Myers et al., 2005, p. 654.

5 Myers et al., 2005, p. 655.

6 Myers et al., 2005, p. 657.

7 Levin, 2008.

8 Tracy & Rix, 2017.

9 *The Los Angeles Times* (September 22, 2002): www.latimes.com/archives/la-xpm-2002-sep-22-me-hillside22-story.html.

10 *History.com* (January 7, 2020): www.history.com/this-day-in-history/the-hillside-stranglers.

11 *The Sacramento Bee* (September 22, 2002, p. 35): www.newspapers.com/image/629555180.

12 Levin, 2008.

13 *The Bellingham Herald* (October 21, 2019): www.bellinghamherald.com/news/local/crime/article236388543.html.

14 Myers et al., 2005; Ostrosky-Solís et al., 2008.

15 *Edmonton Journal* (February 20, 1994, p. 25): www.newspapers.com/image/475876117.

16 Teicher & Samson, 2013.

17 *Centers for Disease Control and Prevention (CDC)* (2020): www.cdc.gov/genomics/disease/epigenetics.htm.

18 Jaffee, 2017.

19 Hickey, 2010, p. 271.

20 Kendall-Tackett, 1991.

21 See Weiss & Alexander, 2013, for review.

22 John-Steiner & Mahn, 2006.

23 DeFronzo et al., 2007; data are on MSKs only.

24 *The Town Talk* (December 2, 2006, p. 17): www.newspapers.com/image/360172592.

25 *The Times* (December 24, 2006, p. 18): www.newspapers.com/image/220290711.

26 Forsyth, 2015.

27 Forsyth, 2015.

28 *Dallas Voice* (December 7, 2006): https://dallasvoice.com/alleged-gay-serial-killer-arrested/.

29 Forsyth, 2015.

30 *NOLA.com* (June 25, 2019): www.nola.com/news/article_45b3a901-8934-5687-bad1-469ef2dac60f.html.

31 Forsyth, 2015.

32 *The Daily Review* (September 24, 2008, p. 7): www.newspapers.com/image/470724229.

33 Forsyth, 2015.

34 *Dallas Voice* (December 7, 2006): https://dallasvoice.com/alleged-gay-serial-killer-arrested/.

35 Forsyth, 2015, p. 864.

36 *The Times* (December 14, 2006, p. 18): www.newspapers.com/image/220290711.

37 Forsyth, 2015.

38 *The Town Talk* (December 2, 2006, p. 17): www.newspapers.com/image/360172592.

39 *The Times Online* (April 8, 2014): www.houmatimes.com/news/bayou-blue-recalls-serial-killer/.

40 Forsyth, 2015, p. 862.

41 Forsyth, 2015.

42 *Houmatoday.com* (September 23, 2008): www.houmatoday.com/story/news/2008/09/23/serial-killer-gets-eight-life-sentences-for-local-murders/27020250007/; *The New York Times* (September 24, 2008): www.nytimes.com/2008/09/24/us/24brfs-PLEAINSERIAL_BRF.html.

43 *The Daily Review* (September 24, 2008, p. 7): www.newspapers.com/image/470724229.

44 Vygotsky, 1929/1994.

45 Bronfenbrenner, 1979.

46 Forsyth, 2015.

47 Jewkes & Linneman, 2018.

48 Rios & Ferguson, 2020.

49 Rios & Ferguson, 2020.

50 For example, Simpson, 2020.

51 Duwe, 2000.

52 Duwe, 2000, p. 364.

53 Jenkins, 1994.

54 Wiest, 2016.

55 Wiest, 2016, p. 337.

56 Schmid, 2005.

57 *Associated Press News* (February 9, 2019): https://apnews.com/article/fda5c470e49540ec9f7f5910bb07bd8b.

58 *The New York Times* (December 10, 1978): www.nytimes.com/1978/12/10/archives/allamerican-boy-on-trial-ted-bundy.html.

59 *SFGATE* (January 28, 2019): www.sfgate.com/crime/article/conversations-with-a-killer-review-netflix-13567369.php.

60 Penfold-Mounce, 2009.

61 Jewkes & Linneman, 2018, p. 1.

62 Holmes & Holmes, 2010, p. 6.

63 *Cambridgeshire Live* (July 5, 2020): www.cambridge-news.co.uk/news/history/mayra-hindley-depraved-sadistic-serial-18531468.

64 *News-Record* (November 18, 1957, p. 1): www.newspapers.com/image/444945183.

65 *Albuquerque Journal* (May 4, 1975, p. 2): www.newspapers.com/image/157934815.

66 *The Escalon Times* (June 1, 1988, p. 1): www.newspapers.com/image/488022638/; *The San Francisco Examiner* (August 16, 2015, p. A8): www.newspapers.com/image/570196074.

67 *NBC News* (August 17, 2005): www.nbcnews.com/id/wbna8983224.

68 *CBS News* (August 17, 2005): www.cbsnews.com/news/chilling-testimony-at-btk-hearing/.

69 *CNN* (June 27, 2005): www.cnn.com/2005/LAW/06/27/rader.transcript/; *NBC News* (February 17, 2005): www.nbcnews.com/id/wbna6988048; *The New York Times* (August 18, 2005): www.nytimes.com/2005/08/18/us/in-gory-detail-prosecution-lays-out-case-for-tough-sentencing-of-btk.html; *The Parsons Sun* (October 27, 1987, p. 3): www.newspapers.com/image/610651560; *Reader's Digest Canada* (July 28, 2020): www.readersdigest.ca/culture/surviving-btk-killer/.

70 *CNN* (February 17, 2005): www.cnn.com/2005/US/02/17/btk.package/index.html; *History.com* (January 22, 2021): www.history.com/this-day-in-history/btk-killer-sends-message.

71 *The Wichita Eagle* (March 23, 2012): www.kansas.com/news/special-reports/btk/article1003859.html; *The Seattle Times* (August 19, 2005): www.seattletimes.com/nation-world/killer-humbled-at-sentencing/.

72 *The Parsons Sun* (October 27, 1987, p. 3): www.newspapers.com/image/610651560.

73 *The Manhattan Mercury* (February 17, 1978, p. 8): www.newspapers.com/image/4240 50150.

74 *The Wichita Beacon* (February 16, 1978, p. 42): www.newspapers.com/image/701508356.

75 *CNN.com* (February 17, 2005): www.cnn.com/2005/US/02/17/btk.package/index .html.

76 *NBC News* (February 17, 2005): www.nbcnews.com/id/wbna6988048.

77 *The Bakersfield Californian* (February 12, 2018): www.bakersfield.com/kern-business-journal/btk-serial-killer-power-of-computer-forensics/article_dd8f0ad3-f833-50b6-8e25-dcf6d406d5c4.html.

78 *The Atlantic* (January 16, 2014): www.theatlantic.com/technology/archive/2014/01/the-floppy-did-me-in/283132/.

79 *American Bar Association Journal* (May 1, 2006): www.abajournal.com/magazine/article/how_the_cops_caught_btk; *NBC News* (February 17, 2005): www.nbcnews.com/id/wbna6988048.

80 *CNN* (February 26, 2005): www.cnn.com/2005/US/02/26/btk.investigation/; *NPR* (December 12, 2007): www.npr.org/templates/story/story.php?storyId=17130501; *The Wichita Eagle* (March 4, 2005, p. 7): www.newspapers.com/image/704068738.

81 *NBC News* (February 17, 2005): www.nbcnews.com/id/wbna6988048.

82 *The Seattle Times* (August 19, 2005): www.seattletimes.com/nation-world/killer-humbled-at-sentencing/.

83 *American Bar Association Journal* (May 1, 2006): www.abajournal.com/magazine/article/how_the_cops_caught_btk.

84 *NBC News* (February 17, 2005): www.nbcnews.com/id/wbna6988048.

85 Helfgott, 2015.

86 *CBS News* (August 19, 2005): www.cbsnews.com/news/life-prison-sentence-silences-btk/; *The Wichita Eagle* (June 3, 2017): www.kansas.com/news/local/article154275709.html.

87 *WebMD* (May 17, 2006): www.webmd.com/mental-health/features/portrait-of-psychopath.

88 *NBC News* (February 17, 2005): www.nbcnews.com/id/wbna8929452.

89 *The Kansas City Star* (June 28, 2005, p. 8): www.newspapers.com/image/688469286.

90 *WebMD* (May 17, 2006): www.webmd.com/mental-health/features/portrait-of-psychopath.

91 Murray, 2017.

92 Murray, 2017, p. 717.

93 *The Kansas City Star* (June 28, 2005, p. 8): www.newspapers.com/image/688469286.

94 *The Wichita Eagle* (June 3, 2017): www.kansas.com/article154275709.html.

95 *Oxygen* (June 7, 2021): www.oxygen.com/crime-news/kerri-rawson-says-she-ceased-contact-with-father-dennis-rader.

96 Farrell et al., 2011, 2013.

97 Yardley & Wilson, 2015, p. 37.

98 Haggerty, 2009.

99 *The Boston Globe* (October 9, 2000): http://cache.boston.com/globe/metro/packages/nurse/part2.htm.

100 Makaroun et al., 2018.

101 Kay, 2006.

102 Connolly & Gordon, 2015.

103 *The Californian* (July 19, 1994, p. 2): www.newspapers.com/image/579606543.

104 *The Californian* (March 18, 1994): www.newspapers.com/image/579583112; *The Californian* (March 20, 1994, p. 1): www.newspapers.com/image/579583552; *The Fresno Bee* (March 18, 1994, p. 24): www.newspapers.com/image/706830564; *New York Daily News* (May 31, 2014): www.nydailynews.com/news/crime/justice-story-dana-sue-gray-article-1.1810400 (url geo-restricted).

105 *Rolling Stone* (August 9, 2019): www.rollingstone.com/culture/culture-features/manson-murder-murderabelia-true-crime-collectibles-869058/.

106 *The Washington Post* (July 24, 2020): www.washingtonpost.com/politics/shes-a-veteran-who-killed-seven-other-veterans-at-a-west-virginia-hospital-their-families-want-to-know-why/2020/07/23/78cc38fe-cab3-11ea-b0e3-d55bda07d66a_story.html; *WVNews* (July 25, 2020): www.wvnews.com/news/wvnews/why-families-of-reta-mays-victims-want-to-know-veterans-motive/article_b63b10a7-68cc-57de-9e32-9635702f3f15.html (url geo-restricted).

107 *WSAZ News Channel 3* (May 11, 2021): www.wsaz.com/2021/05/11/former-wva-va-employee-to-be-sentenced-tuesday-for-multiple-deaths/.

108 *WBOY 12* (May 11, 2021): www.wboy.com/news/crime/live-updates-sentencing-for-clarksburg-va-serial-killer-reta-mays/ (url geo-restricted). *West Virginia Public Broadcasting* (May 11, 2021): www.wvpublic.org/government/2021-05-11/reta-mays-convicted-of-murdering-veterans-hospitalized-in-west-virginia-gets-seven-life-sentence-plus-20-years.

109 *The Seattle Times* (February 13, 1998): https://archive.seattletimes.com/archive/?date=19980213&slug=2734334.

110 *The Seattle Times* (October 27, 2000): https://archive.seattletimes.com/archive/?date=20001027&slug=4049951.

111 *ABC57* (August 19, 2020): www.abc57.com/news/the-nightmare-has-ended-victims-address-the-golden-state-killer-in-court.

112 *ABC News* (August 21, 2020): https://abcnews.go.com/US/living-witness-teen-dads-murder-confronts-golden-state/story?id=72473195.

113 *Chicago Tribune* (April 19, 2016): www.chicagotribune.com/news/breaking/ct-gacy-body-dna-test-marino-met-20160419-story.html; *John Wayne Gacy: Devil in Disguise* (March 25, 2021) Documentary on Peacock television: NBC News Studios.

114 Kennedy et al., 2019.

115 *The Daily Review* (September 24, 2008, p. 7): www.newspapers.com/image/470724229.

116 *The Boston Globe* (March 27, 2001, p. 1): www.newspapers.com/image/442962840/.

117 *The Daily Telegram* (November 18, 1957, p. 1): www.newspapers.com/image/299071488; *The Oshkosh Northwestern* (April 10, 1968, p. 1): www.newspapers.com/image/248113444; *The Palm Beach Post* (February 16, 1991, p. 56): www.newspapers.com/image/130203858.

118 *Marshfield News-Herald* (November 18, 1957, p. 1): www.newspapers.com/image/267871529; *Stevens Point Journal* (November 19, 1957, p. 1): /www.newspapers.com/image/250495821.

119 *Chicago Tribune* (December 17, 2018): www.chicagotribune.com/history/ct-john-wayne-gacy-timeline-htmlstory.html.

120 Shortly after sentencing, on July 1, Judge Garippo resigned.

121 Roach et al., 2017.

122 *Harper's Bazaar* (October 31, 2018): www.harpersbazaar.com/culture/features/a24269889/john-wayne-gacy-kim-byers-lund-interview/.

123 *Harper's Bazaar* (October 31, 2018): www.harpersbazaar.com/culture/features/a24269889/john-wayne-gacy-kim-byers-lund-interview/.

124 *The Philadelphia Inquirer.* www.newspapers.com/image/174493164.

125 *The Capital Journal* (September 30, 1969, p. 1): www.newspapers.com/image/316233391/; *Corvallis Gazette-Times* (March 27, 2009, p. 31): www.newspapers.com/image/383787262; *Daily News* (June 28, 1970): www.newspapers.com/image/464656155.

126 *The Seattle Times* (October 27, 2000): https://archive.seattletimes.com/archive/?date=20001027&slug=4049951.

127 May, 2000; Melendez et al., 2016.

128 Rawson, 2019, p. IX.

129 Rawson, 2019, p. IX*; The Wichita Eagle* (June 3, 2017) https://www.kansas.com/article154275709.html.

130 *ABC News* (January 22, 2019): https://abcnews.go.com/US/btk-serial-killers-daughter-living-normal-life-upended/story?id=60428529.

131 *The Wichita Eagle* (August 19, 2019): www.kansas.com/news/special-reports/btk/article115782553.html.

132 *The Washington Post* (August 18, 2005): www.washingtonpost.com/wp-dyn/content/article/2005/08/18/AR2005081800201.html.

133 *ABC News* (January 30, 2019): https://abcnews.go.com/US/life-changed-instantly-families-victims-murdered-serial-killer/story?id=60686971.

134 *CNN.com* (August 18, 2005): http://transcripts.cnn.com/TRANSCRIPTS/0508/18/bn.02.html.

135 *Greeley Tribune* (May 28, 2020): www.greeleytribune.com/2019/02/01/greeley-resident-author-jeff-davis-son-of-btk-killers-final-victim-part-of-20-20-documentary/.

136 *The Denver Post* (August 18, 2005): www.denverpost.com/2005/08/18/btk-killer-gets-10-life-terms/; *The Washington Post* (August 18, 2005): www.washingtonpost.com/wp-dyn/content/article/2005/08/18/AR2005081800201.html.

137 *CBS News* (August 19, 2005): www.cbsnews.com/news/life-prison-sentence-silences-btk/.

138 *NBC News* (August 17, 2005): www.nbcnews.com/id/wbna8983224.
139 *Daily Mail* (February 5, 2019): www.dailymail.co.uk/news/article-6669831/Son-BTK-killers-victims-tells-family-strangled-bound-age-15.html; *Reader's Digest Canada* (July 28, 2020): www.readersdigest.ca/culture/surviving-btk-killer/.
140 *The Wichita Eagle* (August 21, 2005, p. 6): www.newspapers.com/image/704171840.
141 Connolly & Gordon, 2015.

11 EVOLUTIONARY AND CONVERGING PERSPECTIVES OF SERIAL MURDER

1 Harrison et al., 2015.
2 Dawkins, 1989.
3 Trivers, 1972.
4 Symons, 1979; Trivers, 1972.
5 Gray et al., 2019; Schmitt et al., 2001.
6 Trivers, 1972.
7 Kappelman, 1996.
8 Trivers, 1972.
9 Buss & Shackelford, 2008; Hughes & Aung, 2017.
10 Harrison et al., 2015.
11 Harrison et al., 2019.
12 Harrison et al., 2019.
13 Fisher-Freeman-Halton Exact Test, two-sided, $p = .395$.
14 I was unable to examine the statistical constancy of sex as the primary motive for MSKs, because I collected MSK data purposefully that matched FSKs' years of killing. Still, I suspect sex has always been the primary motive for male-perpetrated serial murder. In fact, at one time, experts believed that serial killings were limited to sex-based crimes. Accordingly, at one time, experts believed there were no FSKs (Farrell et al., 2011; Holmes et al., 1991).
15 Hill et al., 2011.
16 Bowlby, 1969; Pagel, 2016; Tooby & Cosmides, 1990.
17 Harrison et al., 2019; There are virtually no studies that directly compare, with statistics, the crimes and victims of FSKs and MSKs. Some books and other sources approach the topic from a "yes, we know that" perspective, but they do not provide empirical support for their "facts." We therefore collected our own data for a scientific, statistically validated verification of sex differences.
18 Ames & Maschner, 2000.
19 Kanazawa, 2010.
20 McKenzie, 1995.
21 Raine, 2013.

12 OUR UNDERSTANDING OF SERIAL KILLERS EVOLVES

1 *Daily Arkansas Gazette* (July 27, 1919, p. 41): www.newspapers.com/image/141596789.

2 *USA Today* (May 11, 2021): www.usatoday.com/story/news/nation/2021/05/11/serial-killer-reta-mays-sentenced-va-hospital-murders-west-virginia/5023366001/.

3 *United States Department of Justice, USAttorney's Office, Northern District of West Virginia* (May 11, 2021): www.justice.gov/usao-ndwv/pr/former-va-hospital-nursing-assistant-sentenced-seven-consecutive-life-sentences.

4 *BBC News* (May 11, 2021): www.bbc.com/news/world-us-canada-57070025; *CBS News* (May 11, 2021): www.cbsnews.com/news/reta-mays-va-hospital-second-degree-murder-sentenced-life-prison/; *USA Today* (May 11, 2021): www.usatoday.com/story/news/nation/2021/05/11/serial-killer-reta-mays-sentenced-va-hospital-murders-west-virginia/5023366001/.

5 *WOWK CBS13* (March 3, 2020): www.wowktv.com/news/west-virginia/clarksburg-va/person-of-interest-identified-in-va-clarksburg-suspicious-deaths/ (url geo-restricted).

6 *NPR* (May 11, 2021): www.npr.org/2021/05/11/995885699/woman-who-murdered-7-veterans-in-va-hospital-gets-multiple-life-sentences.

7 *International Business Times* (July 25, 2020): www.ibtimes.sg/who-reta-mays-nursing-assistant-kills-7-vets-lethal-jabs-watch-them-die-49016.

8 *NPR* (May 11, 2021): www.npr.org/2021/05/11/995885699/woman-who-murdered-7-veterans-in-va-hospital-gets-multiple-life-sentences.

9 *CBS News* (May 11, 2021): www.cbsnews.com/news/reta-mays-va-hospital-second-degree-murder-sentenced-life-prison/; *WBOY 12* (May 11, 2021): www.wboy.com/news/crime/live-updates-sentencing-for-clarksburg-va-serial-killer-reta-mays/ (url geo-restricted).

10 *Detroit Free Press* (October 12, 2020, p. A10): www.newspapers.com/image/687620823.

11 *CBS News* (May 11, 2021): www.cbsnews.com/news/reta-mays-va-hospital-second-degree-murder-sentenced-life-prison/; *WBOY 12* (May 17, 2021): www.wboy.com/news/crime/watch-live-clarksburg-va-serial-killer-reta-mays-receives-7-consecutive-life-sentences/ (url geo-restricted).

12 *United States Department of Justice, USAttorney's Office, Northern District of West Virginia* (May 11, 2021): www.justice.gov/usao-ndwv/pr/former-va-hospital-nursing-assistant-sentenced-seven-consecutive-life-sentences.

13 *WBOY 12* (May 17, 2021): www.wboy.com/news/crime/watch-live-clarksburg-va-serial-killer-reta-mays-receives-7-consecutive-life-sentences/ (url geo-restricted).

14 *USA Today* (May 11, 2021): www.usatoday.com/story/news/nation/2021/05/11/serial-killer-reta-mays-sentenced-va-hospital-murders-west-virginia/5023366001/.

15 *United States Department of Justice, US Attorney's Office, Northern District of West Virginia* (May 11, 2011): www.justice.gov/usao-ndwv/pr/former-va-hospital-nursing-assistant-sentenced-seven-consecutive-life-sentences.

16 *International Business Times* (July 25, 2020): www.ibtimes.sg/who-reta-mays-nursing-assistant-kills-7-vets-lethal-jabs-watch-them-die-49016; *KDKA CBS2* (May 11, 2021): https://pittsburgh.cbslocal.com/2021/05/11/west-virginia-va-serial-killer-reta-mays-setenced/.

17 *NPR* (May 11, 2021): www.npr.org/2021/05/11/995885699/woman-who-murdered-7-veterans-in-va-hospital-gets-multiple-life-sentences.

18 *CBS News* (May 11, 2021): www.cbsnews.com/news/reta-mays-va-hospital-second-degree-murder-sentenced-life-prison/; *WBOY 12* (May 11, 2021): www.wboy.com/news/crime/live-updates-sentencing-for-clarksburg-va-serial-killer-reta-mays/ (url geo-restricted); *USA Today* (May 11, 2021): www.usatoday.com/story/news/nation/2021/05/11/serial-killer-reta-mays-sentenced-va-hospital-murders-west-virginia/5023366001/.

19 *International Business Times* (July 25, 2020): www.ibtimes.sg/who-reta-mays-nursing-assistant-kills-7-vets-lethal-jabs-watch-them-die-49016.

20 *WBOY 12* (May 11, 2021): www.wboy.com/news/crime/live-updates-sentencing-for-clarksburg-va-serial-killer-reta-mays/ (url geo-restricted).

21 *BBC News* (May 11, 2021): https://www.bbc.com/news/world-us-canada-57070025.

22 *NPR* (May 11, 2021): www.npr.org/2021/05/11/995885699/woman-who-murdered-7-veterans-in-va-hospital-gets-multiple-life-sentences.

23 *WBOY 12* (May 11, 2021): www.wboy.com/news/crime/live-updates-sentencing-for-clarksburg-va-serial-killer-reta-mays/ (url geo-restricted).

24 In Harrison et al. (2019), we purposefully chose MSKs who committed crimes in those same years for our comparison.

25 $r(53) = -0.36$, $p = .006$.

26 $r(53) = -0.20$, $p = .14$; since there are so many differences between FSK and MSK crimes, I analyzed them separately.

27 For example, Toates et al., 2017.

28 *Biography.com* (August 13, 2021): www.biography.com/crime-figure/jeffrey-dahmer.

29 Loftus, 2001.

30 Jentzen et al., 1994.

31 Davis, 1998.

32 As reported by CNN, Dahmer also had a dark sense of humor, not tolerated well by fellow prison inmates. He would turn prison food into fake body parts and cover them with ketchup to resemble blood, leaving these installations around prison for inmates and staff to find. In 1994, Christopher Scarver, a fellow inmate, confronted Dahmer about his gruesome humor and the crimes he committed. Scarver then killed Dahmer. He bludgeoned Dahmer with a metal bar. Scarver was serving time for a previous murder and received an additional life sentence for killing Dahmer. *CNN* (April 30, 2015): www.cnn.com/2015/04/30/us/feat-jeffrey-dahmer-killer-explanation/index.html; *The Orlando Sentinel* (December 16, 1994): www.newspapers.com/image/233946645.

33 *Pew Research* (June 25, 2020): www.pewresearch.org/global/2020/06/25/global-divide-on-homosexuality-persists/.

34 Frederick Toates and O. Coschug-Toates have authored a book about serial murder, *Understanding Sexual Serial Killing* (Cambridge, UK: Cambridge University Press).

35 *Ipsos* (January 29, 2018): www.ipsos.com/en/global-attitudes-toward-transgender-people.

36 Hare, 1999.

37 *Cambridge Dictionary, Cambridge University Press* (2021): https://dictionary.cambridge.org/us/dictionary/english/sanity.

38 *Merriam-Webster* (October 8, 2021): www.merriam-webster.com/dictionary/sanity.

39 Young & Widom, 2014.

40 Blanco et al., 2015.

41 Cleckley, 1941/1988.

42 Farrington & Bergstrøm, 2018.

43 *NPR* (May 11, 2021): www.npr.org/2021/05/11/995885699/woman-who-murdered-7-veterans-in-va-hospital-gets-multiple-life-sentences.

44 Harrison et al., 2019; Hickey, 2016.

References

Abdalla-Filho, E., & Völlm, B. (2020). Does every psychopath have an antisocial personality disorder? *Brazilian Journal of Psychiatry*, 42(3), 241–242. https://doi .org/10.1590/1516-4446-2019-0762

Abdurrachid, N., & Marques, J. (2020). Munchausen syndrome by proxy (MSBP): A review regarding perpetrators of factitious disorder imposed on another (FDIA). *CNS Spectrums*, 1–11. https://doi.org/10.1017/S1092852920001741

Abel, G. G., & Osborn, C. (1992). The paraphilias: The extent and nature of sexually deviant and criminal behavior. *Psychiatric Clinics of North America*, 15(3), 675–687. https://doi.org/10.1016/S0193-953X(18)30231-4

Aggrawal, A. (2009). A new classification of necrophilia. *Journal of Forensic and Legal Medicine*, 16(6), 316–320. https://doi.org/10.1016/j.jflm.2008.12.023

Alexander, R., Smith, W., & Stevenson, R. (1990). Serial Munchausen syndrome by proxy. *Pediatrics*, 86(4), 581–585.

Allely, C. S., Minnis, H, Thompson, L., Wilson, P., & Gillberg, C. (2014). Neurodevelopmental and psychosocial risk factors in serial killers and mass murderers. *Aggression and Violent Behavior*, 19(3), 288–301. https://doi.org/10.1016/j .avb.2014.04.004

American Academy of Pediatrics. (2014). *Adverse childhood experiences and the lifelong consequences of trauma.* https://cdn.ymaws.com/www.ncpeds.org/ resource/collection/69DEAA33-A258-493B-A63F-E0BFAB6BD2CB/ttb_aces_ consequences.pdf

American Psychiatric Association. (2013). *Diagnostic and statistical manual of mental disorders* (5th ed.). https://doi.org/10.1176/appi.books.9780890425596

Ames, K. M., & Maschner, H. D. G. (2000). *Peoples of the Northwest coast: Their archeology and prehistory.* London, UK: Thames & Hudson.

Anderson, N. E., Widdows, M., Maurer, J. M., & Kiehl, K. A. (2021). Clarifying fearlessness in psychopathy: An examination of thrill-seeking and physical risk-taking. *Journal of Psychopathology and Behavioral Assessment*, 43, 21–32. https://doi.org/10.1007/s10862-020-09847-y

Angrilli, A., Palomba, D., Cantagallo, A., Maietti, A., & Stegagno, L. (1999). Emotional impairment after right orbitofrontal lesion in a patient without cognitive deficits. *NeuroReport: For Rapid Communication of Neuroscience Research*, 10(8), 1741–1746. https://doi.org/10.1097/00001756-199906030-00021

Angrilli, A., Satori, G., & Donzella, G. (2013). Cognitive, emotional and social markers of serial murdering. *The Clinical Neuropsychologist*, 27(3), 485–494. https://doi.org/10.1080/13854046.2013.771215

Anton, M. E., Baskin-Sommers, A. R., Vitale, J. E., Curtin, J. J., & Newman, J. P. (2012). Differential effects of psychopathy and antisocial personality disorder symptoms on cognitive and fear processing in female offenders. *Cognitive, Affective & Behavioral Neuroscience*, 12(4), 761–776. https://doi.org/10.3758/s13415-012-0114-x

Arnett, J. (1994). Sensation seeking: A new conceptualization and a new scale. *Personality and Individual Differences*, 16(2), 289–296. https://doi.org/10.1016/0191-8869(94)90165-1

Baumeister, R. F., Bratslavsky, E., Finkenauer, C., & Vohs, K. D. (2001). Bad is stronger than good. *Review of General Psychology*, 5(4), 323–370. https://doi.org/10.1037/1089-2680.5.4.323

Beaver, K. M., DeLisi, M., Vaughn, M. G., & Barnes, J. C. (2010). Monoamine oxidase A genotype is associated with gang membership and weapon use. *Comprehensive Psychiatry*, 51(2), 130–134. https://doi.org/10.1016/j.comppsych.2009.03.010

Beaver, K. M., Wright, J. P., Boutwell, B. B., Barnes, J. C., DeLisi, M., & Vaughn, M. G. (2013). Exploring the association between the 2-repeat allele of the MAOA gene promoter polymorphism and psychopathic personality traits, arrests, incarceration, and lifetime antisocial behavior. *Personality and Individual Differences*, 54(2), 164–168. https://doi.org/10.1016/j.paid.2012.08.014

Bebbington, K., MacLeod, C., Ellison, T. M., & Fay, N. (2017). The sky is falling: Evidence of a negativity bias in the social transmission of information. *Evolution and Human Behavior*, 38(1), 92–101. https://doi.org/10.1016/j.evolhumbehav.2016.07.004

Bell, R. (2016). 'Thence to Patty Cannon's': Gender, family, and the reverse Underground Railroad. *Slavery & Abolition*, 37(4), 661–679. http://dx.doi.org/10.1080/0144039X.2016.1163136

Bennett, K. (2018). Environment of evolutionary adaptedness (EEA). In V. Zeigler-Hill, T. K. Shackelford (eds.), *Encyclopedia of Personality and Individual Differences*, Springer Reference Live. https://doi.org/10.1007/978-3-319-28099-8_1627-1

Benton, A. L. (1994). Neuropsychological assessment. *Annual Review of Psychology*, 45, 1–23. https://doi.org/10.1146/annurev.ps.45.020194.000245

Berke, J. D., & Hyman, S. E. (2000). Addiction, dopamine, and the molecular mechanisms of memory. *Neuron*, 25(3), 515–532. http://dx.doi.org/10.1016/s0896-6273(00)81056-9

Bishopp, D., & Hare, R. D. (2008). A multidimensional scaling analysis of the Hare PCL-R: Unfolding the structure of psychopathy. *Psychology, Crime, & Law*, 14(2), 117–132. https://doi.org/10.1080/10683160701483484

Black, D. W. (2015). The natural history of antisocial personality disorder. *Canadian Journal of Psychiatry*, 60(7), 309–314. https://doi.org/10.1177/070674371506000703

Black, D. W. (2017). The treatment of antisocial personality disorder. *Current Treatment Options in Psychiatry*, 4, 295–302. https://doi.org/10.1007/s40501-017-0123-z

Blair, C. (2017). Educating executive function. *Wiley Interdisciplinary Reviews: Cognitive Science*, 8(1–2), 1–7. https://doi.org/10.1002/wcs.1403

Blanco, L., Nydegger, L. A., Camarillo, G., Trinidad, D. R., Schramm, E., & Ames, S. L. (2015). Neurological changes in brain structure and functions among individuals with a history of childhood sexual abuse: A review. *Neuroscience & Biobehavioral Reviews*, 57, 63–69. https://doi.org/10.1016/j.neubiorev.2015.07.013

Boggess, J. (1979). Troop male membership changes and infant killing in langurs (Presbytis entellus). *Folia Primatologica: International Journal of Primatology*, 32(1–2), 65–107. https://doi.org/10.1159/000155906

Book, A., Methot, T., Gauthier, N., Hosker-Field, A., Forth, A., Quinsey, V., & Molnar, D. (2015). The mask of sanity revisited: Psychopathic traits and affective mimicry. *Evolutionary Psychological Sciences*, 1, 91–102. https://doi.org/10.1007/s40806-015-0012-x

Boschelli, B. (2008). *Johnny and me: The true story of John Wayne Gacy, a memoir*. Bloomington, IN: AuthorHouse.

Bowers, T. G., Holmes, E. S., & Rohm, A. (2010). The nature of mass murder and autogenic massacre. *Journal of Police and Criminal Psychology*, 25, 59–66. https://doi.org/10.1007/s11896-009-9059-6

Bowlby J. (1969). Attachment. *Attachment and loss: Vol. 1. Loss*. New York, NY: Basic Books.

Bronfenbrenner, U. (1979). *The ecology of human development: Experiments by nature and design*. Cambridge, MA: Harvard University Press.

Brook, M., & Kosson, D. S. (2013). Impaired cognitive empathy in criminal psychopathy: Evidence from a laboratory measure of empathic accuracy. *Journal of Abnormal Psychology*, (1), 156–166. https://doi.org/10.1037/a0030261

Brower, M. C., & Price, B. H. (2001). Neuropsychiatry of frontal lobe dysfunction in violent and criminal behaviour: A critical review. *Journal of Neurology, Neurosurgery, and Psychiatry*, 71(6), 720–726. https://doi.org/10.1136/jnnp.71.6.720

Brown, T. R. (2019). Why we fear genetic informants: Using genetic genealogy to catch serial killers. *The Columbia Science & Technology Law Review*, 21(1), 114–181. https://pubmed.ncbi.nlm.nih.gov/33709088/

Brüne, M. (2003). Erotomanic stalking in evolutionary perspective. *Behavioral Sciences & the Law*, 21, 83–88. http://dx.doi.org/10.1002/bsl.518

Brush, J. (2007). Does income inequality lead to more crime? A comparison of cross-sectional and time-series analyses of United States counties. *Economics Letters*, 96(2), 264–268. https://doi.org/10.1016/j.econlet.2007.01.012

Buss, D. M. (2000). *The dangerous passion: Why jealousy is as necessary as love and sex*. New York, NY: Simon & Schuster.

Buss, D. M. & Shackelford, T. K. (2008) Attractive women want it all: Good genes, economic investment, parenting proclivities, and emotional commitment. *Evolutionary Psychology*, 6(1), 134–146. https://doi.org/10.1177/147470490800600116

Buss, D. M., Shackelford, T. K., Kirkpatrick, L. A., & Larsen, R. (2001). A half century of mate preferences: The cultural evolution of values. *Journal of Marriage and Family*, 63(2), 491–503. https://doi.org/10.1111/j.1741-3737.2001.00491.x

Campbell, J. P., & Alvarez, J. A. (1989). Acute arsenic intoxication. *American Family Physician*, 40(6), 93–97.

Carretié, L., Albert, J., López-Martín, S., & Tapia, M. (2009). Negative brain: An integrative review on the neural processes activated by unpleasant stimuli. *International Journal of Psychophysiology*, 71(1), 57–63. https://doi.org/10.1016/j.ijpsycho.2008.07.006

Carter, K. E.; Izsak, E.; & Marlow, J. (2006). Munchausen syndrome by proxy caused by ipecac poisoning. *Pediatric Emergency Care*, 22(9), 655–656. https://doi.org/10.1097/01.pec.0000227871.69309.d7

Castle, T., & Hensley, C. (2002). Serial killers with military experience: Applying learning theory to serial murder. *International Journal of Offender Therapy and Comparative Criminology*, 46(4), 453–465. https://doi.org/10.1177/0306624X02464007

Catalan, A., Díaz, A., Angosto, V., Zamalloa, I., Martínez, N., Guede, D., Aguirregomoscorta, F., Bustamante, S., Larrañaga. L., Osa, L., Maruottolo, C., Fernández-Rivas, A., Bilbao, A., & Gonzalez-Torres, M.A. (2020). Can childhood trauma influence facial emotion recognition independently from a diagnosis of severe mental disorder? *Journal of Psychiatry and Mental Health*, 13(3), 140–149. https://doi.org/10.1016/j.rpsm.2018.10.003 (In Spanish)

Celada, P., Puig, M. V., & Artigas, F. (2013). Serotonin modulation of cortical neurons and networks. *Frontiers in Integrative Neuroscience*, 7, 25. https://doi.org/10.3389/fnint.2013.00025

Cerasa, A., et al. (2010). Morphological correlates of MAO A VNTR polymorphism: New evidence from cortical thickness measurement. *Behavioural Brain Research*, 211(1), 118–124. https://doi.org/10.1016/j.bbr.2010.03.021

Christian, J. D., Lamm, T. C., Morrow, J. F., & Bostwick, D. G. (2005). Corpora amylacea in adenocarcinoma of the prostate: Incidence and histology within needle core biopsies. *Modern Pathology*, 18(1), 36–39. https://doi.org/10.1038/modpathol.3800250

Clasen, M., Kjeldgaard-Christiansen, J., & Johnson, J. A. (2020). Horror, personality, and threat simulation: A survey on the psychology of scary media. *Evolutionary Behavioral Sciences*, 14(3), 213–230. https://doi.org/10.1037/ebs0000152

Cleckley, H. (1941/1988). *The mask of sanity. An attempt to clarify some issues about the so-called psychopathic personality.* C.V. Mosby Co.

Connolly, J., & Gordon, R. (2015). Co-victims of homicide: A systematic review of the literature. *Trauma, Violence, & Abuse*, 16(4), 494–505. https://doi.org/10.1177/1524838014557285

Costa, V. D., Tran, V. L., Turchi, J., & Averbeck, B. B. (2014). Dopamine modulates novelty seeking behavior during decision making. *Behavioral Neuroscience*, 128(5), 556–566. http://dx.doi.org/10.1037/a0037128

Craig, L. A., & Bartels, R. M. (2021). *Sexual deviance: Understanding and managing deviant sexual interests and paraphilic disorders*. Hoboken, NJ: Wiley.

Cristofori, I., Zhong, W., Mandoske, V., Chau, A., Kruger, F., Strenziok, M., & Grafman, J. (2016). Brain regions influencing implicit violent attitudes: A lesion-mapping study. *The Journal of Neuroscience*, 36(9), 2757–2768. https://doi .org/10.1523/JNEUROSCI.2975-15.2016

Cross, C. P., Cyrenne, D. M., and Brown, G. R. (2013). Sex differences in sensation-seeking: A meta-analysis. *Nature*, 3, 2486. https://doi.org/10.1038/srep02486

Dalley, J. W., & Roiser, J. P. (2012). Dopamine, serotonin and impulsivity. *Neuroscience*, 215, 42–58. https://doi.org/10.1016/j.neuroscience.2012.03.065

Daly, M., & Wilson, M. (1988). *Homicide*. Hawthorne, NY: Aldine.

Darwin, C. (1859). *On the origin of species by means of natural selection, or, the preservation of favoured races in the struggle for life*. London, UK: J. Murray.

Davis, J. A. (1998). Profile of a sexual predator: A psychological autopsy of an American serial killer. *The Forensic Examiner*, 7(1–2), 28–33.

Davison, K., Mann, K. K., & Miller, W. H., Jr. (2002). Arsenic trioxide: Mechanisms of action. *Seminars in Hematology*, 39(2), 3–7. https://doi .org/10.1053/shem.2002.33610

Dawkins, R. (1989). *The selfish gene* (2nd ed.). New York, NY: Oxford University Press

De Brito, S. A., Viding, E., Kumari, V., Blackwood, N., & Hodgins, S. (2013). Cool and hot executive function impairments in violent offenders with antisocial personality disorder with and without psychopathy. *PLoS One*, 8(6), e65566. https://doi.org/10.1371/journal.pone.0065566

DeFronzo, J., Ditta, A., Hannon, L., & Prochnow, J. (2007). Male serial homicide: The influence of cultural and structural variables. *Homicide Studies*, 11(1), 3–14. https://doi.org/10.1177/1088767906297434

Di Maio, D. J., & Di Maio, V. J. M. (1989). *Forensic pathology* (1st ed). New York, NY: CRC Press.

Di Maio, V. J. M., & Bernstein, C. (1974). A case of infanticide. *Journal of Forensic Sciences*, 19(4), 744–754. https://doi.org/10.1520/JFS10464J

Dion, K., Berscheid, E., & Walster, E. (1972). What is beautiful is good. *Journal of Personality and Social Psychology*, 24(3), 285–290. http://dx.doi.org/10.1037/h0033731

Dion. K. L., & Dion, K. K. (1987). Belief in a just world and physical attractiveness stereotyping. *Journal of Personality and Social Psychology*, 52(4), 775–780.

Di Tella, R., Freira, L., Gálvez, R. H., Schargrodsky, E., Shalom, D., & Sigman, M. (2019). Crime and violence: Desensitization in victims to watching criminal events. *Journal of Economic Behavior & Organization*, 159, 613–625. https://doi .org/10.1016/j.jebo.2017.10.005

Dietz, P. E. (1986). Mass, serial and sensational homicides. *Bulletin of the New York Academy of Medicine*, 62(5), 477–491. www.ncbi.nlm.nih.gov/pmc/articles/PMC1629267/

Dogra, T. D., Leenaars, A. A., Chadha, R. K., Manju, M., Lalwani, S., Sood, M., Lester, D., Raina, A., & Behera, C. (2012). A psychological profile of a serial killer: A case report. *Omega Journal of Death and Dying*, 65(4), 299–316. https://doi.org/10.2190/OM.65.4.d

Donohew, L., Zimmerman, R., Cupp, P. S., Novak, S., Colon, S., & Abell, R. (2000). Sensation seeking, impulsive decision-making, and risky sex: Implications for risk-taking and design of interventions. *Personality and Individual Differences*, 28(6), 1079–1091. https://doi.org/10.1016/S0191-8869(99)00158-0

Doucet, S., Dennis, C., Letourneau, N., & Blackmore, E. R. (2009). Differentiation and clinical implications of postpartum depression and postpartum psychosis. *Journal of Obstetric, Gynecological, & Neonatal Nursing*, 38(3), 269–279. https://doi.org/10.1111/j.1552-6909.2009.01019.x

Dryer-Brees, E. (2012). Neat, plausible, and wrong: Examining the limitations of typologies in the study and investigation of serial murder. *Internet Journal of Criminology*. https://958be75a-da42-4a45-aafa-549955018b18.filesusr.com/ugd/b93dd4_4f77738e016a48eba3fca73b34ab20dd.pdf

Dube, S. R., Felitti, V. J., Dong, M., Giles, W. H., & Anda, R. F. (2003). The impact of adverse childhood experiences on health problems: evidence from four birth cohorts dating back to 1900. *Preventive Medicine*, 37(3), 268–277. https://doi.org/10.1016/S0091-7435(03)00123-3

Duntley, J. D. (2005). Adaptations to dangers from humans. In D. M. Buss (ed.), *The handbook of evolutionary psychology*, 224–249. New York, NY: Wiley.

Duntley, J. D., & Buss, D. M. (2012). The evolution of stalking. *Sex Roles*, 66, 311–327. https://doi.org/10.1007/s11199-010-9832-0

Duwe, G. (2000). Body-count journalism: The presentation of mass murder in the news media. *Homicide Studies*, 4(4), 364–399. https://doi.org/10.1177/1088767900004004004

Eaton, N. R., Keyes, K. M., Krueger, R. F., Balsis, S., Skodol, A. E., Markon, K. E., Grant, B. F., & Hasin, D. S. (2012). An invariant dimension liability model of gender differences in mental disorder prevalence: Evidence from a national sample. *Journal of Abnormal Psychology*, 121(1), 282–288. https://doi.org/10.1037/a0024780

Ebensperger, L. A. (2007). Strategies and counterstrategies to infanticide in mammals. *Biological Reviews*, 73(3), 321–346. https://doi.org/10.1111/j.1469-185X.1998.tb00034.x

Egginton, J. (1989). *From cradle to grave: Why did a mother's nine babies have to die?* London, UK: Virgin Books.

Eisenegger, C., Haushofer, J., & Fehr, E. (2011). The role of testosterone in social interaction. *Trends in Cognitive Sciences*, 15(6), 263–271. https://doi.org/10.1016/j.tics.2011.04.008

Faedda, N., Baglioni, V., Natalucci, G., Ardizzone, I., Camuffo., M., Cerutti, R., & Guidetti, V. (2018). Don't judge a book by its cover: Factitious disorder imposed on children-Report on 2 cases. *Frontiers in Pediatrics*, 6, 110. https://doi .org/10.3389/fped.2018.00110

Farrell, A. L., Keppel, R. D., & Titterington, V. B. (2011). Lethal ladies: Revisiting what we know about female serial murderers. *Homicide Studies*, 15, 228–252. https://doi.org/10.1177/1088767911415938

Farrell, A. L., Keppel, R. D., & Titterington, V. B. (2013). Testing existing classifications of serial murder considering gender: An exploratory analysis of solo female serial murderers. *Journal of Investigative Psychology and Offender Profiling*, 10, 268–288. https://doi.org/10.1177/1088767911415938

Farrer, T. J., & Hedges, D. W. (2011). Prevalence of traumatic brain injury in incarcerated groups compared to the general population: A meta-analysis. *Progress in Neuro-Psychopharmacology and Biological Psychiatry*, 35(2), 390–394. https://doi .org/10.1016/j.pnpbp.2011.01.007

Farrington, D. P., & Bergstrøm, H. (2018). Family background and psychopathy. In C. J. Patrick (ed.), *Handbook of psychopathy*, 354–379. New York, NY: The Guilford Press.

Fazel, S., Wolf, A., Chang, Z., Larsson, H., Goodwin, G. M., & Lichtenstein, P. (2015). Depression and violence: A Swedish population study. *The Lancet Psychiatry*, 2(3), 224–232. https://doi.org/10.1016/S2215-0366 (14)00128-X

Firstman, R., & Talan, J. (1997). *The death of innocents*. New York, NY: Bantam.

Fisher, K. A., & Hany, M. (2020). *Antisocial personality disorder*. Treasure Island, FL: StatsPearls Publishing. www.ncbi.nlm.nih.gov/books/NBK546673/

Fjell, A. M., Sneve, M. H., Grydeland, H., Storsve, A. B., & Walhovd, K. B. (2017). The disconnected brain and executive function decline in aging. *Cerebral Cortex*, 27(3), 2303–2317. https://doi.org/10.1093/cercor/bhw082

Flórez, G., Ferrer, V., Garcia, L. S., Crespo, M. R., Pérez, M., Saiz, P. A., & Cooke, D. J. (2020). Comparison between the Psychopathy Checklist-Revised and the Comprehensive Assessment of Psychopathic Personality in a representative sample of Spanish prison inmates. *PLoS One*, 15(2), e0228384. www .ncbi.nlm.nih.gov/pmc/articles/PMC7001946/

Forsyth, C. J. (2015). Posing: The sociological routine of a serial killer. *American Journal of Criminal Justice*, 40(4), 861–875. https://doi.org/10.1007/s12103-014-9287-x

Fox, B., & Farrington, D. P. (2018). What have we learned from offender profiling? A systematic review and meta-analysis of 40 years of research. *Psychological Bulletin*, 144(12), 1247–1274. https://doi.org/10.1037/bul0000170

Fox, J. A., & Levin, J. (2011). *Extreme killing: Understanding serial and mass murder*. Thousand Oaks, CA: Sage.

Freedman, D., & Hemenway, D. (2000). Precursors of lethal violence: A death row sample. *Social Science & Medicine*, 50(12), 1757–1770. https://doi .org/10.1016/S0277-9536(99)00417-7

Friedel, E. E., & Fox, J. A. (2018). Too few victims: Finding the optimal minimum victim threshold for defining serial murder. *Psychology of Violence*, 8(4), 505–514. https://doi.org/10.1037/vio0000138

Gao, Y., & Raine, A. (2010). Successful and unsuccessful psychopaths: a neurobiological model. *Behavioral Sciences & the Law*, 28(2), 194–210. https://doi.org/10.1002/bsl.924

Galea, S., Nandi, A., & Vlahov, D. (2005). The epidemiology of post-traumatic stress disorder after disasters. *Epidemiological Reviews*, 27, 78–91. https://doi.org/10.1093/epirev/mxi003

García-Sáinz, J. A. (2002). Adrenaline junkies: Addicted to the rush? *The Biochemist*, 24(5). https://doi.org/10.1042/BIO02405019

Geary, D. C. (2000). Evolution and proximate expression of human paternal investment. *Psychological Bulletin*, 126(1), 55–77. https://doi.org/10.1037//0033-2909.126.1.55

Giordano, J., Kulkarni, A., & Farwell, J. (2014). Deliver us from evil? The temptation, realities, and neuroethico-legal issues of employing assessment neurotechnologies in public safety initiatives. *Theoretical Medicine and Bioethics*, 35(1), 73–89. https://doi.org/10.1007/s11017-014-9278-4

Glenn, A. L., & Raine, A. (2009). Psychopathy and instrumental aggression: Evolutionary, neurobiological, and legal perspectives. *International Journal of Law and Psychiatry*, 32(4), 253–258. https://doi.org/10.1016/j.ijlp.2009.04.002

Glenn, A. L., Johnson, A. K., & Raine, A. (2013). Antisocial personality disorder: A current review. *Current Psychiatry Reports*, 15(12), 427. https://doi.org/10.1007/s11920-013-0427-7

Glenn, A. L., Kurzban, R., & Raine, A. (2020). Evolutionary theory and psychopathy. *Aggression and Violent Behavior*, 16(5), 371–380. https://doi.org/10.1016/j.avb.2011.03.009

Goetschius, L. G., Hein, T. C., Mitchell, C., Lopez-Duran, N. L., McLoyd, V. C., Brooks-Gunn, J., McLanahan, S. S., Hyde, L. W., & Monk, C. S. (2020). Childhood violence exposure and social deprivation predict adolescent amygdala-orbitofrontal cortex white matter connectivity. *Developmental Cognitive Neuroscience*, 45, 100849. https://doi.org/10.1016/j.dcn.2020.100849

Gómez, J. M., Verdú, M., González-Megías, A., & Méndez, M. (2016). The phylogenetic roots of human lethal violence. *Nature*, 538(7624), 233–237. http://dx.doi.org/10.1038/nature19758

Gray, P. B., Garcia, J. R., & Gesselman, A. N. (2019). Age-related patterns in sexual behaviors and attitudes among single U.S. Adults: An evolutionary approach. *Evolutionary Behavioral Sciences*, 13(2), 111–126. https://doi.org/10.1037/ebs0000126

Gross, J. J., Uusberg, H., & Uusberg, A. (2019). Mental illness and well-being: An affect regulation perspective. *World Psychiatry*, 18(2), 130–139. https://doi.org/10.1002/wps.20618

Gunn, J. F., White, J., & Lester, D. (2014). Twice the evil: A comparison of serial killers who killed with a partner and those who killed alone. *American Journal of Forensic Psychology*, 32(1), 5–17.

Haggerty, K. D. (2009). Modern serial killers. *Crime, Media, Culture*, 5(2), 168–187. https://doi.org/10.1177/1741659009335714

Häkkänen, H. (2008). A study of offense patterns and psychopathological characteristics among recidivistic Finnish homicide offenders. In R. N. Kocsis (ed.) *Serial murder and the psychology of violent crimes*, 51–62. Totowa, NJ: Humana Press.

Hare, R. D. (1980). A research scale for the assessment of psychopathy in criminal populations. *Personality and Individual Differences*, 1(2), 111–119. https://doi.org/10.1016/0191-8869(80)90028-8

Hare, R. D. (1984). Performance of psychopaths on cognitive tasks related to frontal lobe functions. *Journal of Abnormal Psychology*, 93(2), 133–140. https://doi.org/10.1037/0021-843X.93.2.133

Hare, R. D. (1991/2003). *The Hare Psychopathy Checklist-Revised (PCL-R)*. Toronto, Ontario, Canada: Multi-Health Systems.

Hare, R. D. (1996). Psychopathy and antisocial personality disorder: A case of diagnostic confusion. *Psychiatric Times*, 13(2). www.psychiatrictimes.com/view/psychopathy-and-antisocial-personality-disorder-case-diagnostic-confusion

Hare, R. D. (1999). *Without conscience: The disturbing world of psychopaths among us*. New York, NY: The Guilford Press.

Hare, R. D. (2001). Psychopaths and their nature: Some implications for understanding human predatory violence. In J. Sanmartin & A. Raine (eds.), *Violence and psychopathy*, 5–34. Boston, MA: Kluwer.

Hare, R. D. (2020). The PCL-R assessment of psychopathy. In A. R. Felthous & H. Sass (eds). *The Wiley international handbook on psychopathic disorders, (2nd ed.)*, 63–106. Hoboken, NJ: Wiley and Sons. https://doi.org/10.1002/9781119159322.ch4

Hare, R. D., & Neumann, C. S. (2005). Structural models of psychopathy. *Current Psychiatry Reports*, 7, 57–64. https://doi.org/10.1007/s11920-005-0026-3

Harpending, H. C., & Sobus, J. (1987). Sociopathy as an adaptation. *Ethology and Sociobiology*, 8(1), 63–72. https://doi.org/10.1016/0162-3095(87)90019-7

Harrison, M. A., & Bowers, T. G. (2010). Autogenic massacre as a maladaptive response to status threat. *Journal of Forensic Psychiatry & Psychology*, 21(6), 916–932. https://doi.org/10.1080/14789949.2010.506618

Harrison, M. A., & Frederick, E. J. (2020). Interested in serial killers? Morbid curiosity in college students. *Current Psychology*. https://doi.org/10.1007/s12144-020-00896-w

Harrison, M. A., & Hughes, S. M. (2020). *Judging a book by its cover: The connection between physical traits and psychology*. Authors: Kindle Direct Publishing.

Harrison, M. A., Hughes, S. M., & Gott, A. J. (2019). Sex differences in serial killers. *Evolutionary Behavioral Sciences*, 13(4), 295–310. https://doi.org/10.1037/ebs0000157

Harrison, M. A., Murphy, E. A., Ho, L. Y., Bowers, T. G., & Flaherty. C. C. (2015). Female serial killers in the United States: Means, motives, and makings. *The Journal of Forensic Psychiatry & Psychology*, 26(3), 383–406. https://doi.org/10.1080/1 4789949.2015.1007516

Helfgott, J. B. (2015). Criminal behavior and the copycat effect: Literature review and theoretical framework for empirical investigation. *Aggression and Violent Behavior*, 22, 46–64. https://doi.org/10.1016/j.avb.2015.02.002

Helmchen, H. (2016). Fuzzy boundaries and tough decisions in psychiatry. In G. Keil, L. Keuck, & R. Hauswald (eds.), *Vagueness in psychiatry*. Oxford, UK: Oxford University Press. https://doi.org/10.1093/med/9780198722373.003.0007

Herman, D. H., Morrison, H. L., Norman, J. A., & Neff, D. M. (1984). People of the State of Illinois vs. John Gacy: The functioning of the insanity defense at the limits of the criminal law. *West Virginia Law Review*, 86(4), 1169–1273. https://researchrepository.wvu.edu/wvlr/vol86/iss4/8

Herzberg, M. P., & Gunnar, M. R. (2020). Early life stress and brain function: Activity and connectivity associated with processing emotion and reward. *NeuroImage*, 209. https://doi.org/10.1016/j.neuroimage.2019.116493

Hickey, E. (1986). The female serial murderer, 1800–1986. *Journal of Police and Criminal Psychology*, 2(2), 72–81.

Hickey, E. (1991). *Serial murderers and their victims* (1st ed.). Belmont, CA: Thomson Wadsworth.

Hickey, E. (2010). *Serial murderers and their victims* (5th ed.) Belmont, CA: Cengage.

Hickey, E. (2016). *Serial murderers and their victims* (7th ed.) Boston, MA: Cengage.

Hickey, E. W., Walters, B. K., Drislane, L. E., Palumbo, I. M., & Patrick, C. J. (2018). Deviance at its darkest: Psychopathy and serial murder. In: C. J. Patrick (ed.), *Handbook of Psychopathy, 2nd ed.*, 570–584. New York: Guilford Press.

Hill, K. R., et al. (2011). Co-residence patterns in hunter-gatherer societies show unique human social structure. *Science*, 331(6022), 1286–1289. https://doi.org/10.1126/science.1199071

Hiraiwa-Hasegawa, M. (1988). Adaptive significance of infanticide in primates. *Trends in Ecology and Evolution*, 3(5), 102–105. https://doi.org/10.1016/0169-5347(88)90116-4

Holmes, R. M., & DeBurger, J. (1988). *Serial murder*. Newbury Park, CA: Sage.

Holmes, R. M., & Holmes, S. T. (2010). *Serial murder* (3rd ed.). Thousand Oaks, CA: Sage.

Holmes, S. T., Hickey, E., & Holmes, R. M. (1991). Female serial murderesses: Constructing differentiating typologies. *Journal of Contemporary Criminal Justice*, 7, 245–256.

Hooven, C., Nurius, P. S., Logan-Greene, P., & Thompson, E. A., (2012). Childhood violence exposure: Effects on adult mental health. *Journal of Family Violence*, 27(6), 511–522. https://doi.org/10.1007/s10896-012-9438-0

Hornor, G. (2021). Medical child abuse: Essentials for pediatric health care providers. *Journal of Pediatric Health Care*, 35(6), 644–650. https://doi.org/10.1016/j.pedhc.2021.01.006

Horwitz, A. V., & Grob, G. N. (2011). The checkered history of American psychiatric epidemiology. *The Milbank Quarterly*, 89(4), 628–657. https://www.ncbi.nlm.nih.gov/pmc/articles/PMC3250636/

Hosker-Field, A. M., Gauthier, N. Y., and Book, A. S. (2016). If not fear, then what? A preliminary examination of psychopathic traits and the Fear Enjoyment Hypothesis. *Personality and Individual Differences*, 90, 278–282. https://doi.org/10.1016/j.paid.2015.11.016

Hrdy, S. B. (1979). Infanticide among animals: A review, classification, and examination of the implications for the reproductive strategies of females. *Ethology and Sociobiology*, 1(1), 13–40. https://doi.org/10.1016/0162-3095(79)90004-9

Hughes, S. M., & Aung, T. (2017). Modern day female preferences for resources and provisioning by long-term mates. *Evolutionary Behavioral Sciences*, 11(3), 242–261. https://doi.org/10.1037/ebs0000084

Hunt, E., Bornovalova, M. A., Kimonis, E. R., Lillenfeld, S. O., & Poythress, N. G. (2015). Psychopathy factor interactions and co-occurring psychopathology: Does measurement approach matter? *Psychological Assessment*, 42(3), 241–242. https://doi.org/10.1037/pas0000055

Jaffee, S. R. (2017). Childhood maltreatment and risk for psychopathology in childhood and adulthood. *Annual Review of Clinical Psychology*, 13, 525–551. https://doi.org/10.1146/annurev-clinpsy-032816-045005

Jakubczyk, A., et al. (2017). Paraphilic sex offenders do not differ from control subjects with respect to dopamine- and serotonin-related genetic polymorphisms. *The Journal of Sexual Medicine*, 14(1), 125–133. https://doi.org/10.1016/j.jsxm.2016.11.309

James, W. (1890). *The principles of psychology*. New York, NY: Henry Holt.

Jarvis, B. (2007). Monsters Inc.: Serial killers and consumer culture. *Crime, Media, Culture: An International Journal*, 3(3), 326–344. https://doi.org/10.1177/1741659007082469

Jenkins, P. (1994). *Using murder: The social construction of serial homicide*. Hawthorne, NY: Aldine de Gruyter.

Jentzen, J., Palmero, G., Johnson, L. T., Khang-Cheng, H., Stormo, K. A., & Teggatz, J. (1994). Destructive hostility: The Jeffrey Dahmer case. *The American Journal of Forensic Medicine and Pathology*, 15(4), 283–294.

Jewkes, Y., & Linnemann, T. (2018). *Media and crime in the US*.Thousand Oaks, CA: Sage.

John-Steiner, V, & Mahn, H. (2006). Sociocultural approaches to learning and development: A Vygotskian framework. *Educational Psychologist*, 34(3/4), 191–206. https://doi.org/10.1080/00461520.1996.9653266

Johnson, L., Petty, C. S., & Neaves, W. B. (1980). A comparative study of daily sperm production and testicular composition in humans and rats. *Biology of Reproduction*, 22(5), 1233–1243. https://doi.org/10.1093/biolreprod/22.5.1233

Johnston, E. L., & Leahey, V. T. (2021). The status and legitimacy of M'Naghten's insane delusion rule. *University of California, Davis, Law Review*, 54, 1777–1852. https://ssrn.com/abstract=3834608

Kafka, M. (2003). The monoamine hypothesis for the pathophysiology of paraphilic disorders: An update. *Annals of the New York Academy of Sciences*, 989, 86–94.

Kamenskov, M. Y., & Gurina, O. I. (2019). Neurotransmitter mechanisms of paraphilic disorders. *S.S. Korsakov Journal of Neurology and Psychiatry*, 119(8), 61–67. https://doi.org/10.17116/jnevro201911908161 (in Russian)

Kanazawa, S. (2002). Bowling with our imaginary friends. *Evolution and Human Behavior*, 23(3), 167–171. https://doi.org/10.1016/S1090-5138(01)00098-8

Kanazawa, S. (2010). Evolutionary psychology and intelligence research. *American Psychologist*, 65(4), 279–289. https://doi.org/10.1037/a0019378

Kappelman, J. (1996). The evolution of body mass and relative brain size in fossil hominids. *Journal of Human Evolution*, 30(3), 243–276. https://doi.org/10.1006/jhev.1996.0021

Kawasaki, R., Cheung, N., Mosley, T., Islam, A., Sharrett, A. R., Klein, R., Coker, L. H., Knopman, D. S., Shibata, D. K., Catellier, D., & Wong, T. Y. (2010). Retinal microvascular signs and 10-year risk of cerebral atrophy: The ARIC study. *Stroke*, 41(8), 1826–1828. https://doi.org/10.1161/STROKEAHA.110.585042

Kay, J. (2006). Murder victims' families for reconciliation: Story-telling for healing, as witness, and in public policy. In D. Sullivan & L. Tifft (eds.), *Restorative justice*, 230–245. New York: Routledge.

Keeney, B. T., & Heide, K. M. (1994). Gender differences in serial murderers: A preliminary analysis. *Journal of Interpersonal Violence*, 9(3), 383–398. https://doi.org/10.1177/088626094009003007

Kelleher, M. D., & Kelleher, C. L. (1998). *Murder most rare: The female serial killer*. Westport, CT: Praeger.

Kendall-Tackett, K. A. (1991). How many children lie about being sexually abused?: A survey of mental health and law enforcement professionals. Paper presented at the *Annual Meeting of the American Professional Society on the Abuse of Children* (San Diego, CA, January 23–26). https://files.eric.ed.gov/fulltext/ED332135.pdf

Kennedy, C., Deane, F. P., & Chan, A. Y. C. (2019). In limbo: A systematic review of psychological responses and coping among people with a missing loved one. *Journal of Clinical Psychology*, 75(9), 1544–1571. https://doi.org/10.1002/jclp.22799

Keuper, K., Terrighena, E. L., Chan, C. C. H., Junghoefer, M., & Lee, T. M. (2018). How the dorsolateral prefrontal cortex controls affective processing in the absence of visual awareness – Insights from a combined EEG-rTMS study. *Frontiers in Human Neuroscience*, 12, 412. https://doi.org/10.3389/fnhum.2018.00412

Khokhar, J. Y., Dwiel, L. L., Henricks, A. M., Doucette, W. T., & Green, A. I. (2018). The link between schizophrenia and substance use disorder: A unifying hypothesis. *Schizophrenia Research*, 194, 78–85. https://doi.org/10.1016/j.schres.2017.04.016

Kidd, C., & Hayden, B. Y. (2015). The psychology and neuroscience of curiosity. *Neuron*, 88(3), 449–460. https://doi.org/10.1016/j.neuron.2015.09.010

Kocsis, R. N., & Palermo, G. B. (2015). Disentangling criminal profiling: Accuracy, homology, and the myth of trait-based profiling. *International Journal of Offender Therapy and Comparative Criminology*, 59(3), 313–332. https://doi.org/10.1177/0306624X13513429

Kondo, N. (2008). Mental illness in film. *Psychiatric Rehabilitation Journal*, 31(3), 250–252. https://doi.org/10.2975/31.3.2008.250.252

Kovner, R., Oler, J. A., & Kalin, N. H. (2019). Cortico-limbic interactions mediate adaptive and maladaptive responses relevant to psychopathology. *The American Journal of Psychiatry*, 176(12), 987–999. https://ajp.psychiatryonline.org/doi/10.1176/appi.ajp.2019.19101064

Krasowska, A., Jakubczyk, A., Czernikiewicz, W. M., Wojnar, M., & Nasierowski, T. (2013). Impulsivity in sexual offenders. New ideas or back to basics? *Psychiatria Polska*, 47(4), 727–740.

Kraus, R. T. (1995). An enigmatic personality: Case report of a serial killer. *Journal of Orthomolecular Medicine*, 10(1), 11–24.

Kröber, H. (2016). Mental illness versus mental disorder: Arguments and forensic implications. In G. Keil, L. Keuck, & R. Hauswald (eds.), *Vagueness in psychiatry*. Oxford, UK: Oxford University Press. https://doi.org/10.1093/med/9780198722373.001.0001

Kumari, V., Barkataki, I., Goswami, S., Flora, S., Das, M., & Taylor, P. (2009). Dysfunctional, but not functional, impulsivity is associated with a history of seriously violent behaviour and reduced orbitofrontal and hippocampal volumes in schizophrenia. *Psychiatry Research: Neuroimaging*, 173(1), 39–44. https://doi.org/10.1016/j.pscychresns.2008.09.003

Labrode, R. T. (2007). Etiology of the psychopathic serial killer: An analysis of antisocial personality disorder, psychopathy, and serial killer personality and crime scene characteristics. *Brief Treatment and Crisis Intervention*, 7(2), 151–160. https://doi.org/10.1093/brief-treatment/mhm004

Labrum, T., Zingman, M. A., Nossel, I., & Dixon, L. (2021). Violence by persons with serious mental illness towards family caregivers and other relatives: A review. *Harvard Review of Psychiatry*, 29(1), 10–19. https://doi.org/10.1097/HRP.0000000000000263

Lachmann, A., & Lachmann, F. K. (1995). The personification of evil: Motivations and fantasies of the serial killer. *International Forum of Psychoanalysis*, 4(1), 17–23. https://doi.org/10.1080/08037069508409511

Lea, R., & Chambers, G. (2007). Monoamine oxidase, addiction, and the "warrior" gene hypothesis. *The New Zealand Medical Journal*, 120(1250), U2441. https://pubmed.ncbi.nlm.nih.gov/17339897/

Leibman, F. H. (1989). Serial murderers: Four case histories. *Federal Probation: A Journal of Correctional Philosophy and Practice*, 53(4), 41–45. www.ojp.gov/pdffiles1/Digitization/122280NCJRS.pdf

Levin, J. (2008). *Serial killers and sadistic murderers-up close and personal*. Amherst, NY: Prometheus Books.

Lilienfeld, S. O., Watts, A. L., Smith, S. F., Patrick, C. J., & Hare, R. D. (2018). Hervey Cleckley (1903–1984): Contributions to the study of psychopathy. *Personality Disorders: Theory, Research, and Treatment*, 9(6), 510–520. https://doi.org/10.1037/per0000306

Linder, P., Savic, I., Sitnikov, R., Budhiraja, M., Liu, Y., Jokinen, J., Tihonen, J., & Hodgins, S. (2016). Conduct disorder in females is associated with reduced corpus callosum structural integrity independent of comorbid disorders and exposure to maltreatment. *Translational Psychiatry*, 6(1), e714. https://doi.org/10.1038/tp.2015.216

Lipman, A. G. (1994). The end of the grain: The long awaited move to metric. *Journal of Pharmaceutical Care in Pain & Symptom Control*, 2(3), 59–61. https://doi.org/10.1300/J088v02n03_05

Litman, J. A. (2005). Curiosity and the pleasures of learning: Wanting and liking new information. *Cognition Emotion*, 19(6), 793–814. https://doi.org/10.1080/02699930541000101

Loftus, J. (2001). America's liberalization in attitudes toward homosexuality, 1973-1998. *American Sociological Review*, 66(5), 762–782. https://doi.org/10.2307/3088957

Luauté, J. P., Kopp, N., Saladini, O., Nespor, C., & Luauté, J. (2011b). Le cerveau de Vacher et les savants, deuxième partie. Résultats de l'autopsie. *Annales Médico-Psychologiques*, 169(9), 545–551. https://doi.org/10.1016/j.amp.2011.07.004

Luauté, J. P., Kopp, N., Saladini, O., Nespor, C., & Luauté, J. (2011a). Le cerveau de Vacher et les savants, deuxième partie. Résultats de l'autopsie. *Annales Médico-Psychologiques*, 169(9), 552–558. https://doi.org/10.1016/j.amp.2011.07.005

Lund, J. I., Toombs, E., Radford, A., Boles, K., & Mushquash, C. (2020). Adverse childhood experiences and executive function difficulties in children: A systematic review. *Child Abuse & Neglect*, 106, 104485. https://doi.org/10.1016/j.chiabu.2020.104485

Lynam, D. R., & Gudonis, L. (2005). The development of psychopathy. *Annual Review of Clinical Psychology*, 1, 381–407. https://doi.org/10.1146/annurev.clinpsy.1.102803.144019

Makaroun, L. K., Taylor, L., & Rosen, T. (2018). Veterans experiencing elder abuse: Improving care of a high-risk population about which little is known. *Journal of the American Geriatrics Society*, 66(2), 389–393. https://doi.org/10.1111/jgs.15170

Manthorpe, S. (2019). Physical attractiveness in the courts: The "what is beautiful is good" theory as bias in juries. *California Legal Studies Journal*, 61–70. www.ocf.berkeley.edu/~blsa/wp-content/uploads/2019/12/BLSA-Journal-2019-Final-.pdf#page=61

Markovic, N., & Markovic, O. (2008). The female reproductive system in health and disease. In N. Markovic & O. Markovic (eds.) *What every woman should know about cervical cancer*, 1–22. Rockville, MD: Springer Science. https://link.springer.com/chapter/10.1007/978-1-4020-6937-6_1

May, H. (2000). Murderer's relatives: Managing stigma, negotiating identity. *Journal of Contemporary Ethnography*, 29(2), 198–221. https://doi.org/10.1177/089124100129023873

McCauley, C. (1998). When screen violence is not attractive. In J. Goldstein (ed.), *Why we watch: The attractions of violent entertainment*, 144–162. New York, NY: Oxford University Press.

McClure, R. J., Davis, P. M., Meadow, S. R., & Sibert, J. R. (1996). Epidemiology of Munchausen syndrome by proxy, non-accidental poisoning, and non-accidental suffocation. *Archives of Disease in Childhood*, 75(1), 57–61. https://doi.org/10.1136/adc.75.1.57

McDermott, R., Tingley, D., Cowden, J., Frazzetto, G., & Johnson, D. D. P. (2009). Monoamine oxidase A gene (MAOA) predicts behavioral aggression following provocation. *Proceedings of the National Academy of Sciences (PNAS)*, 106(7), 2118–2123. https://doi.org/10.1073/pnas.0808376106

McKenzie, C. (1995). A study of serial murder. *International Journal of Offender Therapy and Comparative Criminology*, 39(1), 3–10. https://doi.org/10.1177/0306624X9503900102

Meadow, R. (1977). Munchausen syndrome by proxy the hinterland of child abuse. *The Lancet*, 310(8033), 343–345. https://doi.org/10.1016/S0140-6736(77)91497-0

Meadow, R. (1995). What is, and what is not Munchausen syndrome by proxy? *Archives of Disease in Childhood*, 72(6), 534–538. https://doi.org/10.1136/adc.72.6.534

Meadow, R. (2002). Different interpretations of Munchausen Syndrome by Proxy. *Child Abuse & Neglect*, 26(5), 501–508. https://doi.org/10.1016/S0145-2134(02)00326-5

Meijers, J., Harte, J. M., Meynen, G., & Cuijpers, P. (2017). Differences in executive functioning between violent and non-violent offenders. *Psychological Medicine*, 47(10), 1784–1793. https://doi.org/10.1017/S0033291717000241

Melendez, M. S., Lichtenstein, B., & Dolliver, M. J. (2016). Mothers of mass murderers: Exploring public blame for the mothers of school shooters through an application of courtesy stigma to the Columbine and Newtown tragedies. *Deviant Behavior*, 37(5), 525–536. https://doi.org/10.1080/01639625.2015.1060754

Melton, G. B., Petrila, J., Poythress, N. G., Slobogin, C., Otto, R. K., Mossman, D., & Condie, L. O. (2018). *Psychological evaluations for the courts: A handbook for mental health professionals and lawyers*. New York, NY: The Guilford Press.

Meyer, J. H., et al. (2006). Elevated monoamine oxidase A levels in the brain: An explanation for the monoamine imbalance of major depression. *Journal of the American Medical Association (JAMA) Psychiatry*, 63(11), 1209–1216. https://doi.org/10.1001/archpsyc.63.11.1209

Meyer-Lindenberg, A., et al. (2006). Neural mechanisms of genetic risk for impulsivity and violence in humans. *Proceedings of the National Academy of Sciences (PNAS)*, 103(16), 6269–6274. https://doi.org/10.1073/pnas.0511311103

Miles-Novelo, A., & Anderson, C. A. (2020). Desensitization. *The International Encyclopedia of Media Psychology.* https://doi.org/10.1002/9781119011071.iemp0056

Miller, L. (2014). Serial killers: II. Development, dynamics, and forensics. *Aggression and Violent Behavior*, 19(1), 12–22. https://doi.org/10.1016/j.avb.2013.11.003

Milroy, C. M., & Kepron, C. (2017). Ten percent of SIDS cases are murder – or are they? *Academic Forensic Pathology*, 7(2), 163–170. https://doi.org/10.23907/2017.018

Min, M., Farkas, K., Minnes, S., & Singer, L. T. (2007). Impact of childhood abuse and neglect on substance abuse and psychological distress in adulthood. *Journal of Traumatic Stress*, 20(5), 833–844. https://doi.org/10.1002/jts.20250

Moran, M. E., Pol, H. H., & Gogtay, N. (2013). A family affair: Brain abnormalities in siblings of patients with schizophrenia. *Brain*, 136(11), 3215–3226. https://doi.org/10.1093/brain/awt116

Morana, H. C., Stone, M. H., & Abdalla-Filho, E. (2006). Personality disorders, psychopathy, and serial killers. *Revista Brasileira de Psiquiatria*, 28, S74-S79. http://dx.doi.org/10.1590/S1516-44462006000600005

Morgan, M. (2015). *Delmarva's Patty Cannon: The devil on the Nanticoke.* Charleston, SC: The History Press.

Mullins-Nelson, J. L., Salekin, R. T., & Leistico, A. R. (2012). Psychopathy, empathy, and perspective-talking ability in a community sample: Implications for the successful psychopathy concept. *International Journal of Forensic Mental Health*, 5(2), 133–149. https://doi.org/10.1080/14999013.2006.10471238

Murray, J. L. (2017). The role of sexual, sadistic, and misogynistic fantasy in mass and serial killing. *Deviant Behavior*, 38(7), 735–743. https://doi.org/10.1080/01639625.2016.1197669

Myers, W. C., Gooch, E., & Melow, J. R. (2005). The role of psychopathy and sexuality in a female serial killer. *Journal of Forensic Sciences*, 50(3), 652–657.

Nelson, E. E., & Guyer, A. E. (2011). The development of the ventral prefrontal cortex and social flexibility. *Developmental Cognitive Neuroscience*, 1(3), 233–245. http://dx.doi.org/10.1016/j.dcn.2011.01.002

Nock, M. K., Kazdin, A. E., Hiripi, E., & Kessler, R. C. (2006). Prevalence, subtypes, and correlates of DSM-IV conduct disorder in the National Comorbidity Survey Replication. *Psychological Medicine*, 36(5), 699–710. https://doi.org/10.1017/S0033291706007082

Norton, C. (1994). *Disturbed ground: The true story of a diabolical female serial killer.* New York, NY: W. Morrow and Co.

Ogilvie, J. M., Stewart, A. L., Chan, R. C. K., & Shum, D. H. K. (2011). Neuropsychological measures of executive function and antisocial behavior:

A meta-analysis. *Criminology: An Interdisciplinary Journal*, 49(4), 1063–1107. https://doi.org/10.1111/j.1745-9125.2011.00252.x

Oosterwijk, S. (2017). Choosing the negative: A behavioral demonstration of morbid curiosity. *PLoS One*, 12(7), e0178399. https://doi.org/10.1371/journal.pone.0178399

Ostrosky-Solís, F., Vélez-García, A., Santana-Vargas, D., Pérez, M., & Ardlia, A. (2008). A middle-aged female serial killer. *Journal of Forensic Science*, 53(5), 1223–1230. https://doi.org/10.1111/j.1556-4029.2008.00803.x

Pagel, M. (2016). Lethal violence deep in the human lineage. *Nature*, 538, 180–181. http://dx.doi.org/10.1038/nature19474

Palermo, G. B. (2008). Narcissism, sadism, and loneliness. In R. N. Kocsis (ed.), *Serial murder and the psychology of violent crimes*. 85-100. Totowa, NJ: Humana Press. https://doi.org/10.1007/978-1-60327-049-6_6

Palermo, M. T., & Bogaerts, S. (2015). The dangers of posthumous diagnoses and the unintended consequences of facile associations: Jeffrey Dahmer and autism spectrum disorders. *International Journal of Offender Therapy and Comparative Criminology*, 59(14), 1564–1579. https://doi.org/10.1177/0306624X14550642

Papalia, N., Ogloff, J. R. P., Cutajar, M., & Mullen, P. E. (2018). Childhood sexual abuse and criminal offending: Gender-specific effects and the role of abuse characteristics and other adverse outcomes. *Child Maltreatment*, 23(4), 399–416. https://doi.org/10.1177/1077559518785779

Parfitt, C. H., & Alleyne, E. (2020). Not the sum of its parts: A critical review of the MacDonald Triad. *Trauma, Violence, & Abuse*, 21(2), 300–310. https://doi.org/10.1177/1524838018764164

Parker Jones, O., Alfaro-Almagro, F., & Jbabdi, S. (2018). An empirical, 21st century evaluation of phrenology. *Cortex*, 106, 26–35. https://doi.org/10.1016/j.cortex.2018.04.011

Patel, K. R., Cherian, J., Gohil, K., & Atkinson, D. (2014). Schizophrenia: Overview and treatment options. *Pharmacy & Therapeutics*, 39(9), 638–645. https://www.ncbi.nlm.nih.gov/pmc/articles/PMC4159061/

Patrick, C. J., Hicks, B. M., Krueger, R. F., and Lang, A. R. (2005). Relations between psychopathy facets and externalizing in a criminal offender sample. *Journal of Personality Disorders*, 19(4), 339–356. https://doi.org/10.1521/pedi.2005.19.4.339

Pearson, P. (1998/2021). *When she was bad: How and why women get away with murder*. Toronto, Canada: Random House.

Penfold-Mounce, R. (2009). *Celebrity culture and crime: The joy of transgression*. New York, NY: Palgrave MacMillan.

Pera-Guardiola, V. (& 10 other authors). (2016). Modulatory effects of psychopathy on Wisconsin Card Sorting Test performance in male offenders with Antisocial Personality Disorder. *Psychiatry Research*, 235, 43–48. https://doi.org/10.1016/j.psychres.2015.12.003

Perri, F., & Lichtenwald, T. (2010). The last frontier: Myths & the female psychopathic killer. *The Forensic Examiner*, 19(2), 50–67.

Pershagen, G. (1981). The carcinogenicity of arsenic. *Environmental Health Perspectives*, 40, 93–100. https://doi.org/10.1289/ehp.814093

Pinizzotto, A. J. (1984). Forensic psychology: Criminal personality profiling. *Journal of Police Science & Administration*, 12(1), 32–40.

Porter, S. (1996). Without conscience or without active conscience? The etiology of psychopathy revisited. *Aggression and Violent Behavior*, 1(2), 179–189. https://doi.org/10.1016/1359-1789(95)00010-0

Prentky, R. A., Burgess, A. W., Rokous, F., Lee, A., Hartman, C., Ressler, R., & Douglas, J. (1989). The presumptive role of fantasy in serial sexual homicide. *The American Journal of Psychiatry*, 146(7), 887–891. https://doi.org/10.1176/ajp.146.7.887

Rad, M. S., Martingano, J., & Ginges, J. (2018). Toward a psychology of *Homo sapiens*: Making psychological science more representative of the human population. *Proceedings of the National Academy of Sciences of the United States of America (PNAS)*, 115(45), 11401–11405. https://doi.org/10.1073/pnas.1721165115

Raine, A. (2013). *The anatomy of violence: The biological roots of crime*. New York, NY: Random House.

Raine, A., & Yang, Y. (2006). Neural foundations to moral reasoning and antisocial behavior. *Social Cognitive and Affective Neuroscience*, 1(3), 203–213. https://doi.org/10.1093/scan/nsl033

Raine, A., Meloy, J. R., Bihrle, S., Stoddard, J., LaCasse, L., & Buchsbaum, M. S. (1998). Reduced prefrontal and increased subcortical brain functioning assessed using positron emission tomography in predatory and affective murderers. *Behavioral Sciences and the Law*, 16(3), 319–332. https://doi.org/10.1002/(SICI)1099-0798(199822)16:3<319::AID-BSL311>3.0.CO;2-G

Ratnaike, R. N. (2003). Acute and chronic arsenic toxicity. *BMJ: Postgraduate Medical Journal*, 79(933), 391–396.

Rawson, K. (2019). *A serial killer's daughter: My story of faith, love, and overcoming*. Nashville, TN: Nelson Books.

Read, J., Fosse, R., Moskowitz, A., & Perry, B. (2014). The traumagenic neurodevelopmental model of psychosis revisited. *Neuropsychiatry*, 4(1), 65–79.

Rees, A. (2009). *The infanticide controversy: Primatology and the art of field science*. Chicago, IL: University of Chicago Press.

Reid, S. (2017). Developmental pathways to serial homicide: A critical review of the biological literature. *Aggression and Violent Behavior*, 35, 52–61. http://dx.doi.org/10.1016/j.avb.2017.06.003

Ressler, R. K., & Shachtman, T. (1992). *Whoever fights monsters: My twenty years tracking serial killers for the FBI*. New York, NY: St. Martin's Press.

Rios, V., & Ferguson, C. J. (2020). News media coverage: Coverage of crime and violent drug crime: A case for cause or catalyst? *Justice Quarterly*, 37(6), 1012–1039. https://doi.org/10.1080/07418825.2018.1561925

Roach, J., Cartwright, A., & Sharratt, K. (2017). Dealing with the unthinkable: A study of the cognitive and emotional stress of adult and child homicide investigators on police investigation. *Journal of Police and Criminal Psychology*, 32, 251–262. https://doi.org/10.1007/s11896-016-9218-5

Roalf, D. R., & Gur, R. C. (2017). Functional brain imaging in neuropsychology over the past 25 years. *Neuropsychology*, 31(8), 954–971. https://doi.org/10.1037/neu0000426

Roberti, J. W. (2004). A review of behavioral and biological correlates of sensation seeking. *Journal of Research in Personality*, 38(3), 256–279. https://doi.org/10.1016/S0092-6566(03)00067-9

Robinson, T. E., & Berridge, K. C. (1993). The neural basis of drug craving: an incentive-sensitization theory of addiction. *Brain Research Reviews*, 18(3), 247–291. https://doi.org/10.1016/0165-0173(93)90013-p

Role, A. (1998). A great Cadurcian, Alexandre Lacassagne (1843–1924). *History of Medical Sciences*, 32(4), 409–415. https://pubmed.ncbi.nlm.nih.gov/11625448/

Rosenthal, R. (1979). The file drawer problem and tolerance for null results. *Psychological Bulletin*, 86(3), 638–641. https://doi.org/10.1037/0033-2909.86.3.638

Rushin, S., & Michalski, R. (2020). Police funding. *Florida Law Review*, 72, 277–330. www.floridalawreview.com/wp-content/uploads/3_Rushin_Michalski7098.pdf

Ryan, S., Willmott, D., Sherretts, N., & Kielkiewicz, K. (2017). A psycho-legal analysis and criminal trajectory of female child serial killer Beverley Allitt. *European Journal of Current Legal Issues*, 23(2). https://webjcli.org/index.php/webjcli/article/view/574/749

Sass, L., Borda, J. P., Madeira, L., Pienkos, E., & Nelson, B. (2018). Varieties of self disorder: A bio-pheno-social model of schizophrenia. *Schizophrenia Bulletin*, 44(4), 720–727. https://doi.org/10.1093/schbul/sby001

Savic, I., Garcia-Falgueras, A., & Swaab, D. F. (2010). Sexual differentiation of the human brain in relation to gender identity and sexual orientation. *Progress in Brain Research*, 186, 41–62. https://doi.org/10.1016/B978-0-444-53630-3.00004-X

Schlesinger, L. B. (2008). Compulsive-repetitive offenders. In R. N. Koscis (ed.), *Serial murder and the psychology of violent crimes*, 15–33. Totowa, NJ: Humana Press.

Schmid, D. (2005). *Natural born celebrities: Serial killers in American culture*. Chicago, IL: University of Chicago.

Schmitt, D. P., Shackelford, T. K., & Buss, D. M. (2001). Are men really more 'oriented' toward short-term mating than women? A critical review of theory and research. *Psychology, Evolution, and Gender*, 3(3), 211–239. https://doi.org/10.1080/14616660110119331

Schurman-Kauflin, D. (2000). *The new predator: Women who kill*. New York, NY: Algora Publishing.

Schwartz, J. A. (2021). A longitudinal assessment of head injuries as a source of acquired neuropsychological deficits and the implications for criminal persistence. *Justice Quarterly*, 38(2), 196–223. https://doi.org/10.1080/07418 825.2019.1599044

Seidel, E., Pfabigan, D. M., Keckeis, K., Wucherer, A. M., Jahn, T., Lamm, C., & Derntl, B. (2013). Empathic competencies in violent offenders. *Psychiatry Research*, 210(3), 1168–1175. https://doi.org/10.1016/j.psychres.2013.08.027

Shapero, B. G., Hamilton, J. L., Liu, R. T., Abramson, L. Y., & Alloy. L. B. (2013). Internalizing symptoms and rumination: The prospective prediction of familial and peer emotional victimization experiences during adolescence. *Journal of Adolescence*, 36(6), 1067–1076. https://doi.org/10.1016/j.adolescence.2013.08.011

Shearer, W. M. (1960). The evolution of premedication. *British Journal of Anaesthesia*, 32(11), 554–562. https://doi.org/10.1093/bja/32.11.554

Shin, D. D., & Kim, S. (2019). Homo curious: Curious or interested? *Educational Psychology Review*, 31, 853–874. https://doi.org/10.1007/s10648-019-09497-x

Silva, J. A., Leong, G. B., & Ferrari, M. M. (2004). A neuropsychiatric developmental model of serial homicide behavior. *Behavioral Sciences and the Law*, 22, 797–799. https://doi.org/10.1002/bsl.620

Simpson, P. (2020). *Psycho paths: Tracing the serial killer through contemporary American film and fiction*. Carbondale, IL: Southern Illinois University Press.

Singhrao, S. K., Neal, J. W., & Newman, G. R. (1993). Corpora amylacea could be an indicator of neurodegeneration. *Neuropathology & Applied Neurobiology*, 19(3), 269–276. https://doi.org/10.1111/j.1365-2990.1993 .tb00437.x

Sit, D., Rothschild, A. J., & Wisner, K. L. (2006). A review of postpartum psychosis. *Journal of Women's Health*, 15(4), 352–368. https://doi .org/10.1089/jwh.2006.15.352

Smith, S. M., McIntosh, W. D., & Bazzini, D. G. (1999). Are the beautiful good in Hollywood? An investigation of the beauty-and-goodness stereotype on film. *Basic and Applied Social Psychology*, 21(1), 69–80. https://doi .org/10.1207/s15324834basp2101_7

Snowden, R. J., Smith, C., & Gray, N. S. (2017). Risk taking and the triarchic model of psychopathy. *Journal of Clinical and Experimental Neuropsychology*, 39(10), 988–1001. https://doi.org/10.1080/13803395.2017.1300236

Starr, D. (2010). *The killer of little shepherds: A true crime story and the birth of forensic science*. New York, NY: Knopf/Random House

Stetler, D. A., Davis, C., Leavitt, K., Schriger, I., Benson, K., Bhakta, S., Wang, L. C., Oben, C., Watters, M., Haghnegahdar, T., & Bortolato, M. (2014). Association of low-activity MAOA allelic variants with violent crime in incarcerated offenders. *Journal of Psychiatric Research*, 58, 69–75. https://doi .org/10.1016/j.jpsychires.2014.07.006

Stone, M. H. (2001). Serial sexual homicide: Biological, psychological, and sociological aspects. *Journal of Personality Disorders*, 15(1), 1–18. https://doi .org/10.1521/pedi.15.1.1.18646

Stone, M. H. (2009). *The anatomy of evil.* Amherst, NY: Prometheus Books.

Stone, M. H. (2018). The place of psychopathy along the spectrum of negative personality types. *Contemporary Psychoanalysis*, 54(1), 161–182. https://doi .org/10.1080/00107530.2017.1420376

Stuart, G. L., Moore, T. M., Gordon, K. C., Ramsey, S. E., & Kahler, C. W. (2006). Psychopathology in women who commit domestic violence. *Journal of Interpersonal Violence*, 21(3), 376–389. https://doi.org/10.1177/ 0886260505282888

Stuart, H. (2003). Violence and mental illness: An overview. *World Psychiatry*, 2(2), 121–124. www.ncbi.nlm.nih.gov/pmc/articles/PMC1525086/

Suárez-Meaney, T., López, A. J. P., Becerril, L. C. (2017). Predictibilidad locacional y perfilamiento geográfico en el homicidio serial con gvSIG. Caso Barraza. *Revista Mapping*, 26(82), 52–63.

Suris, A., Holliday, R., & North, C. S. (2016). The evolution of the classification of psychiatric disorders. *Behavioral Sciences*, 6(1), 5. https://doi .org/10.3390/bs6010005

Symons, D. (1979). *The evolution of human sexuality.* New York, NY: Oxford University Press.

Tagge, C. A., and 45 other authors. (2018). Concussion, microvascular injury, and early tauopathy in young athletes after impact head injury and an impact concussion mouse model. *Brain*, 141(2), 422–458. https://doi.org/10.1093/ brain/awx350

Tapio, S. & Grosche, B. (2006). Arsenic in the aetiology of cancer. *Mutation Research/Reviews in Mutation Research*, 612(3), 215–246. https://doi .org/10.1016/j.mrrev.2006.02.001

Taylor, P. J., & Gunn, J. (1999). Homicides by people with mental illness: Myth and reality. *British Journal of Psychiatry*, 174(1), 9–14. https://doi .org/10.1192/bjp.174.1.9

Taylor, S., Lambeth, D., Green, G., Bone, R., & Cahillane, M. A. (2012). Cluster analysis examination of serial killer profiling categories: A bottom-up approach. *Journal of Investigative Psychology and Offender Profiling*, 9(1), 30–51. https://doi .org/10.1002/jip.149

Taylor, S. E. (1991). Asymmetrical effects of positive and negative events: The mobilization-minimization hypothesis. *Psychological Bulletin*, 110(1), 67–85. https:// doi.org/10.1037/0033-2909.110.1.67

Teicher, M. H., & Samson, J. A. (2013). Childhood maltreatment and psychopathology: A case for ecophenotypic variants as clinically and neurobiologically distinct subtypes. *The American Journal of Psychiatry*, 170(10), 1114–1133. https://doi .org/10.1176/appi.ajp.2013.12070957

Tengström, A., Grann, M., Långström, N., & Kullgren, G. (2000). Psychopathy (PCL-R) as a predictor of violent recidivism among criminal offenders with schizophrenia. *Law and Human Behavior*, 24(1), 45–58. https://doi .org/10.1023/A:1005474719516

Toates, F., & Coschug-Toates, O. (2022). *Understanding sexual serial killing*. Cambridge, UK: Cambridge University Press.

Toates, F., Smid, W., & van den Berg, J. W. (2017). A framework for understanding sexual violence: Incentive-motivation and hierarchical control. *Aggression and Violent Behavior*, 34, 238–253. https://doi.org/10.1016/j.avb.2017.01.001

Tooby, J., & Cosmides, L. (1990). The past explains the present: Emotional adaptations and the structure of ancestral environments. *Ethology and Sociobiology*, 11, 375–424. http://dx.doi.org/10.1016/0162-3095(90)90017-Z

Torregrossa, M. M., Quinn, J. J., & Taylor, J. R. (2008). Impulsivity, compulsivity, and habit: The role of orbitofrontal cortex revisited. *Biological Psychiatry*, 63(3), 253–255. http://dx.doi.org/10.1016/j.biopsych.2007.11.014

Tournel, G., Houssaye, C., Humbert, L., Dhorne, C., Gnemmi, V., Bécart-Robert, A., Nisse, P., Hédouin, V., Gosset, D., & Lhermitte, M. (2011). Acute arsenic poisoning: Clinical, toxicological, histopathological, and forensic features. *Journal of Forensic Sciences*, 56(S1), S275-S279. https://doi.org/10.1111/j.1556-4029.2010.01581.x

Tracy, D. K., & Rix, K. J. B. (2017). Malingering mental disorders: Clinical assessment. *BJPsych Advances*, 23(1), 27–35. https://doi.org/10.1192/apt.bp.116.015958

Trivers, R. (1972). Paternal investment and sexual selection. In B. Campbell (ed.), *Sexual selection and the descent of man*, 136–179. Chicago, IL: Aldine-Atherton.

Tuomi, T., Agrell, J., & Mappes, T. (1997). On the evolutionary stability of female infanticide. *Behavioral Ecology and Sociobiology*, 40(4), 227–233. https://doi.org/10.1007/s002650050337

Uchitel, J., et al. (2019). The rights of children for optimal development and nurturing care. *Pediatrics*, 144(6), e20190487. https://pediatrics.aappublications.org/content/pediatrics/early/2019/11/22/peds.2019-0487.full.pdf

Unal, E. O., Unal, V., Gul, A., Celtek, M., Diken, B., & Balcioglu, I. (2017). A serial Munchausen syndrome by proxy. *Indian Journal of Psychological Medicine*, 39(5), 671–674. https://doi.org/10.4103/0253-7176.217017

van Aken, C. (2015). The use of criminal profilers in the prosecution of serial killers. *Themis: Research Journal of Justice*, 3(1), 127–149. https://scholarworks.sjsu.edu/themis/vol3/iss1/

van Haren, N. E., Cahn, W., Hulshoff Pol, H. E., & Kahn, R. S. (2008). Schizophrenia as a progressive brain disease. *European Psychiatry*, 23(4), 245–254. https://doi.org/10.1016/j.eurpsy.2007.10.013

van Steenbergen, H., Band, G. P. H., & Hommel, B. (2011). Threat but not arousal narrows attention: Evidence from pupil dilation and saccade control. *Frontiers in Psychology*, 2, 281. https://doi.org/10.3389/fpsyg.2011.00281

Viding, E., & Frith, U. (2006). Genes for susceptibility to violence lurk in the brain. *Proceedings of the National Academy of Sciences of the United States of America (PNAS)*, 103(16), 6085–6086. https://doi.org/10.1073/pnas.0601350103

Vitello, C. J., & Hickey, E. W. (2006). *The myth of a psychiatric crime wave: Public perception, juror research, and mental illness*. Durham, NC: Carolina Academic Press.

Vygotsky, L. S. (1929/1994). The problem of the cultural development of the child. In R. van der Veer and J. Valsiner (eds.), *The Vygotsky reader*, 57–72. Oxford, UK: Blackwell.

Wahl, O. F. (2003). *Media madness: Public images of mental illness*. New Brunswick, NJ: Rutgers University Press.

Wakefield, J. C. (2005). Biological function and dysfunction. In D. M. Buss (ed.), *The handbook of evolutionary psychology*, 878–902. Hoboken, NJ: Wiley.

Wang, T. (2012). Presentation and impact of market-driven journalism on sensationalism in global TV news. *International Communication Gazette*, 74(8), 711–727. https://doi.org/10.1177/1748048512459143

Wang, Y. Wang, X., Wang, K., Zhao, B. & Chen, X. (2020). Decision-making impairments under ambiguous and risky situations in patients with prefrontal tumor: A neuropsychological study. *Brain and Behavior*, 11(1), e01951. https://doi.org/10.1002/brb3.1951

Warf, B., & Waddell, C. (2002). Heinous spaces, perfidious places: The sinister landscapes of serial killers. *Social & Cultural Geography*, 3(3), 323–345. https://doi.org/10.1080/1464936022000003550

Weiss, K. J., & Alexander, J. C. (2013). Sex, lies, and statistics: Inferences from the child sexual abuse accommodation syndrome. *The Journal of the American Academy of Psychiatry and the Law*, 41(3), 412–420. www.nationalcac.org/wp-content/uploads/2016/10/Sex-lies-and-statistics-Inferences-from-the-child-sexual-abuse-accommodation-syndrome.pdf

Weissenbacher, B. K. H. (1987). Infanticide in tree squirrels – a male reproductive strategy? *South African Journal of Zoology*, 22(2), 115–118. https://doi.org/10.1080/02541858.1987.11448031

Wensley, D., & King, M. (2008). Scientific responsibility for the dissemination and interpretation of genetic research: lessons from the "warrior gene" controversy. *Journal of Medical Ethics*, 34, 507–509.

Wiest, J. B. (2016). Casting cultural monsters: Representations of serial killers in U.S. and U.K. news media. *Howard Journal of Communications*, 27(4), 327–346. https://doi.org/10.1080/10646175.2016.1202876

Williams, W. H., Chitsabesan, C., Fazel, S., McMillan, T., Hughes, N., Parsonage, M., & Tonks, J. (2018). Traumatic brain injury: A potential cause of violent crime? *Lancet Psychiatry*, 5(10), 836–844. https://doi.org/10.1016/S2215-0366(18)30062-2

Wilson, E. G. (2012). *Everyone loves a good train wreck: Why we can't look away*. New York, NY: Sarah Crichton Books.

Wilson, W., & Hilton, T. (1998). *Modus operandi* of female serial killers. *Psychological Reports*, 82(2), 495–498. https://doi.org/10.2466/pr0.1998.82.2.495

Yaksic, E., Harrison, M., Konikoff, D., Mooney, R., Allely, C., De Silva, R., Matykiewicz, B., Inglis, M., Giannangelo, S. J., Daniels, S., & Sarteschi, C. M. (2021). A heuristic study of the similarities and differences in offender characteristics across potential and successful serial sexual homicide offenders. *Behavioral Sciences and the Law*. https://doi.org/10.1002/bsl.2510

Yardley, E., & Wilson, D. (2015). *Female serial killer in social context: Criminological institutionalism and the case of Mary Ann Cotton.* Bristol, UK: Policy Press.

Yorker, B. C. (1994). Munchausen syndrome by proxy as a form of family violence. *Family Violence and Sexual Assault Bulletin,* 10(3–4), 34–39. www.ojp.gov/ncjrs/virtual-library/abstracts/munchausen-syndrome-proxy-form-family-violence

Young, J. C., & Widom, C. S. (2014). Long-term effects of child abuse and neglect on emotion processing in adulthood. *Child Abuse & Neglect,* 38(8), 1369–1381. https://doi.org/10.1016/j.chiabu.2014.03.008

Zillmann, D. (1998). The psychology of the appeal of portrayals of violence. In J. Goldstein (ed.), *Why we watch: The attractions of violent entertainment,* 179–211. New York, NY: Oxford University Press.

Zuckerman, M. (1994). *Behavioral expressions and biosocial bases of sensation seeking.* New York, NY: Cambridge University Press.

Zuckerman, M. (2007). *Sensation seeking and risky behavior.* Washington, DC: American Psychological Association.

Zuckerman, M., & Litle, P. (1986). Personality and curiosity about morbid and sexual events. *Personality and Individual Differences,* 7(1), 49–56. https://doi.org/10.1016/0191-8869(86)90107-8

Zuckerman, M., Kolin, E. A., Price, L., & Zoob, I. (1964). Development of a sensation-seeking scale. *Journal of Consulting Psychology,* 28(6), 477–482. https://doi.org/10.1037/h0040995

Index

Page numbers in *italics* refer to source titles/proper nouns.

Gall, Franz Joseph, 147
Gallup, Gordon G., 200
Garippo, Louis, 126, 196
Garret, Brad, 173
Garrett family, 98, 101
Geberth, Vernon, 136–137
GEDMatch, 171
Gein, Ed, 14, 19, 108–112, *109*, 185,
  195–196, 212
Gein, Henry, 108
genes for violence, 168–170
genesmanship, 95, 200
Gentry, John, 93
Genty, Daniel, 123–124
Gibbs, Mary D., 42
Gilbert, Kristen, 1–4, *2*, 66, 83, 87–88,
  192, 195
Gilligan, Michael, 51–52
Gipson, Talmadge J., 98–99
Glenn, Andrea, 166
Godejohn, Nicholas, 65
Golden State Killer. *See* DeAngelo, Joseph
  James
Goodyear, James, 92, 93
Goodyear, Michael, 92–93
Gordon, Ronit, 193
Gott, Adam, 112
Gray, Dana Sue, 17, 86, 193
Grimm, Fred, 49
Gunness, Belle, 21–26, *25*, 66, 85, 202, 213
  remains of victims, 28, 82, 133
Gunness, Peter, 22

Häkkänen, Helinä, 117
halo effect, 10
Hannibal (2013–2015), 18
Harder, William, 34
Hardstark, Georgia, 174
Hare, Robert, 13, 15, 124, 127, 165, 166, 212
Harper's Bazaar, 196
Harrelson, Frank, 78, 79
Hartford Courant, xii–xiii, 19, 52–55,
  103, 104
Hartley, Greg, 12
Hawn, Stacy, 136
Hays, Jim, 10
Hazel, Dovie, 79
Hazel, Lou, 79
head injuries, 117, 148–149, 151–152,
  156, 160
  and general violence, 168
  John Wayne Gacy, 119, 128–129

Hedge, Marine, 188
Helfgott, Jacqueline, 189
Helgelien, John, 23
Hell's Belle. *See* Gunness, Belle
Hickey, Eric, 4, 9, 15, 18, 106–107, 118,
  131, 137, 145–146, 173
Hickman, Martha Sperry, *12*
Hilton, Tonya, 78
Hindley, Myra, 185
hippocampus, 167, 169
Ho, Lavina, xi
Ho, Thienvu, 172
Hogan, Mary, 108, 109
Holden, Benedict, 54
Holes, Paul, 174
Hollingsworth, Wanda, 85
Holmes, Ronald, 86
Holmes, Stephen, 4, 86
homosexuality, attitudes toward,
  211–212
horror media. *See* media, role of
Howell, Nic, 126
Hrdy, Sarah, 97
Hudon, Henry, 195
Hughes, Susan, 112
hunter-gatherer model, 202–204
Hurlburt, Dennis, 103

income inequality, 132
infanticide, 5, 26, 95–97, 102–103, 133
  Martha Woods case study,
    58–61
  Marybeth Tinning case study,
    61–65
Innocence Project., 20
insulin, 207, 208
intelligence level statistics, 38–39
Isenberg, Sheila, 28

J. B., 154–157, 170, 179
Jakubczyk, Andrzej, 170
James, Cyrus, 6
James, William, 26
Jaws (1975), 18
jealousy, evolution of, 89–90
Jelly, George F., 43
Jentzen, Jeffrey, 211
Jewkes, Yvonne, 185
Johnson, Joe, 5
Jolly Jane. *See* Toppan, Jane
Jones, Genene, 75–78, *77*, 82, 83
Jones, Patricia, 10

mental illness (cont.)
  history and current developments,
    55–58
  Jane Toppan, 43–44
  Jerome Henry Brudos, 143–144
  John Wayne Gacy, 125–126
  Joseph James DeAngelo, 172
  Kristen Gilbert, 88
  Lydia Sherman, 105
  male serial killer comparisons, 114–118
  Margie Velma Barfield, 68–71
  Marybeth Tinning, 61–65
  Nannie Doss, 80–81
  Reta Mays, 209
  Rhonda Belle Martin, 99–101
  statistics and prevalence, 65–68
  Tammy Corbett, 73
  treatment of, 71
Meriden Morning Record, 53
methods-of-crime statistics, 134
Miami Herald, The, 49
Miller, Dorothy, 34
Mindhunter (2017–2019), 18
Mitchell, David, 182
Moise, Judy, 33
monoamines, 168–169
Monster (2003), 8, 50
Montgomery Advertiser, The, 98
Montoya, Bert, 33
Morana, Hilda, 13
morbid curiosity, xi, 26–30, 52, 74, 210
Moreth, Vince, 73
Morgan, Mike, 6
Morning News, The, 6–7
morphine, 42, 52, 55
Morris, Bobby Joe, 92, 93
Morton, Richard, 78
motives, 34, 61
  Aileen Wuornos, 191
  Belle Gunness, 202
  classification of, 86–89
  Ed Gein, 110
  Genene Jones, 77
  J. B., 155
  Jane Toppan, 44
  Joseph James DeAngelo, 173
  Joseph Vacher, 154
  Judy Buenoana, 94
  killing for profit, 89–91, 94
  Kimberly Clark Saenz, 84
  Kristen Gilbert, 87–88
  Lydia Sherman, 103, 105, 202

male serial killer comparisons, 138,
    200–202
  Martha Woods, 59
  Nannie Doss, 79–80
  Rhonda Belle Martin, 99
  Ronald Dominique, 181
  Tammy Corbett, 73
movies. *See* media, role of
MRI scans, 160
Munchausen syndrome by proxy (MSBP),
    60–61, 65
  case of Marybeth Tinning, 61–65
murderabilia, 17–19, 34, 190
Murderpedia, 37
Murfin, Melody, 135, 194
Murphy, Erin, x–xi, 21
Murray, Jennifer, 190
Museum of Death, California, 18
My Favorite Murder (podcast), 174

National Center for Missing and
    Exploited Children, 124
National Institute of Mental Health
    (NIMH), 56–57, 116
NBC News, 189
NBC/Peacock, 123
necrophilia, 111, 144
negative stimuli, 27–28
neuropsychological tests, 157–158
New York Herald, The, 103, 104, 105
New York Post, The, 141
New York Times, The, 22, 184
New Yorker, The, 120, 128
'no female serial killers' theory, 4–5
Norton, Carla, 35
Nurses Who Kill (2016–present), 208

O'Dell, Diane, 141
O'Neill, Courtney Lund, 196
offender profiling. *See* female serial killer
    profiling
Ogilvie, James, 164
Oliver, Patrick, 136
Olson, Jennie, 22, 23
Oosterwijk, Suzanne, 27, 29
Open University Psychological Society,
    211
orbitofrontal cortex (OFC), 164,
    165, 169
Oster, Sunny Gale, 194
Ostrosky-Solís, Feggy, 154–156
Otero family, 186, 198

paired serial killers, 37–38
Palermo, Mark, 167
Palmer, Betty, 34
Pandher, Moninder Singh, 159
paraformaldehyde, 93
paraphilia, 118, 136, 169
Paredes Ordonez, Francisco, 11
parental investment theory, 90, 201, 202
Pearson, Patricia, 9
Peck, George, 104
Peeples, Carlton, 208
Pera-Guardiola, Vanessa, 166
Perr, Belvin, 94
Perrault, Jim, 1, 3, 87
physical appearance, perception of, 9–10
Piest, Robert, 123, 124, 196
Plapp, Beverly, 198
Poersch, John, 63
poison. *See also* arsenic
  ant and roach killer, 68
  bleach poisoning, 84
  flurazepam as, 32
  as most common murder method, 78
  rat poison, 68, 81
  strychnine, 40
postpartum psychosis (PP), 67, 100–101
Poughkeepsie Journal, 62
prefrontal cortex (PFC), 128, 163–165, *163*, 167, 169
protective vigilance, 27, 74
proximate motivators, 92, 203
Psycho Killers (1999), 19
psychopathy, 66, 119, 164, 176
  Aileen Wuornos, 48, 177–178
  behavioral neuroscience, 165–167
  Belle Gunness, 26
  Dennis Rader, 189
  J. B., 156
  John Wayne Gacy, 124, 127–128
  Joseph James DeAngelo, 173
  Lydia Sherman, 105
  primer, 12–15
  Ronald Dominique, 183
  Surinder Koli, 160
Psychopathy Checklist-Revised (PCL-R), 14, 165–166, 177
psychosis, 12–15, 100–101
psychosocial factors, 175
  clinical perspective, 175–179
  effects of serial killers on others, 192–199
  sociocultural perspective, 180–191
  traumagenic perspective, 179–180

psychotherapy, 213–214
Puente, Dorothea, 28, 32–35, *33*, 81, 83, 138, 141, 191

Rader, Dennis, 185–190, *188*, 197–199
Raine, Adrian, 205
RAINN (Rape, Abuse & Incest National Network), 145
Ramirez, Richard, 17
Rappaport, Richard, 126
rat poison, 68, 81
Rawson, Kerri Rader, 188, 190, 197
Reasonable Doubt (2017–present), 20
Reid, Sasha, 160, 162
relationship status statistics, 39, 113–114
religious affiliation statistics, 38
Remember Me (1994), 93
research study, overview of, 35–38
  demographics, 38–40, 44–45
  developmental history, 45–47, 50
Ressler, Robert, 4, 132
reward sensitivity, 46
Reye's syndrome, 62
Ridgway, Gary, 185
Rignall, Jeff, 122
Roberts, June Elizabeth, 193
Robillard, Ron, 55
Rodgers, Garry, xi–xii
Rolling Stone, 17
Rossman, David, 4
Ryan, Annie, 54

Saenz, Kimberly Clark, 84–85
Saint Paul Globe, The, 82
Salee, Linda Dawn, 143
Saltz, Gail, 110
Santa Cruz Sentinel, 35
Savage, Susan, 136
Sawyer, Joshua, 76
schizophrenia, 43–44, 47, 55, 71, 99–100, 110, 117
Schmid, David, 184
Schurman-Kauflin, Deborah, 9, 78
Scott, Darla Sue, 194
selective serotonin reuptake inhibitors (SSRIs), 170
sensationalism, 36–37
sensation-seeking, 28–30
Sensation-Seeking Scale, 29–30
Serial Killer's Daughter, A (2019), 197